Nch'i-Wána
"The Big River"
*Mid-Columbia Indians
and Their Land*

Nch'i-Wána
"The Big River"

*Mid-Columbia Indians
and Their Land*

EUGENE S. HUNN

with James Selam and Family

UNIVERSITY OF WASHINGTON PRESS

Seattle and London

Library of Congress Cataloging-in-Publication Data
Hunn, Eugene S.
Nch'i-wána, "the big river" : Mid-Columbia Indians and their land /
Eugene S. Hunn with James Selam and family.
p. cm.
Bibliography: p.
Includes index.
ISBN: 978-0295-971193
1. Shahaptian Indians—Social life and customs.
2. Salishan Indians—Social life and customs.
3. Indians of North America—Columbia River Valley—Social life and customs.
I. Selam, James. II. Title. III Title: big river.
E99.S325H86   1989   89-14779
979.7'004979—dc20   CIP

To my mother
1907–1986
and
to the elders
of all cultures

Contents

Acknowledgments

I OWE MOST to James Selam and the other Indian elders who entrusted their knowledge of their world to me. I hope that what I have written does them justice. This book is the result of more than a decade of collaboration between myself, an anthropologist, and James Selam, a Columbia River Indian elder. I wrote the book. James informed and inspired it, and now he reads it with a sharply critical eye. Though the proofs are nearly ready for the printer, he calls frequently to argue a point. I try to achieve a resolution of our different points of view, but he fears that his voice may be lost in the chorus of academic commentary I have drawn upon. Perhaps he is right, though the academic voices speak of the global context.

Such relationships are complex. I am James's student, as well as his friend and colleague. James is my teacher, sponsor, colleague, friend, and critic. And these relationships do not exist in isolation but are tangled in a web of relationships each of us has with our own families, our students, and our Indian and academic colleagues, who have their own ideas of what we should write and how we should write it. This is the stuff of ethnography. Searching for common ground on which we both can stand.

I have particularly benefited from the assistance and encouragement of the following Columbia River and Yakima Indian people: Josephine Smartlowit Andrews, Sally Buck, Mary Jim Chapman, Harold Culpas, Virginia Beavert Martin, Elsie Pistolhead, Sara Albert Quaempts, Elmer Schuster, Delsie Albert Selam, James Selam, Lonnie Selam, Otis Shiloh, Ambrose Smartlowit, Gilbert Smartlowit, Donald Umtuch, Hazel Umtuch, and Gary Young.

I have also learned a great deal and profited from the advice and criticism of many academic colleagues, in particular Pamela Amoss, John Atkins, John Barker, Robert Boyd, James Chatters, Melinda Denton, David and Kathrine French, Yvonne Hajda, Virginia and Dell Hymes, Patrick Keely, Dale Kinkade, Arthur Kruckeberg, Alan Marshall, Charlene Martinsen,

Brien Meilleur, Helen Norton, Robert Pace, Jack Reber, Bruce Rigsby, Helen Schuster, and Nancy Turner. The interpretation placed on statements, facts, and events in this book is mine, however, and is not to be blamed on those whose advice I may have neglected to heed.

The drawings of plants in this book, taken from *Vascular Plants of the Pacific Northwest* (Hitchcock et al., University of Washington Press, vols. 1–5), were done by the expert hand of Jeanne Janish, to whom I give my thanks.

Funding for the research has come from a variety of sources, among them the National Science Foundation, the Melville and Elizabeth Jacobs Research Fund, the Phillips Fund of the American Philosophical Society, and the University of Washington Graduate School Research Fund.

The author's royalties will be reserved exclusively for the support of future research that documents and helps preserve Plateau Indian cultural traditions.

Indian Words in the Text

INDIAN WORDS written in phonemic orthography—a special alphabet devised by linguists in which each significant sound unit of the native languages is represented by a single symbol—are set in sans serif type. The symbols used are mostly familiar English letters, but these in many cases are pronounced in an unfamiliar way, for example, "x" represents a guttural sound like the "ch" of German "ach"; "q" is like "k" but is pronounced far back in the throat. Other symbols are English letters with diacritical marks, e.g., "š" is pronounced like English "sh"; "č̓" is pronounced like English "ch" but glottalized, as in nčí'wána ("the big river"), which is spelled Nch'i-Wána when adapted to normal English orthography (as in the title of this book); "ł" is pronounced roughly as English "thl." A Greek lambda with a bar across the stem (λ) represents a lateral affricate sound not found in English, while the "ʔ" symbol stands for a glottal stop. (See Table 4 and chapter 3, pp. 67–80, for a more detailed discussion.)

In most cases the Indian terms cited are from the Columbia River dialect group of the Sahaptin language (which includes Umatilla, John Day River, Rock Creek, Celilo, Tenino, and Tygh Valley dialects). Terms from other dialects, such as those of the Northwest or Northeast groups of Sahaptin, will be indicated by the abbreviations NWS and NES, respectively; those from the related Nez Perce language will be specified as NP. Indian words often will be hyphenated to indicate their internal structure. Such hyphenation is not meant to be exhaustive of significant morphemic contrasts and may not always be shown.

Nch'i-Wána
"The Big River"

*Mid-Columbia Indians
and Their Land*

1

Introduction

THE COLUMBIA RIVER—known to the Indian people of its middle course as nč̓i-wána, "the Big River"—cuts a deep gash through the Miocene basalts of the Columbia Plateau. The river courses deeply through the lives of these Indians as well. It forms the spine of their land, the core of their habitat, and thus profoundly shapes their lives. The land is the stage on which the human drama unfolds, it provides the sets and lighting for the play of human action, as much so today as before the first Euro-American adventurers came upon the scene. But the script has changed.

Culture is the script, providing the dramatic outline brought to life by individual human actors. Human culture is the subject matter of anthropology, and the complex interplay of Indian and Euro-American cultures on the Columbia Plateau is the subject matter of this book. I attempt here an analysis of that cultural drama, an appreciation of its characterizations, the intricacies of its plot, and its tragic denouement.

The land through which the Big River runs is in fact more than a stage; the land is protagonist. The Indian people have always seen the land that way. They speak of the earth as their Mother upon whose nurturing breast they rest. This is a powerful ecological image. Euro-Americans view "Mother Nature" in a different light, as an enemy to be contested: either we rule the land or we are defeated in the attempt. In this Euro-American world view the land is a power to be set in harness—as the mighty Columbia River has been tamed in the service of the burgeoning demands of a rapidly expanding population. The land is a commodity to be sold, an instrument for the production of wealth.

Ecological issues dominate this text. They are central to chapters 4 (ecology) and 5 (resources), and they provide a strong undercurrent throughout the discussions of history (chapter 2), society (chapter 6), religion (chapter 7), and even language (chapter 3). Ecological issues are also prominent in

3

contemporary Indian life in the Plateau (chapter 8). This ecological emphasis reflects my bias as author: my own research on Plateau ethnobiology, the relationships between people and the plants and animals of their cultural landscape, is reported here in some detail for the first time. But I emphasize ecology for another reason. I believe a solid grasp of the ecological details is essential for understanding the anthropocentric topics, that is, history, social organization, and religious and aesthetic expression. I believe that human social and spiritual life cannot be understood outside of its natural environment, and that human ecology does not have meaning divorced from the full range of human strivings.

This ethnography focuses on the Native American peoples of the Columbia River between Celilo Falls and Priest Rapids in what is now eastern Oregon and Washington. Their native language is Sahaptin and their contemporary descendants live on or near the reservations of the Yakima, Umatilla, and Warm Springs Indians. Their traditional way of life and the history of their interaction with Euro-American explorers, traders, missionaries, soldiers, and settlers differ in only minor ways from the experience of their Sahaptin-speaking neighbors such as the Yakimas, Klikitats, and Paluses, and from their close linguistic kin, the Nez Perces. They participated with the Salish speakers farther upriver—the Columbia, Wenatchee, Okanagan, Colville, Spokane, Pend Oreille, Kalispell, Flathead, and Coeur d'Alene peoples—in a large, loose social web strengthened by their shared experience of the Columbia River Basin ecosystem. They also interacted with western Washington and Oregon groups. Their downstream neighbors (with whom they shared the Columbia River gorge), the Upper Chinookan Wasco-Wishrams, provided a coastal link; while their distant enemies, the "Snakes" (Northern Paiutes and Shoshones) of the northern Great Basin and the Blackfeet of Montana's high plains, defined the outer edge of their experience of humanity prior to the arrival of the whites (fig. 1.1).

The Indians of the mid-Columbia were not a tribe. They owed allegiance to no one chief, nor did they join in defense of their territory, except as part of a loosely organized reaction to the danger presented by the pioneer invasions of the 1840s and 1850s. Rather, they were people who cherished their individual autonomy, the right of each family to choose where to hunt, fish, or gather foods and with whom to associate. Families came together for the winter in villages strung along the Big River where they recognized the authority of a headman (miyáwax/miyúux). They also congregated when and where food was abundant—at rich camas meadows in early summer, at

Fig. 1.1. Map of the Pacific Northwest showing territory utilized by Sahaptin-speaking peoples (Hunn 1982:22). The heavy solid line includes the territory where Sahaptin speakers predominated. The dotted line includes additional areas used by Sahaptin speakers in common with speakers of neighboring languages.

points of constriction in the salmon's migratory path, and in the huckleberry
meadows in early fall. They dispersed at other times to exploit more effectively the rich diversity offered by the land.

Archaeology confirms that Native Americans have lived at The Dalles and
on the lower Snake River for at least ten thousand years (Cressman 1977;
Borden 1979). The earliest certain occupations correspond to the last act of
the glacial drama of the ice ages. Ten thousand years ago all the world's
human beings made their living by gathering wild plants, catching fish, and
hunting large and small game. They moved camp with the seasons, though
in more richly endowed habitats they might maintain more or less permanent home bases strategically located within their range.

The Neolithic transformation set civilization in motion in Asia, along the
Nile, and in the highlands of the American hemisphere to the south. This
set the stage for the inevitable cultural confrontation between the Old and
New worlds precipitated by Columbus. The hunting and gathering economies of Northwest Indians evolved more slowly. Isolated as the Indians
were from the competitive stimulus of expanding agricultural populations,
their adaptations to the Northwest environment endured remarkably. Archaeological evidence does document a progressive refinement of productive tools and techniques and a variety of responses to large-scale environmental fluctuations, such as those of the exceptionally warm and dry
altithermal era which lasted from 5500 to 2000 BC. (Cressman 1977; Ames
and Marshall 1980–81).

My account focuses on the life ways of the mid-Columbia Indians as
Lewis and Clark found them on their pioneering journey of exploration to
the Pacific Ocean in 1804–6. I will also trace their subsequent history and
assess their present prospects. I will document their sufferings at the hands
of history but also note their tenacity and the imaginative responses they
have made to the overwhelming transformation of their ancestors' world.

The mid-Columbia Indians are poorly known ethnographically. They
have been treated as poor cousins of their more conspicuous Nez Perce and
Cayuse neighbors. The truth, as we will see, is quite otherwise. At the turn
of the nineteenth century the Columbia River peoples controlled a rich
salmon harvest that they skillfully combined with abundant root foods to
support a large population, substantial winter villages, and summer in-
gatherings numbering in the thousands. Their meticulous accumulated
knowledge of the land and its creatures is a rich heritage not only for their
descendants but for all of us who live on or visit the Columbia Plateau. Their

myths condense, in poetic expression and high drama, their collective wisdom. In response to the multiple shocks of virulent new diseases and aggressive foreign invaders, they produced a religious revival that reverberated throughout the region. This religious revival lives on in a vigorous contemporary Indian church, that of the wáašat, or "sacred dance."

This book is written for the Northwest Indians in the hope that it will show the strength of their traditions. It is written also for the larger audience of those who wish to understand better the reality of American history and to appreciate more deeply the vitality of human diversity. It is intended as more than a summary of current scholarship. It is also a personal statement. My description of the Sahaptin Indian way of life along the Columbia River, though drawn in part from reports, histories, and travelers' accounts, published and unpublished, is grounded as well in my experience. I have spent many days exploring the land that is the focal point of this culture. I have come to recognize its plants and animals and their habitats, to know them in their winter, spring, summer, and fall aspects; I have through persistent repetition learned to name these features: in English, in Latin, and in the Indian languages. I have been apprenticed to an Indian man, James Selam. His life has spanned the gap between the traditional seasonal round of hunting, fishing, and gathering he experienced as a young boy and the contemporary realities of global war, tribal political survival, and poverty in a land of plenty, relieved still as in the past by unbreakable family ties.

Through this continuing apprenticeship I have acquired more than factual knowledge (essential and valuable as that may be), but as well, a sense of the mystery of a way of life radically different from my own. My perspective has changed fundamentally: what I now see from my speeding car on Interstate 82 is more than the big sky of the Columbia Plateau, the sagebrush flats, hackberry on the rimrock, or the now restrained power of the Big River. I can see busy villages, fishermen hard at work with their nets in the swift waters, women carefully stockpiling winter's food, children fearfully seeking spiritual guidance on a lonely prominence, and the dead—a hundred generations and more of the dead—resting in the land, supporting the living. The plants and mammals, birds, fish, and insects are all named, familiar partners in the enterprise of survival. The mystery of this traditional way of life as it was 250 years ago is deepened by the fact that it owes nothing to our civilization. Despite this grand autonomy, I can see myself reflected in the faces of these Indian people. Almost like meeting for the first time intelligent life of another planet and being startled to find them human.

The mid-Columbia Indians are our long-lost brothers and sisters. Too bad that we for too long mistook them for strangers.

I was introduced to the Plateau Indians by Helen Schuster, who had just completed a doctoral dissertation in anthropology at the University of Washington on Yakima Indian traditionalism (1975). I had recently moved to Seattle from California fresh out of graduate school at the University of California at Berkeley. I was an avid traveler in those days, having lived and worked in Germany (as a college student), in Ethiopia (as a Peace Corps volunteer), and in southern Mexico (as an anthropological researcher). My scholarly interests had narrowed to the intersection of language and ecology and my Mexican researches were published as a book with the imposing title, *Tzeltal Folk Zoology: The Classification of Discontinuities in Nature* (Academic Press, 1977). The Tzeltal are Mayan Indians, peasant farmers of a humid tropical highland. The Mayans proved to be expert folk biologists. The fact that they saw the world of nature in much the same terms as expert Western scientists see it (though not necessarily as they understand it) inspired me to test the generality of that conclusion by investigating the folk biological knowledge of a culture living in sharply contrasting circumstances. The Sahaptin-speakers of the Columbia Plateau are hunter-gatherers who live in a temperate semi-desert. Thus their lives differ dramatically from those of their distant relatives, the Maya.

Dr. Schuster introduced me to a number of her friends and Indian colleagues at a 1975 conference on Indian education held at Yakima. She also put me in touch with Gary Young, director of the group seeking funding for the future Yakima Nation Cultural Heritage Center/Museum project. Meanwhile I had written to Dr. Deward Walker, Jr., well known for his Nez Perce research (e.g., Walker 1967). He put me in touch with his former student Larry Porter, a Plains Indian then studying tribal administration at the University of Washington. Porter's wife was a Yakima Indian involved with the local Johnson-O'Malley (JOM) citizens' committees on the reservation.[1] Through them I met Elmer Schuster, JOM director, and was invited to present my research proposals to the JOM committee. When the National

1. The Johnson-O'Malley Act (a.k.a. The Indian Welfare Act) of 1934 was part of the so-called Indian New Deal (see chapter 8). It provided, among other things, for financial assistance to be made available for the public school education of Indian children of recognized tribes. This source of education funding was supplemented by the Indian Education Act of 1972 (Title IV). On the Yakima Reservation in the mid-1970s these funds were allocated on the advice of a local Consortium of Johnson-O'Malley Committees composed of local Indian people.

Science Foundation funded my proposal to investigate "Sahaptin Ethnobiology," I offered my services on JOM bilingual efforts and in museum research and planning. In September 1976, my family and I moved to Toppenish for a full year's work.

My initial contact was with the late Donald Umtuch through the Museum project. We worked long hours together in the house trailer in Toppenish that served as the Museum planning office, reviewing plant and animal names, accounts of their uses, and stories of their adventures in the Myth Age. We pored over topographical maps of the reservation trying to pinpoint the locations of old villages and campsites recorded by Verne Ray (1936b) in the 1930s or that Don Umtuch had learned of and visited in his younger days. When Don was feeling well enough we would take a run in his new pickup down to the river or up into the foothills looking for instructive points of interest. Together we interviewed eighty-year-old, nearly blind Otis Shiloh at his home near Wapato, letting him touch and smell the plant specimens I brought with me. He and his wife, Alice, recorded eight hours of commentary and stories of his life in the early days up the Naches River and down the Yakima.

In early October 1976, Elmer Schuster arranged a meeting between me and James Selam (fig. 1.2), in response to my expressed interest in documenting traditional environmental and ecological knowledge. I remember that meeting well. James Selam certainly looked the part of the elder, with his long black hair streaked with gray, braided in a style strongly reminiscent of old photos I had admired of the great Nez Perce Chief Joseph. He was clearly examining me carefully, testing my motives. He agreed to work on the project and I soon learned that he was a man of strong intelligence committed first of all to the faithful documentation of the truth of what he had been taught and of what he had seen as a Columbia River Indian. We have collaborated in this effort for thirteen years and his dedication is as strong as ever. For my part I see the task of recording his story as a life-long, if part-time occupation for both of us, for the story is still unfolding.

As the first year progressed I was introduced to James's brothers and sister, daughter and sons, and to his sister-in-law Delsie Albert Selam (fig. 1.3), to her cousin, friend, and neighbor, Sara Quaempts, with whom she had grown up at Alderdale, their home village on the Columbia, and to Elsie Pistolhead, their senior.

Together that winter we recorded Elsie Pistolhead's presentation of their full repertoire of Coyote stories, carefully rehearsed by the three women,

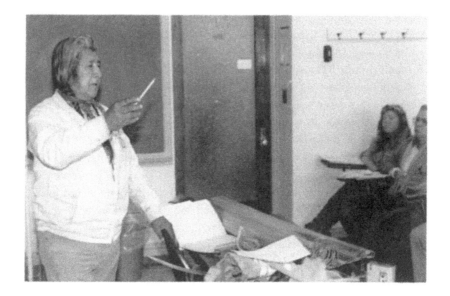

Fig. 1.2. James Selam lecturing at the University of Washington, April 1986.

filling over fifteen hours on tape in Sahaptin. That spring and summer was full as I sought to document the family's knowlege of every plant and animal we could contrive to encounter. We traveled in search of roots and berries north to Badger Mountain, west nearly to Mount St. Helens, and south into Oregon's Blue Mountains, retracing the peregrinations of their youth. Loose ends aside, I have been able to define over four hundred categories of plants and animals that they named in Sahaptin; about each plant or animal one could write a long, fascinating, and intricate story. I hope to someday. In this book I will try to give the reader just a hint of the richness of their folk ecology.

Though the bulk of my information has come from this one extended family, I have had the opportunity to compare notes with a number of other knowledgeable Sahaptin elders in order to assess the importance of local social and ecological contrasts in shaping their varied experience of their culture. A culture cannot be reduced to a list of facts. It is a living process in which individuals pit what they have learned of the world against the daily challenges they must face. What I have written down here reflects just a few facets of the jewel that is Plateau culture.

Fig. 1.3. Delsie "Elsie" Albert Selam, 1986.

Anthropologists and Indians

Anthropologists have a rather poor reputation among the more sophisticated Indian people today (see, for example, Deloria 1969). They have been characterized as a band of cultural thieves whose selfish interests are foremost in their pursuit of the Indians' knowledge. In this view anthropologists exploit Indian people, taking advantage of their customary generosity and their quiet, polite acceptance of others, a cultural ideal of interpersonal relations in many American Indian communities. As the story goes, the typical Navajo family consists of father, mother, brother, sister, and anthropologist, suggesting the ubiquitous intrusiveness of cultural anthropologists. Archaeologists may be even less appreciated as they are seen as professional grave diggers, liking nothing better than to find old Indian graves complete with skeletons and associated characteristic artifacts that may be duly tallied and recorded for storage on the dusty shelves of some university museum.

Indians understandably may feel rather like laboratory animals when subjected to the intense scrutiny of academic research. Nevertheless, I believe in the discipline of anthropology; I believe in its mission. Since the founding of American academic anthropology by Franz Boas before the turn of the century, anthropologists have been committed to the battle Boas (1940) waged against the racism of the European and American societies of his day. He fought that racist ideology with scientific data showing that peoples of all cultures, "races," and language groups were fully human. Furthermore, he argued that cultures should be judged not on some simple-minded scale of advancing civilization but in their own terms.

The primary goal of anthropology remains to promote an empathetic appreciation of all humanity, an appreciation that should bring people closer together in common understanding. Certainly, there have been cases of anthropologists who have strayed from this vision or been victimized by the prejudices of their day. However, I believe that in balance anthropologists have made a positive contribution in defense of the continuing existence of Indian cultural and social life. Furthermore, I believe that Indian people need anthropologists just as anthropologists need Indians.

Anthropologists need Indians, of course, because anthropology is the comparative study of human life and culture. If all humans were culturally indistinguishable, comparison would yield no insight into the human condition. Anthropology needs the contrasts that Indian cultures so richly provide. On the other hand, I maintain that Indians need anthropologists because they need allies in the heart of the politically and economically dominant white majority within the United States, a majority to which most American anthropologists belong.

Professional anthropologists are committed to support and defend the interests of the communities where they work, communities that have traditionally been relatively poor and powerless in the larger national and international political and economic arena. The American Anthropological Association "Statements on Ethics" (1976) asserts that,

> In research, anthropologists' paramount responsibility is to those they study. When there is a conflict of interest, these individuals must come first. Anthropologists must do everything in their power to protect the physical, social, and psychological welfare and to honor the dignity and privacy of those studied.

However, professional anthropologists recognize other commitments as well. These will not always be identical to the goals of the people they study, especially in view of the fact that such goals vary among the individuals of the study communities and between those individuals and their families, communities, and tribes. Anthropologists also have a public responsibility—a responsibility to the entire human community—to document the variety of human cultural adaptations in order to advance scientific understanding and intellectual appreciation of the human condition and to educate the public in that understanding. Again quoting the American Anthropological Association "Statements on Ethics," professional anthropologists owe the public,

> . . . a commitment to candor and to truth in the dissemination of their research results and in the statement of their opinions as students of humanity. . . . As people who devote their professional lives to understanding people, anthropologists bear a positive responsibility to speak out publicly, . . . on what they know and what they believe as a result of their professional expertise gained in the study of human beings.

Anthropologists at times will be torn between protecting what may be seen as a community's privileged store of cultural knowledge and publicly sharing that information to further the scholar's goal of expanding human awareness. On the one hand, we say that "Knowledge Is Power." From this point of view the knowledge revealed in this book may be seen as weakening the Indian community, depreciating the value of its cultural stock. On the other hand, we say that "The Truth Shall Set You Free." If the general public comes to better appreciate an Indian way of life by reading this book, does that not strengthen both the Indian culture and the culture of the nation?

I believe that the aphorism "Knowledge Is Power" is the more limited truth. Knowledge is power only in situations that may be described as "zero-sum games," where one player can gain only at the expense of another. For such to be the case knowledge must hold the key to controlling a scarce resource, a resource that everyone needs or wants but that not everyone can obtain: the stuff of insider trading. But is that true of human awareness? The cultural knowledge we share in the following pages—the language, mythology, ecological sense, and religious values—has more in common with a work of art, which is mute if it is not shown, pondered, appreciated, and acclaimed. To admire a work of art—or to appreciate another people's culture—is not to take possession of it but to gain in understanding. But does this benefit the Indian people who produced the culture we admire? I trust that it does; I believe that we are less likely to destroy what we understand than what we are ignorant of.

Ethnohistory

The reports of anthropologists who witnessed Plateau Indian culture in the first decades of this century are invaluable. They are, nevertheless, several steps removed from the autochthonous cultural reality that evolved on the Plateau prior to the onset of Euro-American influences. That elusive "pristine" Plateau culture is of great interest and importance to anthropology. It represents an experiment in human survival by which our ideas about the essentials of human life may be tested, reformulated, and refined. To get closer to this precontact cultural reality we must match the later anthropological accounts with the often incidental and distorted reports of earlier witnesses. If allowance is made for the refractory properties of the lenses through which these early historical observers viewed Plateau Indian life, valuable confirmation and qualification of contemporary ethnographic accounts can be obtained. Ethnohistory is the use of such materials to reconstruct a past ethnographic reality.

As we will see, we have no true eyewitness accounts for the Plateau as it existed free of Euro-American influence. Significant influences in the form of the horse and smallpox preceded the first white observers, members of the Lewis and Clark expedition. Lewis and Clark passed down the Snake and Columbia rivers in October 1805, spent the winter at the Columbia's mouth, then returned more or less as they had come in late April and May of 1806 (fig. 1.4). Their journals are a goldmine (Thwaites 1959 [1904]). David Thompson's transect of the mid-Columbia region in 1811 on fur company business is also full of surprising ethnographic detail (Glover 1962). Lewis, Clark, and Thompson were under orders to assess the "ethnographic" reality as accurately as possible. Other early journals are disappointing by comparison, as their authors had no interest in understanding the Indians' view of things (e.g., Cox 1831; Work 1923). Sources such as fur company records, carefully sifted with a specific goal in mind, produce valuable social, demographic, and economic data (e.g., Chance 1973; Boyd 1985; Boyd and Hajda 1987).

The first missionary records, Protestant and Catholic, though colored strongly by the missionaries' moral aspersions and spiritual ambitions, reflect long and close association with the Indians. Noteworthy are diaries recorded by Samuel Parker (1846), Henry Spalding and Asa Bowen Smith (Drury 1958), Daniel Lee and Joseph Frost (1968 [1844]), and Henry Perkins (n.d. [1838–43]). The Catholics in particular made a point of learning the

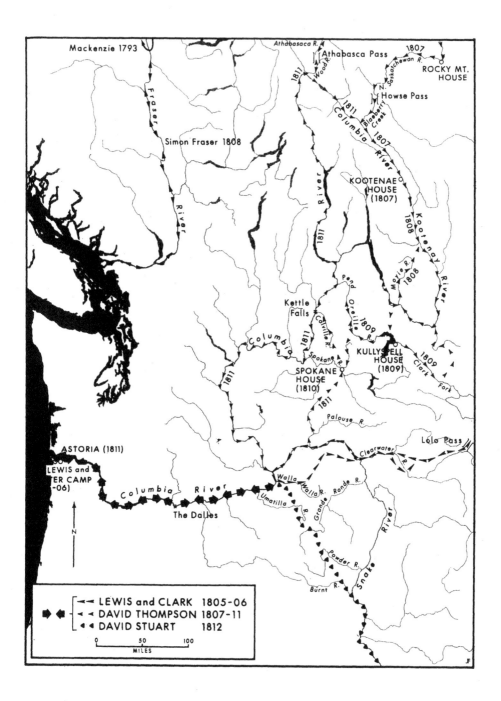

Fig. 1.4. Map of early explorations of the Northwest (reprinted from Meinig 1968:27).

native languages. Father Marie Pandosy's Yakima dictionary (1862) remains, incredibly, the only published Sahaptin lexicon. We may study civil government and military reports, such as those of the Wilkes expedition (Wilkes 1845), of McClellan and Gibbs' railroad survey of 1853 (McClellan 1854; Gibbs 1978 [1854]), military correspondence relating to the treaty councils and their aftermath (Doty 1978 [1855]), and MacMurray's interviews with Smohalla and his contemporaries (Mooney 1896). Bureau of Indian Affairs and Census Bureau documents may be combed for data relevant to particular points of interest.

Historians, of course, are well versed in the use of such materials, while anthropologists have all too often failed to appreciate their value. Plateau Indian life is poorly documented ethnographically, but it has been subjected to a measure of historical overkill. The number of histories of Nez Perce Chief Joseph's heroic campaign would fill a small library, and we have numerous blow-by-blow accounts of the minor skirmishes that pass for Plateau Indian wars. Several historical treatments, such as A. Josephy's *The Nez Percé Indians and the Opening of the Northwest* (1965), stand out as valuable analytical summaries. D. W. Meinig's *The Great Columbia Plain* (1968) is an excellent introduction to Plateau history since contact, emphasizing cultural, geographic, and economic processes. Most recently C. Miller's *Prophetic Worlds* (1985) digs beneath the surface events and superficial motives of missionaries and Indian prophets to show the complexity of their historical confrontation. Robert Ruby and John Brown's three popular Plateau Indian histories (1965, 1970, 1972) are full of lively detail but short on ethnographic perception.

Ethnography

Truly ethnographic work began late in the nineteenth century. In 1883 Dr. Will Everette (n.d. [1883]) elicited answers to an extensive ethnographic inventory distributed by J. W. Powell, director of the newly established Bureau of American Ethnology. The document lay unnoticed in the archives of the Smithsonian Institution until Bruce Rigsby discovered it and had it microfilmed about 1965. The plant and animal terms Everette recorded at Fort Simcoe in 1883 are virtually unchanged today (Hunn 1979).

Herbert Spinden's Nez Perce ethnography (1908) is the first published Plateau ethnographic account. Edward Curtis, the famous photographer of American Indians, wrote thumbnail sketches of several Plateau groups based on his visits in the early 1900s (Curtis 1911a, b). Boas encouraged ethnographic work in the Plateau; he helped edit the amateur accounts of James Teit for several Interior Salish groups (1900, 1906, 1909, 1928, 1930) and guided Melville Jacobs's studies of Sahaptin language and myth (1929, 1931, 1934, 1937a).

A field school organized by Jacobs in the summer of 1930 at Umatilla brought a number of now well-known linguistic fieldworkers to the Plateau, including Carl Voegelin and Morris Swadesh (Rigsby, personal communication). Another of Boas's students, Leslie Spier, coordinated a brief but intense ethnographic blitz of the Okanagan-Colville during the mid-1930s (1938), collaborated with Edward Sapir on studies of the Wishram (1930), and carefully documented the ethnohistorical material available on the Plateau Prophet Dance (1935), a problem pursued further by Cora DuBois (1938). George Murdock, best known for his statistically based global comparative analyses, also did fieldwork here in the mid-1930s, investigating kinship and social organization and shamanism at Warm Springs (1938, 1958, 1965, 1980). Archie Phinney's case is most noteworthy. Phinney was a Nez Perce Indian who earned a Ph.D. at Columbia University from Boas, the first Plateau Indian doctoral degree in anthropology. His collection of *Nez Percé Texts* (1934) was recorded from his mother. Additional Plateau ethnography of this vintage is Turney-High's Flathead and Kootenay material (1937, 1941) and Verne Ray's Sanpoil-Nespelem (1933) and comparative Plateau studies (1936, 1937, 1939, 1960).

Thereafter, Plateau ethnography is scant. Angelo Anastasio's University of Chicago dissertation on Plateau intertribal task groups and other interrelations has been influential (1972 [1955]), but recent work is dominated by Deward Walker's studies of Nez Perce religious acculturation (1967b, 1969, 1970, 1985 [1968]) and the work of his students both at Nez Perce and at Colville (e.g., Ross 1968). Walker has also collaborated with his Nez Perce colleague, Allen Slickpoo, on several publications. David French's ethnobotanical work at Warm Springs is legendary, while Kathrine French has written several key papers on Warm Springs social organization; they have other Sahaptin (and Chinookan) data on language and general ethnography. We must note also the extensive linguistic work of Haruo Aoki on Nez Perce, of Bruce Rigsby and Virginia Hymes on Sahaptin, and of William Elmendorf, Dale Kinkade, Laurence and Terry Thompson, and Anthony Mattina on various Interior Salish linguistic issues (L. Thompson 1973).

Recent studies include Nancy Turner's Northern Plateau ethnobotanical work (e.g., Turner, Bouchard, and Kennedy 1980, Turner et al., n.d.), Gary Palmer's Shuswap and Coeur d'Alene material (1975, 1978, 1985), dissertations by Helen Schuster on Yakima traditional religion (1975), by Alan Marshall on Nez Perce social ecology (1977), and by Lillian Ackerman on Plateau sex roles (1982). Schuster's Yakima bibliography (1982) is a useful resource. Popular accounts by archaeologists provide some ethnographic background (Daugherty 1973; Uebelacker 1984). Craig Lesley's award-winning novel, *Winterkill* (1984), gives us a vivid appreciation of a Umatilla Indian's contemporary reality.

Notwithstanding the above valuable works, no accessible, contemporary ethnographic account exists for any Plateau Indian culture. This book is intended to fill that gap.

2

History

ETHNOGRAPHY HAS often been written as if the ethnographic present—cultural conditions in effect, or presumed to be in effect, at the time of first Euro-American contact—had existed unchanged throughout the indefinite past. For some, this assumption rests on a view of traditional cultures as products of rigid habit, maintained by a fear of change. I believe such an assumption is unfounded. I believe that the dizzy pace of cultural change we have grown accustomed to is due not to any progress in human creativity but rather to the accelerating pace of change in the conditions to which people must adapt.

In fact, archaeological evidence suggests that the Plateau Indian way of life had remained fundamentally the same for ten thousand years prior to the first Euro-American influences of the eighteenth century. What demonstrable changes did occur during that long period of time can be traced to two factors: the biogeographical consequences of climatic change[1] and innovation in resource harvest strategies and techniques. The resulting changes represent subtle shifts of emphasis rather than profound redesign of Plateau economic and social patterns.

Geologists tell us that some fifteen thousand years ago massive sheets of ice bulged southward from great cordilleran ice fields centered in the rugged mountains of what is now British Columbia. South of the ice a veritable zoo of prehistoric animals flourished: mammoths, mastodons, giant ground sloths, camels, horses, sabre-toothed tigers, and huge condor-like birds. Familiar animals such as bison and elk were present also, but were "larger-than-life" size. The wholesale extinction that came with the retreat of the ice

---

1. C. Miller (1985:24–26) builds an elaborate argument for cultural changes in the Plateau due to a "Little Ice Age" said to have lasted from about A. D. 1550 until about 1690. However, there appears to be no clear archaeological support for his contention that this climatic "blip" had a significant impact on Plateau culture history.

has generated intense speculation, most particularly on the question of whether people had anything or everything to do with it (Martin 1973; Grayson 1977).

The ice sheets cut the American super-continent off from continued contact with the Eurasian land mass. But did human beings slip through the ice gate before it slammed shut? In short, was *Homo sapiens* a part of the Ice Age ecosystem of the New World? The issue is still hotly contested. What is certain is that Pleistocene (that is, Ice Age) human occupation of the Americas was sparse, at best, and has left few if any incontrovertible traces of human occupation in the Pacific Northwest (Borden 1979:964).

By 9,000 B.P. ("before the present"), rich archaeological deposits occurred virtually throughout the Columbia Plateau from the Dalles (Cressman et al. 1960), east to the Snake River (at Windust Cave and Hell's Canyon; see Kirk and Daugherty 1978, Ames and Marshall 1980–81), north to Kettle Falls, and west to the Fraser River canyon (the Milliken Site; Borden 1979:965–66). These early Plateau peoples harvested fish, including salmon and suckers (Ames and Marshall 1980–81:41), gathered plant foods in quantity, hunted large ungulates, and traded with coastal peoples for decorative shells (Kirk and Daugherty 1978:37), as they did in Lewis and Clark's time.

Archaeologists contest the relative significance of these major food sources at various periods in Plateau prehistory. Borden, for example, argues that the earliest Plateau peoples "concentrated on large game," and that "fowling and fishing were of negligible significance" (1979:964). He attributes the "strong emphasis on salmon fishing in addition to hunting" that later characterizes the Plateau, to an "Early Boreal Tradition" that spread south through interior British Columbia from Alaska as the ice sheets melted. The complex of features he associates with this "new tradition" are evident at the Ryegrass Coulee site near Vantage by 6,500 B.P. (pp. 967–68). Excavations near The Dalles well south of Vantage, however, disclose "huge quantities of salmon bones" by 7,700 B.P. (though none was found in the earliest levels there, dating to 9,800 B.P. [Borden 1979:965]). Ames and Marshall note that though "fishing tackle and fish remains [are] generally rare in [southeastern Plateau] sites, [they] are present throughout the regional sequence" (1980–81:41). Kettle Falls archaeology reveals evidence of fishing as early as 9,000 B.P., though it is not certain that people were drying the fish for winter rations at that early date (Kirk and Daugherty 1978:67).

Nelson (1973) has put forward a Salish-expansion theory, asserting that intensive fishing arrived—and with it, the historically documented Plateau winter village settlement pattern—with the invasion of the Plateau by Salish-speaking peoples. This movement originated in the Fraser Canyon area, and is estimated on linguistic grounds to have begun about 4,500 B.P. at the end of the Altithermal, a period of hotter and drier conditions than is typical today (Elmendorf 1965). Ames and Marshall dispute this diffusionist theory, arguing that pit-house villages first appear by 5,000 B.P. in the southeastern part of the Plateau, far from the center of Salish expansion (1980–81:43, 47). They ascribe this new residential pattern not to improved fishing techniques imported from the coast, but to an increased intensity of root food collection which emphasized a preexisting Plateau subsistence alternative. This shift in emphasis, they argue, might have been a response to some aspect of Plateau social dynamics rather than to outside influences. They cite an apparent shift in the types of grinding implements present at different levels of Snake River village sites as support for their views (pp. 41, 44). Kirk and Daugherty suggest, however, that though "milling stones seem rare until the Altithermal, . . . roots, berries, and greens must have been major foods before then. Milling stones and a quantity of chokecherry pits found in the earliest levels of the Marmes deposits bear this out" (1978:67).

In sum, despite competing theories as to the origins and antiquity of various features of the immediate precontact Plateau socioecological system, there is a consensus among prehistorians that "culture change on the Plateau proceeded at a modest pace through the millennia to historic time" (Kirk and Daugherty 1978:68). Projectile points, for example,

> . . . arranged by age, . . . show a progression in form and manufacturing technique, not necessarily an improvement through time—for early workmanship was as good as what came later—but a definite and ordered change. . . . Points became gradually smaller . . . reflecting the change in weaponry from spears that were thrust to those thrown with atlatls [i.e., spear-throwing boards], and finally to bows and arrows. (Kirk and Daugherty 1978:68)

Ames and Marshall conclude that "the available data indicate a generalized, broad spectrum adaptation . . . over the last 11,000 years: fishing, fowling, hunting, and gathering of both terrestrial and riverine resources" (1980–81:40).

Such cultural stability certainly belies the conclusion of one scholar, who remarked that the Flathead way of life "was neither stable nor durable, but a culture in transition, fragile, and out of equilibrium with its environment"

(Fahey 1974:xi). In direct contrast, we should conclude that Plateau culture worked, and as the saying goes, "If it ain't broke, don't fix it."

How do we know that the cultural persistence suggested by ten millennia of eating the same foods and making the same tools was not simply force of habit, the result of an inbred resistance to change? Proof to the contrary is found in the dramatic response of western Indians to Spanish horses. Creatures of habit confronted by such an animal, never seen before, might have been expected either to run away in fear or to hunt it as if it were bison or elk, following long established patterns of action. Instead they quickly learned to ride like the wind, to hunt at full gallop; some learned to geld their stallions (*n.b.:* in the Spanish, not the English, manner, as Osborne [1955] has shown) and to control both the behavior and the genetics of their herds. They learned what wealth could be, wealth in horses by the hundreds, by the thousands. They adopted patterns of raid and counterraid on a vastly expanded scale, with the horse the primary motive and means of these adventures. All this and more in the space of just two or three generations, so that the first whites to meet Plateau people face to face on their home ground met them as already transformed people. Clearly, Plateau Indians were not resistant to changes that they judged advantageous. A similar opportunism has been demonstrated for the Coast Salish people who adopted potato cultivation prior to direct Euro-American contact—with no outside encouragement or instruction and without prior experience with agriculture (Suttles 1953).

In fact, the horse is such a central part of traditional Plateau life that James Selam finds it very hard to believe (in fact, he still does not believe it, and I haven't been able to convince him) that Plateau Indians have not always had horses. His grandparents recalled that their grandparents had lots of horses and were expert at horse husbandry (at twenty-five years per generation that dates to 1820 or so) and that the Indian "cayuses" were smaller horses with other characteristics differentiating them from the horses of later white settlers. I suggest that in the absence of written histories modern Americans might find it hard to swallow the fact that there have not always been cars on our highways. In fact, the horse was as rapidly and thoroughly adopted by Plateau Indian society as the automobile has been by modern American society. In sum, a lack of dramatic cultural change does not demonstrate a lack of ability or receptivity to change. (Major events subsequent to first Euro-American contact are listed in chronological order in the *Plateau Historical Time Line,* see pp. 52–57.)

Outside Impacts I: The Horse

Smohalla, the Indian prophet from Priest Rapids, asserted that horses did not come from the white man but had been known to Indians long before white settlers arrived. As I have noted, James Selam believes the same. While it is true that a species of horse flourished in Ice Age North America, none appears to have survived the wave of extinctions that befell so many large mammals and birds as the last ice advance receded. Those first horses went the way of the mammoth, mastodon, North American camel, giant ground sloth, and the predators (e.g., the sabre-toothed cat) and scavengers (e.g., several "elder brothers" of the surviving California condor, now fighting for a last precarious foothold on earth) that lived off the great herds. At least there is no fossil evidence for horses for over ten millennia until, abruptly, they are everywhere in evidence just prior to contact.

We also have eyewitness accounts told by grandparents to their grandchildren, thence written down, of first encounters with the horse by Plateau Indians (Teit 1930:350–52; Haines 1938:434–36). Francis Haines has scoured the early diaries of explorers and fur traders in order to trace the spread of horses from their presumed source in the Spanish colonies in what is now New Mexico. The Spaniards had settled here early and were established before 1600. But they jealously guarded their prized stock, their extensive herds of cattle, sheep, and horses. Cattle provided red meat for their tables (and many of the frontiersmen considered all other foods scarcely worth eating), and they provided skins to be shipped for good profits to Europe. Sheep provided wool for a weaving industry. Horses as mounts symbolized the Spaniards' colonial domination. It was forbidden under severe penalty throughout Mexico for an Indian to ride a horse (Wolf 1959:212). Yet the Spanish seventeenth-century colonial empire had fallen on hard times and the Indian Pueblos, sensing this weakness, revolted in 1680, driving the Spaniards out for a time. Thousands of liberated Spanish horses spread up both sides of the Rockies: on the Plains from Apaches to Comanches, from Pawnees to Kansas Indians, reaching the upper Missouri Mandan villages by 1740; on the west from the Utes on the Colorado Plateau to the Shoshones of the Upper Snake, then to the Flatheads by 1720 and on to the Nez Perces and Cayuses sometime after 1730. Lewis and Clark encountered horses all along the Snake and Columbia to the edge of timber below The Dalles (e.g., Thwaites 1959 [1904], 3:119, 127, 132, 137, 140, 151; 4:280, 295, 301, 318, 322, 323, 327, 342, 344).

The horse was adopted as if the Indians had long awaited its coming. They had always been mobile people, as their lives depended on an extensive seasonal round up and down the mountain slopes from winter village to fishery to root digging flats to high mountain berry fields and hunting grounds. The horse was mobility epitomized. It did not radically change Plateau life so much as it accelerated existing patterns by enhancing this mobility.

The spread of horses among western Indians involved another dynamic element essential to our understanding of the speed with which horses were adopted: competition. A group without horses could not long withstand the pressure of mounted neighbors who began to use their horses to attack the weaker groups nearby. Verne Ray saw Plateau peoples as "pacifists" with the tendency exhibited most clearly by the Sanpoil, a group he considered archtypically Plateau (1933). They had remained isolated from the disruptive influences of Plains and coastal contacts longer than their neighbors. They were as well one of the last peoples on the Plateau to get horses. There is reason to doubt that this "pacifism" was a matter of cultural values (cf. Kent 1980). More likely Plateau peoples maintained largely peaceful intervillage relations because intermarriage and trade were more effective ways of gaining access to mates and useful supplies and of extending one's political influence than violence pursued on foot over large distances. The horse seems to have tipped the scales in favor of violence in many cases.

Lewis and Clark noted that the Columbia River villages from the Umatilla to The Dalles were mostly located on the north shore or on islands in the stream, for fear of the depredations of "Snake Indian" raiders. River Indians today delight in tales of courageous, miraculous escapes of their ancestors from these cruel attacks. Who were these waxpúš-pal (literally, the "rattlesnake people")? Like rattlesnakes they were powerful, deadly, and capricious. They were clearly Numic speakers from the south and southeast, but the Northern Paiutes of southern Oregon at that time were peaceful "digger Indians," preoccupied with gathering their annual supplies from a land considerably less generous than that of the Plateau. The evidence points to another group of Northern Paiutes, known subsequently as "Bannocks," and to their Shoshone colleagues. At an early date, they had adopted horses and a wide-ranging predatory life style, hunting bison herds up the headwaters of the Snake, Missouri, and Yellowstone rivers. Much later a similar mobile, predatory life style became the norm among Northern Paiutes of northern Nevada and southern Oregon, but with white migrant trains as the targets (cf. Steward and Wheeler-Voegelin 1974). The early Bannock penetrated Montana east of the continental divide and harrassed Blackfeet and Sioux groups, as yet still foot Indians. In response, certain Sioux asked for and received horses from their Flathead allies. Nez Perces and Cayuses, and soon after, Walla Wallas, Umatillas, and Yakimas, learned to retaliate in kind, joining this new arena of social intercourse. Their young men (sometimes with support groups of women) proved themselves in daring penetrations of Snake and Blackfeet territory in search of bison and the enemy.

Another piece of this historical puzzle is the gun. Not long after horses enlarged the scope of intergroup raiding (as well as expanding the range of less sanguinary interactions), fur traders began extending their frontier outposts toward the eastern base of the Rockies. Alexander Mackenzie of the Northwest Company pushed across the continental divide and down the Fraser and Bella Coola rivers to the sea in 1793 in the vanguard of this commercial expansion. In exchange for furs they provided—among other novel items of great interest to the Indians—guns and ammunition (Giannettino 1977). Just as the Indians quickly perceived the value of horses to their way of life, they could appreciate guns as vastly superior to their own hunting and fighting equipment. As each group acquired guns from the fur traders, they put them to use to press their newfound advantage over their unarmed western neighbors. The latter in turn were forced to obtain guns for themselves, for defense on their eastern flank and for offense on their western borders. Horses and guns, once made available, spread inevitably, the desire for them feeding on the consequences of their possession.

This new pattern of warfare, while a dramatic innovation, probably had little effect on the basic ecological relations of people and resources along the mid-Columbia River. Bison hunting may have substantially increased game in the diet of groups on the eastern borders of the Plateau—of Flatheads, Nez Perces, and Cayuses (cf. Farnham 1906 [1841]:329). These were the Plateau peoples most active in the bison-hunting "task groups" (Anastasio 1972 [1955]), all groups with limited access to the salmon resources of the mid-Columbia. For mid-Columbia Indians, however, bringing bison meat home would have been like "carrying coals to Newcastle" in light of the abundance of salmon at their doorsteps. More important for them, I suspect, was the value of bison skins for robes and blankets, which might then be traded for surplus food or given in marriage exchanges. James Selam still keeps an old bison robe obtained by trade from Montana, which was handed down from his grandmother's grandmother.

Horses soon became accepted as standards of wealth, movable wealth that needed only to be set loose to feed on the nutritious range grasses (referred to collectively in Sahaptin as waskú), abundant on the low plains and into the mountains. Such wealth gave impetus to ambition, in most hunting-gathering societies severely restrained in the interests of band harmony (cf. Lee 1979).

The word for horse in Sahaptin is ḱúsi; dog is ḱusi-ḱúsi, or "little horse." (Curiously we find the same equation in a number of other, unrelated Indian languages such as Blackfeet, Sioux, and Cree [Roe 1955:61, 104].) It seems safe to assume that before there were horses, dogs were called ḱúsi. (Alternatively, we might interpret this linguistic evidence as support for James Selam's belief in the autochthonous horse.) Horses, when first encountered, might have been described as ḱusi-wáakułł, "dog-like," which was a common linguistic convention (Hunn and French 1984). Only later would the horse have co-opted the dog's name as its own, leaving the dog as the junior partner. But why horse and dog? Why not, as in the case of the Pomo of California, relate the horse to the deer (Bright 1960:217), a biologically more defensible position, as both horse and deer are ungulates while the dog is a carnivore? The similarity of dog and horse is clearly one of cultural role rather than of morphological or behavioral resemblance, the latter principle constituting the basis for modern scientific biological taxonomy. Dogs and horses were more nearly human than their wild counterparts, coyote and deer. They lived with humans as pets (kákya) and helped humans at their labors—dogs for twelve millennia as hunting partners, camp guards, and garbage collectors, and horses in the ways I have noted. Neither was considered edible by most Plateau peoples, who were rather disgusted at the fact that Lewis and Clark's men much preferred dog and horse flesh to the Indians' dried roots and fish.

Horses remain, ironically, a symbol of the old Indian way of life. Several hundred run wild over the Yakima Reservation foothills. The tribe protects them against the urgings of stockmen who see wild horses as economic competitors. James Selam fondly recalls rounding up wild horses as a young man. In the old days, horses were recognized individually and their owners' rights respected. Branding was thus unnecessary before whites arrived. James believes that Indians had a special way with wild horses, an empathy that allowed them to walk right up to a mustang and to break it with ease. He regrets that the traditional Indian horse, small and hardy, has been so interbred with other stock that the true "cayuse" is now rarely seen. His

Sahaptin vocabulary is rich with horse terminology, including terms for at least thirty "breeds" (see Appendix 1).

Outside Impacts II: Pestilence

The new life promised by the coming of the whites and widely prophesied brought a very high price. As far as can be ascertained at present the first bill came due about 1775. Robert Boyd believes, based on a meticulous survey of early documents, that the first wave of smallpox might have come from the west about 1775 from ships exploring for furs along the north Pacific coast (1985:81–90), rather than up the Missouri in 1782, date of a well-documented epidemic that swept across the Plains. Perhaps that later epidemic exhausted itself among the immune survivors of the earlier outbreak on the Plateau.

Smallpox again rampaged along the Columbia in 1801, attacking a new generation of susceptibles grown up since the first visitation (Boyd 1985:99–100). This likely carried off another 10 to 20 percent, reducing the original population to about one half by the time of Lewis and Clark's exploration. In their journals Lewis and Clark describe old men with pockmarked faces among the Upper Chinooks of the Lower Columbia River and were told that the disease had struck a generation before (Thwaites 1959 [1904], 4:241; see also Boyd 1985:78–80, 91–92, 102–3). Smith documents its ravages among the Nez Perces at about the same time (Drury 1958:136). Two more waves of smallpox may have afflicted Indian people on the mid-Columbia. An outbreak of disease reported in 1824–25 (Boyd 1985:338–41) may have been smallpox. The epidemic of 1853 was documented in detail by the McClellan railroad survey party as they conducted their explorations for a cross-Cascades rail route (McClellan 1854; see Table 1.).

Smallpox was devastating, but proved not to be the worst killer of Indians. That distinction is awarded to a disease described as "fever and ague" that broke out at the Hudson's Bay Company's Fort Vancouver headquarters in the summer of 1830 (Cook 1955; Boyd 1985:112–45). It raged unchecked for four years before abating. It was clearly seasonal, dying back in winter only to flare out again each summer. It emptied the Chinookan villages of the lower Columbia and decimated Indian populations throughout the Willamette Valley and in the densely settled Central Valley of Califor-

TABLE 1

Plateau Epidemic History (Boyd 1985:336–37)

Epidemic Area/ Ethnolinguistic Unit	1770s smallpox	1801 smallpox	1807–8 "distemper"	1824–25 "mortality"	1831–37 respiratory diseases	1844 pertussis, scarlatina	1848 measles	1853 smallpox	1853 smallpox
(Subarctic)									
Carrier					X[c]				X
Chilcotin									X
Northeast Area									
Lillooet									X
Thompson									
Lower									
Upper			X						X
Nicola									
Shuswap									
Fraser									X
Northwest Area									
North Thompson									
Kamloops			X						
Kutenai			X						
Upper									
Flatbow									

Central Area								
Salish group								
Flathead			X		X		X	
Pend Oreille/								
Kalispel								
Spokan			X[a]	(X)		S	X	X
Coeur d'Alene			(X)[a]	X				X
Okanagan group								
Colville/Lake					X		X	X
Nespelem/				(X)				
Sanpoil/Sinekalt								
Sinkaietk/Methow								X
Okanagan/				X				
Similkameen								
Columbia group								(X)
Chelan								(X)
Wenatchee								(X)
Sinkiuse							X	X
NW Sahaptin								(X)
Kittitas								(X)
Yakima				X			X	X
Klikitat							(X)	X

TABLE 1 (continued)

Epidemic Area/ Ethnolinguistic Unit	1770s smallpox	1801 smallpox	1807–8 "distemper"	1824–25 "mortality"	1831–37 respiratory diseases	1844 pertussis, scarlatina	1848 measles	1853 smallpox	1853 smallpox
Central Area									
CR Sahaptin						P	X		
Tenino-Tygh	◄———————————————►	◄———————————————►				P	X		
Wayam/Skin						P	X	X	
Umatilla/John Day						P	X		
NE Sahaptin							(X)		
Walla Walla				X	X	P	X		
Wanapam				X			(X)		
Palus							(X)		
Southeast Area									
Nez Perce	◄———————————————►	◄———————————————►			X	S			
Lower Snake									
Clearwater									
Upper snake									
Cayuse				X	X	P	X		

a 1819 "Grate Sickness"
b 1827 pertussis
c 1836 smallpox
X = documented; (X) = undocumented; P = pertussis (whooping cough); S = scarlatina (scarlet fever)

nia. Sober estimates of the mortality directly or indirectly attributable to this scourge in the four-year span of 1830 to 1833 is 90 percent!

Historical epidemiologists are largely in accord on the identity of this disease as malaria, though it was no doubt frequently complicated by influenza and other exotic diseases ready to take advantage of a body weakened by the struggle against malaria. The requisite anopheline mosquitoes thrived along the Columbia east to near The Dalles and required only the introduction of the disease agent in the blood of an infected passenger of one of the numerous trading vessels arriving from the Mexican coast, where malaria had arrived with the African slaves brought to work colonial plantations in the sixteenth century. But the "fever and ague" did not spread much above The Dalles, sparing the Plateau peoples the near total extinction suffered downriver. Nor did it spread north to Puget Sound or Canada. There are no suitable mosquito species in those areas. Oregon's major cities bear names such as Portland, Astoria, Eugene, and Salem, while Washington's have Indian names such as Seattle, Tacoma, Spokane, and Yakima (Ramsey 1977:xxi), reflecting the distribution of malaria.

Though spared from malaria, the Plateau people next found themselves in the path of thousands of immigrants crossing the continent over the Oregon Trail (see Table 2). Seasonal respiratory diseases had become commonplace among the Indians who congregated at fur trading posts each winter (Boyd 1985:341–48), a pattern repeated at the missions. In 1843 after a tour east, Marcus Whitman returned to his Walla Walla mission at the head of a train of one thousand settlers. This scene was to be repeated each subsequent year. With the immigrants came a potpourri of diseases against which the Indians had no resistance. In 1844 there was scarlet fever and whooping cough, in 1846 more scarlet fever, and so forth (Boyd 1985:349–50). Many white settlers saw this mortality of the Indians as an act of God,

TABLE 2
Immigrants at the Whitman Mission, 1841–47

1841	1842	1843	1844	1845	1846	1847
25	100	800	1,500	3,000	1,500	5,000

Note: From National Park Service, Whitman National Historical Monument.

clearing the rich bottomlands of the Willamette for Christian settlement (Scott 1928).

The coincidence of Whitman's hosting the hordes of settlers arriving late each fall from their arduous overland journey and the outbreak of new epidemics was not lost on the Indians. When measles erupted about the time of the immigrants' arrival in 1847, the Indians concluded that Whitman's murderous influence must be stopped. Ironically, in this case it is more likely that measles was introduced earlier that summer by Indians returning from an expedition to California (Heizer 1942).

On November 29, a group of Cayuses attacked the mission, killing Whitman, his wife, and eleven other whites, and taking some fifty captives, subsequently ransomed by Peter Ogden of the Hudson's Bay Company. This brought an abrupt end to the initial period of missionary activity in the Plateau. The massacre inspired revenge and fear among the settlers and initiated a series of violent confrontations—the Cayuse, Yakima, and Palouse "wars"—between whites and the remnants of the Plateau peoples. These conflicts were concluded some thirty years later with the effective confinement of the majority of the Indians to reservations.

The history of Indian-white relations in the Columbia Plateau has been first and foremost a history of the ravages of disease, for the most part inadvertently transmitted by Old World immigrants to defenseless New World populations (see fig. 2.1), which drastically reduced aboriginal populations and disrupted the social and spiritual fabric of Indian life. After the treaties were signed and the Indians confined to reservations, the significance of introduced diseases faded and political events affecting Indian life took center stage.

Outside Impacts III: The Fur Trade

Elegant fur clothing was in demand among European and Chinese elites late in the eighteenth century. Staggering profits could be made with luck, industry, daring, and access to the untapped potential of the North American forests. The Hudson's Bay Company (HBC) claimed first rights to the furs of the boreal forests of the Arctic-bound rivers west to the MacKenzie and had a secure foothold on the Northwest Coast.

The Northwest Company (NWC), also British-owned, controlled the St. Lawrence–Great Lakes axis and was rapidly expanding west across the

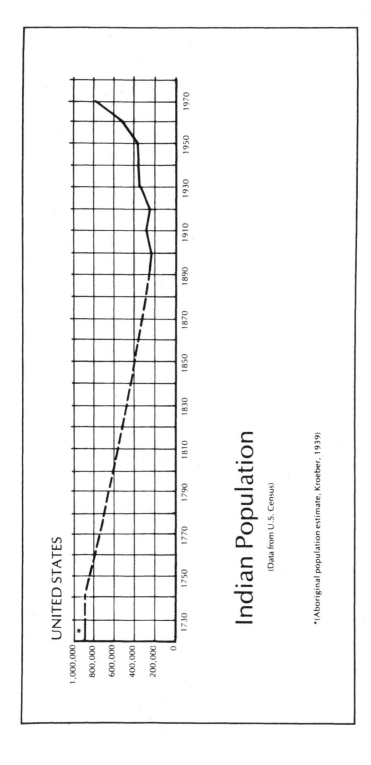

Fig. 2.1. Indian population trends (reprinted from *Oregon Indians*, Zucker et al. 1983:152, with permission of the Oregon Historical Society Press).

continent at the southern edge of the great northern forests, portaging from Lake Superior to Lake Winnipeg and thence up the Saskatchewan and Athabaska rivers toward the Rocky Mountains. Alexander Mackenzie crossed the divide in 1793 exploring for this company, and Simon Fraser persevered down the Fraser to its mouth in 1808. David Thompson laid the foundation for the Northwest Company's dominant trading position in the northern Plateau during his travels of 1807–11, a truly remarkable exploration and careful mapping of the Columbia's headwaters. His maps are of striking detail and accuracy. He also established good working relations with local native peoples and founded a series of posts in Kootenai, Flathead, Spokane, and Pend Oreille territory before pushing down the Columbia River to Astoria in 1811.

These British companies, relying heavily on French-Indian trappers who had learned the fur business during an earlier period of French colonial hegemony, were busily engaged in setting up long overland supply routes and communication lines (the NWC's route passed through Red Deer and Montreal, to London while the HBC's route went via York Factory on Hudson Bay, thence by ship to London). Simultaneously, the Americans were pursuing a daring alternative bankrolled by John Jacob Astor. Astorian ships (of the Pacific Fur Company) out of New York rounded Cape Horn, touched base in Hawaii (the "Sandwich Islands") where native seamen were recruited (some of whom subsequently married Northwest Indian women and were absorbed into local Indian society), then turned northwest seeking out the Columbia River mouth. After crossing the river's treacherous bar, Astor's ships docked at their outpost, Astoria, established in 1811 just before Thompson's arrival from upriver.

Northwest furs were collected here from throughout the Columbia drainage basin for shipment to China. There they were exchanged for rare spices, silks, and tea for resale in New York and Boston (see fig. 2.2). Thus, the Americans came to be known to the Indians as "Boston men" (páštin).

The Astorian operation involved an overland link for rapid communications. The first Astorian overland party met a series of misadventures seeking a way down the Snake River, but it eventually won through to the Columbia. In the process the party discovered the South Pass route and defined what subsequently became the Oregon Emigrant Trail, artery of Northwest colonization. The budding rivalry between Britons and Americans for the Northwest fur trade was aborted by the War of 1812. Astor, fearful of a British blockade, chose to sell his entire Columbia operation to

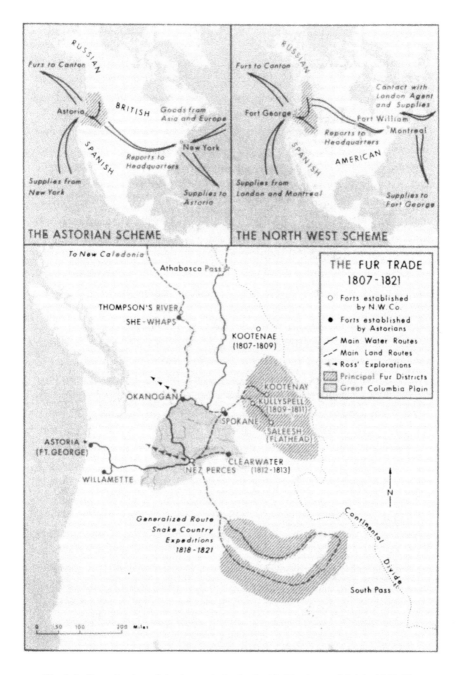

Fig. 2.2. Organization of the fur trade in the Pacific Northwest (Meinig 1968:49).

his Northwest Company rivals. Many of Astor's employees stayed on to work for the NWC, notably Alexander Ross, David Stuart, and Donald Mackenzie, important figures in the next two decades of Northwest fur trade history (Meinig 1968:48–95).

The Columbia Department never proved a great producer of furs. In part this may be attributed to the fact that a good fraction of the territory is not forested and supported relatively few fur bearers. Equally significant is the fact that Plateau Indian people were simply not interested in trapping furs for trade (G. Simpson in Merk 1968:42, 54). Nez Perces considered it beneath their dignity; they "spurned the idea of crawling about in search of furs" as a life "only fit for women and slaves" (quoted in Meinig 1968:52). More important perhaps is the fact that mid-Columbia River Indians relied primarily on roots and fish for an ample subsistence, while hunting and trapping had been much more central to the aboriginal subsistence strategies of the boreal forest Indians with whom the fur traders had been dealing east of the Rockies.

The Plateau was nevertheless strategically located for fur extraction from the highly productive New Caledonian (forest region of the headwaters of the Fraser, Yukon, and Peace rivers) and upper Snake River territories. Furs from New Caledonia could be shipped more economically via a short portage at Kamloops to the Okanogan and by that river to the Columbia, down the Columbia to the sea and to market by ship, than overland to the east.

Meanwhile, following the 1818 agreement between Britain and the United States to share the "Oregon country," the Northwest Company embarked on an aggressive Snake River strategy designed to deny that region's furs to the Americans (G. Simpson in Merk 1968:46). "Brigades" of trappers (not local Indians) were provisioned each summer at Astoria (renamed Fort. George after the British takeover in 1813 and moved to Fort Vancouver in 1825 under Hudson's Bay Company control). They packed their provisions up the Columbia to the Walla Walla by canoe, then loaded their goods on horseback for the overland passage to the upper Snake. Here they devoted the winter to intensive trapping on all the Snake's tributaries, returning with their furs to Astoria (or Fort Vancouver) in June of the following year. (The journals of several Snake River brigades have been published, as, for example, that of John Work for 1826–27.) At Astoria the joint fur production of New Caledonia, the upper Columbia, and the upper Snake was loaded on a London-bound ship.

The Plateau Indians' role in this operation was more that of spectator than participant, though they were essential sources of horses used by the overland brigades and—curiously—they were major providers of venison for fur company personnel, who disdained fish and native roots. The Columbia River was the main link in these commercial chains and Fort Nez Perce— established at the mouth of the Walla Walla River by Donald Mackenzie in July of 1818—eventually became the nerve center of the entire inland operation, located as it was at the strategic junction of the Snake and Columbia-Fraser shipping routes. Fort Nez Perce retained this importance until the 1846 treaty established 49° N as the U.S.–Canadian boundary. The post here—"fort" is a more descriptive term—became known as the "Gibraltar of the Columbia" and saw some of the most intense Indian-white interactions of the period.

Indian–fur trader relations were relatively benign, since the goal of the trade was a profitable business in furs. To that end the Indians had to tolerate the traders' presence, even be willing to assist by providing trading posts with horses and venison. The Indians were otherwise free to pursue their seasonal rounds and traditional social relations. Traders actively discouraged intergroup warfare, however, as an impediment to free movement of the trapping brigades. (This warfare was originally inspired—or at least exacerbated—by the guns and ammunition provided to the Indians by the traders.)

Social and cultural impacts were substantial, but largely unintentional. Foreign diseases have been mentioned as one consequence of the fur traders' presence. Also important and unintended was the sometimes fatal attraction that fur posts had for nearby Indian people as a source of material goods and food. Fur posts soon formed the nucleus of large winter concentrations of Indians, as many found it easier to rely on the obvious abundance in the fur traders' larder than on their own subsistence efforts. Crowds of poorly nourished Indian people provided ideal conditions for the spread of influenzas, and increased winter mortalities were noted in the neighborhood of the fur posts as early as 1810 (Boyd 1985:341–48).

Marriages between Indian women and European or Métis trappers had the effect of expanding the Plateau Indian social network to include individuals of radically different world views. Some twenty Catholic Iroquois trappers married into Flathead society about 1820 and are credited with providing the eastern Plateau Indians with their first instruction in Christian ritual practice (Frisch 1978). The openness to intermarriage continues today, as shown by Walker's Nez Perce marriage statistics (1967c), maintaining the

traditional indeterminacy as to the boundaries of "tribal" and Indian identity. This indeterminacy today has new consequences because ethnic or
"tribal" membership has become the legal basis for access to a variety of
valuable rights and property.

Outside Impacts IV: Missionaries

Fur traders were at least nominally Christian and, as we will see in chapter 7, provided models for the emerging prophet dance rituals of worship,
superficial but conspicuous borrowings. The fur traders' resistance to diseases that decimated the Indians was attributed to their spiritual powers
and to the power of the writing in their books. Following the Hudson's Bay
Company's takeover in 1821 and HBC Governor Simpson's inspection tour
of the Columbia Department in 1825 (Merk 1968), several chiefs' sons were
brought to the Company's Red Deer headquarters to be educated in the
English manner.[2] Disease took the lives of most of these young men, but
one, "Spokan Garry," returned to a position of influence bolstered by his
ability to read from the Book and to communicate with the foreigners in
their own language (Jesset 1960).

Inspired by Garry's success, a delegation of four Nez Perce and Flathead
young men set out eastward intending to petition directly to the whites for a
teacher of their own (Haines 1937; Smith in Drury 1958:106–7). They strag-
gled into St. Louis in the summer of 1832, riding a cresting wave of messianic zeal and piety that spread throughout the young United States in the
wake of the publication of William Walker's "Macedonian cry" (1833; Haines
1955:57–70).[3] Historical accounts indicate that these Plateau emissaries were
well received by none other than William Clark, of Lewis and Clark fame,
now elevated to the rank of general. Yet, the spectre of disease intrudes

2. Simpson also encouraged—rather, demanded—that HBC posts establish farms
to reduce the cost of provisioning personnel and at the same time reduce their dependence on the local Indians for food. To that end he ordered the headquarters of the
Department moved from Astoria (known as Fort George since the British buyout in
1813) to Fort Vancouver, where the land was better suited to farming.

3. As Christopher Miller (1985) has shown, the apocalyptic visions of the Indian
prophets were strangely reflected in the apocalyptic visions of the Americans of that
day, who saw in the heathen Indians a golden opportunity to prove that America was
to be the governmental seat of the Millennium before Christ's triumphant and eagerly
awaited return.

again. All four of the petitioners sickened and died before they could bring their news back home.

The missionary societies responded. The Methodists sent Jason Lee with Nathaniel Wyeth's fur brigade in 1834. Lee took one look at the arid Plateau and proceeded apace to the lush (and largely Indianless, thanks to the "fever and ague" of 1830–33) Willamette Valley, where he established a mission that served the immigrants. The rival ABCFM (American Board of Commissioners for Foreign Missions, a joint Presbyterian, Congregational, and Dutch Reform effort, active in Hawaii since 1820) sent Samuel Parker and Marcus Whitman with an 1835 brigade. Parker visited the Nez Perces while Whitman returned overland to recruit a permanent missionary contingent for the following year.

Parker explored mission opportunities among the Nez Perces' neighbors before proceeding down the Snake River to the Columbia and Fort Vancouver where he caught a ship for home. His published travelog (1846 [1838]) is of ethnohistorical value, but was of no help to the Whitmans and Spaldings who returned overland in the summer of 1836 just as Parker was setting sail.

The Whitmans established their mission on the Walla Walla in Cayuse territory; the Spaldings moved on to Lapwai to address the Nez Perces. In 1838 the Walkers and Eellses arrived to set up the Tshimakain mission to the Spokanes, and the Methodists sent Perkins to join with Jason and Daniel Lee in founding a station at The Dalles. Like the Hudson's Bay posts, the mission compounds were supported by farming operations. Self-sufficiency, however, was only a secondary goal of the missionary farmers. Uppermost in their minds was the goal of transforming their nomadic charges into "civilized" farmers. As Henry Spalding noted, "no savage people . . . have ever become Christianized on the wing . . ." (quoted in Meinig 1968:123). The Indians' mobility was a great impediment to the missionaries' efforts at schooling the Indian children in "civilized ways" and in eradicating sinful practices, such as the polygamy of chiefs and other influential men. As spiritual shepherds they were intent on corraling their restless flock.

Whitman and Spalding had considerable initial success. By 1843 they reported 234 children in school and 140 Nez Perces farming wheat, corn, and potatoes at Lapwai, and 60 Cayuses farming at the Waiilatpu mission (Meinig 1968:136). Perkins and Lee are credited with 1,000 conversions in their great winter revival of 1839–40 at The Dalles (Perkins 1843, 1850). However, settled farming life represents a radical break from the social and ecological patterns familiar to hunting-gathering peoples, and the Indians soon reverted to their time-tested seasonal rounds, leaving the missionaries with empty pews.

Yet the missionaries' example was not ignored and Indians miles from the missions took up farming and the rearing of cattle as an adjunct to their traditional economic activities. (They were already highly knowledgeable about plants, their life cycles, and the conditions favoring plant growth.) Joel Palmer, subsequently named Indian agent for Oregon, noted in 1845 that Indians camped on the Umatilla River were peddling their farm produce to passing immigrants on this branch of the Oregon Trail (1906 [1847]:111). Clearly, in this case the Indian farmers had no intention of growing all their own food but rather adopted farming as a means to obtain the white man's goods through exchange.

The heyday of this first round of missionary activity on the Plateau was brief, beginning with Whitman and Spalding's arrival in 1836 and ending abruptly after the death of the Whitmans in 1847. The "massacre" at Waiilatpu led to the precipitous abandonment of most existing mission stations, Protestant and Catholic alike. It marked the beginnings of military pacification, the forced Indian resettlement on reservations, and the onslaught of white settlement, a process essentially complete in the Plateau by the early 1880s.

Indian disillusionment with the missionaries, who first had been hailed as the miraculous realization of hopeful prophecy, was due to several factors. Foremost among these must be counted the progressive certainty in the Indians' minds of the association of epidemic disease and the presence of whites, an association interpreted quite reasonably as resulting from the superior spiritual forces controlled by the missionaries. This belief that an excess of spiritual power leads to *murderous* power is a deep article of Plateau Indian faith. An Indian doctor with too much power eventually becomes a watay-ɬam, "one who kills people with power." So the Cayuses killed Whitman in self-defense to prevent the final extermination of the Indians by his power. As Smohalla said, "Dr. Whitman many years ago made a long journey to the east to get a bottle of poisen (*sic*) for us. He was gone about a year [1842–43], and after he came back strong and terrible diseases broke out among us. The Indians killed Dr. Whitman, but it was too late. He had uncorked his bottle and all the air was poisoned" (Mooney 1896:724–25). Disease was simply the symptom of a deeper spiritual cause.

In truth, in 1842 Whitman had returned to ABCFM headquarters in Boston to appeal the board's order dismissing Spalding and closing the missions at

Waiilatpu and Lapwai (Drury 1958:241, 335). This radical decision on the part of the ABCFM Prudential Committee had been transmitted in a letter of February 1842, received at the Oregon missions that October. The decision—rescinded the following year—was based largely on a series of highly critical letters sent to the ABCFM by Asa Smith, an ABCFM missionary sent west in 1838 to join the Whitmans and Spaldings. He pushed for an independent station and was authorized to establish a mission at Kamiah, upstream from Spalding's mission at Lapwai and deep in the heart of Nez Perce country.

Smith's letters reveal a deep skepticism about the entire Northwest Indian missionary enterprise, doubts not entirely reducible to Smith's ingrained pessimism. Smith was a well-educated man trained in Latin and Greek, and he took the task of learning the native language seriously. "Without a knowledge of the language we are useless," he intoned, and "the difficulty of translation seems almost insurmountable" (Drury 1958:104, 138). He worried at length over how to faithfully convey the true meaning of such words as "baptism" (Drury 1958:112). (Perkins at The Dalles similarly puzzled over how to translate "prophet," "hallowed," and "blessed" into Sahaptin, n.d. [1838–43], Book 1:6–8.) Smith chastised Spalding for admitting two Nez Perces, Timothy and Joseph (father of Chief Joseph of later fame), into the church: ". . . those individuals were admitted to the church without any articles of faith or covenant *in their language* [author's emphasis] & no one is able to explain the articles of faith & covenant satisfactorily in the Nez Perce language. Consequently they know not what they are required to believe" (Drury 1958:143).

Smith finally despaired of his mission to the Nez Perces because of the language problem. He calculated that it would require years of effort at substantial expense to translate the scriptures into a language which he estimated was spoken by less than 2,500 people and which was, in his judgment, doomed soon to die out altogether. (A prophecy not yet realized!) How could such a mission be justified when, "The same array of means . . . is necessary here for 3000, as needed for the millions of Siam, or of China" (Drury 1958:141).

Smith also took issue with Spalding's insistence on converting the Nez Perce Indians to a settled farming life. He argued on the basis of a rather astute ecological analysis that settling the Nez Perces would prevent them from providing for their own subsistence, which he correctly judged required a highly dispersed and mobile settlement pattern (Drury 1958:134–35, 182). The missionaries would thus be forced to feed them as well, at great expense and at the cost of destroying their self-reliance, a moral value esteemed highly by the Calvinist denominations of the ABCFM. Clearly, Smith's doubts were worthy of serious consideration by the mission board, ad hominem attacks aside.

Smith's departure from the mission field in the spring of 1841, however, removed an irritant from the Plateau mission community, and the Cayuse and Nez Perce missions were allowed to continue, despite increasingly hostile relations with the local Indians.

Schisms among Christian denominations were another source of Indian disillusionment. Other Protestants were tolerated by Whitman and Spalding, but Catholics were viewed as agents of the anti-Christ. Papal paranoia was a strong force in the early American world view, and the successes of the itinerant "black robes," as the missionary Catholic priests were known to the Indians, inspired Protestant missionaries to ever more aggressive proselytizing. Catholic influence originated with the French Canadian fur trappers in the Hudson's Bay Company's employ long before Fathers F. N. Blanchet and M. Demers passed through the Plateau in 1838. Subsequent Catholic missions were established along the Flathead River in the Bitterroot Valley, on the St. Joe River in Coeur d'Alene country, on the Umatilla River (where Father A. N. Blanchet moved in with a chief's family), and on Ahtanum Creek among the Yakimas. They also set up camp opposite the Methodist mission at the Dalles, making the mid-Columbia a battleground for Indian allegiance (see fig. 2.3).

Religious conflicts masked underlying national rivalries, pitting Protestants, symbolic of American "Manifest Destiny," against Catholics who symbolized European colonial control. Some historians suspect that Whitman's return at the head of a party of 1,000 emigrants was part of an official strategy of American preemptive settlement of the (then) disputed Oregon Territory (Miller 1985:142–43)—which was not incorporated into the United States until 1846—to forestall British designs there. So Whitman did bring back the "bottle of poison" in his role as emigrant guide and host. His mission at Waiilatpu—and Perkins' at The Dalles also—came to be primarily a travelers' hostel, until the Cayuses took their desperate action.

Though Ogden of the Hudson's Bay Company ransomed the Whitman hostages, the HBC was already in the process of selling its assets south of the 49th parallel and redirecting its coastal transshipment operation via Fort Langley on the Fraser delta. So ended both the era of the early missions and the era of the fur trade. So began the hegemony of the United States.

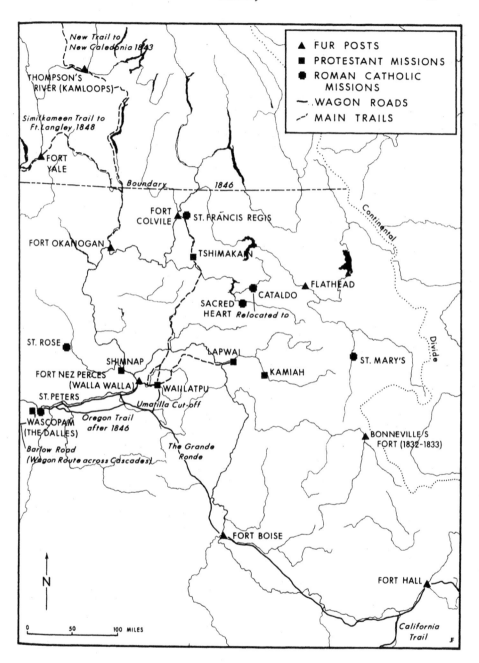

Fig. 2.3. Early missions and fur posts (Meinig 1968:113).

The "Indian wars" of the Northwest have fascinated history buffs for a long time and the literature on the subject is voluminous. The Indians' fate, however, was already sealed before those conflicts began. The heroism of Chief Joseph of the Nez Perces and of the Yakima leader Kamiakin must be understood in the context of their despair at the destruction already accomplished by virus and protozoan. A "different kind of man" had come and the world was indeed falling to pieces (Miller 1985:ii). Governor Isaac I. Stevens of the recently created Washington Territory (carved in 1853 from the Oregon Territory that had been established in 1848) was motivated by one goal, to gain legal title to the land so that settlement might proceed unhindered by the "dying race" of Indians. The chiefs who signed Stevens' treaties had no chips left with which to bargain. They did not know how the paper they were marking with their "X" marks would determine the fate of their twentieth-century descendants. How could they? They knew well that the whites coveted their lands. They also sensed the hopelessness of their position as defenders of their ancestral homes. Selling their birthright in the name of their fellow Indians was certainly an act they could scarcely contemplate or understand. We will never know what was in the chiefs' thoughts as they made those marks on the treaty papers. We do know, however, what those marks mean today.

Treaties

Between 1778 and 1871 the government of the United States negotiated and signed 371 treaties with Indian groups of the present-day United States (Zucker, Hummel, and Høgfoss 1983:69). Many were never ratified by the U.S. Senate, the body constitutionally empowered to make treaties in the name of the United States. Others were rescinded, modified, misapplied, or ignored in the years that followed, until Congress voted in 1871 that "no treaties shall hereafter be negotiated with any Indian tribe within the United States as an Independent Nation or People." Subsequent Indian reservations were established (and rescinded) by executive order (as in the case of the Colville, Spokane, and later Nez Perce reservations).

The earliest treaties reflected the reality of a balance of power between *sovereign* Indian governments and the still-tenuous power of the youthful United States. By the mid-1800s the balance of power had shifted dramatically, and treaty-making had degenerated into a legal ritual directed by government agents as a means to acquire title to the Indian land base. Newly appointed Washington Territorial Governor Isaac Stevens had a carefully laid plan that in just one or two years would free up the entire territory for white settlement, leaving the surviving Indians tucked safely away on reservations off the lines of travel and land development. This plan reflected both Stevens' ambition and his Washington, D.C., superiors' instructions. Then federal Indian Commissioner George Manypenny wrote to Stevens directing him to "enter at once upon negotiations . . . having for principle [*sic*] aim the extinguishment of the Indian claims to the lands . . . so as not to interfere with the settlement of the territories" (in Relander 1962:39). Stevens responded that "the large reserve [i.e., that of the Yakima] is in every respect adapted to an Indian reservation. . . . It is off from the wagon route to the sound over the Cascades" (Relander, p. 44).

The treaties he offered the chiefs and headmen who gathered to hear his proposals in the Walla Walla Valley in June 1855 were virtually word-for-word the same as those offered the previous year to western Washington tribes at Medicine Creek, Point Elliot, and Point No Point. Only the signatories' names, the boundaries, and a few compromise provisions differed. The boundaries of the lands to be ceded to the United States (see Appendix 5, Article I) were already drawn so that, if and when all his proposed treaties were signed, every square inch of the territory would be covered (see fig. 2.4). These land cessions were to be granted *by the Indians* in exchange for a guarantee of exclusive use of a reservation and its resources (see Appendix 5, Article II) and of *use in common* with the settlers of traditional resources at "usual and accustomed places" (Article IV), plus grants of technical and economic support (Articles IV and V).

The special relationship established by treaty between the members of an Indian "tribe" and the federal government has been defined more precisely by a series of court cases—most notably a decision of the U.S. Supreme Court handed down in 1832 by Chief Justice John Marshall in the case of *Worcester* vs. *State of Georgia*. These "consider the several Indian nations as distinct, political communities within which their authority is exclusive, and having a right to all the lands within those [reservation] boundaries, which is not only acknowledged, but *guaranteed* [my emphasis] by the United States" (in Zucker, Hummel, and Høgfoss 1983:68). Subsequent Supreme Court decisions declared the fundamental principle that whatever rights were not specifically ceded by treaty were reserved by the signatory Indians.

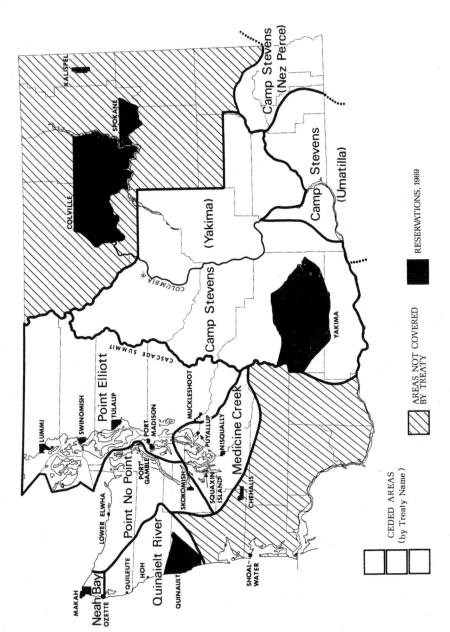

CEDED AREAS
(by Treaty Name)

AREAS NOT COVERED
BY TREATY

RESERVATIONS, 1969

Fig. 2.4. Treaty cessions and reservations (American Friends Service Committee 1970:22).

Thus, the special "privileges" that treaty Indians appear to have been given by the U.S. government are rather their prior and inextinguishable rights, not granted to them on the basis of their "racial" origin—as some contemporary critics of Indian treaty rights assert—but *reserved to them* by virtue of their prior legal claim as "first citizens" of this land.

Opponents of the continued existence of distinct Indian communities make much of the alleged "paternalism" of the government's role as legal guardians of their Indian wards. This is based on a fundamental misconception. Indians are not wards as individuals; rather Indian bands, tribes, and nations are recognized as dependent governments. The Yakima treaty (see Appendix 5, Article VIII) states, "the aforementioned confederated tribes and bands of Indians acknowledge their *dependence* [my emphasis] upon the government of the United States." Wardship is a relationship between governments, with the more powerful and physically encompassing United States government pledging to protect the internal political integrity of the less powerful dependent Indian states.

Opponents of treaty rights also interpret the Indians' special benefits as a form of government *welfare.* This is an even more pernicious misunderstanding. Some of the federal government services reserved for Indian people today may be seen as an attempt to live up to the spirit of the original treaty language. Consider Article V of the Yakima treaty (Appendix 5). In partial compensation for the value of the lands (some 10,000,000 acres) and other rights ceded by this treaty, the U.S. government promised to build and maintain two schools on the Reservation, providing the necessary "furniture, books, and stationary" and teaching staff, to be provided "free to the children of the said confederated tribes and bands of Indians." No expiration date is cited for this commitment. No such schools are being maintained on the Yakima Reservation today. So federal funds that have been made available in support of Indian education through the Johnson-O'Malley legislation of 1934 and subsequent acts of Congress should be seen not as "welfare," a word to raise the hackles of all red-blooded Americans, but as part of the federal government's payment for the ceded lands. This is not welfare; this is a minuscule annual installment paid toward a national debt.

Article V also promises "to build two blacksmith shops to one of which shall be attached a tin shop and to the other a gunsmith's shop; one carpenter's shop, one waggon and ploughmaker's shop, and to keep the same in repair . . ." and furnished with tools and craftsmen, who should instruct the Indians in these trades. A hospital is also promised, as are medicines and a physician. The personnel are to be maintained at these jobs for twenty years after ratification (which came at last in 1859, by the hand of President James Buchanan). Clearly the language of these standardized treaty agreements presumed a federal interest in and responsibility for preparing the Indian people to deal with the new circumstances they must confront in the post-treaty era, as part of the U.S. government's promise to protect tribal autonomy and continued political existence.

Indian Responses to White Pressure

Indian responses to "treating" with the whites ranged widely. Three positions may be recognized along the continuum of divided opinion. There were intransigents, who held a position that very often led to their early death at the hands of armed whites or by capture and hanging after a preemptory trial. Such was the fate of Qualchan, hotheaded young son of Owhi (NWS: áwxi), a Kittitas chief. Many intransigents appear to have been young men acting out a rite of passage to adulthood recalling Plains Indian bravado. Their deaths were devoid of tragedy, as they were culturally meaningful. Such young men thus avoided being witness to subsequent events. However, their defiance often brought heavy-handed retribution from an equally hotheaded but much more numerous vigilante militia who did not often stop to inquire if they had gotten the right man.

At the opposite extreme were the cooperators. Best known in this role is the Nez Perce chief, Lawyer (Haines 1955:139–40, 159; Drury 1979). Mountain men for whom he served as guide gave him the name Lawyer for his shrewdness. His home village was Kamiah, where he served as Asa Smith's primary linguistic informant (1838–40). Lawyer clearly had established a position as a cultural mediator. It is instructive to note, however, that Smith makes no mention of Lawyer being a "chief," though he does identify others with that title. It seems clear that Lawyer successfully manipulated his position as cultural go-between to enhance his social position. He traded his cooperation at the treaty council (he alone among the Plateau leaders argued for signing the treaties forthwith) for political prominence and control of what ultimately remained as the heart of the Nez Perce Reservation, which included his home at Kamiah, site of the present-day Nez Perce agency (see fig. 2.5).

Lawyer is portrayed by some white historians as a traitor to his people. He

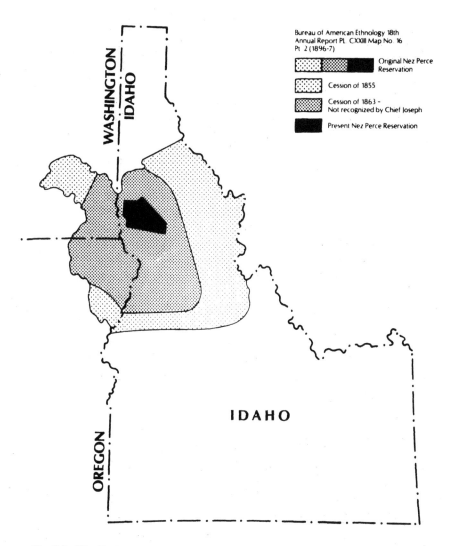

Fig. 2.5. Nez Perce reservation lands and ceded territory (Walker 1985 [1968]:47; reprinted with permission of the University of Idaho Press).

is held up as a contrary example to highlight the proud independence of the young Chief Joseph of the Wallowa band, who led the Nez Perce flight in 1877, eluding for months three United States armies. This judgment presumes that the Indians should have demonstrated their first loyalty to their own "Indian" people; that if they had "all hung together" they might not have each hung separately. This attributes an unrealistic sense of common purpose to Plateau Indian society and leadership and presumes as well that the Indians' defeat was somehow the result of their strategic errors rather than the inevitable consequence of their small numbers.

Had Lawyer withheld his suppport of the proposed treaties at the Walla Walla council, would the course of American history have been deflected from its path of explosive Euro-American expansion? One could more convincingly argue that had the Indians refused to sign in 1855, they would have suffered greater losses in the next decades in confrontations with territorial militias, lawless gold seekers, and the U.S. Army, and would find themselves today with no land base and no legally defensible fishing rights. Ironically, Lawyer's self-serving defection may ultimately have assured the survival of the Plateau Indians.

Lawyer was motivated by no such far-seeing altruism. His acceptance of the treaties and later conversion to Protestantism gave him a leg up in competition with his Nez Perce rivals for the favor of the powerful white "chiefs." He was using Governor Stevens for his own ends, a shortsighted strategy (when considered from certain twentieth-century vantage points), but a familiar and sensible one in the context of the political and cultural realities of his day.

A third stance vis-à-vis the whites was indecision. This was the dominant attitude of Chief Kamiakin of the Yakimas and Paluses and of the Young Chief Joseph of the Nez Perces. Both were mature leaders who felt strongly the heavy responsibility of their chiefly position for the welfare of their respective village groups. They were driven by neither bravado nor ambition to force the issue with the whites, so they hung back, maintaining a "low profile," speaking with painful reserve or keeping silent at the treaty councils. They cooperated with the whites only when they saw that resistance would be disastrous for their people. Both eventually led their people in resistance to the whites when they realized that their cooperation would require that they abandon the heart of their traditional responsibility to their people and to their land.

We are tempted to idealize Indian leaders of this era and to pass moral judgment on their actions. In this regard, it is instructive to solicit the opinions of contemporary Plateau Indians as to the reputations of these famous men among the descendants of their own relatives, allies, and rivals. I was surprised by Mary Jim Chapman's account of the Whitman massacre (generally attributed to the actions of Cayuse intransigents) as self-defense against Whitman's genocidal poisoning campaign—a view she shares with Smohalla. I was equally unprepared for James Selam's pride in the role of his Warm Springs relations as Army scouts in the fight against Captain Jack, leader of the Modoc resistance. James has long pursued a campaign to get the U.S. Army administration to grant at last to these Indian scouts recognition for their military contribution in the Modoc Wars, and thus to award the appropriate pensions to their surviving families. The fact that the Warm Springs scouts contributed to the defeat of their "fellow Indians" carried little weight with James (his ancestors often raided the Klamath-Modoc for horses) as no sense of "racial" common cause governed Indian loyalties at that time.[4] I was also somewhat taken aback when James informed me that Smohalla was distrusted for allegedly abusing his spiritual powers. In each of these cases we see that Euro-American concepts of praise-worthy or contemptible behavior in the political arena are at odds with those of the Plateau Indians' judgments of their own leaders.

4. A sense of common cause as "American Indians" is now strongly developed. In recent years this common cause has been extended to Indians in Central and South America, as shown by the editorial thrust of *America Indigena* and the organization of Native American conferences to generate mutual support and counsel for the struggle of indigenous ethnic minorities throughout the hemisphere.

Plateau Historical Time Line

1680   Pueblo revolt in New Mexico; Spanish stock freed

ca. 1710   Horses to the Flatheads

ca. 1730   Horses to the Cayuses and Nez Perces

ca. 1775   Smallpox throughout, from coastal contacts?

1782   Smallpox on the Plains

1793   Alexander Mackenzie explores the upper Fraser and Bella Coola rivers for the Northwest Company

1801   Smallpox throughout

1805   Lewis and Clark expedition descends the Snake and Columbia rivers in October

1806   Lewis and Clark return upriver in April and May

1807–10 David Thompson of the Northwest Company explores the upper Columbia, Kootenay, Clark Fork, and Coeur d'Alene rivers; establishes fur-trading posts

1807–08 "Distemper" spreads among the Interior Salish

1808   Simon Fraser descends the Fraser River to the mouth

1811   Astorians of the Pacific Fur Company establish Astoria at the Columbia River mouth, arriving by sea from Boston

           David Thompson descends the Columbia to Astoria; returns via the Palouse and Spokane rivers

           D. Stuart and A. Ross of the Pacific Fur Company accompany Thompson up the Columbia, then proceed up the river to establish posts at Okanogan and Kamloops

1812   Pacific Fur Company attempts to establish posts at Lapwai and Spokane, but arouses ire of Indians

           War of 1812 between Britain and the U.S.A. breaks out

1813   Pacific Fur Company sells out to the Northwest Company under threat of war

1818   Donald Mackenzie, now of the Northwest Company, moves key interior post from Spokane to the mouth of the Walla Walla River (Fort Nez Perce = Fort Walla Walla) to support Snake River fur brigades; Indians remain unsympathetic

1821   Hudson's Bay Company (HBC) buys out the Northwest Company

1824–25	Epidemic, probably smallpox, throughout
	Sir George Simpson, HBC director, tours Columbia district; returns taking sons of Spokane and Kootenay chiefs for schooling
1825	P. Ogden leads HBC Snake River brigade to Great Salt Lake, Humboldt River, Shasta and Klamath areas
1830–33	Malaria ravages Indians of the lower Columbia and Willamette valleys
1831	Nez Perce delegation travels to St. Louis to request missionaries
1832–33	Capt. B. L. E. de Bonneville explores the upper Snake River for U.S. fur interests
1834	Jason Lee, first missionary, accompanies Nathaniel Wyeth party; goes on to the Willamette
	N. Wyeth establishes Fort Hall in Idaho to trade furs in competition with HBC; post abandoned in 1836
1835	Revs. S. Parker and M. Whitman arrive to scout Nez Perces and neighbors for mission posts (American Board of Committees for Foreign Missions)
1836	Whitman returns with his wife and H. Spalding family; establish ABCFM misions at Waiilatpu (Cayuses: Whitmans) and at Lapwai (Nez Perces: Spaldings)
1838	F. Blanchet and M. Demers (Catholic) establish itinerant mission
	Revs. H. Perkins and D. Lee (Methodist) establish Wascopam mission at the Dalles
1839	Revs. E. Walker and M. Eells (ABCFM) set up Tshimakain mission near Spokanes/Colvilles; have little contact with Indians
1839–40	"Wonderful Work of God" Methodist revival among Upper Chinookans and Sahaptins at The Dalles; many converts
1841	Father P. DeSmet establishes St. Mary's mission (Catholic) to the Flatheads in the Bitterroot valley
1840–43	Some 250 Nez Perces and Cayuses farming; similar numbers of children in school at Lapwai and The Dalles at height of mission success
1842	F. Point (Catholic) establishes Sacred Heart Mission to Coeur d'Alenes; moved to Cataldo in 1846
	First immigrants over the Oregon Trail

1843–45	Heavy use of the Oregon Trail by immigrant wagon trains; 5,000 Americans settled in the Willamette Valley by 1845
1844	Scarlet fever and whooping cough hit the Columbia River Sahaptins, Cayuses, and Nez Perces on the heels of the immigrant trains
1846	U.S.A. and Britain establish 49° N. boundary; HBC abandons operation south of the boundary
	Scarlet fever hits the Cayuses
1847–48	Measles epidemic throughout central and southern Plateau
1847	Father Chirouse establishes St. Rose mission at present-day Wapato
	Whitman "massacre" on Nov. 29; 13 whites killed; P. Ogden ransoms 48 captives; beginning of end of mission era
1848	Whites mount punitive expeditions to Walla Walla area
	Gold discovered in California
1849	Chirouse joined by Fathers Pandosy, d'Herbomez, and Blanchet; they establish St. Joseph's mission on Ahtanum Creek; Kamiakin friendly but refuses to convert, remains polygynous
1850	U.S. Army post set up at The Dalles
	U.S. Congress passes Donation Act, prematurely opening Northwest lands for settlement
1851–52	Traffic heavy on the Columbia River at The Dalles
1853	Washington Territory separated from Oregon; I. I. Stevens named governor and Indian agent
	Smallpox throughout
	McClellan railroad survey party (with G. Gibbs) explores Klikitat and Yakima country
	First wagon train through Yakima valley en route to Puget Sound over Naches Pass
1854	Intertribal council in the Grand Ronde (northeast Oregon) called by Kamiakin to map out strategy of response to Stevens' land grab
1855	Treaty council convened by Stevens at Walla Walla in June; treaties signed that established Yakima, Umatilla, and original Nez Perce reservations; later treaty signed at The Dalles sets up Warm Springs Reservation

	Stevens prematurely announces area east of Cascades open for settlement
	Gold discovered at Colville
	Indian agent A. I. Bolon killed by Yakimas; punitive expedition defeated; St. Joseph mission at Ahtanum burned by vigilantes
1856	Ft. Simcoe established by U.S. Army in Yakima country
1856–58	"Indian wars": a series of skirmishes in the Yakima, Walla Walla, and Palus country; Col. G. Wright defeats resistance of Paluses, Coeur d'Alenes, and Spokanes (1858)
	U.S. Army attempts to prevent settlement east of the Cascades pending treaty ratification
1859	Treaties ratified
	Military withdraws from Ft. Simcoe; Yakima Indian Affairs agency takes over
1860–64	J. Wilbur first Yakima agency teacher, then school superintendent; dismissed for challenging ethics of agent
1863	Second Nez Perce treaty eliminates Wallowa country; drives wedge between Lawyer's pro-white faction and Joseph's anti-treaty group
1865	U.S. Civil War ends
	Second (invalid) Warm Springs treaty (the "Huntington treaty") signed in effort to confine Indians to the reservation
1865–83	J. Wilbur serves as Yakima agent, commissioned by President Lincoln; reservation population estimated at 3,400
1867	Ahtanum mission rebuilt; Father N. St. Onge in charge
1871	President Grant assigns Yakima Reservation to Methodists
1872	Colville Reservation established by executive order
	Massive earthquake rocks the region
1877–78	The "Nez Perce War": anti-treaty group led by Joseph eludes three U.S. armies; finally trapped in north-central Montana; taken as POWs to Oklahoma Indian Territory
1879	543 N. Paiute POWs brought to the Yakima Reservation for confinement after "Bannock Wars"; subsequently moved to Warm Springs where now resident

1880–81	Severe Plateau winter wipes out herds of livestock
1882	J. Slocum's vision starts Indian Shaker Church at Mud Bay on Puget Sound
1883	N. Pacific Railroad begins operating through Yakima valley bringing tide of settlement
1884	Lieutenant MacMurray tour of inspection; he interviews Smohalla
	Homestead Act extended to Indians; 100 Indian homesteads established in Klikitat country by 1891
1885	Umatilla Reservation reduced in size
1887	Dawes Severalty Act (General Allotment Act) passed
1899	First Shaker Church east of Cascades at White Swan
1904	Jake Hunt founds the Feather Dance religion
1905	Fishing rights case, U.S. v. Winans, decided by U.S. Supreme Court affirming Yakima treaty rights of access to off-reservation fishing sites
1906–07	Townsites of Toppenish, Wapato, and Parker established on allottments sold to whites; leasing of trust lands at Yakima begins; violent conflict over sale of allotted lands
1914	Allotment rolls closed; allotments stopped after 440,000 acres at Yakima allotted, 90,000 of those in fee patent, and 27,000 acres sold
1919	U.S. Supreme Court decision in Seufert Brothers v. U.S. extends U.S. v. Winans ruling beyond the Yakima treaty
1924	Indian Citizen Act grants Indians the vote
1928	Merriam Survey Report documents problems of Indian people
1934	Indian "New Deal" legislation: Johnson-O'Malley Act provides support for education, health, and welfare; Wheeler-Howard (Indian Reorganization Act or IRA) provides for local option tribal government
	John Collier named Commissioner of Indian Affairs; serves until 1945
1938	Bonneville Dam completed; Grand Coulee under construction
	Warm Springs adopts IRA

1942	U.S. Supreme Court decision in *Tulee* v. *Washington* rules out state license fees for Indian fishing
1944	Yakimas adopt IRA; establish General Council and Tribal Council of 14 elected "chiefs"
1946–78	Indian Claims Commission in operation; attempts to resolve outstanding claims
1949	Umatillas accept IRA
1953	Termination Act defines Eisenhower policy; Klamath, Siletz, and Grand Ronde reservations in Oregon terminated (1954)
	States granted wide jurisdiction on Indian reservations in six states including Oregon (except at Warm Springs)
1957	The Dalles Dam completed
1958	The Dalles Dam settlement
1965	Yakima enrollment at 5,700
1969	Judge R. Belloni decides *U.S.* v. *Oregon* (*Sohappy* v. *Smith*) fishing rights case; orders "a fair and equitable share of all fish . . ." be guaranteed Indian fishermen on the Columbia River
1972	Indian Education Act grants Title IV funds for Indian education programs
	McQuinn strip returned to Warm Springs Reservation
1974	The Boldt decision defines treaty fishing rights on Puget Sound
1975	Indian Independence Act passed
1977	Columbia River Inter-tribal Fish Commission established
1978	Native American Religious Freedom Act passed
1979	U.S. Supreme Court upholds Boldt ruling; *Confederated Tribes* v. *Kreps* ruling orders reductions in ocean trolling to help preserve treaty fisheries
1980	Judge R. Orrick issues first decisions in Boldt Phase II defining rights of Indians to hatchery-reared fish and to protection of habitat
1983	Cook's Landing Indians convicted of illegal fishing in "Salmonscam" sting operation
1987	Yakima Nation jury acquits Salmonscam defendants

3

Language

sínwit, "speech"

PEOPLE MAY BE variously distinguished. We are male and female, of course, young and old, rich and poor, more or less smart, strong, or beautiful. But such distinctions, invidious or otherwise, most often apply within societies, and they provide a framework for social relations. Ethnic distinctions tend rather to form a basis for "foreign relations." Those of another culture or "race" are set apart as a group. The hostility and fear that characterized Columbia Indians' accounts of their traditional enemies, the Northern Paiute/Shoshone or "Snake" Indians, are illustrative. Paiute raiders are reported to have committed inhuman atrocities against Columbia River villages and are portrayed in Sahaptin stories as fair targets in a young man's quest for fame and honor. The same held for distant enemies in the northern Great Plains, as is shown graphically in the Cayuse story of "How Fish-Hawk Raided the Sioux" (Ramsey 1977:25–27).

Closer to home, Indians might be known by their characteristic habitat, as in the Columbia River Sahaptin term pápš-pal, "tall fir people," applied to the Salish-speaking Wenatchee Indians. Or they might be known by a characteristic food, as was customary in the northern Great Basin (Fowler 1986 [1982]). Still closer to home, peoples were distinguished by their characteristic place, normally their winter village, which might be named in turn for a prominent local landmark, as in the case of the Rock Creek people, the q̓miⱡ-ⱡáma, that is, "people of the rocky defile."

The peoples so named, of course, tended to be more finely discriminated the closer they were to home. Confusion resulted when outsiders interpreted such named peoples as "tribes," a term that connotes an organized political unit, a primitive nation. The Euro-American view of the social landscape—cut apart into national political pieces as in a jigsaw puzzle—failed to reflect the flexible reality of local ethnic distinctions. Even Snake Indian enemies could be trading partners, and the descendants of captured enemies were accepted as full citizens of their adopted group. Marriage routinely linked peoples of different places, even of different language areas, and "citizenship" was dual through one's parents, quadruple through one's grandparents, consequently multiple for virtually all Plateau Indians (see Table 21).

The social boundaries so strongly emphasized by territorial administrators were bridged by enduring ties of kinship constantly reinforced by the exchange of valued goods. Even conflicts fostered a grudging appreciation of the distant enemy and provided an opportunity for cultural exchange. As we have seen, the Spanish horse spread rapidly north in just that manner, from raider to raider.

The fluidity of social and political boundaries within the larger Plateau region has led to a primary reliance by ethnographers on linguistic distinctions as a basis for classifying indigenous cultures. Languages are like species of living things in some key respects. They are defined by a mutual intelligibility that includes a barrier to the outside exchange of information. Likewise, species are defined by the existence of barriers to the exchange of genetic information. In both cases these barriers arise gradually as a consequence of isolation and distance. Hybrid languages are practically nonexistent, rarer than hybrid plants or animals. Most human individuals can be readily assigned to one and only one native language group, just as most individual plants or animals may be assigned without ambiguity to their proper species category. Thus, language provides the scholar with a convenient classificatory framework.

Mutual intelligibility requires social intercourse. Thus, social barriers often coincide with language barriers. But not always. Language distinctions may well reflect ancient geographic or social barriers long since torn down, and multilingualism (frequent among Plateau Indians) is a ready means to overcome language differences. Sign languages and trade jargons—as in the Chinook Jargon that flourished in the Pacific Northwest in the early contact period—are other means employed to overcome linguistic impediments. Still, human languages are such complex and powerful creations of the human mind and spirit that language differences must have a substantial impact on cultural perception and cultural expression. We will look closely at the Sahaptin language as spoken on the middle Columbia River, indicate its place on the map of contact-period language distribution in the Plateau (see fig. 3.1), and briefly review scholarly attempts to reconstruct the history of these languages as clues to major events in the prehistoric past of Plateau peoples.

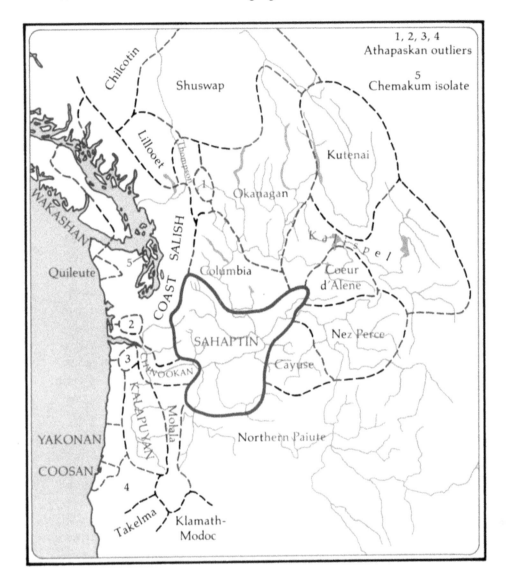

Fig. 3.1. Language areas of northwestern North America.

Languages also resemble species of plants and animals in that they evolve. As all living species—according to the Darwinian theory of evolution—are descended from a single ancestral life form, so are all languages presumed to be the descendants of a single prototypical human tongue. Historical linguists, like their biologist counterparts, attempt to reconstruct the evolutionary history of languages by comparing contemporary languages. In this way families as well as larger "stocks" and "phyla" of languages are proposed to account for similarities among contemporary languages. For example, the Indo-European language phylum is judged to include three to four hundred living languages, as diverse as English and Hindi, and to have descended from a common Proto-Indo-European language spoken in Central Asia about seven thousand years ago. Lacking written records, students of Northwest Indian languages have not been able to prove such distant relationships. There is agreement, however, on the basic classificatory framework (see Table 3).

The mid-Columbia Indians speak a dialect of Sahaptin. The Sahaptin language includes three main dialect divisions set apart by distinctive vocabulary items, pronunciation, and grammatical paradigms. Bruce Rigsby, a linguistic anthropologist who studied Sahaptin in detail during the 1960s, describes fourteen extant dialects (see fig. 3.2), which he classifies as follows:

The Northwest Cluster: Klikitat, Upper Cowlitz or Taitnapam, Yakima, and Kittitas or Pshwanwapam;

The Northeast Cluster: Priest Rapids or Wanapam, Walla Walla, Snake River, and Palus; and

The Columbia River Cluster: Umatilla, John Day, Rock Creek (Washington), Wayámpam (Celilo), Tenino, and Tygh Valley.

Sahaptin is closely related to Nez Perce, spoken along the Snake River and its tributaries above the Palouse River junction, and the two languages together form the small Sahaptian language family. The terms *Sahaptin* for the language and *Sahaptian* for the family are corruptions of the Columbia Salish name for the Nez Perce Indians, sháptanoxʷ (Rigsby 1965:24). The term is clearly misapplied in the case of Sahaptin (and older reference works often use "Sahaptin" or "Shahaptin" for Nez Perce) but is nevertheless generally understood by scholars. Native speakers of Sahaptin refer to their language or dialect as "Indian," as in the English sentence, "He's speaking Indian," or, in Columbia River Sahaptin, čiškín, literally, "this way [of speaking]." I use Sahaptin here for lack of any better means to refer to the language and the people who use it.

Table 3

Plateau Language Relationships

Stock	Family	Language	Dialect
Na Dene————Athapaskan———Carrier, Chilcotin			
Isolate————————?——————Kutenai			
Salishan————Interior Salish		Lillooet	
		Thompson	
		Shuswap	
		Okanagan—————	Sinkaietk, Sanpoil-Nespelem, Colville, Lakes
		Columbia—————	Columbia, Wenatchee, Chelan, Methow
		Kalispel——————-Spokane, Kalispel, Pend Oreille, Flathead	
		Coeur d'Alene	
Penutian ?	Chinookan	Kiksht (Upper Chinook)	
	Sahaptian	Sahaptin	
		NW Sahaptin——Kittitas, Yakima, Klikitat, Upper Cowlitz	
	?	CR Sahaptin——Tenino-Tygh, Celilo, Rock Creek, John Day River, Umatilla	
		NE Sahaptin——Walla Walla, Snake River, Palus, Priest Rapids	
		Nez Perce	
		Klamath——————Klamath, Modoc	
	?———————— Cayuse		
	?————————— Molala		
Uto-Aztekan——Numic—————— Northern Paiute			

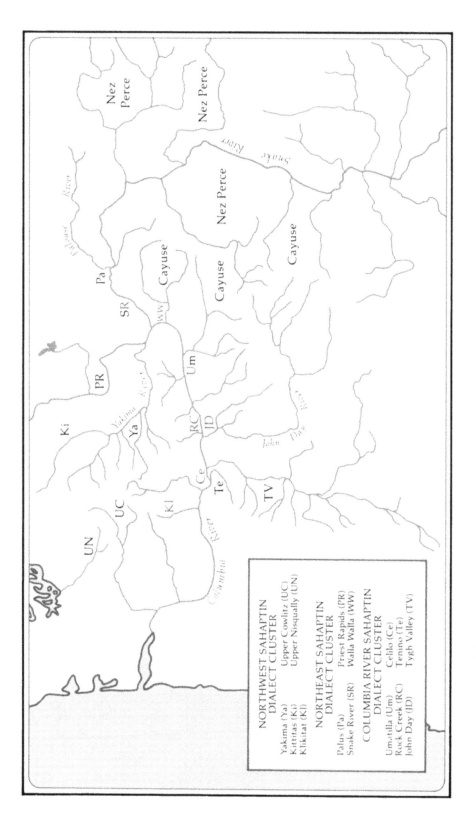

Fig. 3.2. Relative locations of the Sahaptin dialects, Nez Perce, and Cayuse (Rigsby 1965:22; reprinted with permission).

NORTHWEST SAHAPTIN
DIALECT CLUSTER

Yakima (Ya)   Upper Cowlitz (UC)
Kittitas (Ki)   Upper Nisqually (UN)
Klikitat (Kl)

NORTHEAST SAHAPTIN
DIALECT CLUSTER

Palus (Pa)   Priest Rapids (PR)
Snake River (SR)   Walla Walla (WW)

COLUMBIA RIVER SAHAPTIN
DIALECT CLUSTER

Umatilla (Um)   Celilo (Ce)
Rock Creek (RC)   Tenino (Te)
John Day (JD)   Tygh Valley (TV)

It is generally agreed that the Sahaptian languages are related to Klamath and Modoc (Rude n.d. [1986]) and perhaps to Cayuse and Molala as well (see Rigsby 1965, 1969). They may also be related more distantly to the Chinookan languages of the lower Columbia River. All have been grouped in the Penutian stock together with the Tsimshianic languages of the northern British Columbia coast and adjacent interior, the Kalapuyan languages of the Willamette Valley, and the California Penutian languages, such as Miwok (cf. Sapir 1929). Speculative scholars claim yet more distant ties to the languages of the Maya (Ruhlen 1987; Greenberg 1987). The ancient diaspora that produced the pattern of language distributions we now see inspires reflection. It suggests a dynamic history of peoples in motion, seeking new opportunities in new lands, and it hints at the extinction of many languages that will forever remain unknown.

Sahaptin survives in the memories of several hundred elders because it has served its people well, and it may yet survive to serve their descendants in a world dominated by languages of empire, such as English, Spanish, Arabic, and Mandarin Chinese. We have noted how the missionary Asa Smith doubted the value of devoting scarce church resources of time and energy to the study of Nez Perce, a language he believed would soon be extinct. Modern language scholars harbor no such doubts, as each human language may reveal a key to unlock the mystery of human language, and all human languages guard the cultural treasures of their people. We mourn the loss of a human language as we mourn the extinction of a species of living thing or the destruction of a great work of art.

Nez Perce still lives but Cayuse has now vanished. A few brief lists of Cayuse words were recorded by Horatio Hale about 1840 and in the second quarter of the twentieth century by Melville Jacobs, Verne Ray, and Theodore Stern from elderly speakers bilingual in Nez Perce or Sahaptin, but these were sufficient to show only that it was likely to have been distantly related to Sahaptin and Nez Perce. Rigsby could find no one who knew Cayuse in 1965, though Indian people today identify "Cayuse" individuals (in Sahaptin, wáylat-pam) among their grandparents. What happened to this language? Why did it disappear? What caused the Cayuse people to be absorbed by their neighbors?

Ruby and Brown's popular history of the Cayuse Indians (1972) characterizes them as "Imperial Tribesmen of Old Oregon." The truth seems otherwise. The Cayuse Indians excelled as horsemen and used their equestrian mobility effectively to harry early white settlers in the manner of the mounted warriors of the Plains. The notoriety they gained as perpetrators/ victims of the Whitman incident assured their reputation among whites as proud and dangerous adversaries. Sociopolitically, however, they had no special status among Plateau Indians (see chapter 6); they occupied an ecologically marginal position off the main salmon migration path. The marginality of their language accords with other evidence to suggest that at the time of Lewis and Clark's exploration they were being absorbed by their more populous Nez Perce, Umatilla, and Walla Walla neighbors through peaceful intermarriage.

The extinction of languages such as Cayuse does not require that we imagine dramatic conflicts among linguistic "tribes" for dominion over the Plateau populace. Hunter-gatherers do not create empires, they tend rather to mind their own business. Linguistic change is more likely a slow process whereby "successful" languages (that is, those learned by increasing numbers of people) spread at the expense of neighboring languages by *creeping*, not *leaping*. Melville Jacobs (1937b) proposed such an explanation for the presence of Sahaptin speakers west of the Cascade Crest on the headwaters of the Lewis, Cowlitz, and Nisqually rivers (Klikitat, Taitnapam, and the extinct Mishalpam dialects). According to Jacobs's hypothesis, intermarriage of Coast Salish Indians of the western slopes of the Cascades and Sahaptin speakers to the east led to an asymmetrical exchange of spouses, more wives moving downstream toward the productive lower reaches of coastal streams than moving upstream; in other words, women drifted in a direction opposite to the flow of surplus wealth. Such a pattern is to be expected where wives relocate with their husbands' families more often than not (a patrilocal bias in postmarital residence). This assumes also that mothers have a stronger influence on the early language training of their offspring than do fathers.

The Eastward Spread of Interior Salish Languages

Comparative studies of the Interior Salish sub-family of languages suggest an earlier expansion in the opposite direction and on a grander scale than that Jacobs described (though the process at work on the Cowlitz River in A.D. 1800 might have wrought changes on a scale comparable to that of the interior Salish expansion if continued for several millennia). As a consequence of this expansion, Sahaptin is now bordered on the north and north-

east by Interior Salish languages, and on the northwest by languages of the
Coast Salish stock found throughout Puget Sound and the Straits of Georgia. All told there are some twenty languages in this family, seven in the
interior Fraser–Columbia River basins.[1]

South of the Plateau—past the broken lava barrens of south central Oregon and Idaho's Snake River plain—even more dynamic speech shifts were
underway. The mid-Columbia Indians' traditional enemies, the Snakes, represent the northern fringe of a vast desert range occupied in 1850 by three
closely related Numic languages, distant kin of the Nahuatl language
spoken by the Imperial Aztecs of Mexico. (In this instance the adjective
"imperial" is amply warranted.) Of these, Northern Paiute spread north and
northeast from the region of Mono Lake at the eastern base of the Sierra
Nevada range in southern California. Shoshone spread more easterly from
near Death Valley through central Nevada to the northern shores of the
Great Salt Lake; it spilled over the imperceptible divide to occupy the Snake
River Basin above formidable Hell's Canyon, a substantial barrier to Nez
Perce or Sahaptin advance southward. An offshoot of the Shoshone pushed
far east to become the feared Comanche of the southern Great Plains. A
third movement carried Southern Paiute and Ute from the Panamint Valley
near Las Vegas east to the Colorado River canyon lands and to the southeastern shores of Great Salt Lake. The uniformity of these three languages over
such an immense territory suggests a rapid spread, estimated by Lamb
(1958) to have occurred sometime after A.D. 1100.

Salishan and Numic speakers did not expand into unoccupied territory. In
both cases there must have been other peoples speaking other languages
inhabiting these regions. We can only speculate at this late date as to their
identities. One point seems clear, however; the mid-Columbia Sahaptins are
not recent immigrants to the Plateau, despite misleading speculations to the
contrary inspired by James Teit's Columbia Salish account (1928). The antiquity of Sahaptin occupation on the middle Columbia is indicated by many
lines of evidence, notably the compact Sahaptian range, the dialectal diversity within Sahaptin (indicating at least a millennium of slow expansion in
their present locale), the existence of elaborate Sahaptin terminologies for
local places and for the flora and fauna characteristic of these places, and the

---

1. Elmendorf (1965) uses the techniques of lexicostatistics (Swadesh 1959) to reconstruct a likely history of Interior Salish expansion from a presumed point of origin in
the Fraser River canyon area now home to the Thompson Indians.

fact that Lewis and Clark placed the linguistic boundaries at precisely their later historic locations (cf. Ray 1938; Murdock 1928; Rigsby 1965:81, 221–28).

The Sahaptin language at the time of first white contact was well entrenched from just above The Dalles to Sentinel Gap above Priest Rapids on the main Columbia, throughout the Yakima Basin, and up the Snake to just above the Palouse River junction. In addition, Sahaptin speakers had spread west to occupy the headwaters of the Klickitat, White Salmon, Lewis, Cowlitz, and Nisqually rivers, the lower basins of which they shared with Chinookan- and Coast Salish-speaking Indian peoples. Patterns of seasonal resource exploitation reconstructed for this period also point to regular Sahaptin utilization of all but the headwaters on the Walla Walla, Umatilla, John Day, and Deschutes rivers, southern tributaries of the Columbia.

The Sahaptin Language: How It Works

The Sahaptin language is difficult for a native English speaker to learn. I can attest to that, as I have struggled to grasp the organizing principles of Sahaptin for ten years with limited success. There are two major contributing factors to this difficulty. First, virtually nothing is available in print to assist the beginner in the learning task. Dictionaries are limited to one originally composed in French by Father M. Pandosy, priest to the Yakima at the Ahtanum Mission, 1849–55, and published in English translation in 1862. David and Kathrine French have unpublished lexical files. A provisional word list has been prepared by Virginia Hymes for the Warm Springs tribe (1976), and a prototype for an English-Sahaptin dictionary has been compiled for the Yakima Nation by Virginia Beavert and Bruce Rigsby under the auspices of the regional Johnson-O'Malley program (Beavert and Rigsby 1976), a federally funded effort to promote Indian education. Lexicographic work is in progress on the Warm Springs Reservation and at the University of Oregon (as of 1987). Most of these materials are not available to the general public. Thus the scarcity of materials on the language is not due entirely to a lack of scholarly effort. A reluctance on the part of contemporary Indians to share freely their cultural heritage with outsiders is also important. Russell Jim, Yakima tribal councilman during the late 1970s and early 1980s when he served as chairman of the committee of the tribal government responsible for educational matters, put it to me this way: "First the whiteman takes our land, then he takes our fish, now he wants to take our language." My argument that a language is not something so readily alienated as land or fish did not convince him. Students who wish to learn Sahaptin should appreciate the historical basis for these feelings and approach the study of the language with respect for the rich cultural tradition it embodies.

Grammatical accounts are as difficult to obtain as vocabularies. Melville Jacobs's 1931 doctoral dissertation (pursued under the direction of Professor Franz Boas at Columbia University in the late 1920s) is a grammatical analysis of the northwestern dialects of Sahaptin, Klikitat and Taitnapam, in particular. It is both highly technical and out of date. Serious students will find much of interest in it, but it is no substitute for an "Introduction to Sahaptin Grammar." Bruce Rigsby has written just such an introduction for the volume on language of the new Smithsonian Institution *Handbook of North American Indians,* the publication of which is still in the future. I attempt below to communicate to you what I have learned from Rigsby's grammatical sketch, though he must not be blamed for my misapprehensions.

Rigsby's dissertation (1965) describes patterns of dialectal variation in Sahaptin and provides basic word lists comparing Sahaptin with Nez Perce and Klamath. Melville Jacobs's three volumes of myths and stories are a goldmine for the serious student (1929, 1934, 1937a). Close comparisons of his English and Sahaptin texts, which are cross-indexed sentence by sentence, allow one to compile a crude working dictionary and a rough grammatical sketch on one's own. These texts also suggest the power of the language and contain a wealth of ethnographic detail, as illustrated in Jim Yoke's geographic text, which Jacobs recorded in the late 1920s from an Upper Cowlitz Indian. Jacobs comments on Yoke's tour de force: "[Yoke] plunged spontaneously into this peculiar text, the motivation apparently being to parade knowledge derived from a lifetime of travel in the local region, in the hope that both the visiting ethnologist and the younger natives squatting about the tipi might be properly edified and impressed" (Jacobs 1934:228). The full text describes nearly three hundred named places familiar to Mr. Yoke, their order tracing the main routes of his travels.

The second difficulty with Sahaptin is that it is radically different from English. The basic sounds used to form Sahaptin words sprain the tongue of one raised to speak English. It is next to impossible to describe these foreign sounds. They must be learned by patient practice, of both ear and tongue. However, it is possible to write Sahaptin words so as to render faithfully the distinctions relevant to native speakers of the language. Several "alphabets" have been invented for this purpose and proponents of each staunchly defend the inherent superiority of their favorite. In most cases the differences among them are matters of style or convenience. I will use here my own preferred mode of transcription, a variant of the linguists' standard orthography. There are thirty-two consonant symbols and seven vowels for writing the thirty-nine *phonemes* of the language (see Table 4). Virtually all of the symbols have been borrowed from the English alphabet and represent sounds familiar to the English speaker's ear. A few, however, are strange.

The most difficult for native English speakers are the glottalized consonants, variants of familiar p, t, k, c ("ts"), and č ("ch"), which are accompanied by a glottal "explosion," a popping sound that sharply emphasizes the consonant. Such glottalized consonants are sometimes called "hard" consonants and are customarily marked with an apostrophe following or super-

TABLE 4

The Sahaptin Alphabet (adapted from Rigsby 1965:156, with permission)

CONSONANTS

Simple stops	p	t			k	kʷ	q	qʷ	
Glottalized stops	ṗ	ṭ			k̓	k̓ʷ	q̓	q̓ʷ	ʔ
Simple affricates		c	ƛ	č					
Glottalized affricates		c̓	ƛ̓	č̓					
Spirants		s	ɬ	š	x	xʷ	x̣	x̣ʷ	h
Sonorants:									
Nasals	m	n							
Liquids			l						
Glides	w			y					

VOWELS

high, short	i			u
mid, short			ɨ	
low, short			a	
high, long	ii			uu
low, long			aa	

UPPER COWLITZ GEOGRAPHIC NOTES

Jim Yoke

1. In this country, when the country had its beginning, in the myth age, he (Coyote) ordained it (all). He named all these places in this land, (such as) the rivers, (and the) places where fish were to be obtained (and so on).

2. There is a place there named Ohanapecash. There is that (little) stream or lake for the people to get fish at, which stream flows out (as the) wa'inpas (it empties into the Clear Fork above Lewis). (2) Below there it is named ləka'lwit (Indian name of both the Clear Fork River and of the camp at its mouth), and there are also fish (caught) at that place. (3) He who named it said there would be fish netting right here to get salmon. Another (site) is named p̓na' ("water worn rock pocket under the falls"), a (good) place to catch (club) salmon, for us to get salmon. (4) On his route he (Coyote) came out of the water to shore, and he said at this place, "People will dwell here." At that place he set up a rock. (named) alε'l, long and high. (5) When a person became tired out. he could sit there on top of it. And he also set up so large (rather small) a rock, for small children to sit on. (6) He thought of a mountain, he named it nəq̓u't ("breast", Mt. Tatoosh). At that place he determined there would be lots of berries, that people would climb up it, gather those berries, dry them, and descend again to the same place where they were drying fish. (7) He named (a creek) for getting fish ctcu·'c (near Ohanapecash). He named another (creek) pcuwi'nc, a creek that flows from the mountains past here (Lewis) into the big river (Cowlitz). (8) And again another

1. i'tcik ti·tca'm, anaku u·'ya ti·tca'm, ku wat̓i't̓acpa itama'n-wiya. ku i'tcε·nak ti·tca'mnan t̓ła'x̱ᵘ iwi'wanika, tcε·'cnan, waika'nacai ku'tai.

2. iwa' iwani'kca a'ux̱anapaikac. kuk iwa' k̓pə'n tcε'ic wata'm ti·nmi'yai ku'tai waika'nacai, kwnə'k iwa'ipx̱nma tcε'ic wa'inpas. (2) iwani'kma mi'tiknink ləka'lwit, ku'cx̱i kwnə'k itx̱a'nax̱a waika'nac. (3) ku k̓pə'nk anił̓a' itε·'nana i'tcnək nəx̱ana'c wənə'ptai nu'sux̱ai. a'nat'cax̱i iwani'ka na'x̱c p̓na', wənəptpama' nusux̱pama', nəmikaya'i wənə'ptai nu'sux̱ai. (4) kuk iwiya'pyukm̓a a'x̱miyau, ku itε·'nana i'tcna, "kuk i'tcnək ti·'n inica'ikata." kuk kwnə'k ipa'tuka pcwa·'n, alε'l, ku ka·'Dnam x̱w̓ε·'mi. (5) ku-pa'ic ła'k̓əp ti·'n itx̱a'nax̱ata, ku kwnə'k ayi'ḵx̱ata x̱w̓ε·'mi. kuk i'kwa·la a'nat'ca pcwa' ipa'tuka, iksiksnmi'yai miyanacnmi'yai a'yiktai. (6) ku ipx̱wi'na pə't̓x̱anunan, kω·nə'k iwani'ka nəq̓u't. kwnə'k ipx̱wi'na iwa'ta ələ'x̱ təmani'D, kuk ipana'tita ti·'n, ku iku'ta kω·nə'k təmani'tnan, ilə'x̱iyawita, kuk iha'ikta i'kwnx̱i anakwnə'k ilə'x̱i-yawix̱a nu'sux̱nan. (7) iwani'ka waika'nacai ku'tai ctcu·'c. a'wa-nika na'x̱c pcuwi'nc, pə't̓x̱anuknink iwa'ipx̱ca kaskε·'s i'tcən nt'ci'yau a'Dwanayau. (8) a'nat'cax̱i na'x̱c iwa'ipx̱ca, iwani'kca

(creek) flows out, named t'cqε·'ᴅ, (good) for catching fish. There is a mountain named waqa'q́k (frog croaking), also (good) for berrying. Right here (at Lewis) there flows (a creek) named tamxɛ·'x̣, also (good) for fishing. (A creek below Lewis) is named qwa'qwatəm. (There is a mountain) named wactcaini', a huckleberry patch. (9) There is another (creek) named cucaincacnmi' ("place of steelhead", below Lewis). There is a mountain named əx̣a''əx̣a ("alder"). (10) At that place there flows out mulainmi' (creek). That mountain (right there) is named tiska'ya ("Skunk", three or four miles below Lewis). (11) Opposite there (and below) there is (a mountain) named k̓a'cinu ("elbow"), a place at which to get berries. Another creek empties out named cicu'. (12) And another is named lax̣pəᴅnmi' (a water moss). (Another) flows out, kaya'x̣əm. A mountain there is named takta'k ("small prairie"). a place for berrying. (13) They name a place there where it (a spring) comes up out of the ground, it is named mulmulła' ("bubbles person"). Another spring is named plu's ("brains"), it is white. ni'łᵘ (Silver Creek) flows out. (14) On the opposite side (of the Cowlitz) from it there flows out that (creek) named taita'i (a tree moss; at Randle), it is also a salmon fishing place. (15) There is a place named cə'q́k, it is also a salmon fishing place (at the Kiona farm a mile below Randle), long ago a great many people used to be there. (16) There is another place named tca'kumac ("fern root place", below Randle). Another is named ikkɛ·tacnmi' ("place of the children"). Another is named tu'łq́pc ("scratch", above Cispus R.). Another is named k̓iya'nxᵘ (on Cowlitz R. southeast of Morton). (17) Another is named k̓wsə's (at mouth of Cispus R.). At that place the ci'cpac (Cispus R.) flows out.

3. Further below there it is named sx̣ə'tsaikt (name of creek and adjacent camp). There is (a creek) named k̓wə'p ("falls"). On

---

t'cqɛ·'ᴅ, waika'nacai ku'tai. iwani'kca pə't̓x̣anu waqa'q́k təmani'taix̣i. iwani'kca i'tci wa'naca tamx̣ɛ·'x̣, waika'nacaix̣i. iwani'kca qwa'qwatəm. iwani'kca wactcaini', a't̓it̓ac. (9) wani'kca na'x̣c cucaincacnmi'. iwani'kca pə't̓x̣anu əx̣a''əx̣a. (10) iwa'ipx̣camc kwnə'k mulainmi'. i'k̓wak iwani'kca pə't̓x̣anu tiska'ya. (11) ku kwnəkpama' iwani'kca k̓a'cinu, təmanitpama' kutpama'. na'x̣c iwa'ipx̣ca kaskɛ·'s iwani'kca cicu'. (12) ku-iwani'kca na'x̣c lax̣pᴅnmi'. iwa'ipx̣ca kaya'x̣əm. kwnə'k iwani'kca pə't̓x̣anu takta'k, təmanitpama' kutpama'. (13) iwani'kca kwnə'k iwɛ·na't.ca, k̓pə'nk iwani'kca mulmulła'. na'x̣c wɛ·na'tt iwani'kca plu's, plə'c. iwa'ipx̣ca ni'łᵘ. (14) i'catknink kwni'nk iwa'ipx̣ca iwani'kca k̓pə'nk taita'i, k̓pə'nkx̣i nusux̣pama'. (15) iwani'kca cə'q́k k̓pə'nkx̣i iwa' nu'sux̣as, kwnə'k itx̣a'nax̣ana palala'i ti·'n mi'wi. (16) na'x̣c ti·tca'm iwani'kca tca'kumac. iwani'kca na'x̣c ikkɛ·tacnmi'. iwani'kca na'x̣c tu'łq́pc. iwani'kca na'x̣c k̓iya'nxᵘ. (17) iwani'kca na'x̣c k̓wsə's. iwa'ipx̣caikc i'kwnk ci'cpac.

3. kwnə'k iwani'kca maimi'ti sx̣ə'tsaikt. iwani'kca k̓wə'p. iwani'kca i'catkwnink pa'pc kutpama'x̣i nusux̣pama'. (2) kwnə'k

imposed on the consonant symbol. Another problem is posed by the k and x̣ sounds. The k is pronounced more or less as in English while the x̣ has a harsh guttural quality familiar to students of German as the "ch" in "Dachau" or in the Scottish "Loch Lomond." Moreover, there are two "k" 's in Sahaptin, the "front" or English k (k) and the "back" k (q) formed with the root of the tongue pressed against the far rear portion of the palate, as if the speaker were trying to swallow the sound. Both k and q may be either "plain" or glottalized. To further complicate matters there are both front and back "x" 's, but we may be thankful that the front x is rare. In addition, all these k's and x's may be pronounced with the lips rounded, in which case a "w" superscript is added (for example, the English word "quick" would look like kʷik).

Finally, there are the laterals. The "thl" sound we find in the middle of the word "athlete" may occur in Sahaptin at the beginning, middle, or end of words. It is often called the "barred l" sound because it is customarily written ɬ. It reminds me of the sound of someone preparing to spit. For example, the Sahaptin word for "head" is ɬámtax̣. A sharper affricate consonant likewise made with the edge of the tongue (thus a "lateral") is usually rendered by the Greek letter lambda crossed by a "bar." Barred lambda may also be pronounced plain (ƛ) or glottalized (ƛ̓). The glottal stop, a consonant in its own right, is written as a question mark without the dot (ʔ), or in some systems as the numeral "7." It sounds like a catch in the throat. In English it is the sound we hear in the admonition, "únhʔunh." In Sahaptin it appears in the word for "crow," áʔa.

Put the above sounds together in Sahaptin words like "blackbird," x̣iƛámx̣ʷ, "pig," húq̓huq̓, "corn," sɬx̣ʷs-wáakuɬ, or "they are getting married," pápatkʷalšix̣ša, and you may wonder that any human could string such sounds together. Many non-English speakers, on the other hand, feel exactly the same way about English.

Moving on to grammar, the plot thickens. English grammar relies heavily on word order to define the syntactic role of each word. English words are generally short, with compounds as elaborate as "antidisestablishmentarianism" quite unusual. Sahaptin, by contrast, is polysynthetic (mildly so, according to Rigsby) and agglutinative, in that words, especially the verbcomplex, are rarely simple. They are constructed of many smaller monosyllabic elements, each of which adds something to the meaning of the whole word but which may mean nothing by itself (cf. Sapir 1921:123–43). Rigsby cites the example of the sentence, i-šapá-tuti-yay-ša-na-aš niit, which requires two "words" in Sahaptin but eight in the English translation, "He was putting up my tent for me." This sentence may be analyzed as follows (Rigsby n.d.:15):

i-	pronominal prefix, third person singular
šapá-	causative prefix
tuti-	"stand," intransitive verb stem
-yay-	benefactive suffix
-ša	imperfect aspect suffix
-na	past tense suffix
=aš	pronominal enclitic, first person singular
niit	house

Pronouns rarely stand alone. Most are affixed to some other sentence element, as in the query, Míš=nam waʔ ("How are you?"), in which the pronominal element -nam ("you") is attached to the interrogative miš ("how?"). In this case, the pronoun is an "enclitic" element, that is, it is attached not to a particular word but is inserted at a particular position, specfically, attached to the end of the first word of the sentence. We use the equals sign (=) to highlight such particles.

Word order is flexible, allowing subtle shifting of emphasis by reordering sentence parts. This is possible because the "parts of speech" are usually obligatorily marked by a combination of prefixes and suffixes that allow the listener to deduce the proper interpretation. As a novice Sahaptin student my attempts at communication are normally restricted to a few pat phrases, such as "How are you?" or "Good morning" (niix máycqi). By the time I figure out how to put a novel sentence together (more or less correctly) the conversational opportunity has long since passed.

With study, however, I have come to a growing appreciation for the logical order of Sahaptin grammar. It makes excellent sense once its own logic is grasped. It exhibits features common to all human languages: Sahaptin sentences are composed of nominal and verbal elements, for example, of nominal subjects and objects and verbal predicates. In English the subject normally comes first, followed by the verb, then by the object (s v o order), as in the sentence, "The old man gave me a horse." The same order is frequently used in Sahaptin, as for example in the translation of the above sentence (this example is from Rigsby n.d.:19–23): X̣ʷɨsaat-nɨm=naš i-ní-ya in-áy k̓úsi. Step by step this translates as follows:

xʷɨsaat	"(the) old man"
-nɨm	subject case marker
=naš	first person singular subject/object pronoun
i-	third person singular subject pronoun
ní-	"give," the verb stem
-∅	unmarked, completed verb aspect
-ya	past tense marker
in-	first person singular pronoun
-áy	objective case marker
k̓úsi	"(a) horse"

Note, however, that the subject and indirect object are "tagged" as such allowing the sentence to be rearranged as one shifts emphasis from the old man to the act of giving or to the recipient or to the gift as the primary topic of the sentence:

Iníya=aš xʷɨsaatnɨm ináy k̓úsi.
"He **gave** [me] (the) old man [subject] to me [object] (a) horse."

Iná=aš xʷɨsaatnɨm iníya k̓úsi.
"To **me** [me] (the) old man [subject] he gave (a) horse."

k̓úsi=naš xʷɨsaatnɨm iníya ináy.
"(A) **horse** [me] (the) old man [subject] he gave to me [object]."

Note also that the first person pronoun enclitic, =(n)aš, always attaches to the end of the first word of the sentence. In this case the first person so indicated may be either subject or object of the verb depending on how the remainder of the sentence is read. Sahaptin speakers do not distinguish "the horse" from "a horse." Our required distinction between the definite and indefinite articles is either irrelevant to their discourse or inferred from its context. Finally, note that Sahaptin employs three words where English needs seven. This exemplifies again the polysynthetic quality of this Indian language, a feature shared by Finnish and other unrelated languages.

At the heart of any sentence is the verb. Let us consider an example to illustrate how Sahaptin verbs are inflected as subject, object, tense, and aspect shift. Let us begin with an intransitive verb stem such as wína-, "go." This stem cannot stand alone but forms the core around which a complete sentence is built. Prefixes are attached when the subject is third person, i- if singular, pa- if plural. If there is no prefix, the subject is first or second person. Suffixes are attached in a certain order (see Table 5).

First, one selects an appropriate aspect marker. If the action of the verb is continuing, attach -ša; if repeated or habitual action, attach -xa; if conditional, -taxna. A single completed action is indicated by "attaching" the null affix, Ø, that is, the position is left blank. Next in line is the tense marker. The "default

TABLE 5
Sahaptin Verb Inflection (adapted from Rigsby n.d.)

The verb	wína-, "go"	
Inflected for subject	wína-ša=aš	"I am going"
	wína-ša=nam	"You (singular) are going"
	i-wína-ša	"He/she is going"
	wína-ša=na	"We (you, too) are going"
	wína-ša=ataš	"We (but not you) are going"
	wína-ša=pam	"You (plural) are going"
	pa-wína-ša	"They are going"
Inflected for tense and aspect	i-wína-Ø-Ø	"She goes"
	i-winá-Ø-ta	"She will go"
	i-winá-Ø-na	"She went"
	i-wína-ša-Ø	"She is going"
	i-wína-ša-na	"She was going"
	i-wína-ša-ta	"She will be going"
	i-wína-xa-na	"She used to go"
	i-wína-taxnay	"She would have gone"
Context specified	wína-ša=aš k̓usi-pa	"I am going on horseback"
	wína-ša=aš átmupil-ki	"I am going by car"
	wína-ša=aš tkʷátat-yaw	"I am going for food"
	wína-ša=aš wána-kan	"I am going toward the river"
Verbal nouns	wína-t	"to go, going"
	wina-ɬá	"one who goes"
	wina-át-ša	"come out quickly," a place name[†]
	winá-at-ša-pam	"people of Wenatchee"

† In this case, winá- is a related but distinct, homophonous morpheme, an adverbial prefix meaning "quickly," "rapidly" (Rigsby, pers. comm.). James Selam notes that the verb form glossed "she was going" is more appropriately interpreted as "she went and came back."

option," marked by the null affix, is the present tense. The future is marked by suffixing -ta and the past is shown by -a, -na, -ya, or -ča depending on the sound preceding the suffix. Verb stems may also be modified to serve as nouns, much as in the English infinitive and gerund constructions such as, "To err is human." and, "Working in the hot sun is hard." Familiar place names such as those rendered in English as "Wenatchee" and "Wenas Creek" are corruptions of Sahaptin nouns derived from the verb stem wína-, "go."

To complete the idea of "going" we need to add, for example, a destination (to answer the question, "Where?") or a conveyance, e.g., "by car" (to answer the question, "How?"). In English such details which complete the picture drawn by the sentence are set off by prepositions. Sahaptin speakers attach suffixes to the nouns of place or of means to achieve the same purpose, as is illustrated in Table 5.

Transitive sentences add considerable complexity to our grammatical sketch. I will give but a brief outline here. In English the contrast between transitive and intransitive verbs is subtle. We know that "The bird flew" means something rather different from "The pilot flew (the plane)." The verb in the first instance is intransitive; in the second it is transitive. We recognize the absurdity of saying "The bird flew the plane," because we share a view of the world in which such an event is impossible. The verb "to fly" is transitive or intransitive according to context.

In Sahaptin a verb must be either transitive or intransitive, and distinct grammatical rules apply in each case. It is not always obvious to me whether a particular verb is one or the other. I must first see how a native Sahaptin speaker inflects it. For example, "to hunt" (more properly, "to go hunting"), tkʷáynp-, is an intransitive verb. "To shoot," however, is transitive. Thus one says, ín=aš tkʷáynp-ša yáamaš-yaw ("I am (going) hunting (for) mule deer"), but ín=aš á-tuxna-ša yáamaš-na ("I am shooting mule deer").

The mule deer's role is indicated by the postpositional suffix (rather than by a "preposition" as in English) -yaw in the intransitive sentence (since intransitive verbs, by definition, take no direct objects), but is indicated by the object case marker -na in the transitive sentence. Note also that a stressed verb prefix á- is required in the transitive case. This particular prefix is attached to the transitive verb stem whenever the subject is first or second person (here, "I") and the object is third person (here, "mule deer").

Use your newly acquired knowledge of Columbia River Sahaptin to appreciate the following excerpts (somewhat simplified) from a short text by Delsie Selam on how to make string from Indian hemp (see Text).

Sample Sahaptin Text: Making Twine of Tax̣ús

(by Delsie Selam, January 1977)

špam   anakúk i-lá-xyawi-x̣a aykúk patá-šaq'qɨn-x̣a
Autumn   then   it is dried up.   Then   they cut it

kʷaaná patá-šapa-lk̓ʷ ayt-ša-nx̣a, kúš-x̣ay pata-ʔí-x̓pi-x̣a
that one   they bury it,   or   they sprinkle it

čúuš-ki kʷaaná awku á-miik-ša, kʷaaná á-wila-xyawi-ša
with water that one now   peel it,   that one   dry it

mɨɬ   wáwtukt,   mɨɬ   mɨɬtaat, pínapt wáwtukt kʷaaná
so many   days,   that many three   four   days   that one

á-x̣amši-ša, kʷaaná á-tɋini-ša.   kuʔánay awku ku-nam
is scraped, is made into strands. Afterwards then   you

awku-tun   x̓áax̣ʷ   á-wi-ani-ša kúnki wisx̣áwas. awku
then   everything is made   with it (the) string. Then

i-qáwačič anam-tún-tya á-tɋiix̣-ša   aní-t   kúnki.
it is done whatever you   want   to make with it.

wápas   tunx̣-túnx̣   awku pa-wí-ʔani-x̣a-na kúnki awx̣ɨɬun,
Bags of many kinds then they used to make with it   nets,

ašúx̣nay x̓áax̣ʷ-awtun anak̓úš-x̣i awku-tun wisx̣áwas-tun.
eel nets every kind.   likewise   then   kinds of string.

šuyapuu-nmí wátisas   pá-ʔani-x̣a-na.   aw   ay.
White man's   rope   they used to make it. That's all.

The Sapir-Whorf Hypothesis

Learning a foreign language such as Sahaptin involves more than learning a strange set of sounds, getting used to unfamiliar grammatical patterns, and memorizing a new vocabulary. It also requires learning a new way of thinking and adopting a different perspective on reality. The problem of translating from the conceptual world of language X to that of language Y has been sharply drawn by Edward Sapir and his protégé Benjamin Lee Whorf. The hypothesis of linguistic relativity associated with these men was put strongly by Sapir when he asserted that people who grow up speaking different languages do not live in the same world with just the labels for things changed, but live in unique worlds (Sapir 1921:218).

The semantic discontinuities between languages emphasized by linguistic relativists are found both in grammar and in vocabulary. Some languages, such as Spanish, require that nouns be "male" or "female"; others, such as English, do not. Does requiring the things of the world to be of masculine or feminine gender subtly alter how the world is perceived and how one acts within it? Sapir might argue that it does. Whorf's best-known case involved Hopi: he argued that the Hopi language lacks verb tenses. Instead of past, present, and future, Hopi speakers classify events as known or imagined (Whorf 1950). Linguistic relativity in vocabulary is exemplified by the oft-repeated example of the proliferation of words for "snow" in Eskimo languages.

Though appealing at first encounter and obviously to some degree valid, linguistic relativity is only partial. If it were total, one could never hope to learn another language and communicating with a native-speaker of a foreign language would be like conversing with a humpback whale! I choose to stress here how all human languages, Sahaptin among them, provide people with a consistent and powerful means of grasping the nature of the world in which they live. To a degree the worlds of human experience are everywhere alike: the sun shines, rain falls, and gravity pulls on all of us; birds fly, fish swim, and trees grow more or less in like fashion everywhere. We should expect all languages to reflect those common elements of experience.

The reality of experience is also subject to diverse interpretations. Here we should look for experiential discontinuities. A well-known example is the naming of colors. Is our basic English color vocabulary God-given? Will every language label black, white, red, yellow, green, blue, purple, pink, orange, brown, and gray as we do? The answer is, "No, but . . ." Sahaptin, for example, has basic terms[2] for black, white, red, yellow, blue, and gray (Hunn and French n.d. [1977]). "Green" is usually translated maxáš-pyat, a term applied originally to Hudson's Bay company blankets and which is derived from the term for "yellow," maxáš. But grass is described as lamt, "blue," just as is the color of the sky. This lumping of green and blue is very common in American Indian languages (Berlin and Kay 1969). "Purple," "pink," and "brown" may be distinguished but are labeled less directly as "huckleberry-like," "pale-red," and as the color of a particular kind of horse, respectively.

The translation of Sahaptin names for plants and animals also poses problems, but not because the Sahaptin-speaking Indians choose to see the biological world in some exotic fashion. Rather, the translation problem lies with English: English lacks widely recognized terms for much of the local flora and fauna. (English speakers have had less than two hundred years to get acquainted with the local environment, and the English-speaking settlers have always relied primarily upon plants and animals brought from Europe.) Sahaptin terms for plants and animals are readily translated into scientific Latin, with a very few interesting exceptions (see chapter 4).

But colors and the flora and fauna are aspects of the world the objective reality of which is hard to deny. We must be able to respond appropriately to these things or qualities or die trying. In our social and spiritual lives, however, there is less agreement on the nature of reality and wider scope for cultural interpretation. This is apparent when we attempt to learn the Sahaptin kinship terms, analyzed in some detail in chapter 6 (see also Appendix 4). Consider the implications of the fact that Sahaptin-speaking people refer to the Creator, not as "Our Father," but as naamí pyap, "Our Elder Brother." The messages in these metaphors are not entirely consistent—though in both cases the ultimate deity is equated with a senior male kinsman. The connotations sharply contrast. The Plateau Indian people clearly

2. In Berlin and Kay's influential analysis (1969), "basic color terms" are defined in a special way in order to differentiate the basic "core" of color vocabulary from the numerous secondary terms. Basic terms are (1) not included in any other basic color term, unlike "scarlet" which is a kind of "red," the basic term; (2) named "monolexemically," unlike "bluish purple" or "blue-green"; (3) are universal in their application, unlike "blonde" or "silver" which can be applied only to certain objects; and (4) are psychologically salient and widely recognized within the community of speakers. They argue that there are no more than eleven basic colors recognized by the languages of the world, that languages name from two to eleven of these colors, that which colors receive basic color names is highly predictable, and that the focal points of basic colors in terms of hue and brightness are invariant.

had difficulty appreciating the missionaries' view of God as a fiercely righteous patriarch.

Beneath the great superficial disparity of English and Sahaptin kinship terms lies a common conceptual ground of biological descent and the sociological imperatives of human family life. Likewise, there may exist some common ground beneath the disparate spiritual realities posited by Plateau Indian people on the one hand and Christian missionaries on the other. Henry Perkins struggled to find the right Sahaptin words to translate the scriptures, but he noted as well that "the opinions of the Greeks, Romans, and Jews, with regard to evil spirits, or demons formerly, appear to have been almost precisely what the opinions of these Indians [at Celilo Falls] are now" (Perkins n.d. [1838–43], Book 1:25–26).

The Many Uses of Sahaptin

Human language sets people apart from all other animals. Recent experiments have shown that chimpanzees and gorillas—our closest natural kin—have the mental capacity to acquire minimal proficiency in sign language and to use artificial codes to accomplish certain communicative tasks. However, the fact that fully complex human languages are both essential to human survival and universal in our species underscores the fundamental importance of understanding what language is if we are to comprehend what it means to be human. Why did the language capacity evolve in the human species? The Columbia River Indians as hunter-gatherers may more closely reflect the original evolutionary context for the origin of human language than would a highly literate society. How do Sahaptin speakers use their linguistic gifts?

Language, of course, is a tool of communication. As such it *limits* intercommunication to those who speak the same language. It is useful thus for exchanging messages with relatives, neighbors, and friends. With enemies and strangers communication usually takes a more primitive form. Language is also useful for the internal communication that accompanies much of our thinking. Just as language links one mind with another, aligning their thoughts and calling upon common experience, so also does language align memory with present perception and future possibility. It is essential to the displacement of thought and imagination from immediate reality. Language dramatically increases memory capacity by labeling our thoughts and images so we may call them up by name at will.

The typical sentence, complete with inflected verb and subject and object nouns, is a symbolic representation of an event. An event is a unit of interaction between an individual and his or her environment, in short, an ecological unit. Human survival hinges on the outcome of such ecological events as finding food, eating, killing, escaping, meeting, mating, feeding, and dying. With language we can describe, catalog, and analyze a very large number of such events as well as imagine, and thus perhaps create, new ecological realities. Language is thus not merely a means of self-expression but also a tool of survival more powerful than bow-and-arrow, net, or plow. In language we construct our battle plan for our daily skirmish with hard reality. For example, the sentence, Ín-aš npíwi-ta tkʷínat-yaw awx̣át-ki wána-pa ("I will fish for Chinook salmon by dip net in the River"), is a recipe for recreating an event that has proved life-sustaining many times before. The elements of this plan link up with other plans necessary to its accomplishment or assume prerequisite knowledge and skills. Chinook salmon occur in abundance but briefly and periodically. They are huge and fat, provide efficient returns to the skilled fisherman, and, if not too oily, may be dried for use in the manufacture of salmon meal (člay), a highly regarded food.

The sentence spoken represents but the tip of the iceberg of cultural knowledge about the event it describes. The use of a dip net is one option for fishing for Chinook salmon. But one might also use a spear, set net, or weir. Only certain of the possible combinations of means, ends, times, and places are feasible, however. Weirs will not work in the main channel of the Columbia River, for example, and spears are useful only in clear, shallow water. This knowledge must be acquired, remembered, and passed on.

We now come to a second critical aspect of the survival value of language, the social transmission of information. Mid-Columbia River Indian mothers, camped in late spring near the Blue Mountain root-digging ground, might have instructed their daughters: Wína-k-nam x̣ní-ša x̣áwš-na yuk-pa p̓uštáy-pa, ku niʔíix̣ piná-q̓inu-k háti-yaw ("Go dig cous roots on yonder hill, but beware of the háti root"). If necessary, háti, an allegedly poisonous cous lookalike, could be described by color, size, shape, and/or texture of its leaves, flowers, stem, and root to save the neophyte root-digger from a perhaps fatal ecological error.

Long winters were passed in home-bound tasks such as repairing and manufacturing tools, and the long nights passed with celebrations in myth-telling and power dancing. The visiting facilitated by the enforced rest of the winter season was used to good advantage by comparing notes on past experiences and future plans with a series of visitors. "How was the fishing at sk̓in last spring?" "And the hunting above áyunaš?" "Will there be a good crop of camas at k̓íttaas [Kittitas] next June?" "A Paiute war party was engaged south of ttaxšmí." "Chief Yellept's daughters are hardworking and comely and of age." And so the news is passed on, providing essential information by which peoples' plans can be adopted, modified, shared, or abandoned. Language makes it possible for each member of society to benefit from the experience of many others and thus to know a much wider reality (see Text, pp. 70–71).

Language is more than a tool for communicating information. Language can also be used to control and inspire others. Oratory is a gift highly valued in Indian society. The eloquence of Indian chiefs is legendary and that of Plateau leaders is as moving as any. Smohalla (šmúxala), prophet of Priest

Text: Sahaptin Subsistence Activities Described

Subject	Verb	Object	Instrument	Location
wínš-in	pá-tuxna-na	yáamaš-na	twínpas-ki	píɬxanu-pa.
The man	shot	the mule deer	with a gun	in the mountains.
ín=aš	á-tuxna-xa-na	yáamaš-na	wislak̓uskí-ki.	
I	used to shoot	mule deer	with arrows.	
winš	i-tkʷáynp-ša	ƛ́álk-yaw.		
The man	is hunting	for black-tailed deer.		
ím=nam	nip̓íwi-ša	tkʷínat-yaw	awxát-ki	wána-pa.
You	are fishing	for Chinook salmon	with a net	in the river.
tílaaki-in	pá-xni-ta	pyaxí-na	kápɨn-ki	šám-pa.
The woman	is digging	bitterroot	with a digging stick	in rocky soil.
ín=aš	á-tamayt-ša	xmáaš-na	tiičám-pa.	
I	am baking	camas	in the earth.	

Rapids and a major force in the prophet dance religious revival of the mid-nineteenth century, rejected the Euro-American world view with these few words: "You ask me to plow the ground! Shall I take a knife and tear my mother's bosom?/ You ask me to dig for stone. Shall I dig under her skin for her bones? Then when I die I cannot enter her body to be born again./ You ask me to cut grass and make hay and sell it, and be rich like white men. But how dare I cut off my mother's hair?" (quoted in Mooney 1896:721).

Chief Joseph of the Nez Perces ended the heroic retreat of the non-treaty Nez Perces when finally surrounded by the combined armies of Generals Howard, Gibbon, and Miles. "Tell General Howard that I know his heart. What he told me before [that the Nez Perce would be repatriated and guaranteed the safety of their remaining reservation lands—a promise not kept]—I have it in my heart. I am tired of fighting. Our chiefs are killed. . . . The old men are all dead. . . . It is cold, and we have no blankets. My people—some of them—have run away to the hills, and have no blankets, no food. No one knows where they are. . . . I want to have time to look for my children, and to see how many of them I can find; maybe I shall find them among the dead. Hear me, my chiefs, my heart is sick and sad. From where the sun now stands, I will fight no more with the white man" (quoted in Joseph 1983 [1879]:4). (For a reconstruction of that speech by a contemporary native speaker, see Aoki 1979:123–24.)

The power of this simple oratory captured the imagination of whites as well, inspiring in some of them oratorical responses that in their florid sentimentality highlight the discordance of style between Native American speech and that of the pioneers. Compare C. T. Brady's epitaph for Joseph with Joseph's own words cited above: "The other day a gray-headed old chief, nodding by the fire, dreaming perhaps of days of daring and deeds of valor, by which, savage though he was, he had written his name on the pages of history, slipped quietly to the ground and fell into his eternal sleep [Joseph fell dead while sitting before his teepee on the Colville Reservation, 22 September 1904]. Peaceful ending for the Indian Xenophon, the Red Napoleon of the West" (quoted in Joseph 1983 [1879]:7).

Indian oratory drew power not only from speaking the truth with vivid simplicity, but also from silence. At the treaty council convened by Governor Isaac Stevens at the mouth of the Walla Walla River in late May of 1855, "Governor Stevens and General Palmer, in succession, made long speeches to [the assembled Indian chiefs], explaining the benefits they would receive from signing this treaty, and the advantages which would result to them from their removal to the new lands [*sic*, the proposed Nez Perce, Umatilla, and Yakima reservations, which were hardly "new" lands] offered in exchange for their present hunting grounds. The council lasted till three o'clock" (Kip 1971 [1855]:15). This filibuster continued with almost daily harangues that left the unwilling Indians literally speechless. Chief Looking Glass, a Nez Perce, arrived at the proceedings direct from skirmishing with Blackfeet on the bison grounds in Montana. His speech is of three lines: "My people, what have you done? While I was gone you have sold my country [referring to Chief Lawyer's acceptance of the proposed treaty]. I have come home and there is not left me a place on which to pitch my lodge" (Doty 1978 [1855]:28). This had such an effect "that not only the Nez Percés but all the other tribes refused to sign."

Though Kamiakin, outstanding chief among the Yakima present, affixed his X mark to the treaty, his silence at the council speaks louder than words. "Kamiakin spoke for his people, not for himself alone. . . . he was tired of talking and waiting here [at the Walla Walla council grounds] and wished to get back to his garden. . . . Kamiakin . . . was tired of hearing so much talking; he . . . did not wish to be head chief [a role foisted upon him by Stevens]. . . . He would not speak. He would make the treaty; he liked the reservation and wished to collect his people, they were much scattered" (quoted in Pace 1977:13–14). However, he never did accept the monetary inducements the treaties guaranteed to those appointed head chiefs on the new reservations. Governor Stevens forced the Indians' surrender to his treaty terms with a barrage of words that was met with the stony silence of Indian resignation.

Indian people appreciate the power of words. Perhaps for that reason village headmen and chiefs (miyáwax̣/miyúux̣), employed heralds (sɨnwi-ɫá) to repeat the headman's speeches in a loud voice for all to hear (Thompson in Glover 1962:349). "This village crier . . . went through the village each evening announcing the news of the day and activities planned for the next" (Desmond 1952:7, said of the Yakima). This use of an intermediary allowed the chief to assume the appropriate role as a person "reserved, dignified, . . . patient [who] waits to make a decision . . . , then waits to act . . . , slow talking [but with] the power to persuade or convince." In mid-Columbia Indian society individual autonomy was prized, and a leader whose power was exercised without restraint was resented. Thus, the spokesman role took the hard edge off the exercise of power and helped maintain the delicate balance between social order and freedom (see chapter 6).

Finally, language inspires. This is best seen in the social role of myths along the middle Columbia. In America today a "myth" is a species of falsehood. For Indians, myths were and are a species of truth. Modern-day Yakima Indians call the Coyote myths their "Indian Bible," and so they are. Our appreciation of the meaning of Indian myths is complicated by the rancorous debate in American society concerning the nature of Biblical truth: is it literally true, or is it truth of a more subtle nature, divinely inspired nonetheless? Or is it just a catalog of superstitious illusions? These conflicting views might also be applied to Indian mythology. However, let me make a case for a middle ground, that Coyote stories—the core of Plateau Indian mythology—embody inspired truth as is found in all great literature.

Is Shakespeare's work true? Is it inspired? Yes, certainly, to both questions. Coyote myths are cast in the same mold despite the fact that they are the work of no single author, nor were they captured in print until recently (e.g., Curtin 1909; Jacobs 1929, 1934, 1937a; Phinney 1934; Beavert 1974). In fact, in the process of writing myths down much of the force of the original presentation is lost. The context: a dark, frigid night of a Plateau winter, the wind stroking the tule mats covering the lodge, smokey fires with three generations of family gathered around. A grandparent quietly begins the story, becoming progressively animated, drawing the animal people alive into the lodge with deft imitations of their speech and actions. The audience responds warmly, as they are an integral part of the cast, caught up in the drama, whether comic or terrible. Like Aesop's fables, there are morals to be drawn, but they are not didactic. Coyote, rather, teaches by example, and he exemplifies all the good and bad qualities of the human animal. Coyote stories instruct while inspiring obedience to an ethic of mutual respect and concern. They inspire modesty, honesty, generosity, forbearance, forethought, and courage. They etch in the children's memories a living map of their surroundings, a land peopled with creatures and forces of nature that are fully animate and virtually human; in fact, they once were fully human. Here, art clearly serves survival, strengthening the ecological, social, and spiritual balance on which the hunter-gatherer life depends.

The Present Status of and Future Prospects for Sahaptin

The Sahaptin language still lives. Of an estimated twenty-one Indian languages spoken in Oregon at first European contact, however, only four still have substantial numbers of native speakers, four more are in varying stages of moribundity, with from one to twenty elderly speakers left, while twelve are extinct, known from written records if at all (Pierce 1965). In the case of moribund languages, the reality of the language is attested by the failing memories of a handful of elders. These elders had acquired an imperfect command of their language in childhood because of the disruption of Indian family life (circa 1880–1925). A few North American Indian languages, with Navajo the premier example, are thriving today. Infants still learn Navajo at home by the natural learning process, a sort of "osmosis" from the everyday speech of family members. Navajo remains the preferred language for most native speakers in many situations. A literature is being developed as Navajos adopt a writing system adapted from those of professional linguists.

Sahaptin is not yet moribund, nor is it thriving. Very few children speak it, though a substantial number of young people at the Yakima and Warm Springs reservations have a passive knowledge of it, understanding much of what their elders say when speaking "Indian," but unable (or perhaps unwilling) to speak it fluently themselves. Knowledge of Sahaptin among those over fifty years of age is widespread and as late as 1980 a few old women were reputed to speak no English (whether from ignorance or active resistance, I don't know). On the Yakima Reservation one may hear telephone conversations conducted entirely in Sahaptin and some knowledge of the language remains an important de facto qualification for election to leadership positions on the tribal council and in wáašat congregations. In December 1976 I recorded a full repertoire of Coyote stories in Sahaptin from Elsie Pistolhead, a total of sixty-five stories lasting sixteen hours. James Selam and Virginia Hymes are working with me to transcribe, translate, and interpret this invaluable collection.

I believe Sahaptin will survive, and with it much of the cultural knowledge and wisdom it has served to transmit through the centuries. One might assume that the preservation of a language would be a goal sought by everyone. Yet in language is power, and where there is power there will be politics. The continuity of Indian language was seen by the Bureau of Indian Affairs—to which the United States government assigned the responsibility for protecting the interests of the government's Indian *wards*—as a threat to the primary goal of U.S. Indian policy between 1870 and 1930, that of assimilation, a goal pursued sporadically by government officials to the present day. Indian agents correctly surmised that so long as Indian children had the opportunity to learn their ancestral language and culture from their parents, assimilation to the American mainstream would fail. The American Indians would remain recalcitrant in their possession of reservation lands and stubborn in defense of their treaty rights, the exercise of which increasingly rankled their non-Indian neighbors. The establishment of boarding schools for Indian children was calculated to break this bond of tradition (Colson 1953). In such schools, use of Indian languages was severely punished while communication between children and their parents was restricted as far as possible (but see McBeth 1983 and Lomawaima 1987 for a more complex assessment of the impact of the boarding school experience on Native American youth).

The policy shifts introduced by John Collier, commissioner of Indian Affairs under Franklin Roosevelt, eliminated official federal antagonism to the use of Indian languages. In many cases, however, the damage done was irreparable. Languages such as Sahaptin remain in a precarious position in which the traditional processes of linguistic transmission may not be sufficient for its preservation. An active program of instruction, utilizing customized alphabets and printed training materials seems essential. Yet this work has recently become a deeply divisive political issue in the Yakima Nation. The bilingual education work and dictionary writing project pursued in the 1970s by the Consortium of Johnson-O'Malley Committees of Region IV was halted by a General Council resolution imposing a moratorium on bilingual projects. The moratorium reflected a deep distrust among a segment of the reservation community of the effects of such a publically accessible and nontraditional mode of transmission of the language. A few elders insisted that if their children wanted to learn their language they must seek out their parents or grandparents for oral instruction. If they could not bring themselves to that point, let the language die! Others feared that whites would "steal" their language as they had stolen their land and fish before.

By 1987, a renewed commitment to bilingual literacy was beginning to be felt among the Yakimas, while bilingual projects on the Warm Springs Reservation in Oregon received continued support under the watchful eye of the Culture Heritage Committee. The involvement of academic scholars in this work is, in my opinion, essential. Tribal governments hire outside professionals to advise them on technical matters of economic development if the essential expertise is lacking among their own people. Language preservation likewise requires professional expertise. But such involvement is always a delicate political issue given the often conflicting interests and perspectives of native language consultants and their families, the various factions of tribal government, the funding agencies that sponsor such research, and the academic community where the free exchange of information is held as a first principle, with success defined in terms of published output.

In conclusion, language is the key. People are known by the language they speak. The biological necessities of finding food and shelter depend on detailed cultural knowledge of the natural environment, knowledge stored and transmitted by language. Human social life in all its complexity requires language, while moral commitment and spiritual satisfaction come through the inspiration of the spoken word. Let us now explore these further avenues of Indian life on the middle Columbia River.

4

Ecology

tiičám, "land"

MOUNT HOOD rears its head above the busy Celilo Falls fisheries across the roaring Columbia from the village of sḱin. From the ancient pit house rings on the greasewood flats where Toppenish Creek joins the Yakima River, Indian ancestors looked west to the icy dome of pátu, "snow peak," as Mount Adams is known at Yakima. The soft outline of the Blue Mountains southeast from the Walla Walla River (from walawála, "little rivers") provided a less dramatic vista for the citizens of Umatilla, Walla Walla, and Snake River villages. Between the extremes of baked-dry riverside flats and cool mountain forests, the people of the mid-Columbia found the full range of resources they needed to sustain their lives and their culture year after year for many centuries (see fig. 4.1).

In summer the low valleys are hot as furnaces with temperatures regularly rising over 100°F (40°C), yet in sight of the perpetual ice of the dozing volcanic summits. Cool huckleberry meadows near timberline provide a refuge from this heat when the mid-summer fish runs slacken. The low valleys receive on average as little as seven inches (175 mm) of precipitation annually. They lie in the rain shadow of the Cascade range which wrings moisture from the Pacific fronts. By contrast, Paradise on Mount Rainier's southwest shoulder averages 50 feet of snow (equivalent to 150 inches of rain) each year and has recorded 100 feet. The air, cooled at high altitude, then descends the east slope of the range, warming and consequently drying out as it falls, absorbing moisture from the land like a sponge. Only well east toward the Rocky Mountains is there a hint of the convectional summer rainfall pattern characteristic of the Great Plains, Southwest, and Eastern Woodlands. The lack of summer rainfall may help explain the fact that agriculture—with the exception of an occasional patch of tobacco (Davies 1980:47)—was unknown in the Plateau.

The encircling mountains also trap cold air at ground level in winter. For

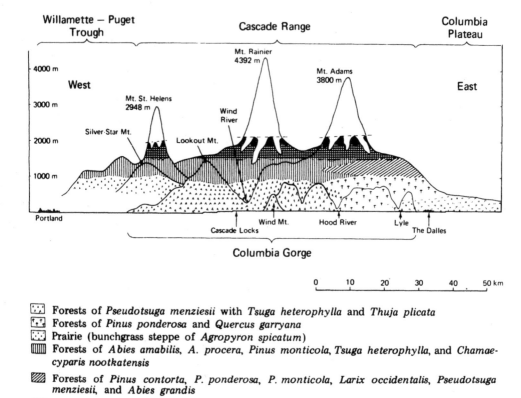

Fig. 4.1. Habitat transect of the Cascade Range (Franklin and Dyrness 1973:311).

weeks on end a monotonous subfreezing overcast reigns, nourishing depression in the people confined to their lodges. Fresh foods are virtually unavailable. No migrant salmon appear between late October and late April, just a few steelhead and resident whitefish which may be caught by hook and line through the ice. The only edible plants at this season are a few tuberous perennials, notably the large-fruited mariposa lily (nuunás; *Calochortus macrocarpus*), found by careful searching amongst the sagebrush near winter villages such as náwawi at the mouth of Alder Creek, where Delsie Selam and Sara Quaempts grew up. This land would support very few people by hunting and gathering were it not for their stores of dried roots, salmon, berries, and venison prepared during many long hard days of spring, summer, and fall, then carefully cached in cellars (wulčí) and in special baskets.

In Sahaptin the earth is tiičám. It is the source of life, the nurturing Mother, on whose breast one's bones are laid at death, in the words of the prophet Smohalla. Death is familiar to the Indians here still. Funerals are the most frequent of ritual performances. Everyone attends or should, as virtually everyone is related to the deceased and owes them this last demonstration of respect. The earth harbors so many of their dead, pulling the living like a magnet to remain close to that special earth.

The sun (an) is Father; water (čuuš), the first sacred food. It is drunk as a sacrament to begin and end each wáašani feast. The winds are each named. The prevailing westerly wind is hulí, which may also be used to refer to wind in general. Myths recount epic battles between the frigid North wind (átya) and the Chinook wind (wináaway), a strong southerly flow of air that can thaw the frozen land in hours and provide relief from the midwinter chill (Beavert 1974:10–24). Hot dry east winds (txáwna) in spring can burn the precious roots, cutting the harvest short. Winds are powers to be reckoned with. Steep temperature gradients in winter and spring between coast and plateau send air rushing through the Columbia Gorge and the lower passes to sweep across the dusty central plain. Indians here may burn the wood of the pallid evening primrose (kalux̲-mí áčaš, "blueback salmon's eyes"; *Oenothera pallida*)—the blooms of which freckle the sandy slopes at low elevations at the end of spring—as a prayer to halt the forceful play of the winds.

The Columbia River Indians' Knowledge of Nature

The precontact Indians of the middle Columbia—in common with hunter-gatherers everywhere—survived by virtue of a detailed, encyclopedic knowledge of their environment. We have noted their appreciation of the basic elements on which life depends. Prominent landforms and habitats were also named (see fig. 4.2).

Such landforms are useful indicators of the location of plant and animal resources. For example, waláas, a plant (as yet unidentified) that produces balls of "Indian chewing gum" on its roots, grows only on steep clay banks, a habitat called iš̲x̲ú in Sahaptin. Specific floral associations may also be indicated explicitly in plant names, as in pix̲anu-pamá ttax̲š, "mountain wil-

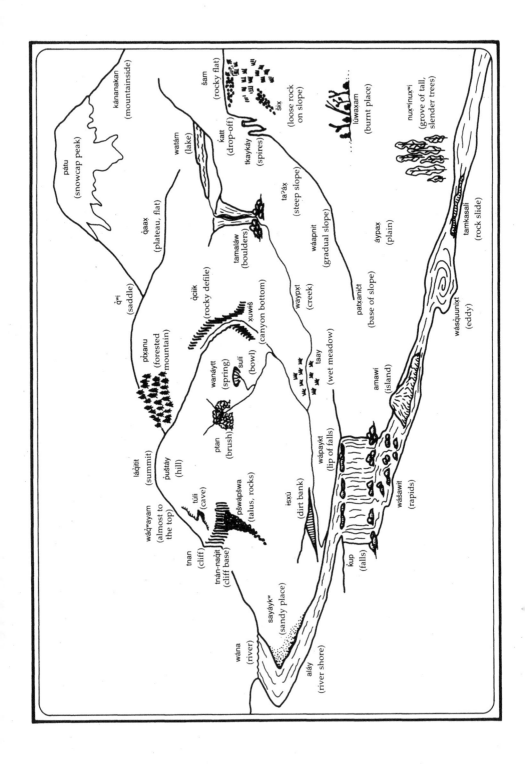

low" (*Salix scouleri* and/or *S. monticola*). More often it is simply taken for granted where resource species may be found. For example, bitterroot and Canby's lomatium are found in productive abundance usually on šam terrain (lithosols); wákamu, or x̣maaš (camas), favors vernal meadows (taay).

Columbia River Indians also named hundreds of specific places. Their ethnogeography differs systematically from the Euro-American in certain telling ways; for example, they did not usually name mountains and rivers as such. For non-Indians, a focus on specific mountains and rivers as things of importance implies a cartographic perspective, one in which the observer is placed above the landscape as if in flight. The Indians' land-based perspective named instead specific places on a mountain or along a river *where things happened*. It was a practical rather than a purely abstract geography, naming culturally significant places, the sites of important events or activities, whether of the present or of the myth age.

The Columbia River was called nči-wána, which means simply "big river," a name I have borrowed for the title of this book. Indian names adopted by the early western explorers for other major rivers, such as the Yakima, Klickitat, Umatilla, Walla Walla, Wenatchee, Okanogan, Sanpoil, Spokane, and Colville, were names for specific villages or other landmarks on or near those rivers, not names for the rivers themselves. Such names did not exist in the Indian lexicons. Mount Adams and Mount Hood were both called pátu, a generic landform designation rather than a name for a specific peak, though today the term is used as a proper name for Mount Adams, which has acquired special significance for the Yakima Indians as a symbol of their tribal lands and identity. Mount St. Helens and Mount Rainier, by contrast, were given proper names long ago. That for St. Helens, lawílayt-ɬá, literally, "the smoker," described its active volcanic state, while that for Rainier, tax̣úma, was likely borrowed from a Coast Salish language.

The degree of elaboration of geographic names in the Indian languages clearly reflected the cultural importance of an area. At the great Celilo Falls fishery dozens of rocky points and ephemeral islands were named (see fig. 5.3 in chapter 5). Each was a valuable fishing station, its time and manner of use governed by the seasonal rise and fall of the Columbia. Traditionally, such points might have been owned by a resident family who erected scaffolding there each year to serve as a fishing platform. Permission to use these facilities—the real limiting resource here being not the salmon but the good fishing places—had to be requested of the owners. The owners felt bound to share their bounty with both relatives and strangers. Strangers were allowed to catch one fish; elders who came to watch the action were also due a fish as a common courtesy (for the Upper Chinookans at The Dalles, see Spier and Sapir 1930:175).

Indian place names give rich clues to the ecological perceptions of the people (cf. Boas 1934). Many names refer to plants or animals characteristic of the place. For example, the lower Crab Creek area north of Priest Rapids was called taxús-as, which is to say "[place] of Indian hemp" (Relander 1956:312). Though Indian hemp might be found in many low-lying areas closer to home, the hemp there grew higher and straighter, and the long strands produced were prized for the strength of the twine made from them. So special was this resource area that violent conflict (otherwise uncommon) occurred between Wanapam Sahaptins and Columbia Salish over access to the hemp (Relander 1956:312).

Áyunaš was a camping place near Mount Adams visited each August by Indians drawn from many miles around. James Selam recounts traveling there by horse and wagon as a child in the 1920s. In August 1983 we retraced a portion of his route, the track now scarcely discernible under the forest growth. Áyunaš means "lovage place," named for a valuable medicinal root (áyun; *Ligusticum canbyi*, fig. 4.3). The best berrying grounds were nearby at kalamát meadow, a center also for summer social activity, for visiting, trading, horse racing, and gambling. A deep trace of the Indian horse-racing track is still evident, now partially obscured by the passage of backpackers' boots. The place has become a registered historic landmark. Kalamát means "yellow pond lily" (*Nuphar polysepalum*). To my surprise I found a few pond lilies growing in a shallow pool in the meadow, though pond lilies are unusual at such a high elevation (4,500 feet). These plants were not important food for Sahaptins (though the Klamath Indians relied very heavily on them). Perhaps their unexpected occurrence on such a high tarn enhanced the mnemonic value of kalamát as a place name.

Many place names refer imaginatively to prominent landmarks. The Yakima village at Union Gap was called paxutakyúut, literally, "head-to-head," as the steep brows of the ridge cut through here by the river suggest two people in close consultation. The large Sahaptin village on the north bank of the Columbia River at Celilo Falls was formerly called sk̓in, literally, "cradle board," an allusion to the shape of a prominent rock nearby; it is now called "Wishram Station" (a misnomer, as the Upper Chinookan village named wíšxami in Sahaptin [or nixluídix in the Kiksht language of its own inhabitants] was situated several miles downstream, somewhat above The Dalles).

Fig. 4.3. Lovage (*Ligusticum canbyi*; áyun).

The ribald humor of the Columbia River Indians is seen at play in such place names as simtay-wáakuɬ, literally, "resembles pubic hair," for a triangular patch of riparian woods at the head of a tributary stream of Satus Creek southwest of Toppenish. The high point of Toppenish ridge south of White Swan is known as čáynač, or "groom" (see fig. 4.4). From certain vantage points, the sensuous curves of the ridges below the peak, silky with golden

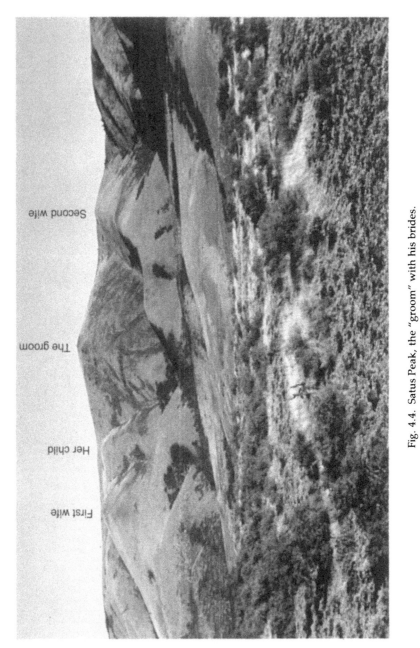

Fig. 4.4. Satus Peak, the "groom" with his brides.

summer grass, suggest a young man flanked by two graceful and naked wives, the "younger" with babe at breast. Such features, imaginatively perceived, might be brought to life in myths (e.g., Beavert 1974) that account dramatically for the feature's creation. Their's is a vivid landscape, still alive for the elders.

The sheer weight of geographical terminology as a component of Sahaptin vocabulary suggests a long period of stable residence on this stretch of river. Clearly indigenous Sahaptin geographic terminology exists for features south as far as Fox Valley (called ímáayi) and the Metolius River (from Sahaptin miłúla, "spawned-out" or "dog salmon") in central Oregon (cf. Suphan 1974a, 1974b), north to the Wenatchee River ("come out quickly," see Table 5, p. 75) in Interior Salish territory, west nearly to old Fort Vancouver, where a meadow is called alašík ("turtle"), and east to the Palouse. Such indigenous terms sketch the boundaries of the land frequented by Sahaptin speakers. An interesting example of the use of place name origins to discover prehistoric language shifts is in Kinkade (1967). He notes that Methow geographic terms are largely of southern Okanaganlinguistic affinity and argues for a rather recent replacement of an Okanagan dialect there by the Methow dialect of Columbia Salish.

Such inferences from Indian place names to historic migrations must be supported by careful comparative linguistic analysis, as superficial resemblances of inaccurately transcribed place names have given rise to mistaken conclusions in the past. The most notorious example is James Teit's theory (1928) that Salish speakers occupied the Columbia River down to near The Dalles in the immediate precontact period. In Teit's scheme the Columbia Salish were but recently displaced on the mid-Columbia by Sahaptin speakers, who had in turn been pushed north by pressure from expanding Numic populations in the Great Basin. The equation by Teit of the "pisch quit pás" of Lewis and Clark (Thwaites 1959 [1904], 3:137)—identified with a village a few miles below and opposite the Umatilla River mouth—with the "pisquouse" of the 1855 treaty—the latter a Columbia Salish self-designation—compounded the error (Rigsby 1965:221–28). "Pisch quit pás" might be a poor attempt at spelling Sahaptin píšxu-pa, literally, "rabbitbrush place" (after a common local shrub, *Chrysothamnus* spp.), which might appropriately describe the terrain about the village of the so-called "Pisch quit pás" of Lewis and Clark, a name no longer recognized by local Indians. Though the mystery of the "Pisch quit pás" remains unsolved, it provides no support for a theory of Salish occupation of the Columbia River below Priest Rapids.

Flora and Fauna

As an ethnobiologist I have pursued a primary interest in the nature and scope of Sahaptin knowledge of their native flora and fauna. An ethnobiological investigation is deceptively simple at first glance. One compares the native name for a plant or animal with the Latin of the biological scientist (appending an English equivalent, if such exists). If every speaker (user) of a language, whether English, Latin, or Sahaptin, used words in the same way, and if everyone, regardless of cultural training, recognized the same categories of living organisms, the task would be reduced to the matching of labels. According to Edward Sapir, a founder of anthropological linguistics, people do not live "in the same world with [just] different labels attached" but rather in different worlds conditioned by the unique perspective acquired in learning their native language. (As noted above, this assertion of linguistic relativity has come to be known as the Sapir-Whorf hypothesis, after Sapir and his pioneering colleague, Benjamin Lee Whorf.)

Ethnobiological evidence, however, sharply qualifies this relativistic position. Close agreement between folk and scientist in the naming of plants and animals is evident. Natural species have an undeniable reality which it can be dangerous to ignore and which it is certainly useful to recognize. On the other hand, there are simply too many species of plants, birds, and insects to justify naming them all, even in the language of modern science (Raven, Berlin, and Breedlove 1971). It is thus of great interest to learn which species are recognized and which ignored or casually dismissed by the folk biologists of a culture, in this case, by the Sahaptin folk biologist.

I have so far recorded names in Sahaptin for approximately 240 basic kinds of animals and for 215 of plants. This is not an overwhelming total, as subsistence farmers in Mexico, Peru, and the Philippines are known to catalog 500 to 1,000 in each kingdom (see Brown 1985 for a cross-cultural summary). The size of the Sahaptin inventory is nevertheless impressive compared to that of the average modern-day Euro-American and is in keeping with the diversity of the local biota, their dependence on hunting, fishing, and gathering for subsistence, and the degree of attrition the language has suffered as a result of Euro-American contact and domination (Hunn and French 1984).

The botanical expertise of the traditional mid-Columbia Indians is best exemplified by their recognition of the many species of "lomatiums," plants all classed in Latin in the genus *Lomatium*, literally, "winged seeds." Hitchcock and Cronquist's regional flora (1973) lists forty species of lomatiums, which constitute nearly 50 percent of all the native species of the Umbelliferae, a large family including such familiar plants as carrots, parsley (hence the name "desert parsley" for some lomatiums), celery, dill, and coriander. The genus *Lomatium* includes a total of some eighty species found throughout the western half of the United States and the southern edge of Canada. Botanists consider it a difficult group to analyze taxonomically. Unlike other genera of comparable size and complexity such as the willows (*Salix*) and lupines (*Lupinus*), the various lomatiums are refreshingly stable, rarely if ever hybridizing in nature. The difficulty scientists have had with the genus—which is apparent in the errors of classification that have crept into Cronquist's expert summary[1]—is perhaps primarily because many *Lomatium* species are restricted in range, being rare and little known relict populations.

Sahaptin-speaking Indians had no such difficulty learning to distinguish and name these species. Fourteen "folk species" are named in Sahaptin (see Table 6), including two "varieties" each of *Lomatium canbyi* (Canby's lomatium), *L. farinosum,* and "*L. gormanii.*" In the last instance the Indians distinguished between Gorman's lomatium proper and Piper's lomatium (*L. piperi,* fig. 4.5), a distinction Hitchcock and Cronquist judged too subtle to be worthy of scientific recognition. Sahaptin speakers who know both plants—now restricted to a few elderly women—find the distinction not all that subtle. To them Piper's desert parsley is mámɨn and is considered a choice root food, a necessary ingredient of high quality root cakes (sapɨl). Gorman's lomatium (the name applied here in the restricted sense) is called sasamíta and is considered food fit only for "ground hogs" (that is, marmots). Mark Schlessman's doctoral thesis (1980) confirms the Indians' judgment in documenting numerous fundamental (if not obvious) differences between these two species.

The summit of Dalles Mountain commands a sweeping view of the Big

1. Cronquist's treatment of the genus *Lomatium* in Hitchcock et al. (1961) should be amended as follows: *Lomatium farinosum* should now include *L. hambleniae* as *L. farinosum hambleniae* (Schlessman 1978); *Lomatium gormanii* should be restricted to those plants with papillate ovaries and seeds, and the smooth seeded plants should be recognized as *L. piperi* (Schlessman 1980); *L. orogenioides* should be renamed *Tauschia tenuissima* (Schlessman 1980); the range of *L. tuberosum* should be extended to include the Priest Rapids area of Benton, Grant, and Yakima counties, and it should be noted that the illustration on page 567 is of *L. columbianum,* not *L. tuberosum;* finally, a new species, *L. quintuplex* must be added (Schlessman and Constance 1979).

TABLE 6

Lomatium Species of Cultural Significance (Hunn and French 1981:90)

Scientific name	(PNRR*)	Sahaptin name/s	Uses	Distribution
L. canbyi C. & R. Type A	(38/39)	sikáywa, sikáwiya (NW) lúkš (CR) lamúš (NE)	Staple, tuber eaten, boiled or dried whole or as "finger cakes"	Lithosols, n. w. Nev. n. to Douglas Co., Wash., where overlaps Type B
Type B		škúlkul (NW, CR, NE)	Staple, tuber eaten, baked underground	Lithosols, Douglas to Spokane Cos., Wash.
L. columbianum M. & C.	(0/17*)	aҳúla (YK)	Plant avoided	Talus slopes, locally, Yakima Co., Wash., to Hood River Co., Oreg.
L. cous (S. Wats.) C. & R.	(16/16)	ҳáwš (NW, CR, NE)	Staple, tuber, eaten, boiled or dried whole or as "finger cakes"	Lithosols, Whitman Co., Wash., s. and w. through Blue Mtns. to e. base Oregon Cascades
L. dissectum (Nutt.) M. & C.	(12/15)	čalúkš (NW, CR, NE)	Medicine for people and horses, fish stupefactant, hide tanning agent, shoots and young roots eaten by Salish and Nez Perce Indians	Talus slopes, throughout

Species	(n)	Native name	Use	Habitat/Distribution
L. farinosum (Geyer ex Hook.) C. & R. var. farinosum	(0/0*)	nikaptát (NE)	Tubers eaten	Lithosols, c. Columbia basin of Wash. e.
var. hambleniae (M. & C.) Schlessman	(2/14)	maxšlí, maxšni (NE)	Tubers eaten	Lithosols, w. of var. farinosum to e. base Wash. Cascades s. to Yakima Co., local, Wasco Co., Oreg.
L. gormanii (Howell) C. & R.	(4/13)	sasamiła, sasamiłaya, łałamit'a (NW, CR, NE)	Tubers eaten (NW) or avoided (CR)	Lithosols, e. c. Wash. w. rarely to e. slope Cascade Mtns., rare, n. Oreg.
L. grayi C. & R.	(16/21)	x̣ásya (NW) latítlatit (CR) atuná (NE)	Sprouts are the first "Indian celery" available in late winter, root eaten formerly	Talus slopes, throughout
L. macrocarpum (H. & A.) C. & R.	(26/33)	púła (NW, CR, NE)	Tuber eaten formerly	Lithosols and slopes, throughout
L. minus (Rose) M. & C.	(4/6)	nak'únk (jd, um)	Tuber eaten formerly, boiled	Basalt drainage channels, n. c. Oreg.
L. nudicaule (Pursh) C. & R.	(28/30)	x̣amsi (NW, CR, NE)	Peduncles and leaf shoots eaten fresh, seeds used as insect repellent, perfume, and medicine	Dry open areas, throughout

TABLE 6 (*continued*)

Scientific name	(PNRR*)	Sahaptin name/s	Uses	Distribution
L. piperi C. & R.	(28/31)	mámɨn, mámɨls (NW, CR, NE)	Favorite, tuber eaten, mixed with *cous* or *canbyi* to make "finger cakes"	Lithosols, e. slope Cascade Mtns
L. triternatum (Pursh) C. & R.	(4/30)	ɬáqimaš (te, ty)	Formerly used as food and medicine, ignored by other Sahaptin speakers	Dry open areas, throughout

Lomatium species clearly named by Sahaptin speakers. Indian language orthography follows Rigsby (n.d.). Distribution of native terms coded as follows: NW, Northwest dialect cluster; CR, Columbia River dialect cluster; NE, Northeast dialect cluster; jd, John Day dialect; te, Tenino dialect; ty, Tygh dialect; um, Umatilla dialect; yk, Yakima dialect. Uses and habitats cited are the most typical only. Information on uses by Salish and Nez Perce Indians is from Marshall (1977), Turner et al., n.d., and Turner, Bouchard, and Kennedy (1980). Plant nomenclature follows Hitchcock et al. (1961).

*PNRR = Positive Naming Response Ratio. This is the ratio of instances of confident recognition and naming of individual specimens by individual informants to all instances in which an informant was shown a specimen of *Lomatium*. In cases citing no positive naming responses, the referential range of the Sahaptin term is inferred from secondary data.

River above the famed Celilo Falls fishery. It was no doubt a goal of spring root-digging expeditions by nearby Indians in centuries past. *Lomatium piperi* and *L. gormanii* grow here side by side without hybridizing and may be closely compared when blooming in late March and April.

The second instance of Sahaptin taxonomic refinement is the case of *Lomatium farinosum*, which is divided into two named varieties. Max̣šní has yellow flowers and a western distribution; nikaptát has white flowers and the more easterly range. The first term applies to the scientific variety *hambleniae* (treated as a distinct species by Hitchcock and Cronquist), while the second names the variety *farinosum* (Schlessman 1978).

Max̣šní is widely known to modern-day Sahaptin root diggers, by name if not by firsthand experience, though its range is largely restricted to the lands traditionally exploited by Kittitas and Priest Rapids groups. It is a rather small plant with a tuberous root that averages just 3.5 grams (compared to the 12-gram average weight for roots of *Lomatium canbyi* and *L. cous*). Children are sent to dig for it on the windswept, thin-soiled flats where it grows in greatest abundance, while adults focus their efforts on more productive and more highly valued species. The white-flowered variety grows east of Priest Rapids and the Grand Coulee. The Nez Perce call it laqáptat (likely the source of the Sahaptin name) and collect its roots as a secondary food item (Marshall 1977:52). Mary Jim, born and raised on the lower Snake River, is the only person I met who knows both, having been raised on the borderline between the ranges of the two varieties.

The third instance in which Sahaptin-speaking Indians surpass the professional botanist in discriminating lomatiums remains something of a mystery. The species "split" in this case is Canby's lomatium, known as a key food source by Indians from northeastern California to southern British Columbia. Its value is rivaled only by "cous" (that is, *Lomatium cous*), made famous by Lewis and Clark. (Cous is the most abundant edible lomatium in the northern Rocky Mountain area and is valued next to camas and bitterroot throughout its range. See fig. 5.12.) Canby's lomatium is known by many Indian names, having gained recognition in at least six Indian languages (see fig. 4.6 and Table 7), but Northeast Sahaptin speakers are unique in dividing Canby's lomatium into two distinct folk species, škúlkul and lamúš (see also Washington n.d. [1976]). The first is described as the larger, its foliage more fern-like, its tuber distinctively shaped. Most important, the oil content of the škúlkul root is high, making sun-drying difficult. For this reason škúlkul must be baked underground after the fashion of

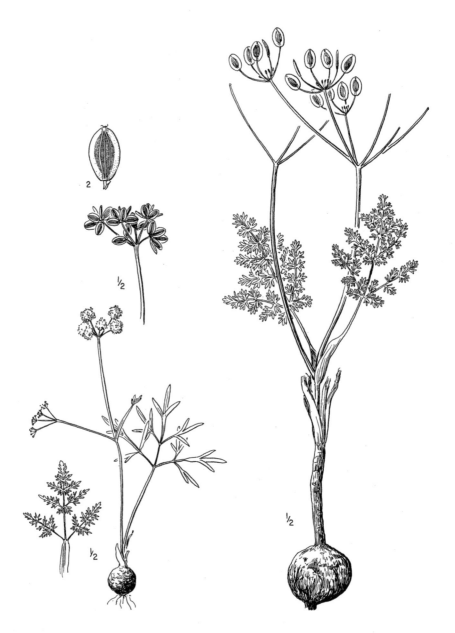

Fig. 4.5. Piper's lomatium (*Lomatium piperi*; **mámin**) (labeled *L. gormanii* in Hitchcock et al. 1961:557).

Fig. 4.6. Canby's lomatium (*Lomatium canbyi*; **lukš**).

TABLE 7
The Many Names of Canby's Lomatium

Columbia River Sahaptin	lukš (+ škúlkul)
Northwest Sahaptin	sikáywa (+ škúlkul)
Taitnapam Sahaptin	sikáwiya (+ škúlkul)
Northeast Sahaptin	
variety A	lamúš
variety B	škúlkul
Nez Perce	q̓eq̓íit (Marshall 1977:48–49)
Upper Chinookan	wa-q̓ʷát
Klamath	"ɬhe-hăs" (Coville 1904:102)
Harney Valley Northern Paiute	cana cuka, literally, "sweet cous" (Couture 1978:43)
Columbia Salish	c̓əxʷəl̓úsaʔ (Kinkade 1981)
Okanagan-Colville Salish	c̓exʷl̓úsa (Turner, Bouchard, and Kennedy 1980:64)

camas. Lamúš, smaller and less oily, is dried whole by stringing on a cord of Indian hemp. Mary Jim asserts that škúlkul and lamúš may be found side by side on Badger Mountain and about Soap Lake, root-digging grounds shared by Northeastern Sahaptins and the Okanagan Salish. As yet I have been unable to obtain definitive collections of these variants and thus cannot say what objective basis exists for the Indians' distinction.

Whatever the biological basis for the recognition of škúlkul, the practical implications of making the distinction are clear. A more elaborate and labor-intensive mode of preparation is called for by škúlkul, which (as in the case of camas, as we will see) precipitates a social event. The underground oven (tamáyč) requires cooperative efforts of adults of both sexes. Thus, preparing the plant for storage or consumption requires careful planning and coordination. The payoff may well have been both "economies of scale" in the production of winter food supplies and social "profits" derived from mutual assistance.

Škúlkul's reputation as a distinctive and valued food of the Wanapum or Priest Rapids people may explain Lewis and Clark's "Sokulk" tribe, which they placed on the Columbia River above the Yakima's mouth. The intriguing resemblance between "Sokulk" and škúlkul, first noted by Relander (1956:28), suggests that the "Sokulks" were Priest Rapids people. In the 1980s škúlkul is still known as a specialty of the Wanapum people worth a trip to Priest Rapids. The abundance of lukš—as Canby's lomatium is known in the area from Yakima south—is irrelevant. It is no substitute for škúlkul.

Lukš—note another odd linguistic coincidence; škúlkul is lukš spelled backwards, then duplicated—is one of three or four root staples of the traditional mid-Columbia Indian diet. It is abundant on lithosols—"bald" patches of exposed basalt with just a thin grout of soil among the rocks—and flowers with the first hint of spring, usually in early March, though unusual weather conditions may stimulate a precocious flowering in January. It is a perennial that has adapted to survival on thin soils in a land alternately frozen, then baked. It succeeds here by storing energy as starch in a tuberous swelling of the root a few inches beneath the ground surface. These plants can "sleep" through the summer drought period as well as through the winter freeze, then draw on their energy bank account to finance a burst of new growth, a mantle of finely dissected leaves that hug the ground, out of the wind but receptive to the sun's energy. The root's store of energy combined with the photosynthetic efforts of the new leaves provide the force for flowering and seed production. By April or early May the seeds are ripe as the leaves turn to the task of replenishing the root's "tanks" for the plant's next period of dormancy.

Enter the Indian in search of food. If the root can store energy for the plant, it can store energy for people as well. And so it does, unwittingly. However, for maximum benefit it is important to know the plant's life cycle well. The root is packed with carbohydrates throughout its dormant period. But at this time it is in hiding, the leaves and seeds having blown away in the dry winds that sweep the Columbia Basin each spring. During the early phase of its growth cycle the root goes "soft," expending much of its stored resources to generate the plant's early spurt of growth. At maturity of the seeds the roots again reach their full capacity, while the plants remain conspicuous. The soil at this time is neither too muddy nor yet baked too hard for easy digging. These optimal conditions for harvest last but a few days at a given locality, as hot east winds in a matter of hours can dry the tops and blow them away, "burn" the roots, and bake the soil to hard pan.

Timing of the harvest is thus critical, as is a careful reading of microhabitat effects on plant growth. Plants mature first on sunny south-facing slopes (án-kni, "sun-ward") and are retarded in their development on shady northfacing slopes (šqíš-kni, "shade-ward"). This opens the harvest "window" a bit wider at each digging site. For an adequate annual harvest, however, a strategy of seasonal upslope mobility is employed. Lukš—and its companion pyaxí (bitterroot, *Lewisia rediviva* [Portulacaceae], fig. 4.7)—may be ready for harvest in early April at 500 feet (150 m) elevation, where it is readily accessible from riverside fishing villages, and is still harvestable in late June at 6,000 feet (1,800 m) elevation on mountain ridges several days' journey from the river. Camps were traditionally established progressively further from and higher above the river from April through June, thus extending the harvest so that a family of four might collect a supply of dried roots sufficient for 60 percent of its winter caloric needs (Hunn 1981; see Table 8 and Table 9).

Lomatiums provide more than calories. The nutritional new year begins with the first "Indian celeries." Along the mid-Columbia and in the Yakima Basin, sprouts of Gray's lomatium (*L. grayi*, fig. 4.8) fill this role. The cultural value ascribed to Gray's lomatium, like that of Canby's, is reflected in the profusion of names applied to the plant. Columbia River Sahaptins call it latít-latit (literally, "little flowers"); Northwest Sahaptins call it xásya; while in northeastern dialects it is known as atuná, a term applied to the plant's (barely) edible root in the other dialects.

At flowering these plants highlight many a dry arroyo with their gray-green, fragrant foliage crowned by golden umbels. The common English vernacular name, "spring gold," captures this aesthetic appeal. By flowering time, however, the plant's food value has dropped sharply as the ascorbic acid (Vitamin C) rich shoots become dry and fibrous. As the plant's economic role is transformed so is its name. Latít-latit becomes wáʔwinu, no longer the source of that delicious, spiced salad centerpiece at the thanksgiving feast held in its honor each year in March at the Rock Creek longhouse.

The "Indian celery" role is played by other lomatiums in other sections of the Plateau, reflecting complex phytogeographic patterns. Nez Perce Indians gather the rare and localized *Lomatium salmoniflorum* from rocky talus slides in the Snake River canyon for their first fresh greens, often as early as February (NP: ílq̓úulx; Marshall 1977:48–49). This species is found only between the Palouse and the Salmon rivers. Thompson and Okanagan Indians, who live north of the centers of abundance of Gray's lomatium, harvest the underground shoots of fern-leaved lomatium (*Lomatium dissectum*), a widespread species normally restricted to medicinal uses because of its toxicity. The underground shoots are apparently safe, though readers are warned that the root of this species is a potent fish poison.

By April Gray's lomatium is past its prime, but the bare-stemmed lomatium (*L. nudicaule*) is now flowering virtually everywhere in the Cascade foothills (fig. 4.9). Both flower stalks (x̣amsí) and leaf petioles (p̓ís̓p̓tis̓) are eaten. X̣amsí is featured at the April salmon-and-root feasts held throughout the Plateau. It is relished by Indian children today as a seasonal snack. The key nutrient in these sprouts and stalks is Vitamin C, a water-soluble vitamin readily lost when foods are cooked or stored for extended periods. Vitamin C may have been a nutrient in short supply in late winter for Plateau peoples who had subsisted for several months on a diet of dried foods. X̣amsí stalks contain up to 67 milligrams/100 grams when harvested early in the flowering cycle—the Indian preference. A sample of mature stalks contained only 11 mg/100 grams (Benson et al. 1973). Such "spent"

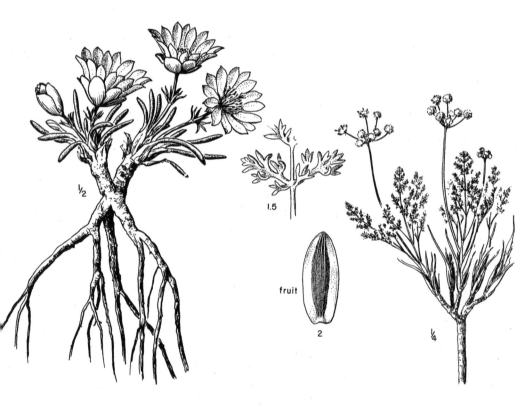

Fig. 4.7. Bitterroot (*Lewisia rediviva*; **pyax̣í**).

Fig. 4.8. Gray's lomatium (*Lomatium grayi*; **latít-latit**).

TABLE 8

Estimates of Plant Food Harvest Rates (kg/woman/day), Total Harvests (kg/woman/year), and Caloric Yields (kcal/person/day) (from Hunn 1981:130–31)

Species	Estimated Daily Harvest	Harvest Period/ Days	Total Annual Harvest	Kcal Yield	Locale
Spring:					
Lomatium canbyi	30	30–40	1050	800	Sanpoil[1]
Lomatium cous	22.7–34.1	ca. 40	1136	988	Nez Perce[2]
	33.3*	ca. 30	999	869	Umatilla[3]
Lewisia rediviva	30.3*	ca. 60	1818	1121	Umatilla[3]
	6.5	7	45	28	Kutenai[4]
Early Summer:					
Camassia quamash	36.4–40.9	14–21	677	524	Nez Perce[2]
	18.2–22.7	14–21	358	277	Nez Perce[2]
			2160	1672	Flathead[5]
Late Summer-Fall:					
Vaccinium spp.		28–42	63.9–80.2	31	Tenino-Wishram[6]
			98	42	Umatilla[3]

Reprinted with permission of the Society of Ethnobiology.
Sources: 1. Ray 1933, 2. Marshall 1977, 3. Hunn and French 1981, 4. Hart 1976, 5. Geyer 1845–46, 6. Perkins n.d. [1838–43].
*Based on extrapolation to 8-hour days. If the average spring root harvest suppled 900 kcal/person/day for the year, the camas harvest added 400 kcal, and berries another 50, the plant food contribution would total 1,350 kcal, or 67.5 percent of needs.

stalks are called ašwaníya, literally, "slaves," which is to say they are worthless, inedible.

Before leaving the subject of the lomatiums I should note also their medicinal value. It is often the case that the same plant families which are major sources of human food are also rich in toxic plants with high concentrations of physiologically active chemical compounds. Such is the case for the Solanaceae, the family of the white potato, tomato, and chili pepper. This

TABLE 9

Contribution of Root Foods to the Diet of the Mid-Columbia River Indians: Plant Food Proximal Analyses Used, per 100 gm (from Hunn 1981:130–31)

Species	Water (gm)	Protein (gm)	Fat (gm)	Carbohydrate (gm)	Kcal
Lomatium canbyi					
av. 6 dried root samples[1]	11.68	2.58	1.48	82.41	352
same, adjusted for water content	71.9	0.9	0.47	26.22	112
1 fresh sample[2]	71.9	0.8	0.12	25.9	108
Lomatium cous					
1 fresh sample[2]	67.9	1.0	0.4	30.0	127
Lewisia rediviva					
1 fresh sample[2]	76.6	0.7	0.1	21.6	90
Camassia quamash					
1 fresh sample[2]	70.0	0.7	0.23	27.1	113
Vaccinium spp.					
blueberries, raw[3]	83.2	0.7	0.5	15.3	62

Reprinted with permission of the Society of Ethnobiology.
Sources: 1. Washington n.d. [1976], 2. Benson et al. 1973, 3. Watt and Merrill 1963.

family also gives us tobacco, deadly nightshade, jimson weed, and belladonna, plants that have the power to alter dramatically how our bodies and minds function, with potentially fatal consequences. Consider also the Leguminosae, the family of the garden pea, chickpea, soy bean, and many varieties of common beans. Yet sweet peas, vetches, and lupines may be poisonous.

The lily family gives us onions, leeks, and garlic, and provides the Plateau Indians with many nutritious bulbs and corms, notably the staple camas (wákamu or x̣maaš; *Camassia quamash*, fig. 4.10) and numerous supplementary

foods. Yet death camas (*Zigadenus* spp.) and false hellebore (*Veratrum* spp.)
can be deadly. Both of the latter are known to Sahaptins for their medicinal
values, mimún (false hellebore) used as a hair rinse for lice, and alapíšaš
(death camas) to treat skin sores. (See Appendix 4.)

The Umbelliferae provide yet another example of this ethnobotanical duality. In the past Plateau peoples obtained a substantial fraction of their annual food energy in the form of *Lomatium* roots, but were exposed as well to

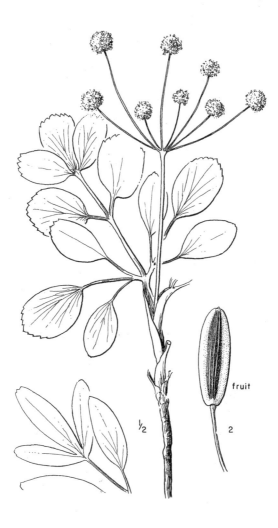

Fig. 4.9. Bare-stemmed lomatium (*Lomatium nudicaule;* x̣amsí).

Fig. 4.10. Camas (*Camassia quamash;* x̣maaš or wáḱamu).

a threat of sudden, violent death if they were so careless as to confuse deadly water hemlock (alamíla; *Cicuta douglasii*) with foods such as cow's parsnip (tx̣u; *Heracleum lanatum*) or water parsley (*Sium suave*). Sahaptin speakers today have no special term for plants of the umbel genus *Angelica* though these are common and quite edible. Perhaps the plant's seductive resemblance to deadly water hemlock, from which it is not readily distinguished, discouraged further experimentation on their part.

Even the genus *Lomatium* has toxic species, most notably, the fern-leaved lomatium (čalúkš; *Lomatium dissectum*, fig. 4.11). Though eaten sparingly in the sprouting stage by Interior Salish Indians, as I noted above, it is respected as a powerful medicine from California to Canada and from the Pacific to the high plains east of the Rockies (Meilleur, Hunn, and Cox n.d. [1989]). Its primary medicinal applications are external. The root is mashed and the pulp applied as a poultice to draw out infection. It may be effective as well as a bactericidal agent. It is considered effective against saddle sores in veterinary medicine. An infusion is drunk for symptoms of cold and flu or applied as a hair rinse for dandruff. At Warm Springs the root is used in processing buckskin (D. French, personal communication).

Columbia River and Yakima Indians use the root as a fish poison. A quantity of the root mashed on streamside rocks will shortly reduce the resident fish to a state of stupefaction. This technique is workable only in small, quiet streams with still pools where the poison will have time and sufficient concentration to operate. James Selam claims that this technique allowed the selection of preferred fish while sparing the rest, as the fish soon recover from the effects of the poison as it is flushed from the stream.

Little is known of the biochemical basis for this toxicity. A preliminary study by Rachel Cox at Reed College (1983) has verified the plant's power to stun and kill fish and has isolated a chemical fraction from the root with coumarin-like properties as most likely containing the active ingredients. Cox describes its effect on fish—mosquito fish (*Gambusia affinis*) and fingerling silver salmon (*Oncorhynchus kisutch*) studied under laboratory conditions—as follows:

> "It took less than one minute for the fish [*Gambusia*] at 1.0 g[ram]/l[iter] (raw, undried root) to show symptoms of intoxication. Affected fish displayed an interesting behavioral fluctuation. At first they were extremely hyperactive, exhibiting furtive bursts of energy, jumping out of the water, displaying overactive gill motion, and frequently hitting against the sides of the bowl. Subsequently, they would slow down, begin to lose equilibrium, float with bellies

up, and sometimes begin to sink. . . . appeared dead, but when nudged gently, they could be coaxed back to hyperactivity. (Cox 1983:50–51)

Another *Lomatium* valued as an Indian medicine is the bare-stemmed lomatium. The seeds of this plant are valued to the point of being a hot trade item on Vancouver Island well northwest of the species' natural limits in the Fraser River delta and along Puget Sound shorelines (Turner and Bell 1973). The highly aromatic seeds have a powerful anise odor and are used on the middle-Columbia as "moth balls" to protect precious ceremonial regalia from the ravages of insects.

Two other lomatiums are considered to be poisonous by my Indian consultants. *Lomatium columbianum*, a robust species found in a limited area from near the eastern end of the Columbia Gorge north to the Naches River west of Yakima, superficially resembles the fern-leaved desert parsley. Josephine Andrews calls it axúla and recounts how her grandmother cautioned her that it was a "bad plant." *L. columbianum* contains columbianin, another chemical compound of the coumarin group notable for their effect as smooth muscle relaxants (Call and Green 1956). Still mysterious is the case of the plant known as háti, described as deceptively similar in outward appearance to the staple food root xawš. I learned of this plant quite by chance while on a root-collecting expedition to the traditional Blue Mountain haunts of my John Day and Alderdale consultants. We camped at Anson Wright county park, once an Indian campsite now used as a base of operations for the spring harvest of pyaxí and xawš. The campsite was pleasantly quiet with little traffic on the state highway that climbs past into the mountains. Set at the base of a north-facing hill covered with ponderosa pine and Douglas fir, the camp has a sweeping view of hillsides carpeted with grass and wildflowers. Along the willow bordered stream we glimpsed an otter in the early morning and James caught a red-sided shiner (pała-lí) with a short line and hook baited on the spot with xamłúy—a caddisfly larva we discovered beneath a rock in the stream.

Elsie Pistolhead interpreted the conversations of a nearby meadowlark that sang from the phone lines on the roadside. Meadowlark is a truth-sayer as well as a tease, a key character in Coyote stories. That evening Mrs. Pistolhead carefully set out soap and matches to appease the "stick Indians" (Sasquatch-like creatures that may romp through camp by night). Elsie Selam and Sara Quaempts, reminiscing, told how as young girls they had learned to avoid confusing xawš (*Lomatium cous*), primary object of local root digging efforts, with the notorious háti. A girl one time came down the hillside opposite, digging stick in hand and wápas bags full. She proudly presented the contents of her bag to her elders only to be rebuked for bringing down a load of háti. As with axúla I was able to learn only that it was a bad plant, not the precise cause of its ill repute. I spent hours scouring that hillside—rather too steep for the women to negotiate at their age—and found besides *Lomatium cous* two other similar *Lomatium* species not otherwise nomenclaturally accounted for in Sahaptin. These were *L. donnellii*, which was common on the hillside, and *L. vaginatum*, of which but a few specimens were found. Háti apparently refers to one or the other or both of these plants; however, I know of no evidence that they are either inedible or toxic. It may simply be that the Indian people recognized them as different from the well-known and loved x̣awš, but had insufficient opportunity to test their potential as food. A strongly reinforced aversion to things "familiar but different" may have survival value where foods and poisons are similarly packaged.

Plateau Indians survived as hunters and gatherers for ten thousand years in a land of strong contrasts by virtue of their encyclopedic knowledge of the local environment. Their knowledge of lomatiums demonstrates that their perceptual and analytical capacities are on a par with those of a modern-day professional botanist. Yet their knowledge of their local ecosystem is in certain key respects quite unlike what the modern professional ecologist or wild-plant enthusiast might choose to learn about the same biogeographical terrain. Literally hundreds of species of "wildflowers" that grow here are known to the Indians as "just flowers" (áwtya ay latít). Some few wildflowers are named on the strength of their peculiar beauty or conspicuousness, as is the case for the scarlet gilia (*Gilia aggregata*), called in Sahaptin "hummingbird's food" (qmámsali tkʷátat), the shooting star (*Dodecatheon* spp.), literally "curlew's beak" (k̓ʷayk̓ʷaynmí núšnu), and the diminutive first-of-spring gold star (*Crocidium multicaule*, see fig. 4.12), which as papč̓iláw plays an important role in the myth of "Coyote's eyes."[2]

By contrast, the showy native wild iris (*Iris missouriensis*) goes unrecognized by many Sahaptin speakers (though it is consistently referred to as

2. The flower in this myth is sometimes referred to in English as "buttercup." At Warm Springs the cognate term papč̓ilú is sometimes applied to *Crocidium*, sometimes to the sagebrush buttercup, *Ranunculus glaberrimus*. Both flowers contribute a splash of color to the rocky flats frequented by the root diggers in early spring.

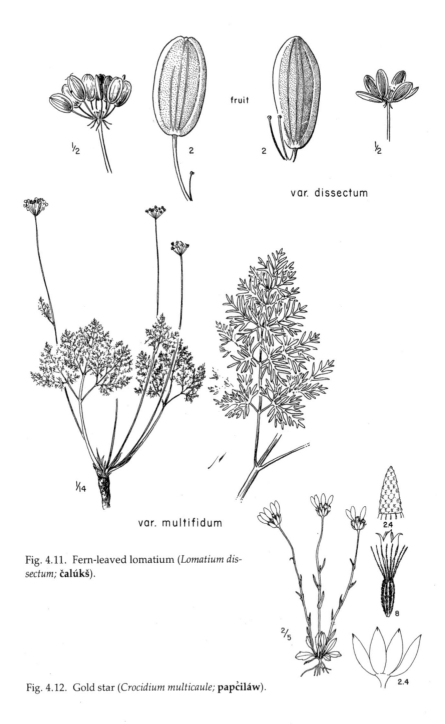

fruit

var. dissectum

var. multifidum

Fig. 4.11. Fern-leaved lomatium (*Lomatium dissectum;* **čalúkš**).

Fig. 4.12. Gold star (*Crocidium multicaule;* **papčiláw**).

nuunas-wáakuɫ, "mariposa lily-like," on the Warm Springs Reservation [D. French, personal communication] and may once have been employed to treat smallpox [Gibbs 1978 [1854]:14]). Nor do the windflowers (*Sisyrinchium* spp.) or violets (*Viola* spp.) have standard names. Showy buckwheats (*Eriogonum* spp.) dominate the sagebrush hills in June as fully as the lomatiums do in April, yet none is named.[3]

We might see in this dismissal of so many pleasing plants as "just flowers," a hard-nosed practicality deficient in aesthetic sensitivity. However, I question the validity of such a judgment. I know the Indian people have a deep reverence for their homeland. I suspect rather that survival placed a premium on knowlege of utilitarian value and a price on knowledge motivated solely by a compulsion to name every living thing. James Selam would never say that a plant "has no use," for he firmly believes that every plant and animal has both a name and a significant role to play in the overall economy of nature. This is an article of his faith. It is just that, in his view, he was born too late and never had the opportunity to learn the true names of these "nameless" organisms.

The Sahaptin Way of Making a Living

Hunting and gathering is an ancient way of life. Our Australopithecine ancestors were hunter-gatherers more than three million years ago. However, a careful study of hunting-gathering as practiced by contemporary humans, as for example the Plateau Indians, proves that the hunting, fishing, and gathering of these Indians differ dramatically in virtually every important respect from the foraging of apes. Some important points of comparison include: tool use, transport, processing of food, sharing and the division of labor, range of food items utilized, and the cultural context of production. While chimpanzees have been shown to construct a few crude implements, such as "termiting sticks" and overnight nests, their technological skills are far surpassed by such "lower animals" as beavers, bower birds, and bees. The technological repertoire of modern hunter-gatherers—like that of our own upper Paleolithic ancestors (I refer here to the peoples of Europe, Asia, and Africa of 35,000 to 10,000 years ago)—is often described as "simple," even as "crude." In comparison to the machinery of the indus-

3. David French reports (personal communication) that tall buckwheat (*Eriogonum elatum*), a conspicuous but scarcely "showy" wild buckwheat, is known as paǫ́ilakaš, "basket-covering plant," at Warm Springs.

trial era those may be apt terms. On closer examination, however, the "crude" tools of hunter-gatherers, such as the boomerang of the Australian aborigines or the Eskimo (Inuit) igloo, often reveal complex underlying conceptual plans. The boomerang is a triumph of aeronautical engineering in a single carved piece of wood, while in the igloo the principle of the true arch is applied in three dimensions to construct an ephemeral shelter of packed snow. (Were you not taught that the Romans "invented" the arch?) Igloos were also commonly improved by an attached subterranean air-lock entryway and skylights of translucent ice for indirect lighting.

Precontact Plateau peoples hunted with bow and arrow. Three thousand years ago they did without this tool, which seems so much a part of being Indian to us. They relied then on the spear-thrower or atlatl, named for its Aztec counterpart. The impact of this particular technological revolution must have been felt throughout Plateau society, though the archaeological record indicates a very gradual transition from atlatl to bow and arrow (Cressman 1977:105–8).

A strong bow and a true-flying arrow are not simple to make or use. Appropriate materials must be selected. On the Plateau oak was most often preferred for the bow, with the bowstring of elk sinew, carefully extracted and treated for this application. It should neither stretch nor break under great strain. Arrows were characteristically of serviceberry wood (*Amelanchier alnifolia*), light and straight, but hard. The bush itself was called kayáasu-waaš in Northwest Sahaptin dialects, literally, the "arrow bush."

Tiny obsidian arrow heads were fashioned by flaking from an obsidian core (obtained in trade from near Bend, Oregon, in an area dominated by enemy Northern Paiutes), then retouched by pressure with an elk antler flaking tool on a protective pad of elk hide, then hafted with Indian hemp bindings sealed with pine pitch. This was an industrial operation that every boy once knew how to perform to perfection. It now can be replicated by only a few old-timers. The bow and arrow has gone the way of the atlatl before, replaced by guns, and with it has gone the old knowledge.

Though hunting is strongly emphasized in most descriptions of hunting-and-gathering economies, the pursuit of big game such as deer, elk, and bear actually contributed but a small fraction to the mid-Columbia Indian food energy budget, somewhere in the order of 10 percent of total calories. Gathering of plant foods and fishing were responsible for the remaining 90 percent. In the global context of human prehistory, fishing technology represents a relatively recent innovation in comparison with that of hunting and gathering. Fishing nets may be less than twice as old as agriculture as a means to exploit more effectively the resources of the natural environment for human sustenance.

There is evidence of complex fishing gear in use on the Columbia River at The Dallas seven to nine thousand years ago. Weights for use with seine nets and points that may have been used on a harpoon or leister (fig. 4.13) for spearing large fish are known from excavations east of The Dalles and date to that period (Cressman et al. 1960:115, 118–19). Lewis and Clark found local fishermen employing such diverse techniques as weirs—elaborate traps of willow and stone (fig. 4.14) broaching the full width of small tributary streams—dip and set nets, baited bone chokers on a hemp line, and fish spears with detachable points of various sorts (Thwaites 1959 [1904], 4:326, 327, 335, 338). A complete list would include as well, fish poisons and gill nets woven to the specific dimensions of the fish sought (cf. Rostland 1952). It is not surprising that native terminology for fishing is highly elaborated, as shown by the sample of Sahaptin terms in Table 10.

The Seasonal Round

ánam, "winter"

The winter season offered ample free time for tool construction and maintenance. James Selam made a three-quarter-scale model dip net for the Yakima Nation Cultural Heritage Center Museum during the winter of 1976 and invited me to photograph the steps involved (see figs. 4.15 and 4.16). A full-sized dip net (twanú) has a fifteen-foot handle trimmed from a Douglas fir sapling. The hoop is formed of two pieces of vine maple or Douglas maple (twanú-waaš, literally, "dip net plant"), which has strong, flexible wood. The hoop-halves are bound together with Indian hemp (taxús) twine and strengthened at the base with a brace of ocean spray (pɨxwayč-pamá, literally, "for [the] dipnet brace," *Holodiscus discolor*) wood, a local "iron wood." The net is knotted of Indian hemp twine using a net gauge to fix the size of the mesh and a bobbin to hold the supply of twine. This twine is laboriously fashioned by women during the long winter confinement, as described in Delsie Selam's text (see chapter 3). The net is closed by a drawstring pulled tight by the weight of the trapped fish, preventing its escape.

Dip-netting involves drawing the hoop through the water with the cur-

Fig. 4.13. A Wishram Indian fishing with a two-pronged spear (Curtis photograph, University of Washington Libraries, neg. 209).

rent and pulling the net up when a fish is felt in the net, because the turbulent water obscures the fisherman's vision. This same net can be used as a set net by holding it in an eddy until a fish is felt. "Roping fish" involves this same net, but held just out of the water at the base of a fall. The fisherman tries to catch the fish that fall back in their attempts to leap the falls.

Traditionally, winter was also a time for visiting and the time for myth-telling, a time of heightened spirituality associated with the winter shamanistic performances. Visiting had not only social but also ecological significance, as visitors shared information essential to the planning of next

Fig. 4.14. A stone weir for suckers in Rock Creek.

summer's harvest strategy. Visiting also served as a mechanism to redistribute food surpluses and to compensate for local shortages, as visiting has always been the occasion for feasting. Generous hosts won wide regard.

wawáxam, "spring"

Most traditional accounts of the local Indian economy note the coming of the spring Chinook salmon as the long awaited event that brought winter to an end. Yet long before their arrival at The Dalles—normally at the end of April—Columbia River Indian women were hard at work stockpiling next

TABLE 10
Sahaptin Terminology for Fishing

I am fishing.	npíwi-ša=aš
I am fishing with hook and line.	waċílak-ša=aš
fishing pole	waċílak-as
fish hook	q̓íya
I am gaff-hooking.	q̓íyak-ša=aš
I am snagging fish.	wawa-q̓íyak-ša=aš
I am fishing with a bone choker.	šapá-ʔax̣č-ša=aš
I am dip-netting.	twalúu-ša=aš
dip net hoop	twanú
vine or Douglas maple	twanú-waaš
dip net pole	sunúus
I am "roping" fish in smooth, shallow rapids.	á-twax̣umk-ša=aš
I am "roping" fish at a waterfall.	sapá-wiilata-ša=aš
I am fishing with a fixed net at a fish jumping place.	sapá-x̣up-waalata-ša=aš
I am seining fish.	išɨm-laytk-ša=aš
I am catching fish at a weir.	sapá-x̣aluu-ša=aš
fish weir	sapa-x̣aluu-ɫáwas
fishing scaffold	sapa-x̣ʷluu-s
I am spearing fish.	tayx̣áy-ša=aš
fish spear	tayx̣áy
I am fishing by torch light (with a spear).	tapwalkʷ-ša=aš
I am fishing with a set net.	tápatuk-ša=aš

year's root supplies. The gathering activities of the women required knowledge, skill, and technological expertise equal to that needed for hunting and fishing. Women also, as we shall see, contributed at least half the total food supply.

Gathering has been vastly underrated by anthropologists in the past. It has been dismissed as an activity scarcely removed from that of apes and other animal foragers. Each ape gathers his or her own food. It is then eaten on the spot without further ado. Human gathering—and that of the Plateau Indians is no exception—involves complex planning. Gathering begins with a decision as to which foods to gather and where to go to look for them. These decisions are constrained by the larger planning framework of the seasonal round. Digging bitterroot would not be contemplated in the fall. Not only is there no bitterroot available, but the family is otherwise engaged fishing on the river or gathering huckleberries high in the Cascades, far from bitterroot habitat. Nor should one dig bitterroot in the spring until the proper thanksgiving rituals (káʔwit) have been performed; a failure to show respect for the Earth's gifts of food would guarantee poor future harvests. Given the appropriate season, the pursuit of bitterroots involves choosing an area where quantities of this and other roots at the proper stage of maturity might be found.

Sara Quaempts describes the plan her people at Alderdale followed each spring when she was growing up. The winter lodges at náwawi were dismantled and all the people moved up along the creek to the first major tributary canyon, a place called aykʷs-mí tánawt, "cottontail's burrow." In early spring this canyon bottom caught the sun's limited heat and deflected the cold winds. Water was readily available and the thick sagebrush of the creekside flats provided ample firewood. The women climbed to the ridges above to dig bitterroot and lomatiums, which they cleaned and prepared for drying each evening back at camp. When the local supplies were exhausted, after perhaps a week's time, the people moved camp further upstream to the next tributary canyon, to a campsite named pnáy-pnay, "many pestles." The process was repeated here and again at xʷíyayč-mí, "sweat lodge place," two miles farther up the canyon. The supplies of dried roots were then hauled back to náwawi for storage in semisubterranean cellars. This process was repeated with local variants by the residents of each riverside winter village.

When the spring Chinook salmon runs began, the women attended to the cleaning and drying of the men's catch. Later in May, as the river rose in spring flood and the fishing sites were covered, mid-Columbia families packed their gear and set off, the men riding, the women generally walking, leading the pack animals (before A.D. 1750, of course, they did without these helpful companions) to the first of another series of familiar way stations that would lead eventually to the camas meadows of the high Blue Mountains.

James Selam's family, for example, was accustomed to camp first at Olex, about twenty miles southeast of their winter village of táwaš at Blalock, on

Fig. 4.15. James Selam making a dip net.

Fig. 4.16. Dip netting in pools, Wishram (Curtis photograph, University of Washington Libraries, neg. 208).

the Columbia just above the John Day River mouth and nearly opposite Rock Creek, Washington. Bitterroot and Canby's lomatium roots were abundant here. As the season progressed they camped next at Condon, then at Fossil, each stop some twenty miles farther south. Beyond Fossil they descended to the John Day River at Spray, then moved up the North Fork to Monument (a corruption, according to James Selam, of the Sahaptin place name, mánmint) where they intercepted a spawning run of "eels" (that is, the anadromous lamprey *Entosphenus tridentatus*). Here they might join forces with families from winter villages at Roosevelt (nišxúawi) or Alderdale whose routes moved south farther to the east, up Willow or Butter creeks, to Heppner or still further east through Pilot Rock and Ukiah. Here the bitterroots grow among the yellow umbels of xawš, a cousin of Canby's lomatium.

The patches of thin šam soils favored by bitterroot and the tuberous lomatiums are common but dispersed, making large encampments at this season impractical. At Fox Valley, Oregon (imáayi), however, the abundant camas mature in late June, bringing many families together for the cooperative effort of the harvest of this favorite bulb. Such gatherings were attended by hundreds, perhaps even thousands of Indians (Ross 1956 [1924]:22–30; Marshall 1977:111, 159). Famous camas meadows include those at Kittitas and at Glenwood in the Cascade foothills of Washington and near Kamiah, Idaho, at the base of the Bitterroot Mountains. The concentrated abundance of vegetable food at such times and places provided a welcome opportunity for socializing, highlighted by the intense excitement of gambling and horse racing, and for the business of regional politics and of mate matching.

In the early days of this century the mid-Columbia Indians modified their traditional path through the Blue Mountains in order to visit the frontier town of John Day for the Fourth of July rodeo—a modern multi-cultural equivalent of their traditional summer gatherings. The contemporary Indian pow-wow may have roots in these ephemeral regional gatherings, occasioned by extraordinary environmental largess. Camas did not provide the only context for such events. We see large, diverse colocations of Indian people at the summer fish runs at Celilo Falls and The Dalles and at Kettle Falls and again at the early spring lomatium concentrations across the Columbia opposite the mouths of the Okanogan and Sanpoil rivers (Ray 1933). Fur trading posts and missions provided comparable material opportunities and motivations, which proved a mixed blessing to these Euro-American entrepreneurs and an unmitigated disaster to the Indians.

The roots collected during the spring, if not eaten on the spot, were dried, cached, then transported to the winter village sites upon the families' return to the river for summer fishing. Horses greatly facilitated this labor, as a single family might have to transport over 1,500 pounds of dried roots over distances of more than one hundred miles to add to their winter supplies. Of equal significance in the labor equation, however, is the fact that the roots were first dried, then transported. This reduced the weight of their loads by two-thirds.

šátam, "summer"

In late June or early July the Big River drops, exposing the summer runs of blueback and Chinook salmon and summer steelhead to the eye of the fisherman. Women put their roots aside in order to clean and dry the quantities of fish being pulled from the river.

Fish runs are at their peak for short periods of a few days or a week with slack time between; during these breaks the women could take time off to gather the early ripening fruits of golden currant (*Ribes aureum;* ҳan), gooseberry (e.g., *Ribes lacustre;* pínuš; see fig. 4.17), dogwood (wíwál, fruit of lučaní), serviceberry, and chokecherry. The currants and dogwood berries ripen first, in June of most years, and as with the first Indian celeries, the first suckers, the first roots, and the first salmon, they are ritually welcomed before the general harvest begins. In the late 1970s this káʔwit cermony for dogwood fruits and golden currants was being revived by Indian congregations at Horn Dam on the lower Yakima and at Satus longhouse.[4]

Chokecherries (*Prunus virginiana;* tmiš, fig. 4.18) remain a great favorite of older Indian women. Today they are frozen for later consumption, in place of the traditional process of grinding (pits and all—exposure to air eliminating the toxic cyanide compounds characteristic of pits of *Prunus* fruits, cf. Timbrook 1982) and drying in the sun.

Henry Perkins, a Methodist missionary posted at The Dalles, was frustrated by the Indians' peripatetic ways, as his fledgling congregation up and left him en masse in mid-August 1842 (Perkins n.d. [1838–43]). They were heading for the huckleberry fields in the high Cascades. Many stayed away

---

4. David French notes (personal communication) that there is much variability among Sahaptins as to preferences and terminology for currants.

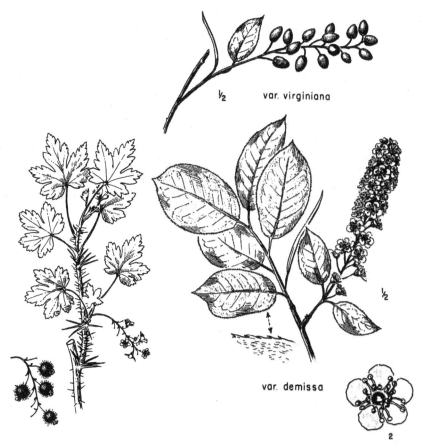

½   var. virginiana

var. demissa

Fig. 4.17. Swamp goosberry
(*Ribes lacustre*; **pínuš**).

Fig. 4.18. Chokecherry (*Prunus virginiana*;
tmiš).

until cold weather in October brought snow to the high country camps.
Today the automobile or pickup truck with camper top makes such extended dislocations unnecessary. Early August remains the occasion for the
first-foods celebration in honor of the Indians' number one fruit, the black
mountain huckleberry (*Vaccinium membranaceum*, known in Sahaptin as
wíwnu). This feast is the obligatory prelude to a series of day, overnight, or
weekend trips to the productive berry fields, the knowledge of which is part
of an Indian family's inheritance. A serendipitous consequence of this phase

of the seasonal migration is that it provides an excuse to escape the summer's most intense heat, when for many days the land bakes at over 100°F on the riverside flats and in the rock-rimmed canyons.

špam, "fall"

James Selam fondly recalls his family's annual trek to "Indian Heaven," as the stretch of subalpine forest, high meadows, and mosquito-infested tarns between Mount Adams and Mount St. Helens in the Gifford Pinchot National Forest is known. The family needed three days to cover the distance by horse and wagon from Celilo Falls where his family owned fishing sites. They stopped overnight west of Goldendale, at Glenwood, and again at Goose Lake, where they stashed their wagons. They climbed on foot and horseback to their campsite at áyun-aš near kalamát, as the meadow with the historic Indian racetrack was known to his people. In August of 1983 we retraced this last portion of his route. James was like a kid again, poking here and there about the meadow's edge for signs of tepee frames or sweat lodge hearths, but we saw little that could be taken as evidence of the intense activity focused here in centuries past, except the deep trace of the horse racing track itself, which ran east to west across the meadow.

The meadow was clearly less extensive than formerly, as could be seen by comparing photos taken there at the turn of the century (Jerman and Mason 1976). Lodgepole pine saplings were sprouting up all around the meadow margins, consuming the open space. This is an inevitable consequence of fire suppression, which has been the law of the land in the national forests for several decades now. An old-time ranger I met at the Naches Ranger Station recalled how he used to rave at the Indians for their "carelessness" with fire, as frequent fires were attributed to them during the late summer season. What the ranger failed to appreciate was the fact that fire is one of the Indians' most powerful tools of food production. Fire creates sunny openings in the forest, creates edges that foster the rapid spread of nutritious herbs and shrubs, most notably the black mountain huckleberry and related species, blueberry and grouseberry (Minore 1972:68). Such zones of increased natural productivity draw deer and elk within the hunter's range as well. Though knowledge of the traditional use of intentional burning to create favorable habitat has been all but forgotten by contemporary Plateau Indians, evidence assembled by Henry Lewis (1973, 1977) shows that the ecological role of fire was known and manipulated in complex ways by Indians from California to Canada.

"Indian Heaven" it was indeed. Cool nights, warm days, and hillsides covered with bushes loaded with grouseberry (*Vaccinium membranaceum* and *V. scoparium*, fig. 4.19), called wiwlú-wiwlu, "little huckleberries," and the sweetest of all, the low mountain blueberry whose Latin name tells it all, *Vaccinium deliciosum* (ililmúk).

Many berries no doubt vanished between hand and basket. The famous Klikitat cedar-root baskets, decorated with beargrass leaves and bitter

Fig. 4.19. Big huckleberry and grouseberry (*Vaccinium membranaceum, V. scoparium*; **wiwlú-wiwlu**).

cherry bark were used (and still are) in these tasks. The surplus berries were dried slowly over a fire kept smouldering in a rotten log (Filloon 1952). This method of drying the berries preserves the bulk of the Vitamin C content in the fruits, as our nutritional analyses indicate (Norton et al. 1984:223). As in the case of fish and roots, drying reduced the water content of the food drastically and thus its weight by 70 percent. H. W. Perkins notes in his journal the results of these efforts of the Indian women:

> "They are usually absent on these excursions, from four to six weeks; during which, each family lays in, for winter use, four or five pecks [ca. four to five gallons] of nice dried berries. These they mix from time to time with pounded salmon, & a good portion of salmon oil, & thus is prepared one of the best dishes of which an Indian can boast." (Perkins n.d. [1838–43], Book 1:10)

The huckleberry fields south of Mount Adams were not so far from the Columbia River that fishing was entirely neglected during August and September. In fact, the most important salmon run of all, that of the fall Chinooks from which the bulk of winter stores was produced, normally passed in early September (see fig. 4.20). Men rode down from "Indian Heaven" to the mouths of the Wind and Little White Salmon rivers to fish for fall Chinook and silver salmon, hauling the fish back to the huckleberry camps so the women could prepare them. Huckleberry season was also prime time for hunting deer and elk, which had retreated to the high country for the rut. The preferred prey in the Cascades was the black-tailed deer (*Odocoileus hemionus columbianus;* x̣alk), distinguished from the closely related common mule deer of the lower eastern slopes (*O. h. hemionus;* yáamaš) (see Table 11).

In October the winter villages were reoccupied while the last of the salmon were salvaged to augment the winter supply. It was this phase of the annual cycle that Lewis and Clark observed on their journey down the Columbia from the mouth of the Snake River to The Dalles between the sixteenth and twenty-fifth of October 1805. They had found the lower Snake River villages vacant, just caches of lodge poles set up on racks out of harm's way to mark their locations. The occupants were apparently off hunting, perhaps for antelope southward or for deer and elk up in the Blue Mountains. But the Columbia was feverish with activity. The explorers found that the salmon the Indians were processing left a lot to be desired. Many were múqʷayč, spawned-out carcasses of fall Chinook salmon which spawned along this stretch of the river, with perhaps some fresh mił úla, the dog or "white" salmon (a term that may also refer to spawning salmon in general).

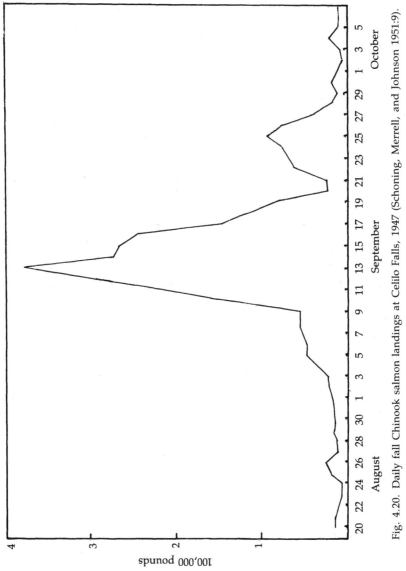

Fig. 4.20. Daily fall Chinook salmon landings at Celilo Falls, 1947 (Schoning, Merrell, and Johnson 1951:9).

Tales of a superabundance of salmon on the Columbia, of salmon so plentiful it was burned for fuel, are based on Clark's surmise (Thwaites 1959 [1904], 3:124). This seems unlikely, given the abundance of fast-burning sagebrush all along the river. The inclusion of fat-depleted and half-rotten fish in the diet—remarked upon by several early Euro-American travelers in the Plateau (see also Thompson in Merk 1968:40)—suggests otherwise: that the margin of safety for winter survival was not overly generous.

Population Size and Density

Lewis and Clark counted winter houses in the hundreds during their descent through Sahaptin territory, noting as best they could how many occupants shared each lodge. From this count a rough estimate can be derived of the Columbia River Sahaptin people present (an important caveat) on the river in late October 1805. These population figures are assembled in Table 11. Adding Lewis and Clark's estimates for the entire Sahaptin-speaking area east of the Cascades, we arrive at a figure of 12,765 people occupying an area of 31,000 square miles, an average of about two persons for every five square miles.

Such densities may be only half of the true precontact values, as two smallpox epidemics are known to have afflicted the middle-Columbia people before 1805—epidemics that may have spread inland from coastal trading ships bringing strange and deadly foreign pestilence with their new wealth or may have been brought back across the Rocky Mountains by bison-hunting parties. Based on losses reported for twenty "virgin-soil" smallpox epidemics by the epidemiologist C. W. Dixon (1962:325), Boyd has calculated the likely population loss in the Plateau between 1770 and 1805 at approximately 45 percent (1985:334). If his inferences are correct—and we have no better basis for inference at present—then Sahaptin-speakers originally numbered more in the range of 23,000 at a density of >0.7 per square mile. (Kroeber estimates 0.1-0.3/square mile for the Plateau, which is much too low [1939:134f].)

Even that density is but 5 percent of the present population of the area, a telling statistic for those who favor a return to the halcyon past. Though one person per square mile seems a thin population by modern standards, it is a high density for a hunting and gathering economy to support, especially given the interior location and moderately high latitude of the Plateau. We

Table 11

Plateau Population and Density Estimates

Group	L & C	Boyd	Area/sq mi	Density
Cayuse	438	788	7710	0.10
Nez Perce	4,627	8,329	24,000	0.35
Northeast Sahaptin	4,185	7,533	<9,590	>0.79
Columbia Sahaptin	3,900	7,020	12,660	0.55
Northwest Sahaptin	4,680	8,424	<8,839	>0.95
Southern Plateau Total	17,830	32,094	<62,799	>0.51
Plateau Sahaptin Total	12,765	22,977	31,089	0.74
Columbia Salish	3,200	5,760	12,225	0.47
Okanagan/Colville	4,361	7,850	25,350	0.31
Kutenai	829	1,492	19,300	0.08
Flathead	4,402	7,924	27,490	0.29
Coeur d'Alene	1,067	1,920	4,350	0.44
Northern Plateau Total	13,859	24,946	88,715	0.28
Columbia Plateau Total	31,689	57,040	153,774	0.37

Adapted from Boyd 1985 and the U.S. Army Corps of Engineers 1952.

Note: "L & C" are Lewis and Clark's estimates as interpreted by Boyd (1985). Boyd's estimates for the precontact period (before ca. 1775) are calculated for each group at 180 percent of Lewis and Clark's figures, allowing for a 45 percent population loss due to early smallpox epidemics. This loss figure is a conservative approximation based upon C. W. Dixon's average mortality for 20 virgin-soil smallpox epidemics (1962:325). Areas are estimated on the basis of drainage basin figures cited by the U.S. Army Corps of Engineers (1952, 1:50–51) with approximate adjustments for basins divided among more than one ethno-linguistic group. The relative rankings of major groups corresponds reasonably well with expectations based on densities of major root and fish species.

may compare this Plateau estimate with estimates of Great Basin Indian population densities published by Julian Steward (1938). These densities range from one person on two square miles in the Owens Valley of California (roughly comparable to the Sahaptin average) to one person per forty square miles on the southwestern fringe of the Great Salt Desert in Utah.

The lower densities in the Basin may best be accounted for by the absence of fish runs comparable to those of the Columbia. These fish are locally unearned resources in the sense that the salmon represent an organic concentration of nutrients derived from the solar energy that falls on the huge area of the Pacific Ocean where the salmon feed during the several years of their pelagic development.

Conclusion

In sum, the gathering, fishing, and hunting economy of the mid-Columbia Indians represents several million years of progress beyond the first known hominid economies. Tools—though limited in scale by the demands of portability and the familial basis of production for most tasks—allow highly efficient harvests of roots, fish, and game otherwise beyond human reach. Imagine catching a struggling fifty-pound salmon with your bare hands, digging tons of roots from stony ground with just your fingers, or hauling nearly a ton of dried roots home over a hundred miles of rugged terrain without carrying devices. Indian hemp nets and bags and cedar-root baskets allowed heavy loads to be carried over the average 600 to 1,000 miles traversed during a typical seasonal round.

Consider also the impact of innovative food processing techniques, all too readily passed over as "women's work." Without the knowledge of how to dry roots, fish, berries, and meat, local populations would have been reduced to the number that could be supported during the meanest season, the lean winter months (an expression of Leibig's Law of the Minimum). This would certainly have been but a small fraction of the populations actually achieved. Dried foods are not only light in weight and thus more efficiently transported, but they also may be kept for up to several years, stored in a carefully lined cellar (the wulčí), providing a margin of safety for the occasional year in which several key resources fail. The technologies of transport and of food preservation are thus among the critical pillars of the Plateau hunting-gathering way of life.

A final point must be stressed. The traditional Sahaptin economy was founded on cooperation between men and women in the tasks of feeding both parents and children. Among our ape brethren the males rarely contribute to feeding their own offspring. In fact, they probably do not know which offspring are their own, thus they are motivated by no genetic interest to help in rearing them. The human family, such a basic social and economic unit on the Plateau, represents a radical departure from the ways of our primate ancestors. Males, through the cultural formalities of marriage ceremonies and marriage exchanges, recognize their equal genetic interest in their offspring and join with their spouses in a division of labor that is far superior in its productive capacity to what each could produce separately. Men hunt and fish, by and large, while women gather plant foods and process the men's harvest. Though we are able to measure the relative caloric contribution of each sex and weigh their relative efforts[5] and thus judge female (as here) or male the more productive, such calculations pit male against female in competition for production quota honors. This is misleading. Neither sex exploited the other in the Plateau (Ackerman 1982). Each held the other's work in high regard and *together* they saw to the continuation of their families and their traditions.

5. Early travelers and settlers frequently remarked on the laziness of the men and the industriousness of the women, but their perceptions may have been distorted by wishful thinking.

5

Animal and Plant Resources

Mammals

nuq̓ʷút ani-ɬá-ma, "milk-makers"

MID-COLUMBIA Indians of the nineteenth century did not have ready access to abundant big game. No great herds of bison or caribou grazed on the Columbia Basin bunch grass. Though the range of the bison extended into the Columbia Plateau between fifteen hundred and five hundred years ago, they did not occur here in more recent times (Schroedl 1973). Pronghorn antelope were hunted on the plains within the "big bend" of the Columbia until shortly after contact, but were not abundant. Thus, hunting contributed much less to the diet than did fishing and gathering.[1]

Hunting prowess was highly valued in a man, however, and a boy's first kill was the occasion of a rite of passage to manhood. This ritual is still occasionally observed. Hunting was pursued year-round, and men who accompanied root- and berry-gathering parties were alert to any game they might encounter. Autumn was the most productive hunting season. At that time berrying camps were established in high mountain meadows, where rutting deer and elk also gathered, attracted by the nutritious browse of the meadow's edge.

Bow-and-arrow was the weapon of choice before guns were known. In fact, guns are known by the same term as is applied to the bow, twínpaš. Bows were of the hard woods—oak being a common choice—and might be sinew-backed for greater strength. They were strung with rawhide. Arrows were by preference of the wood of the "arrow bush," which here is the

---

1. Marshall estimates the contribution of hunting to the diet as 10 to 25 percent for the Nez Perces (1977:71). It was no doubt less for mid-Columbia River peoples whose fisheries were more productive than those of the Nez Perce.

serviceberry (*Amelanchier alnifolia*). Arrows were fletched with hawk flight feathers bound with Indian hemp twine and sealed with spruce pitch.

Ungulates
x̣aax̣ʷ waskú tkʷata-łá-ma, "all the grass eaters"

Prey was most often the mule deer (yáamaš) or black-tailed deer (x̣alk). These two subspecies were distinguished by range, size, and subtle differences of proportion. Game biologists believe that the wapiti, or American elk, was absent from the Cascades in protohistorical times. However, Sahaptin has an elaborate, dialect-specific vocabulary for elk that distinguishes bulls from cows (see Table 15), with additional terms for calf and spike bull that apply as well to deer. This suggests a longstanding familiarity with the species.

Included with mule deer and elk in the general category íwinat—which might best be translated "ungulate" or "ungulate meat"—are the less common native species, the white-tailed deer, mountain goat, and bighorn sheep, as well as the now-extralimital pronghorn and bison. Moose and caribou were not named in Sahaptin by my consultants, though indirect knowledge of their existence is to be expected (see Table 12).

Hunting strategy varied, of course, with the prey, situation, and season. A typical fall deer hunt was a cooperative venture of several men (perhaps including older boys in apprentice roles). Hunting parties usually dispersed widely in an area judged favorable, with contact maintained by agreed upon signals, often imitations of animal sounds. When fresh tracks or other signs were located one man might attempt to drive the deer toward a second hunter who, having circled around ahead of the animal, was waiting in ambush. The hunter whose arrow first struck home was credited with the kill.

The hunting party shared the raw liver and kidney before dressing the carcass and packing it home. There the meat was widely shared and the skin handed over to the hunter's wife for processing. If the kill was credited to a boy and it was his first, the meat would be distributed in a ritual manner. The boy would receive no part of his first kill—a powerful reinforcement of the moral principal that generosity comes first. Such a rite of passage was a traditional prerequisite to marriage, a minimal test of a man's capacity and willingness to contribute substantially to the task of feeding the next generation.

TABLE 12

Native Ungulates (ɨwínat) as Prey

Species	Family/Latin Name	Sahaptin Name	Weights (lbs)
	CERVIDAE		
wapiti/elk	*Cervus canadensis*	♂ wawúukya	♂ 700–1,000
		♀ tašímka	♀ 500–600
mule deer	*Odocoileus hemionus*	yáamaš	♂ 125–400
			♀ 100–150
"mule deer"	*O. h. hemionus*	yáamaš	
"black-tail deer"	*O. h. columbianus*	x̣alk	
white-tailed deer	*O. virginiana*	čatwilí	♂ 75–400
			♀ 50–250
	BOVIDAE		
mountain goat	*Oreamnos americanus*	waw	100–300
big-horn sheep	*Ovis canadensis*	tnuun	♂ 125–275
			♀ 75–150
bison	*Bison bison*	cúułim	800–2,000
	ANTILOCAPRIDAE		
pronghorn	*Antilocapra americana*	wáwataw	75–130

Hunting remains of great interest and cultural value to Plateau Indians, though rifles and pick-up trucks have entirely replaced the traditional hunting equipment. Off-reservation hunting rights on "unclaimed lands" were guaranteed by the treaties as fully as were off-reservation fishing rights. The recognition of those rights has been hard fought for years (Baenen 1968), as non-Indian hunters strongly resent what seems to them an "unfair" advantage granted Indians to hunt "out of season," to exceed bag limits, and to avoid paying for state permits. In this tense climate of opinion rumors of Indians "wasting" game are readily believed and eagerly repeated by non-Indians.

Such reports of the profligacy of Indian hunters date back to the period of first settlement. Gibbs, for example, describing the Klikitat Indian country, says that, "Of game, there is but little left. The deer and elk are almost exterminated throughout the country, the deep snows of winter driving them to the valleys, where the Indians, with their usual improvidence, have slaughtered them without mercy" (1978[1854]:10). First of all, such accounts may or may not be true. If true, they are very likely exaggerated if allowance is made for the biases of the "witnesses." Some wastefulness might be attributable to the new technology, the guns and ammunition that early traders found to be the most lucrative of trade items. Wasteful hunting might also be explained— if it in fact occurred—in part by the breakdown of traditional cultural values.

These values, however, were clear: wasting game was an offense against the animals themselves, against the moral order of nature, and was punished by bad luck in hunting or by sickness (cf. Jacobs 1929:198–200; Feit 1970; Martin 1978; Nelson 1983). That these same conservation values are upheld by contemporary Indians as well is indicated by their careful regulation of hunting by their own tribal members on reservation lands. On both Yakima and Warm Springs reservations considerable land has been set aside by tribal law for game preserves where no hunting is allowed. It is time to accept the fact that there are committed environmentalists among both Indians and whites and selfish poachers in both camps as well. They may even occur in comparable proportions among whites and Indians, but they certainly do not occur in comparable numbers.

James Selam hunts whenever and wherever he can and he may bag two or three deer and an elk in the course of a normal year. The meat is soon gone, a hindquarter given to one brother's family, a forequarter to another relative or friend, one part kept at home in the freezer to feed himself, his family, and any visitors who should happen by. The hide is laboriously cleaned and softened by a female relative and is eventually transformed into moccasins and decorated buckskin clothes. Deer brains are employed in processing hides; hooves are made into dance rattles; antler and bone once served for tools (for example, antler for digging-stick handles and obsidian flaking, and bone for fish hooks). Nor is the hunt simply over and done. The experience is savored and its thrill shared in repeated tellings, in affirmation of being alive, a part of nature, an Indian, and a man.

Rodents and Their Kin

Hunting for most of us means "big game." But the smaller mammals, mostly rodents and rabbits, may represent the larger biomass. Of course, it is more efficient to harvest one's meat in a few large chunks than in many small pieces (Feit 1970; Smith 1983). Under certain circumstances, however, the smaller animals can be worthwhile targets of the hunter's attention. This is most often the case when these animals are concentrated in a small area and have put on fat for their seasonal nap. Two rodents are of particular note as food sources in the Columbia Plateau. The yellow-bellied marmot, a.k.a., "groundhog" or "rockchuck" (čłkčłknu), emerges from hibernation in March and hauls out into the early spring sun that now warms the rock outcrops of his low elevation habitat. By mid-summer the adults and their offspring are busy putting on fat for the long sleep, which in this semi-arid habitat often extends not only through the frigid winter but through the baked-dry late summer and fall as well—a combination of aestivation and hibernation. A full-grown, well-fattened marmot weighs five to ten pounds, a hefty meal. They are readily bagged with bow and arrow and are found in numbers close to the summer fishing camps.

The marmot's alpine elder brother, the hoary marmot (NWS: wáwšiłun), is even larger (eight to twenty pounds), but was apparently not hunted. This is the famous "whistling" marmot of the alpine meadows. In the Indian world view it is associated with preternatural beings, the little people, whose whistling might seduce the lone hunter, calling him ever on until he loses all track of time, space, and identity. This species of "alpine madness" is much feared and, it seems, inhibits the exploitation of the potential resources of the zone above timberline.

A second rodent considered good eating was and is the Townsend's (and Washington) ground squirrel. This picket-post squirrel is best known locally as the "prairie dog" and, like the yellow-bellied marmot, spends most of the year asleep under ground. Between the first days of spring and the dog days of summer, these little guys are hard at work putting on fat. Though it takes fifteen to twenty of them (at 168–280 grams) to equal one marmot, they congregate in large colonies in sandy soils of the plains and foothills. A preferred technique of capture is to divert a stream (or haul water in containers) to flood their burrows, flushing them out where they can be easily shot or clubbed.

Townsend's and Washington ground squirrels are allopatric sibling species occupying opposite sides of the Columbia River in central Washington and Oregon. The very subtle differences between them are not noted by the Indians as both are known in Columbia River Sahaptin as čii-łá (N W S: łímyá). Their larger upland relative, Belding's ground squirrel, found from central Oregon south, is recognized as a distinct but related creature, čiiła-wáakuł, that is, čii-łá-like.

Jackrabbits and cottontails, unlike their European relatives, are not colonial warren-dwellers but typically occupy individual or family territories. Nevertheless, in certain years of abundance an area of sagebrush flat could be so infested with jackrabbits as to make a net drive worthwhile. The traditional Indian jackrabbit hunt was a communal affair involving men, women, and children alike. Rabbit nets were knotted of Indian hemp twine, just as were fish nets, but were about three feet wide by several hundred feet long. If several were available a long fence could be set up by stringing the nets from bush to bush in a semi-circle. As has been described in detail for the Great Basin Paiute and Shoshone (cf. Steward 1938:38–39), a "human fence" angling out in a V-shape from the ends of the net kept the jackrabbits headed toward the trap as beaters drove them in with much noise and shouting. The stampeding rabbits leaped pell-mell into the net where they were clubbed. Rabbit fur was used for socks and a special winter vest.

Trapping techniques were known for taking beaver, muskrat, otter, and other fur-bearers, but mid-Columbia peoples did not take to fur trapping as a major source of income as did the Indians of the northern forests. Trapping appears to have been motivated by the occasional need for furs, as for otter skins to braid in one's hair as a decorative and symbolic ornament, or to obtain the beaver's musk gland as an aphrodisiac and love charm. Trapping, of course, increased in importance as one moved from the river-oriented lowland economies to those of more heavily forested uplands bordering the central Plateau.

Birds

Kákya means "bird" in general and is included in the broader Sahaptin category tamám ani-łá-ma, "egg makers." Kákya also may mean "pet," even when the pet is not a bird, as with the horse and dog, or when a gambler keeps a metallic wood-boring beetle (Buprestidae; x̣ax̣áykʷ, literally, "money") as a good luck charm. A third sense of the term as meaning any animal has currency in some parts of Sahaptin country. This illustrates a common process whereby general terms for plant or animal, tree or bird, are derived from terms with more specific meanings, as the need arises for more abstract, less environmentally specific concepts (cf. Turner 1987).

More than 260 species of birds have been recorded in the Sahaptin area in recent years. Of these, perhaps 220 are of regular and conspicuous occurrence. Elders today recollect 60 to 70 kinds of birds that are named in Sahaptin (see Appendix 1). These are, by-and-large, birds of large size, conspicuous habits, common occurrence, or special note. The rest, if small birds of field or forest, may be dismissed as cikʷá-cikʷa, or "dickey bird." Twenty of the regions' 21 duck species are lumped with the prototypical duck, the mallard, as x̣át-x̣at, the most common, widespread, and conspicuous species here and one of the largest as well. Of the rest, only the common merganser is singled out and awarded its own name. The great variety of migratory shorebirds that pass through the region in small numbers are passed over as "like the killdeer" (tiit), a ubiquitous and inescapable year-round resident. Thus Sahaptin bird naming is selective. Bats (čátaqš) may be included also as "birds of darkness" or "birds of evil."

Grouse

Lewis and Clark encountered hordes of sharp-tailed grouse (known locally as "prairie chickens"; q̓áx̣nu) in the grasslands, and sage grouse (payúmš) on the sagebrush steppes along the Snake and Columbia rivers. Both species are now reduced to fragile remnants of their former abundance as their native habitat is plowed under for farming. Both were considered very good eating and were easily shot with bows and arrows. Payúm-ša means (approximately) "to dance promiscuously," a reference to the male sage grouses' competitive breeding display. The sharp-tailed grouse serves as the conceptual model for the recently established Eurasian gray or Hungarian partridge and chukar, both of which may be known today as q̓ax̣nu-wáakuɬ, literally, like the sharp-tailed grouse. Forest grouse, such as the blue (pti) and ruffed (sapaníca; NWS: s̓impaasá) were also hunted but were not found in large concentrations. The spruce grouse is a rare resident of high mountain forests on the margins of the Sahaptin range. Northwest Sahaptin speakers know it as miyáwax̣ or "chief," an honorific also applied to the black bear. The spruce grouse is the quintessential "fool's hen," steadfast in its refusal to fly from danger. It is curious that a bird considered by whites to epitomize stupidity, should be considered "chiefly" by Indian people, and I speculate that the grouse's disregard for danger is seen as high courage by Indians.

Waterfowl

Waterfowl today are abundant in the nesting season on the potholes (small lakes fed by groundwater) strewn across the center of the plateau. Most of these potholes are artifacts of massive twentieth-century irrigation projects. The Indians, I suspect, preferred Columbia River islands as their primary duck and Canada goose (ákak) hunting sites. Ethnographic reports of waterfowl hunting in the Plateau are sketchy. Egg collecting is also occasionally reported. Clearly, waterfowl were not among the key resources here, despite their seeming ready availability. Adult birds were shot or netted. Waterfowl—including numbers of both tundra and trumpeter swans (both named onomatopoetically, wawqilúk)—were abundant along the river in winter, providing a potential adjunct to dried winter food stocks.

Birds were more significant in other cultural roles than as food. The common merganser, noted above as the only rival to the mallard for nomenclatural recognition, is a large saw-billed duck that is permanently resident on Columbia basin rivers. It is called táš-taš, or in myth, taštáaš-ya. The motive for this special recognition is only partly attributable to its conspicuousness—as other Plateau ducks might be judged equally worthy of note. (In fact, táš-taš has been identified in the literature as both "canvasback" and "wood duck.") The merganser also served as an early warning system to the mid-Columbia villagers. A large flight of mergansers past a village was taken as a sign of the approach of Paiute raiding parties.

Taštáaš-ya in myth is surreptitiously violated by Coyote. She is the alluring maiden bathing on the river's far shore who stimulates Coyote's desire. Devious as always, he impregnates her by means of a botanical "penis extender," the scouring rush (*Equisetum hyemale;* wapáy-wapay, literally, "small reed"; see fig. 5.1). This joint-stemmed plant grows handily at riverside and might, with sufficient imagination, be joined in series like disarticulating tent poles to form a sort of hose extending from his hiding place, across the river, and down to the unsuspecting Merganser maiden.

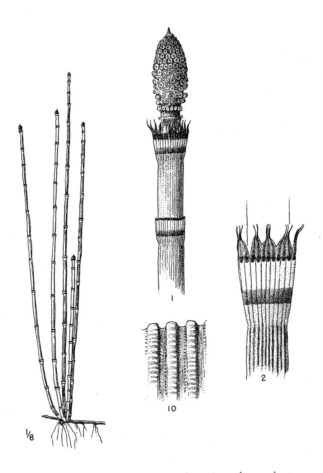

Fig. 5.1. Scouring rush (*Equisetum hyemale;* **wapáy-wapay**).

Other Birds

Feathers (**wáptas**) were collected for technological, aesthetic, and religious purposes. Hawk feathers kept the arrow's flight true. The bright red-orange flight feathers of the flicker (**taxt**; N W S: číya) adorned dancers, and the broad tail feathers of eagles (both bald and golden) were essential to dress the corpse of the deceased for the journey beyond. Eagle feathers have intrinsic power. If a war dancer should drop an eagle feather on the dance floor— perhaps the feathers of his bustle are poorly secured to his costume—the competition is brought to an abrupt halt. Men experienced in war—today

World War II, Korean, or Vietnam War veterans are chosen—ceremonially "hunt" the fallen feather until the strongest among them spear it. The man who captures the feather recounts publicly a memorable war experience, then accepts a generous gift from the family of the dancer who lost the feather. The power of the wayward feather is thus controlled and the dancing can continue.

Birds are prominent in Sahaptin myths. One such tells of Golden Eagle and his five daughters. They come on stage in order of size: first yityíit-ya, "Kestrel" (23-inch wing span), then wapnyawała-yáy, "Prairie Falcon" (42 inches), then qiluš-yáy, "Red-tailed Hawk" (50.5 inches), then itatat-yáy, presumably the "Ferruginous Hawk" (56 inches), and finally qiqinu-yáy, "Osprey" (56 inches). In this orderly progression we can see that the people clearly perceived evolutionary and ecological relationships among the creatures that shared their land. Curiously, the bald eagle (k̓ámamul), totemic symbol of the U.S.A., is scarcely noted in all of Sahaptin mythology. "Eagle" of myth is always the prince of raptors, Golden Eagle. Bald eagles are rather viewed as outsized vultures, feeding as they most often do on dead fish. In this bias of sympathy we can see a hint of Sahaptin hunting values, which, however, did not deter them from harvesting spawned-out salmon themselves.

Birds are important as signs. Some characteristic behavior of a bird might provide an ecological or moral mnemonic, as we saw in the case of the merganser. The canyon wren (x̣ali-x̣áli), said to attack and drive off rattlesnakes in defense of its rimrock nest, exhibits exemplary courage in defense of home and family. Meadowlark's outspoken eloquence gives its flesh "medicinal" power to cure speech impediments, while the mourning dove's heart is eaten to make a person "quiet." Ravens are powerful Indian doctors and messengers. Those with raven's power can interpret the messages they bring of portentous distant events. Perhaps a raven first brought word of the miraculous coming of the whites? Crows, by contrast, though talkative, rarely say anything of significance, being given over to idle gossip, according to James Selam. The contrast is inferred from the contrasting behavior of these close relatives. The raven is a more solitary bird partial to wilderness; the crow is a gregarious camp-follower. Swallows (łíx-łix), as we have noted, signal the return of the spring Chinook salmon, while the oriole represents— most explicitly in Smohalla's theology—the rebirth of life in springtime (Relander 1956:73). The oriole (wawšuk-ła, literally, "throws [fruit] down") does not tolerate taunting imitation by upstart humans. Such disrespect is punished by the failure of the golden currant and serviceberry crops.

Fish

Salmon

The Plateau's abundant anadromous salmon runs give local Indian life a unique flavor. Salmon (núsux̣) have provided an extremely reliable food source along the mid-Columbia. The river was the funnel through which millions of adult fish passed each year en route to their spawning beds throughout the Columbia drainage basin, a territory of 260,000 square miles ranging over ten degrees of latitude. Thus, the variable effects of climate, landslides, or fish diseases would not likely affect more than a small fraction of the breeding populations of the system in any given year. Evidence of commercial fish captures during the heyday of the commercial exploitation of the Columbia River (ca. 1880–1940) demonstrates that quantities available to the Indians precontact at such fishing stations as Celilo Falls far exceeded their needs (see fig. 5.2).

Despite the superabundance of salmon, its dietary contribution has been exaggerated. Nowhere did salmon approximate the 80 to 90 percent of the diet that Haines attributes to it for the Nez Perce (1955:12). A conservative estimate based on Hewes' ethnohistorical survey (1973 [1947])—later modified by Walker [1967a] and Schalk [n.d.])—suggests an average figure for the Plateau of under 30 percent and for the mid-Columbia of no more than 40 percent of caloric needs (Hunn 1981; see Table 13). Why this restraint on salmon consumption if supplies far exceeded demand?

One reason may be found in the fact that salmon are hard to catch except where geological circumstance produces an impediment to their upstream movement, forcing them to leap up through narrow channels or to rest in eddies from their struggle up a difficult stretch of rapids. Such favored fishing sites were few and access to them strictly controlled by the local villagers. The ten mile stretch of the Columbia River between Celilo Falls and The Dalles was the greatest fishery on the whole river, with the Cascades, Priest Rapids, and Kettle Falls also very productive. Between these major fisheries, salmon were caught with gill nets set at right angles to the shore, by seining from canoe and shore, by gaffing spawning fish, by collecting dead spawned-out salmon, or they might be trapped in weirs constructed across the smaller tributaries.

A second limiting factor was timing. The mid-Columbia has five or six distinct salmon runs, with very few fish available between late October and

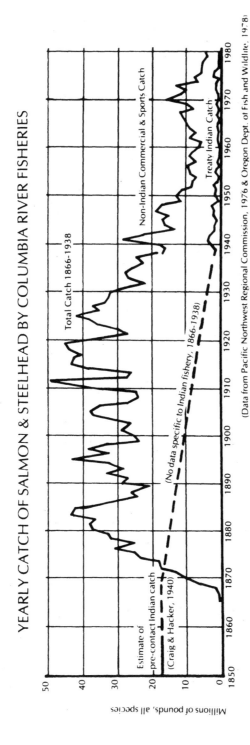

Fig. 5.2. Declining Columbia River fisheries (reprinted from *Oregon Indians*, Zucker et al. 1983:167, with permission of the Oregon Historical Society Press).

TABLE 13

Nutritional Contribution of Salmon: Estimates of Salmon Consumption
(pounds/person/year), Caloric Yields (kcal/person/day), and Percents of
Estimated Minimal Daily Energy Requirement (Hunn 1981:128)

Society	Annual Consumption[1]	Gross Caloric Yield[2]	Calorie Loss Factor[3]	Net Caloric Yield[4]	Percent of MDR[5]
Wishram	400	676	.88	594	30
Tenino	500	676	.87	735	37
Umatilla	500	845	.81	684	34
Nez Perce 1	300	507	.52	264	13
Nez Perce 2	582	983	.52	511	26
Sinkaietk	500	845	.67	566	28
Sanpoil	500	845	.62	524	26
Coeur D'Alene	100	169	.25	42	2
Flathead	100	169	.25	42	2
Kutenai	300	507	.25	127	5
Chilcotin	600	1,014	.64	649	32
Shuswap	500	845	.675	570	28
Lillooet	600	1,014	.80	811	41
Thompson	900	1,521	.81	1232	62

1. Annual consumption figures are from Hewes (1973 [1947]) except for Nez Perce 2, which is from Walker (1967a).

2. Gross caloric yields are derived from annual consumption figures by converting to kg/day, multiplying by 0.8, the edible portion, at 1700 kcal/kg, the average of 20 samples including all five Pacific salmon species and the steelhead trout (Watt and Merrill 1963).

3. Calorie loss factors for the Fraser River groups, Chilcotin, Shuswap, Lillooet, and Thompson, are from Kew (n.d. [1976]). Calorie loss factors for Columbia River groups is calculated as the distance from the mouth of the Columbia River to the center of the particular group's range divided by the length of the main stem of the Columbia or, if the group occupied a tributary, by the distance to the limit of salmon migration on that tributary. The resultant ratio is multiplied by 0.75, the fraction of caloric value lost by salmon in migration, and subtracted from 1.0.

4. The net caloric yield is simply the gross caloric yield times the calorie loss factor.

5. Minimal daily requirement (MDR kcal/person) averaged over men, women, and children is estimated at 2000 (cf. Lee 1979, where caloric *production* by the Dobe !Kung is calculated at 2355 kcal/person/day).

late April (though steelhead and suckers might be running by March and some whitefish might be caught on a line through the ice in winter). High water made fishing impossible from late May to late June in the main river, leaving five months for salmon fishing. However, the runs often peaked for only a few days at a time, with desultory results between. Takes of several hundred fish in a day per fisherman—as have been reported for the Indian fishery—could have been achieved for only a few days each year. A full-time specialization in salmon fishing would thus have been an inefficient use of resources. Such specialization would have required the neglect of the equally abundant edible roots and berries, the well-loved bitterroots, lomatiums, camas, and huckleberries. Except in early spring, such roots and berries are found at a considerable distance from the river. The cost of such a mixed strategy of resource use is high mobility; the benefit is a nutritionally more diverse and reliable economic base.

Sahaptin speakers know their salmon well. They may speak of "anadromous salmonids" in general, that is, of núsux̣, or they may speak of each species in turn (see Table 14). Note that steelhead—anadromous rainbow or cutthroat trout, not true Pacific salmon—are included in the general category núsux̣, while their stay-at-home cousins, the trout (aytmín), are not. In this the Sahaptin folk taxonomy differs from that of the western scientist, but only in recognizing the cultural equivalence of steelhead and salmon, a consequence of their extraordinary size and anadromous habits. This point of cultural difference with white fishermen—for whom the steelhead is a sacred fighting fish and as distinct from a salmon as a deer is from a cow— has created considerable ill-will and misunderstanding.

Sahaptin goes further, however, in distinguishing the jack salmon (most often a small variety of Chinook that spawns a year ahead of schedule) as tkʷilát-tkʷilat, literally, "little Chinook salmon." Otis Shiloh, an octogenarian from the Naches area, further sets apart two varieties of tkʷínat that spawn up the Naches River. A dark variety spawns on the gravels of the Tieton River, while the paler variety returns to the lighter colored sands of the American River. Charles Darwin might have profited from a conversation with Mr. Shiloh! A further complication is the use in Sahaptin of a single term, mitúla, to refer both to the dog salmon species (*Oncorhynchus keta*), which now rarely penetrates past Bonneville Dam, and to the post-spawning life-stage of salmon in general, both characterized by pale or "white" flesh (hence, "white salmon").

The cultural importance of salmon is recognized ritually and in myth, as is

TABLE 14

Sahaptin Fish Taxonomy

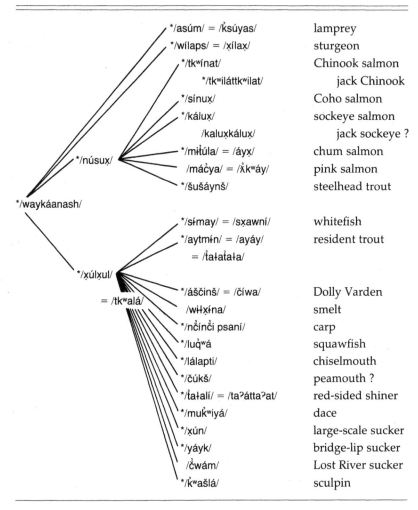

*/asúm/ = /k̓súyas/	lamprey
*/wílaps/ = /x̱ílax̱/	sturgeon
*/tkʷínat/	Chinook salmon
*/tkʷiláttkʷilat/	jack Chinook
*/sínux̱/	Coho salmon
*/kálux̱/	sockeye salmon
/kalux̱kálux̱/	jack sockeye ?
*/mɨłúla/ = /áyx̱/	chum salmon
/mác̓ya/ = /x̓kʷáy/	pink salmon
*/šušáynš/	steelhead trout
*/sɨmay/ = /sx̱awní/	whitefish
*/aytmɨn/ = /ayáy/	resident trout
= /łałałała/	
*/áščinš/ = /číwa/	Dolly Varden
/wɨłx̱ɨna/	smelt
*/nčínči psaní/	carp
*/luq̓ʷá	squawfish
*/lálapti/	chiselmouth
*/čúkš/	peamouth ?
*/łałalí/ = /taʔáttaʔat/	red-sided shiner
*/mukʷiyá/	dace
*/x̱ún/	large-scale sucker
*/yáyk/	bridge-lip sucker
/č̓wám/	Lost River sucker
*/k̓ʷašlá/	sculpin

*/núsux̱/

*/waykáanash/

*/x̱úlx̱ul/

= /tkʷalá/

Note: Terms in the repertoire of James Selam are marked *. Dialect variant equivalent terms are indicated by =. Minor phonological variants are not cited here. A question mark indicates that the term or its gloss is inadequately established.

Reprinted from Hunn 1980:9, courtesy of *Northwest Anthropological Research Notes.*

the case also for suckers (see below). Today the mid-spring longhouse feasts are dedicated to both roots and salmon. In the past, I am told, each seasonal resource was welcomed separately. Erna Gunther describes a traditional salmon renewal ceremony (1926, 1928) that was celebrated in one form or another throughout the Pacific salmon's range. At The Dalles and Celilo the First Salmon Ceremony is less elaborate than among coastal groups. Lewis and Clark observed the ceremony on April 19, 1806, at a Wishram village just above The Dalles:

> There was great joy with the natives last night in consequence of the arrival of the Salmon; one of those fish was caught; this was the harbinger of good news to them. They informed us that these fish would arrive in great quantities in the course of about 5 days. this fish was dressed and being divided into small pieces was given to each child in the village. this custom is founded in superstitious opinion that it will hasten the arrival of the salmon (Thwaites 1959 [1904], 4:300)

Henry Perkins witnessed a somewhat more elaborate ritual among the Sahaptin-speaking residents of wayám at Celilo Falls sometime before 1843:

> . . . the "tu-a-ti-ma" [twáti-ma, "Indian doctors"]—or medicine men—as they are sometimes called by the whites—practice a sort of invocatory ceremony on the first arrival of the salmon in the spring. Before any of the common people are permitted to boil, or even to cut the flesh of the salmon transversely for any purpose, the "tu-a-ti" [twáti]—medicine man of the village, assembles the people, & after invoking the "Tah" [taax] or the particular spirit which presides over the salmon, & who they suppose can make it a prosperous year or otherwise, takes a fish just caught, & wrings off its head. The blood, which flows from the fish, he catches in a basin, or small dish, & sets it aside. He then cuts the salmon transversly into small pieces, & boils. The way is thus opened for any one else to do the same. Joy & rejoicing circulate through the village, & the people now boil & eat to their heart's content.
>
> But I wish to call your attention to the *blood*. This is considered to be "aut-ni" [áwt-ni]—or as we should say sacred, or hallowed, or sanctified, i.e., it is sacredly set apart & carefully garded for five days, when it is carried out, waved in the direction in which they wish the fish to run, & then carefully poured into the water." (Perkins n.d. [1838–1843], Book 1:7)

James Selam recalls only that a strong swimmer was chosen to swim out above the falls with the remains of the first fish caught, where he dove deep to deposit it in mid-river as an invitation to its fellows to come upriver also.

At major fishing sites such as Celilo and Kettle Falls, a salmon chief had authority to open and close fishing on an annual and a daily basis. Such salmon chiefs were considered distinct from the miyúux, or village chiefs.

Tommy Thompson (Indian name: láwat, "Belly"), a wayam-łáma, served in this capacity at Celilo Falls until The Dalles Dam flooded the site in 1957. He inherited the post from his paternal uncle, Stockely (stáqułay). Fishing was closed each night until late the following morning—James says this was done to allow some salmon to escape—and was shut down to honor the dead during funerals. Sunday fishing was also interdicted. These restrictions were increasingly difficult to enforce owing to the breakdown of traditional social relations and the influx of non-local Indians and whites in the twentieth century (Relander 1962).

Coyote brought salmon to the river people during his mythical peregrinations (cf. Beavert 1974:34–38; Ramsey 1977:47–49). Five sisters had blocked their migration with a dam. Coyote heard of this while traveling down the river and decided to do something about it. Coyote was, of course, too well known to approach the sisters directly, so he turned himself into a baby strapped on a cradle board and set himself adrift on the river. Soon he lodged up against the sisters' dam where he was discovered by the youngest of the five. "Oh, look at the poor baby," they all cried, and took him home with them. Next day they all set off to go root digging in the hills (a realistic ethnographic detail), leaving the child.

As soon as they were safely out of sight Coyote turned himself back into his real self and set to work. He made himself five (the Plateau *pattern number*) digging sticks (kápin) and five oak-burl mortars (łáluš). He then attacked the dam with the first digging stick. For four days he worked, each day with a new kápin, stopping only as the sisters approached the village. On the fifth day, as the sisters were digging roots, the youngest's digging stick broke. This being an ill omen, they all dashed back to the village suspecting that something was amiss with the baby. Sure enough!

They found Coyote hard at work with his last kápin, breaking up their dam. Coyote quickly put on the first oak mortar as a helmet to ward off the sisters' attack. They broke first one, then the second, third, and fourth. But Coyote was nearly through the dam, which gave way in a flood just as the fifth mortar helmet cracked. The sisters were defeated and the salmon swam up to join the people. Thereafter, the sisters, as *swallows* (James Selam describes their mud nests, suggesting that the cliff or barn swallow is the type he has in mind), must signal the return of Chinook salmon each spring. Coyote's work is evident at Celilo Falls, where the rock outcroppings from which the Indians fished, each meticulously named, represent the remnants of the Swallow Sisters' dam (see fig. 5.3). Further upriver, among the Okanagan Salish, we find virtually the same story, but with spotted sandpiper sisters (R. Bouchard, personal communication). Both swallows and spotted sandpipers arrive early in spring and frequent the river shores, giving conspicuous testimony to the season.

Suckers

Two very similar species of suckers are common, the large-scale sucker (*Catostomus macrocheilus;* x̲uun) and the bridge-lip sucker (*C. columbianus;* yayk) (see fig. 5.4). Both spawn in late winter or early spring in small tributary streams of the Columbia and Yakima rivers such as Rock and Satus creeks in Washington. At the turn of the nineteenth century they were caught in willow basket traps set in a stone weir designed to force the migrating fish to the center of the stream where the strong current might push them back into the trap. They were also snagged, the preferred technique today. A large, three-pronged hook on a line, a good eye for distance, and a quick hand are what is needed. As many as fifty might be snagged in an hour's work from pools where the fish rest on their upstream course. A sample of large-scale suckers taken from Rock Creek in this fashion in March 1977, averaged two pounds and eighteen inches for the females (loaded with eggs) and one pound and twelve inches for the males. Though suckers are considered "trash fish" by non-Indians and fisheries officials and are systematically eliminated by rotenone poisoning to make way for "game fish," the Indians still value them highly, placing them nearly on a par with salmon.

Why this respect for a lowly bottomfish, full of tetrahedral bones? For one they are tasty and readily captured (with little "sport" involved, of course). Primarily, however, because they provided a reliable "break fast" as the first fresh fish available after months on dried rations. The late February and March runs precede the spring Chinook bounty by two full months. If winter rations were low, such a food resource might make the critical difference between survival and famine. Lewis and Clark's journal records that in late April of 1806 the Indians at The Dalles and Celilo Falls were impatiently awaiting the first salmon of the season, "subsisting [meanwhile] primarily on 'mullet' " (Thwaites 1959 [1904], 4:290, 328), a vernacular term for suckers.

The Indians' respect for these fish is exemplified by a special thanksgiving

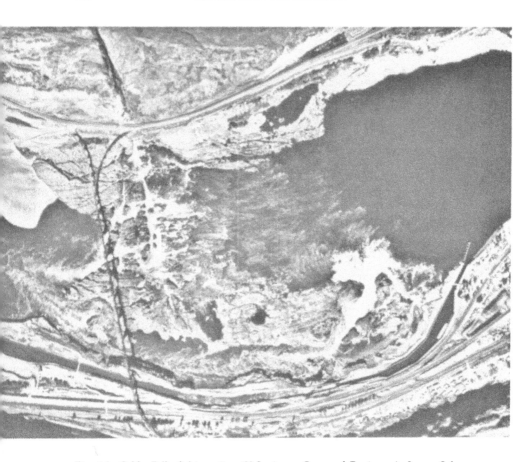

Fig. 5.3. Celilo Falls fishing sites (U.S. Army Corps of Engineers). James Selam named and located these sites in 1987. His family belonged to the community at *sḱin* so he claimed limited knowledge of the fishing places on the Oregon side. He described how he and other children (in the 1920s) used to fish at *tíčas,* one of his family's sites.

The village was built on the rocks above the sandy beach at the foot of the falls. There were many drying sheds (*tyáwtaš*) there. *Sḱin* people seined off the sandy beach and set a gillnet just below *núšnu.* This net was 300–500 feet long and the catch was shared by all families of the village. The village women worked together to make the long net. The *walawála* area was a high water fishing site. At *tayxaytpamá,* a bed of pale flat stones under clear water facilitated spear fishing. At *sapawilalatatpamá,* the river fell 8 to 10 feet. Fishermen held their dipnets below the falls in order to catch the leaping salmon. Drying sheds were set up in summer on *amáwi* (later known as "Big Island" by Wayam (i.e., Celilo) fishermen). The materials and gear were brought across by canoe or boat. *Awxanáyčaš* ("standing place") was a site where seven men stood in a line dipping into the rushing current (the whole island was subsequently

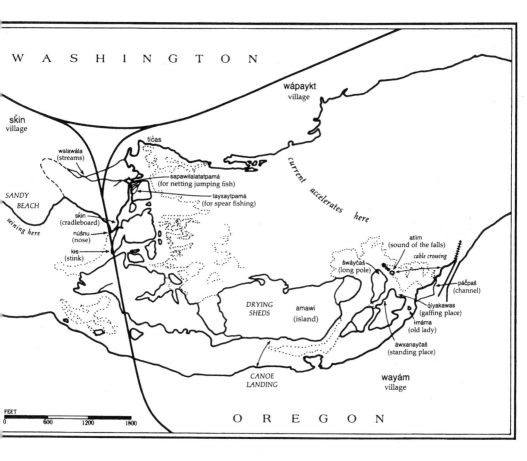

named "Standing Island"). In the early days it was necessary to swim from *awχanáyčaš* to reach *šwáyčaš*. A dipnet on a long pole (over 20 feet long) was needed to reach the current here.

This site belonged to Chief Tommy Thompson's family and thus the island came to be known as "Chief Island." The rock called *atíim* stood at the very lip of the falls. In the early 1930s it came to be called "Albert's Island" after the family that claimed it then. It was accessible at low water by boat, though a cable was stretched across to it from Taffe's fishwheel early in this century. *Páčpaš* was the location of several high-water fishing sites. It was a narrow channel favored for catching "eels," apparently the same as that known as Downes' Channel. The current here turned the best of Taffe's fishwheels (Donaldson and Cramer 1972:110). "Old lady" rock was tabooed.

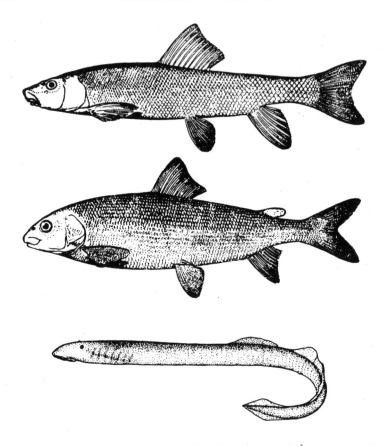

Fig. 5.4. Sucker (x̱uun), whitefish (sɫmay), and lamprey "eel" (k̓súyas or asúm) (reprinted from *Sierra Nevada Natural History*, Storer and Usinger, with permission of the University of California Press; © 1963 The Regents of the University of California).

feast at the Rock Creek longhouse, now held jointly with that for the first Indian celeries (see above), and by a popular myth that recounts how Sucker—shattered by a fall from the sky—was revived and rehabilitated with bones contributed by many other animals so that people might catch them and enjoy them. The sucker's skull is unusual in that its component bones never completely fuse. When cooked, these oddly-shaped bones come apart, providing the Indian storyteller all the opportunity needed to recount the mythical source and identity of each bone: "Grizzly's earrings," "Raven's socks," "Cricket packing her child," "Bluejay," and even the "Soft-basket-woman monster" (Hunn 1980; see fig. 5.5).

Soft-Basket Woman Monster

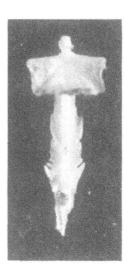

Cricket packing her child

Raven's socks

Steller's jay

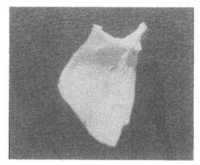

Grizzly's earring

Fig. 5.5. Sucker's head bones.

Eels

The creature known in the local vernacular as the "eel" is a lamprey, a primitive cartilaginous fish with sucking mouthparts and a parasitic way of life (see fig. 5.4, above). (True eels, such as the moray, are unknown in the river.) In Sahaptin it has two names: k̓súyas is preferred above Rock Creek; asúm (asm̓ at Warm Springs) is more familiar below the creek and on the Yakima River. In the Great Lakes, sea lampreys (*Petromyzon marinus*) recently have become a serious pest by heavily parasitizing local lake trout (*Salvelinus namaycush*). They attach themselves to the fish by means of sucker mouths, using their rasplike teeth to lacerate the trout's flesh, then suck its blood.

The situation on the Columbia River is quite different. Here both salmon and "eel"—at least the large anadromous Pacific lamprey (*Entosphenus tridentatus*)—feed only at sea, using their accumulated fat reserves to power their migration home to their ancestral spawning beds. So lamprey and salmon coexist peacefully in the Columbia.

"Eels" are considered a delicacy by local Indians (see fig. 5.6). The Indians have always appreciated their rich fat flesh and harvested them in quantity at favored sites. They were spitted over an open fire just as were salmon, though a smaller size stake (pátpas) of the dense wood of the mock orange (*Philadelphus lewisii*; sáxi) was cut for this purpose. Surplus eels were dried in a shed over alder smoke or by the hot dry winds that blow down the Columbia gorge in summer. For best results the eels were cut in an aesthetic geometric pattern, then spread with cedar splints.

Columbia River people still enjoy eating eels but find it difficult to locate a place to catch them. Holding an eel is like holding a large snake; their strength is uncanny, and in the water they are strong swimmers despite their unfishlike shape. They are most readily caught at rapids and low falls where they are forced to "crawl" up the sides of the rocky channels against the powerful currents using their sucker mouths as feet. Here and in the eddies below such rapids they may be dip-netted easily. Eel fishing is a nighttime activity, when eels are inching their way up the rapids under cover of darkness.

Until the early 1970s, parties had regularly gone to Bonneville Dam in June and July to net eels, but officials there have recently denied access, complaining of interference with their dam operations. Willamette Falls at Oregon City south of Portland is still open but requires a long, arduous trip

Fig. 5.6. James Selam with eel.

from Yakima or Warm Springs. (Warm Springs Indians can still get eels at Sherar's Bridge on the Deschutes River.) My only opportunity to observe eel fishing firsthand was with James Selam in early June 1985 when we visited Rainbow Falls State Park on the upper Chehalis River, a site he knew of by reputation but which he had never visited. The park manager reported that Indians from the nearby Chehalis reservation still fished there for lamprey on occasion and that there were no regulations prohibiting such fishing. Lamprey are certainly not game fish, nor have commercial interests discovered them, thus Indians may seek this traditional delicacy in peace.

We had just a few hours to spare and found only a few eels, managing to net one good-sized individual. It measured twenty-four inches and weighed in at twelve ounces, which James considered about average. Eels are most abundant just after the early summer high water. In fact, a squall the night before our visit to Rainbow Falls roiled the waters and added to the difficulty of locating and catching them.

Lamprey, like their distant shark relatives, have gill slits or pores rather than true gills. There are normally seven slits, although freaks are said to occur with just five slits, the sacred number. To catch such an abberation is an ill omen, and such eels turn into snakes. I see this holy aversion to violations of nature's predictable patterns as a nearly universal human response, and an aversion that may ultimately be adaptive. Monstrosities, the unexpected creatures that violate our well-founded expectations of nature's patterns, might prove to be unpredictable as well in their behavior or in their physiological effects. "Better safe than sorry!"

Other Fish

Suckers, eels, and salmon provided the bulk of the fish traditionally consumed by the river people, but the rest were by no means despised. Table 14 shows how each indigenous fish species was named in some of the river dialects (see also Appendix 1). The language lacked a general term for fish, other than the descriptive phrase "underwater swimmer" (yɨtkʷanayti-ɬá; cf. Everette n.d. [1883]) or the term waykáanaš, used for fish as food in a ritual context. Fish were grouped by Columbia River Indians as either núsux, "salmon," or x̱úl-x̱ul, "small fish," a term apparently a diminutive of x̱uun, "large-scale sucker." At Warm Springs, by contrast, small fish were lumped with trout under the term tkʷalá. I suspect that trout surpassed suckers in value in the foothill country at Warm Springs.

Trout and red-sided shiners were caught by hook-and-line in mountain streams. James Selam demonstrated this technique for me on a June trip to the Blue Mountains in 1977. He took a short stretch of leader (originally the line was of horse-hair or hemp), attached a small metal hook (in the old days made of bone), then turned over a few streamside stones until he found the case of the caddisfly larva (Trichoptera; x̱amɬúy). He deftly extracted the worm-like inhabitant, slipped it on his hook, and dangled it in the stream. In less than a minute he had hooked a three-inch shiner (*Richardsonius balteatus*; paɬa-ɬí). A few minutes' work before breakfast added interest to a meal of roots.

If čalúkš (*Lomatium dissectum;* see fig. 4.11) were found growing nearby—and it is frequent on steep talus slopes on lower canyon walls—a fish poisoning party might be organized. Several of the large roots mashed on streamside rocks to produce a soapy juice that spread into a pool held behind a rough dam would stun whatever fish were in the pool. The fishermen would take those they wanted and let the rest revive as the current flushed out the poison. Mountain whitefish (*Prosopium williamsoni;* sɨmay; see fig. 5.4 above), one of few fresh fish available at that season, were hooked in winter through the river ice.

Not all fish were considered edible. Curiously, mid-Columbia River people disdained the mighty sturgeon (as Lewis and Clark noted, Thwaites 1959 [1904], 4:290), source of fine caviar and sought after by Indian fishermen on the lower Columbia and Fraser rivers. James Selam considers the sturgeon to be a "trash fish," to borrow a term modern fisheries managers apply to native fish of little sport or commercial value. The fact that sturgeon had the nickname, nayšɨa-nmí kákya, literally, the swallowing monster's pet, suggests another interpretation. The mythical nayšɨá, the "Swallower," terrorized the River's residents in the myth age, lurking in the River's deepest hole and swallowing all who came near. Wily Coyote came to the rescue. He induced nayšɨá to swallow him by taunting the monster with unflattering remarks and challenging it to a swallowing contest, which Coyote, of course, lost. Once inside the monster's belly—like Jonah in the whale—Coyote rallied the captive animals and built a fire beneath the beast's heart, then began to cut the heart from its moorings. Suffering great gastric distress, the Swallower evicted its tenants before exploding. (See Beavert 1974:28–31 and Ramsey 1977:9–12 for other versions of this popular tale.) Contemporary Indians of the River identify the Swallower's haunt as the deep pool in the Columbia opposite and just above the mouth of the Deschutes River near the tip of Miller Island, three miles above the old village of skin. Modern charts show a depth here of 164 feet, which puts the bottom a few feet below sea level.

Perhaps the huge bulk of old sturgeon (see fig. 5.7)—the record size on the Columbia River is 12½ feet long and 1,285 pounds (Wydoski and Whitney 1979:18)—and their scavenging habits suggested the possibility that one could—as did its mythological master—swallow a human (cf. Marshall 1977:42). Thus, by the logic of indirect cannibalism, its flesh was abhorrent, just as was the meat of grizzly bear to Plateau peoples. A similar logic may account for an aversion expressed by River people for eating the Dolly

Fig. 5.7. A giant sturgeon (**wílaps**) (Relander Collection, Yakima Valley Regional Library).

Varden char (*Salvelinus malmo;* áščinš). Frogs and mice have reportedly been found in the stomachs of Dolly Vardens, another case of "eating-up," that is, an animal consuming another animal perceived to be closer on the scale of relatedness to humans, a justification for food taboos found throughout the world (cf. Simoons 1961).

Other aquatic species were and are spared because of their spiritual powers. The Columbia River system is home to a taxonomically complex set of sculpin populations (*Cottus* spp.) representing at least eight species. All closely resemble one another in their bull-heads, large full-lipped mouths, and prickly leathery skin (see fig. 5.8), and all are known as k̓ʷašlá. Most are just a few inches long, but all are respected as Indian doctors and weather-changers. I trapped one at Alder Creek one winter day and brought it home to a small aquarium in my house near Toppenish. The aquarium already contained about a dozen native minnows (dace, *Rhinichthys* spp.; muk̓ʷiyá) I had trapped in the irrigation ditch that ran in front of the house. The sculpin immediately took command of the tank, perching on a prominent rock, its rigid spiny pectoral fins used like hands to hold onto its rock perch. All the minnows hid in whatever shelter they could find, and I scarcely saw them for as long as the sculpin ruled the tank.

James Selam warned me that keeping the k̓ʷašlá captive was ill advised and he noted how cold and drear the weather had become since I first got him. Not wishing to tempt fate, I decided to return the sculpin to its native stream, though this meant a drive of some fifty miles. The day after his release the sun appeared on the heels of a warm Chinook wind! Crayfish (k̓astilá) are also treated as Indian doctors, perhaps in recognition of the formidable appearance they share with the sculpins.

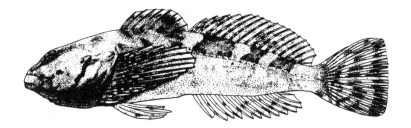

Fig. 5.8. Sculpin or "bullhead" (*Cottus confusus;* k̓ʷašlá) (reprinted from Bailey and Bond 1963:111).

A last river denizen's story needs telling, that of the fresh water mussel (*Margaritifera falcata* and relatives; x̣ístú, NWS: siwáala). Elders recall eating these mollusks, which grow to large size in concentrated masses where river bottom and current conditions are favorable. No one to my knowledge bothers with them today and the knowledge of where to find them and how to harvest and prepare them is being lost. Archaeologists have found deep shell middens at the sites of many old villages, indicating that they once formed an important part of the Plateau diet (Lyman 1984). It may have been the case that villages were strategically located near mussel beds so that they might be harvested to stave off late winter famine.

Herps

"Herps" is a shorthand term derived from "herpetology," the study of reptiles and amphibians. It is used to refer to that otherwise awkwardly labeled category of creatures, as well as, in the form of a verb, the activity of seeking such animals out, as in "herping," i.e., to go out looking for herps. No herps have ever been eaten by Plateau Indians, nor are any reptiles and amphibian species otherwise utilized, though Columbia River Indians tell tales about them, name places for them, and accord them respect. Extraordinary respect is granted the rattlesnake; he is given wide berth as a powerful Indian doctor. Equal respect, but with less an undercurrent of fear, is accorded the diminutive short-horned lizard (*Phrynosoma douglassi*; x̣liłá-wit; see fig. 5.9). He is considered to be a pamispamisi-łá, a variety of Indian doctor who heals by blowing healing breath on the diseased part of the body. If mistreated, Horned Lizard will send bad weather.

Sahaptin herpetological terminology is similar to that of the English vernacular in its generality, perhaps reflecting the limited utility of this class of animal, or as a consequence of a progressive loss of terminological detail by recent generations of native speakers (see Appendix 1). For example, contemporary speakers lump all snakes together as pyuš, with the single exception noted above of the rattler (waxpúš; *Crotalus viridis*). Word lists from early in this century, however, suggest that other types of snake were also named. At that time, the term pyuš may have referred specifically to the abundant garter snakes or it could have been used generically. Melville Jacobs' unpublished field notes cite separate terms for snakes that I suspect are the rubber boa, racer, California mountain king snake, and

Fig. 5.9. Horned lizard (*Phrynosoma douglassi;* xliławit) (reprinted from *Sierra Nevada Natural History,* Storer and Usinger, with permission of the University of California Press; © 1963 The Regents of the University of California).

ring-necked snake, while several scholars have noted special terms for the gopher snake.

Invertebrates

Contemporary Sahaptin speakers recognize some fifty named types of invertebrates (see Appendix 1), including in their vocabulary terms for such diverse creatures as snails, clams, crayfish, horsehair worms, beetles (five distinct kinds), crickets and grasshoppers (five kinds), fleas, flies, ants, wasps, lice, ticks, spiders, scorpions, and centipedes. Other than the freshwater clams noted above and saltwater clams obtained through trade, none was eaten. Crayfish were shunned as food because of their status as Indian doctors, in that respect resembling the bullhead fish. Several types of aquatic insect larvae contributed to the diet indirectly as fish bait, including caddisfly larvae and two others I have not yet been able to identify positively, called úšʔuš and papsiá (most likely larval neuropterans) (see fig. 5.10). Some invertebrates have names that are imaginatively descriptive. Horsehair worms (Aschelminthes, order Gordioidea) are called nawinała-nmí šuu, that is, "Thunder's whiskers," alluding to their seemingly mysterious appearance in pools

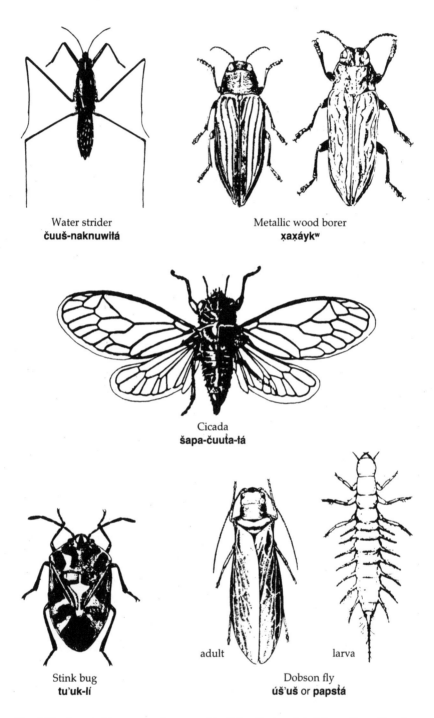

Water strider
čuuš-naknuwiɫá

Metallic wood borer
x̣ax̣áykʷ

Cicada
šapa-čuuɫa-ɫá

adult   larva

Stink bug
tuʾuk-lí

Dobson fly
úšʾuš or **papsɫá**

Fig. 5.10. Assorted insect species named in Sahaptin (reprinted from *Sierra Nevada Natural History*, Storer and Usinger, with permission of the University of California Press; © 1963 The Regents of the University of California).

of rainwater after storms. Metallic word-boring beetles (Coleoptera, family Buprestidae) are called "silver" or "money" (x̱ax̱áykʷ; see fig. 5.10). They may be kept as "pets" for good luck in gambling. One that I found was a brilliant shimmering metallic blue-green (the golden buprestid, *Buprestis aurulenta*). Elsie Pistolhead judged it to be a "male." Another of a dull brownish color she judged a "female" (perhaps a species of *Chalcophora*).

Water striders (Hemiptera, family Gerridae) are called čuuš naknuwi-ɬá, "guardians of the water" (see fig. 5.10). Stinkbugs (Coleoptera, family Pentatomidae; fig. 5.10) are tuʔuk-lí (literally, "stinking"). Centipedes and millipedes are wux̱a-putaaptit-ní, "hundred-legged ones." Cicadas (Homoptera, family Cicadidae; fig. 5.10) are known to some as šapa-čuu-ɬa-ɬá, "thirst makers," calling to mind the burning heat of summer days when the cicadas are at full throttle.

The great diversity of invertebrate species requires that terms cover a wide range of specific types. Examples include wax̱alx̱alí for spiders, atníwa for bees and wasps, kliwisá for ants, and mux̱láy for flies. Species or forms of special note within the normal range of these general designations may be singled out for special nomenclature recognition. The black widow spider (*Latrodectus* spp.) is considered to be not a "spider" (wax̱alx̱alí), but a tišpún, something quite different; that is, the large, deadly female is so-called, while the small yellowish male—which mates with its monstrous consort at considerable personal peril—is tispúl-tispul ("little black widow"). Bumblebees are contrasted with the run of honey bees, yellowjackets, hornets, and wasps as lawašmúk. A tiny black ant variety is distinguished from the majority of ants as tamšúy; I don't yet know why. Horse flies are distinguished as ištx̱ní, while the smaller but equally vicious deer fly is istx̱lí-istx̱li ("little horse fly"). Gnats may be called mux̱láy-mux̱lay ("little fly").

When fine distinctions are required, they are clearly drawn. Head lice are apín; the larger, gray body louse is apúlk. Scientists classify these as distinct subspecies of the human louse species, *Pediculus humanus*, a pan-human scourge that apparently hitchhiked across the Bering Strait land bridge. A great variety of minute free-living larvae are lumped as apíl-apíl ("little lice").

The significance of insects as environmental features is notable in place names such as wawayáš ("place of mosquitoes"), a high meadow near Mount Adams, and apúlk (literally, "body louse") for a louse-infested fishing site on an island opposite Rock Creek, Washington. Tick and mosquito (áčpɬ-yay and wawa-yáy) are mythological cannibals, reduced at Coyote's command to pests that are with us to this day.

Plants

Indian Celeries

Indian celeries (hahán) are eagerly sought in spring, now as in the past. The first to appear along the mid-Columbia are the sprouts of *Lomatium grayi*. (*Lomatium salmoniflorum* plays this role for the Nez Perces on the Snake River, and the sprouts of *Lomatium dissectum* are substituted by Interior Salish Indian people.) Since these sprouts are dug up with the digging stick, they are not strictly speaking a kind of hahán ("stem"), but are included in the next category of plant resources to be considered, x̣nit ("plant foods that are dug"). They are available in February and March, and a special thanksgiving feast is held at the Rock Creek longhouse to celebrate the onset of their harvest. Eaten raw, they are crisp with a lively peppery flavor. It takes about 125 sprouts—a quantity produced by a half-dozen individual plants—to make a 100-gram serving. Such a serving contains 15 milligrams of Vitamin C, about one third of currently recommended daily dietary allowances.

As the season progresses, Gray's lomatium loses its appeal and is replaced in the diet by the stalks and stems of *Lomatium nudicaule*, known as x̣amsí. The leaf stalks of x̣amsí are also relished, but are distinguished as p̓íš-p̓íš. Fifty-six young stems of the bare-stemmed lomatium make a 100-gram serving worth 66 milligrams of Vitamin C, well over the daily recommended dose of 45 milligrams. When the bare-stemmed lomatium stalks dry out by mid-May, substitutes that grow higher in the mountains are found: the stalks of the abundant balsamroot "sunflowers" (*Balsamorhiza careyana/B. sagitatta*; pášx̣aš; see fig. 5.11) that carpet the dry hills in May; those of its relative, the mule's ear (*Wyethia amplexicaulis*; pii; NWS: piik), that favor wet swales; and high in the mountains, the thick succulent stalks of cow's parsnip (*Heracleum lanatum*: CRS, NWS: tx̣u). Cow's parsnip must be carefully peeled, for the skin of the stalk is armed with irritating hairs (Kuhnlein and Turner 1986). A high meadow on the Cowlitz-Tieton divide—a favorite summer camping and berry-picking ground for Northwest Sahaptins—was known as tx̣ú-waš ("cow's parsnip place").

Plants Dug for Food

This is a category of plants defined by the action employed in their harvest, x̣ni- ("to dig food plants"). Closely linked are the essential tools, the

Fig. 5.11. Balsamroot "sunflower" (*Balsamorhiza careyana;* **pášxaš**).

kápɨn, or digging stick, and the wápas, or food collecting bag/basket, hung from a tie around the waist. The term x̱nit indicates not only the edible portion dug up for food but the whole plant as well. Most such plants are small, herbaceous, spring-flowering species. The edible parts may be true tubers, corms, bulbs, tuberous roots, even underground sprouts, distinctions relevant to the botanist but of no great moment for the Indian food gatherer. At least twenty-five species are known. X̱nit also defines a season, as all such plants are harvested between March and July. Tmaaní-t ("plants picked for food") by contrast represent the food-collecting activities of late summer and fall. X̣ni- is a transitive verb stem taking the particular species as direct object: Aw kutas á-x̣ni-x̣a-na piyax̣í-na x̣ʷyayč-mí-pa ("And then we used to dig bitterroot at Sweat-Lodge-Place") (from a text by Sara Quaempts, June 1986).

Any Sahaptin speaker can name the most "famous" root foods:

bitterroot	piyax̣í
camas	x̣maaš or wákamu
cous	x̣awš (fig. 5.12)
Lomatium canbyi	lukš
"Indian carrot,"	sawítk (fig. 5.13)
Perideridia gairdneri	

Several additional species, somewhat less widely recognized and highly regarded, are still frequently sought by root diggers:

"Indian potato,"	anipáš (fig. 5.14)
Claytonia lanceolata	
Lomatium piperi	mámɨn
Lomatium grayi	latít-latit
Brodiaea hyacinthina	sɨt̓x̣ʷs (fig. 5.15)
yellowbell,	sɨkni (fig. 5.16)
Fritillaria pudica	
Lomatium macrocarpum	púɬa

Others are highly localized and closely associated with the people who live within their range:

Lomatium canbyi/part	škúlkul, Priest Rapids only
Tauschia hooveri	pank̓ú, Yakima only
Lomatium "hambleniae"	max̣š-ní, Priest Rapids only
Calochortus macrocarpus	nuunás, winter root of deserts
Lomatium minus	nak̓únk, John Day and Umatilla only

The most knowledgeable elders can recall as well rarely used species that were once valued more highly:

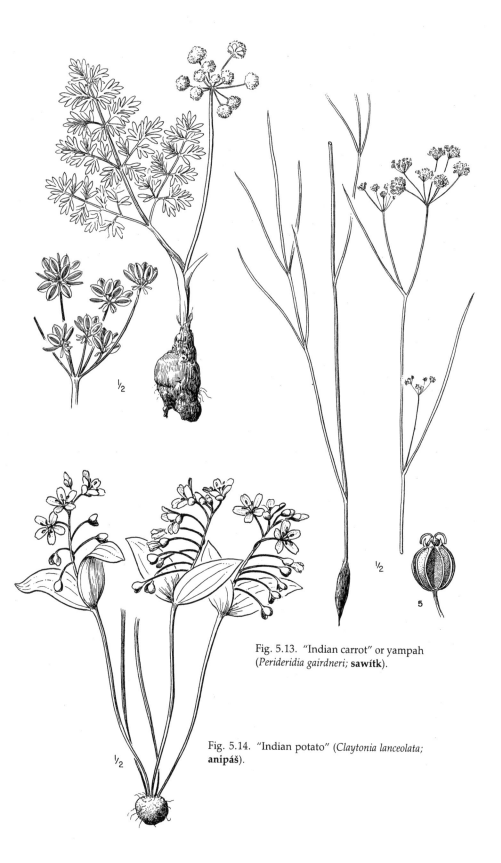

Fig. 5.13. "Indian carrot" or yampah (*Perideridia gairdneri;* **sawítk**).

Fig. 5.14. "Indian potato" (*Claytonia lanceolata;* **anipáš**).

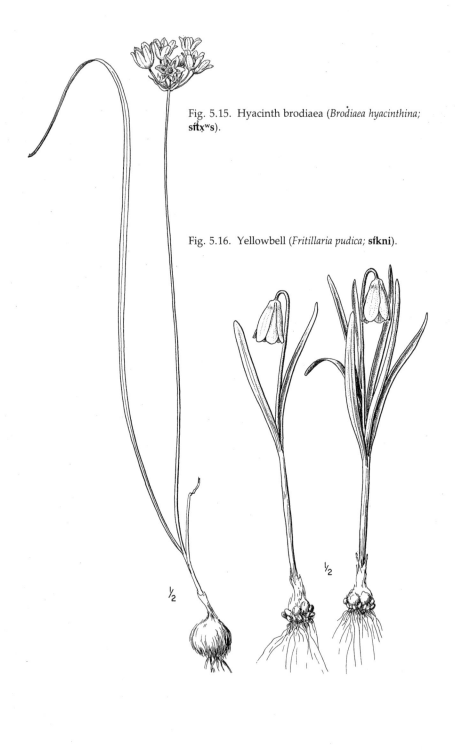

Fig. 5.15. Hyacinth brodiaea (*Brodiaea hyacinthina;* sƛ̓x̌ʷs).

Fig. 5.16. Yellowbell (*Fritillaria pudica;* sɫkni).

½

½

Brodiaea howellii/B. douglasii	anałpípi
Lomatium farinosum	nikaptát, Nez Perce and Palus only
Microseris troximoides	mɨčúna, a "false dandelion"
yellow avalanche lily,	hʷíkʷk
Erythronium grandiflorum	
Lomatium gormanii	sasamíła, like mámɨn but less palatable
Osmorhiza occidentalis	siwíw, more for seasoning than for food value
tiger lily, *Lilium columbianum*	pananát
Valeriana edulis	k̓ʷíya, a strong smelling root
Balsamorhiza hookeri	p̓líwa, tough and stringy
Perideridia sp.	mank, like sawítk but different

The contribution of root staples to the food energy needs of the mid-Columbia Indians may be estimated in several ways. In each case it is necessary to assess:

1. the total weight, in kilograms (one kilogram = 2.2 pounds), of roots of various species harvested by a family each year; we may assume that one adult woman digs roots for herself and three other dependent family members;

2. the edible fraction of that harvest; between 5 and 10 percent of the weight of the roots brought home is lost in cleaning and peeling them;

3. the caloric value per kilogram of each major staple, as prepared for consumption; and

4. the amount of calories available per capita per day averaged over the year; this assumes that such foods may be stored without loss of food energy value.

It is also helpful to measure the quantity of plant food available on each hectare (one hectare = 2.5 acres) of productive land and the distribution of root plant habitat within the range of each village. The total quantities harvested may be estimated from ethnohistorical or ethnographic reports, as for example: "I saw a young woman at the Skitsoe village [Coeur d'Alene] who had collected and prepared sixty sacks of good Gamas [*Camassia quamash*], each sack containing 1⅕ bushel; she was spoken of in the best terms throughout the village" (Geyer [1845–46], quoted in Hart 1976:49).

Several such reports suggest that Indian women could pick approximately a "bushel" of roots in a day's work. Though a "bushel" is scarcely a precise unit of volume, it has been standardized recently as equal to 60 pounds (27 kilograms) of potatoes, a commodity quite comparable to the Indian roots (Webster's *New Collegiate Dictionary*, 1956, p. 521).

An independent assessment of root harvests is based on actual time-and-motion studies of root digging by contemporary Indian women. I have clocked them at 330 to 360 roots per hour for *Lomatium canbyi* and *L. cous*, which at approximately 10 grams per tuber (net weight) comes to 3.5 kilograms per hour or 28 kilograms for an eight-hour day, nearly identical to the figure of a bushel a day reported by early observers.

But how many days' work is available for root-digging each year? As I have noted, roots are harvestable for only a short time at any given locality and elevation, a few weeks at best, due to the plants' maturational cycle. However, by moving camp to progressively higher elevations as spring advances, the harvest season for roots can be extended from March through June. Let us assign the conservative figure of sixty days for root digging, which allows time off for processing roots and fish, for camp maintenance, and for travel. Each woman could thus harvest 60 bushels of roots for her family, or some 400 kilograms per capita for the year.

Staple root foods of the mid-Columbia Indians vary from 900 calories per kilogram for bitterroot to 1,270 for cous. A thousand calories per kilogram seems a conservative average figure for the energy value of these roots, yielding a grand total of 400,000 calories per capita per year or 1,100 calories per man, woman, and child daily throughout the year.

To this we may add the camas harvest, as that normally took place after the bitterroot and lomatium season was spent. If an additional ten bushels of camas are allowed (readily harvested in two weeks time), the grand total daily calorie contribution from roots is closer to 1,300, over 50 percent of current recommended daily dietary allowances (*Encyclopedia Americana*, international ed., 1986, 20:569).

Clearly, root foods were essential fuel for Columbia Plateau Indian populations. But what of another key nutrient, protein? If 1.3 kilograms (2.9 pounds fresh or about one pound dried) of roots were eaten each day, that would provide just 10 grams of protein, less than one quarter of the average recommended daily allowance of protein for body maintenance. The actual contribution may have been considerably less given the usual imbalance among the amino acids of plant proteins. The solution: just over a pound of salmon per day (500 grams) yields over 100 grams of protein and 850 additional calories, enough to balance the protein and energy budgets with room to spare. An exemplary diet of traditional Plateau Indian foods is outlined in Table 15.

A Sample Traditional Plateau Indian Diet

	Quantity (gm)	Calories	Protein (gm)	Carbohydrate (gm)	Fat (gm)	Calcium (mg)	Iron (mg)	Vitamin C (mg)
Bitterroot	500	450	4	108	0.5	223	7.0	—
Lomatium canbyi	500	540	4	130	0.6	179	5.5	—
Camas	300	339	2	81	0.7	151	20.7	—
Roots total	1,300	1,329	10	319	1.8	553	33.2	—
	61%	52%	6%					
Huckleberries	100	62	1	15	0.5	29	0.3	64.5
Plants total	1,400	1,391	11	334	2.3	582	33.5	64.5
	66%	55%	6%					
Salmon	500	850	107	0	43.5	875	4.5	—
Fish total	23%	33%	64%					
Venison	240	302	50	0	9.6	24	—	—
Animal total	740	1,152	157	0	53.1	899	4.5	—
	34%	45%	94%					
Grand total	2,140	2,543	168	334	55.4	1,481	38.0	64.5
RDDA		2,267	45			898	14.0	45.0

Notes: RDDA's are calculated from age and sex specific values in the *Encyclopedia Americana* (International Edition, 1986, volume 20, pg 569), averaging age and sex subgroups, then weighting males, females, and children (<10 years) as equal components of the total population. Nutritional values are from Benson et al. 1973, Keeley et al. 1982, Norton et al. 1984, Hunn 1981, and Watt and Merrill 1963. The quantities of roots are as estimated above. Values whenever possible are for *dried* roots corrected for water content. The quantity of salmon is from Hewes 1973 and Hunn 1981; of huckleberries based on Perkins' observations (n.d. [1838–1843]; and that for venison is based on the assumption that each hunter kills one elk and two mule deer (of average weight) in the course of a year, with a 70% waste factor.

Plants Picked for Food

Just as spring is defined by the activity of root digging and its product, x̣nit, so are summer and fall organized around the activity of "picking" plant foods, fruits, berries, nuts, and even a species of tree lichen that is picked from high country conifers, several gunnysack loads at a time, then baked underground and eaten as a confection. All are classed together as tmaanít. A more rigid collecting container is preferred for fruits and berries than the wápas of twined Indian hemp cord normally employed for collecting roots. Berry-picking containers include "Klikitat baskets" of cedar root decorated with bear grass and bitter cherry bark.

The tmaanít harvest begins in some areas with the sweet golden currants and bitter white dogwood fruits that ripen by the end of June at low elevations along the major rivers. To honor the first fruits, thanksgiving ceremonies were held. These have recently been revived in several communities. Mid-August is the traditional time for the huckleberry feast, still widely celebrated in preparation for the annual harvest of the Plateau Indians' number one fruit, the black mountain huckleberry (wíwnu; *Vaccinium membranaceum*).

Between late June and mid-August the harvest focuses on lowland and foothill species, especially chokecherries (tmiš; *Prunus virginiana*) and serviceberries (ččaa; *Amelanchier alnifolia*). Chokecherries come in three distinct color varieties, but Sahaptin speakers ignore these superficial distinctions in their nomenclature. Thompson Salish speakers, by contrast, distinguish by name nearly a dozen varieties of serviceberries, according to size, color, taste, habitat, and life-history (Turner et al., n.d.).

Sahaptin speakers agree with their Interior Salish colleagues that the most important fruit of all is the black mountain huckleberry (Turner 1987:72). It is distinguished by its large size, exquisite flavor, and general abundance in high mountain clearings. The very similar but less abundant Alaska huckleberry (*Vaccinium alaskaense*) was not distinguished by my consultants, but was considered to be a less choice variant found in more shaded habitats. Grouseberry (*V. scoparium*) is a miniature of its taller huckleberry relations, low in stature, with tiny leaves and diminutive red to burgundy berries, traditionally harvested with a special wooden comb. Appropriately, the grouseberry is called wiwlú-wiwlu, "little black mountain huckleberry."

Associated with black mountain huckleberry nearly throughout its range is the blue huckleberry (*Vaccinium ovalifolium*), the berries of which have a thicker skin and lack the fine flavor of wíwnu. The leaves are noticeably different, smooth-edged and pale. It is called q̓šiš-lí, which James Selam suggested might imitate the sound made when you bite into this thick-skinned berry. On the west slope of the Cascades the red huckleberry (*V. parvifolium*) is common. Columbia River Indians rarely ventured so far west and so gave it a variety of descriptive names, such as lúča-luča wíwnu, "red huckleberry," or cicums-lí, "boil-colored," a graphic image for this shocking pink fruit.

Sweetest of all is the low mountain blueberry (*Vaccinium deliciosum*, apparently including *V. caespitosum*), known as iłiłmúk.[2] Sally Buck, a Klikitat, apparently uses the term iłiłmúk for the bog blueberry, *V. occidentale*, while Dávid French's Warm Springs consultants apply wiwlú-wiwlu to *V. caespitosum*.

Coincident with the huckleberry harvest is a harvest of black tree lichen (k̓unč; *Bryoria fremontii;* see fig. 5.17). While the huckleberries are dried over a slow fire in the waning warmth of October (Filloon 1952), k̓unč receives the full "camas treatment," baked underground to render the airy strands to a pastelike carbohydrate, much concentrated and reduced in volume (Turner 1977). This lichen was not, as has often been claimed, a famine food, but was appreciated as a culinary treat, an "Indian pudding," worth the substantial effort put into its harvest and preparation. It is still eaten today despite the complexity of its preparation.

Trees

The first white immigrants coming down the Oregon Trail to the Columbia River found the land a despairing sight: ". . . forest trees totally disappear, and nothing larger than the common willow is to be seen. This whole intervening tract is one of gravel and sand, with just soil enough to sustain a scanty covering of grass" (quoted in Meinig 1968:103). This "Great Columbia Desert" appeared bleak, dusty, rock hard, treeless, in a word, a desert. The travelers hurried on to the rich partially wooded bottomlands of the Willamette Valley, a more comfortably familiar habitat.

The Indians at home along this arid stretch of river were not ignorant of trees. Their seasonal travels exposed them to over thirty species, most of

---

2. The English terms "huckleberry," "blueberry," and "grouseberry" are applied here in no consistent fashion to name various species of the genus *Vaccinium*. This contrasts with standard usage in eastern North America where "huckleberry" is reserved for the large-seeded *Gaylussacia* berries, which do not occur in the West.

Fig. 5.17. Black tree lichen (*Bryoria fremontii;* ƙunč).

which were known by distinct names. Many contemporary urban Euro-Americans may know perfectly well what a tree is but are unable to say what *kind* of tree they are looking at. The Indians know well the kind of tree but are a bit unsure as to just what is or is not a "tree" in their language. The closest we can come in translating "tree" in Sahaptin is with the word pátat, which has the literal meaning of "thing standing upright." Is a dead snag or a flag pole a pátat? When I asked this question I got hesitant and conflicting opinions in reply. I believe the truth is that for the Indians the most important fact was what *kind* of tree it was, as there were few occasions when any old tree would do.

The specificity of Sahaptin plant nomenclature is striking if we compare

TABLE 16
Pine Tree Names in Sahaptin

Pine in general	*Pinus* spp.	Ø, tápaš
Ponderosa pine	*P. ponderosa*	tápaš
Western white pine	*P. monticola*	paǩinák-aas (NWS only)
Lodgepole pine	*P. contorta*	kalám-kalam
Whitebark pine	*P. albicaulis*	ninník-aaš

Indian names with the standard English terms for pines, to take just one example (see Table 16).

Each species has its own name; binomials are avoided. The suffix -aaš/-aš/-aas, though it never occurs alone, might be translated "plant." Again, each species is useful to the Indians in particular ways. The whitebark pine is a source of pine nuts, ninník, for which the tree itself is named, literally, "pine nut plant." Ponderosa pine produces edible inner bark and sugar, and doubles as a major habitat indicator, marking the lower timberline, called tápaš-naq̓ít, "ponderosa pine edge." The lodgepole pine, as the name indicates, was a preferred species for lodge poles due to its straight, branchless growth where it springs up after a fire (this applies to the Indians of the northern Plains, not to the Plateau, as far as has been recorded).

The classification of willows (*Salix* spp.) demonstrates yet more clearly this functional specificity of plant nomenclature. The willows are a diverse genus of woody plants. Some are honest-to-God trees, large, with heavy trunks. Most, however, are spindly shrubs or, in alpine areas, sprawling ground-covering mats. Whether tree or shrub, willows are called ttáxš in Columbia River Sahaptin. This is apparently derived from i-ttáx̣-ša, "it is growing." There is one exception. The peachleaf willow (*S. amygdaloides*)—a large tree willow of riparian flats east of the Cascades—is singled out as haháw. Like every willow species, this one demonstrates many characteristics shared throughout the willow clan, but it exhibits as well a unique feature that justifies for the mid-Columbia Indians its separate name. It grows straight and tall, upwards for fifty feet sometimes with scarcely a twist or a branch (Peattie 1950:346; see fig. 5.18). In this respect it is quite unlike its large cousin, the Pacific willow (*S. lasiandra*) that is often found

Fig. 5.18. Peach-leaf willow (*Salix amygdaloides;* **haháw**).

with it in streamside groves. It might well have been called the "lodgepole willow" were Sahaptin speakers inclined to use compound names, for its unusual form of growth (for a willow) makes of it the perfect species for constructing longhouse frames. As we have seen, the mid-Columbia people spent their winters in sheltered side canyons just off the big river, an area nearly devoid of trees. Trees that are found here are often sprawling and shrubby like most willows or weak like the cottonwood. The peachleaf willow fills the bill for construction timbers. One need not haul tall, straight trees from the mountain forests at great effort. One need only seek out a good riverside stand of haháw.

If you visit the Yakima Nation Cultural Heritage Center Museum in Toppenish, Washington, you will see a full-sized Plateau Indian longhouse on display. This was built in 1982 by a team including James and Elsie Selam and Sara Quaempts. The women were in charge of making the tule mats (about which more below) and James saw to it that the frame was constructed of peachleaf willow poles in the best traditional manner.

Trees are not often useful as sources of food. I have already noted two that are, the whitebark pine for its nuts and the Ponderosa for its sweet cambium. I must add the Garry oak (ćuníps; fig. 5.19) to this category. It is the only oak that grows naturally this far north on the Pacific slope. It is restricted to the western edge of the Plateau in the Columbia gorge and along the eastern Cascade foothills north to the Naches River. Its acorns (wawačí) are esteemed, though they belong to the bitter white oak group. Leaching is required to eliminate the tannins before they can be eaten. This was traditionally accomplished by burying the acorns in a certain kind of odoriferous mud found along the Columbia at certain spots. They were then baked underground in the manner of camas. If Steller's jays (the local "bluejay"; x̣ʷášx̣ʷay) came to scold the acorn baking party, the acorns would be ruined. Why? A Wasco myth of Raccoon and his grandmother describes how the irresponsible boy, Raccoon, eats up his grandmother's acorn stash, replacing each acorn with his dung to hide his greed. For this antisocial act his grandmother whips him with a stick from the fire: that's how Raccoon got his stripes (see Text, pp. 186–87). (Is it not curious that raccoons are branded as thieves in Sahaptin myth as in Euro-American folklore?) As the saga continues, Raccoon's grandmother, regretting her anger, seeks to make it up with her boy, but he chokes her instead. As she gags, "Kak, kak, kak," she turns into a jay. So the jay is the scolding grandmother, a reminder of the grave necessity to maintain proper familial relations.

Fig. 5.19. Garry oak (*Quercus garryana;* čuníps).

Wood is of great value in native technology, each tree appreciated for the special qualities of its wood. Maple is strong and flexible, ideal for dip net hoops. Hence vine and Douglas maples are called twanú-waaš, literally, "dip-net plant." Hardwoods are singled out for other roles. Ocean spray (*Holodis-cus discolor*), for example, is called piⱡwayč-pamá, literally, "[plant] for braces," referring to its preferred use as the crosspiece that gives strength to the dip net hoop. Similarly, oak is occasionally named kápiⱡ-aaš, literally, "digging stick plant," as it was favored for digging stick shafts.

The "firewood problem" has been much discussed in the context of Plateau ecological adaptation. Large quantities of wood were required to heat the peoples' winter homes when temperatures might drop to −20°F. It has even been suggested that salmon was burned as fuel in lieu of readily obtainable firewood (based on a surmise in Thwaites 1959 [1904], 3:124). This hypothesis ignores an abundant source of fuel wood ready to hand, sagebrush (*Artemisia tridentata;* tawšá; N W S: pišⱪú). Nevertheless, firewood supplies were no doubt a key consideration in village site selection with driftwood concentration points highly favored.

Not all woods are of equal value as firewood, however, and some are worthless or worse. Knowledgeable firewood selection is underscored by the belief that to use blue elderberry wood (*Sambucus caerulea;* mííp) or wood of the sumac (*Rhus glabra;* łantít) would lead to disaster. Elderberry stems are pulpy with little substance at the core, thus useful as "straws" for venting underground ovens, but useless as firewood. Sumac may in fact produce poisonous smoke as is the case with its highly toxic relatives, poison ivy and oak. The roots are used to treat venereal disease.

Several other trees, especially the conifers, are valued as medicines. Pitch (íšxí) is highly regarded in the treatment of wounds and sores. The young foliage of Ponderosa pine and larch (kimíla) is boiled to make teas for treating flu and tuberculosis, respectively. The highly aromatic balsam firs (*Abies* spp.; patátwi) are highly regarded for their cleansing powers, cleansing not only the body but purifying the spirit and the house as well. One sits on the flat sprays of grand and silver fir in the sweat lodge and the healing power of the steam is strengthened by the strongest of all the firs, the subalpine (*A. lasiocarpa;* see fig. 5.20).

Trees even play an active role in myth. Hemlock (*Tsuga* spp.; waqutqut-yáy) is credited with Coyote's rescue from drowning. After Otter and Turtle had failed to rescue him, Hemlock succeeded by hooking Coyote from the bottom of the river using its bent lead shoot. This peculiarity of hemlocks is a well-known field mark that at a glance singles out the hemlocks from the mass of Cascade forest trees (see fig. 5.21). The Indians have also seized upon this distinction, reinforcing its value as a distinguishing feature by highlighting it in myth.

Fibers

Plateau peoples were too mobile to find pottery of much use. They made their containers instead of highly portable and durable plant fibers. The value of such plant materials in the manufacture of essential tools can hardly be exaggerated. Foods keep us alive, it's true, but baskets, nets, and bindings make it possible to collect and transport those foods, while mats and clothing protect the body from hypothermia. Survival on the Plateau depended as much on the knowledge of fiber plants as it did on the knowledge of food plants.

Little Raccoon and His Grandmother

(A Wasco-Warm Springs Story from Ramsey 1977:58–60, modified as requested by Ramsey [1988, pers. comm.]. Told to Ramsey by Mrs. Alice Florendo of Warm Springs, Oregon; courtesy California Folklore Society.)

Little Raccoon lived with his grandmother; he was her *k'itch* [paternal grandson], and she spoiled him. They were gathering acorns over the mountains, and one day she asked Raccoon what he wanted to eat for dinner. "Would you like some wapato?" she asked, and Raccoon answered, "No, I'm tired of wapato." "Some jerky, then?"—"No, I'm tired of jerky."—"How about some dried fish-eyes?"—"I don't like dried fish-eyes!" So Raccoon's Grandmother grew angry and told him to just go out and find his own dinner. "But stay out of the acorns!" she told him.

Well, after awhile Raccoon came to the five pits where his grandmother was storing her winter's acorns. "I'm so hungry!" he said to himself, and after awhile he said. "Grandmother surely won't miss just one acorn." So he reached into the pit, under the dirt covering, and took out one acorn to eat—and then another, and then another, until pretty soon the pit was empty! "Now what shall I do?" he said, "Grandmother will be very angry." So he thought he would crap once for every acorn in the pit, but eating acorns had given him diarrhea, and what he left was a smelly mess—which he covered up. But he was still very hungry, and he went on to the second pit. "Well, maybe I'll just take one more acorn," he said, but after awhile that pit was empty too, and so he filled it up, as before, with his dung. Well, Raccoon just seemed to get hungrier and hungrier, and before long he had eaten every acorn in each of the five pits, and filled each one with his dung.

After awhile his grandmother went out to get some acorns for their supper. But when she reached into the first pit all she felt was Raccoon's smelly mess! "Somebody has been messing around here!" she said. So she went on to the second pit and reached in, and felt the same thing—and so on through all five pits. She was getting angrier and angrier. "I'll bet it was that Little Raccoon!" she yelled, and when she found him by the fire she grabbed a fire-stick [braided willow wands to carry live coals in] and whipped him from his nose to his tail. That is why raccoons have those stripes across their backs.

Little Raccoon ran away then, he thought he would go live with some friends in a village nearby. But when he arrived there everybody came out and jeered at him. "Ha ha, here comes that Little Raccoon; he stole all his grandmother's acorns and replaced them with his dung!" So Raccoon felt silly and went on to another village, but there again all the people ran out and ridiculed him, "Ha ha, here's that Little Raccoon, we've heard how you pilfered your grandmother's acorns and left her only dung!" He was ashamed, and went on to three more villages, but every time he arrived the people would come out and make fun of him. So Raccoon learned how stories about the mean things you do travel ahead of you, and he went off by himself into the woods.

Now about this time his old grandmother began to feel badly about whipping her little k'itch; she felt sorry for him. So she set out to find him, but when she came to the first village, they told her that Raccoon had gone on to the next village, and so on, until she had visited all five villages without finding him. She was feeling pretty bad. Now Raccoon was up in a service-berry bush, eating berries, and he heard his grandmother coming up the hill, crying, "Oh my little k'itch, my little Raccoon, where are you, where are you?" Raccoon yelled, "Here I am, Grandmother, just eating service-berries." Pretty soon she came up, nearly blind from crying so much, and she said, "My k'itch, I'm so hungry, throw me some berries."

Now that his grandmother had found him, that Raccoon was feeling mischievous again, so he threw a whole handful of berries, leaves, and twigs right down her throat, and she began to choke. "Kak-kak," she cried, "my k'itch. I'm choking; here, take my basket-hat and get me some water!" So that Raccoon climbed down, took the hat, and ran to a creek and filled it up, but he was feeling mean again so he poked a hole in the hat and by the time he got back he had only a little water. "Kak-kak!" cried the grandmother, "get me some more water!" So Raccoon went to fetch her water again, but he poked another hole, and brought even less water this time. He was obeying her, but not really. Each time he went he poked another hole into the hat and brought back a little less, and a little less, until the fifth time, when the grandmother could hardly talk, he brought her only one drop of water. And just as he handed her the basket-hat this time, she cried "Kak-kak-kak" once more—and turned into a blue-jay and flew off, scolding the way blue-jays do. Little Raccoon just sat down and cried; it was all his fault.

Fig. 5.20. Subalpine fir or "balsam" (*Abies lasiocarpa;* **patátwi**)

Fig. 5.21. Hemlock (*Tsuga heterophylla;* **waqutqut**)

(Drawings by Ramona Hammerly from *Northwest Trees,* reprinted with permission of The Mountaineers.)

Two species stand out immediately for their exceptional utility: Indian hemp (*Apocynum cannabinum;* taxús; see fig. 5.22) and tule or bulrush (*Scirpus acutus/S. validus;* tⁱku). Indian hemp is widespread on alluvial soils at low elevations, but only rarely attains a size productive of the long fibers that make the strongest twine. Such choice sites today are kept secret by the women who know of them. Indian hemp can be gathered in summer, but then has to be softened by burial in damp earth. By October the standing plants have dried sufficiently for processing. The stalks are crushed to loosen the paper-thin bast from the stem. The bast is then shredded to separate the long fibers. During long winters in the past, women twined literally miles of hemp string from these fibers, rolling the finished string into large balls for later use. Indian women always kept a ball of twine which they knotted in a special way to record the significant events of their lives, as a string diary (Leechman and Harrington 1921).

The salmon harvest would have been much reduced without hemp twine for knotting nets and binding the hoop to the dip net shaft. Objects uncovered at the classic Wakemap (Upper Chinookan: wáq̓map) excavations near Spearfish just above The Dalles have been interpreted as gill net sinkers, which suggests great antiquity for net fishing, and thus, we may assume, for hemp twine manufacture (Cressman 1977:118–19).

Hemp twine played a key role also in root collecting, as the soft "corn husk bags" used by root diggers are actually Indian hemp twined bags decorated in later years with corn husk imbrication. These soft bags conform to the shape of the load of roots. Small bags are worn on the hip to receive the roots fresh from the ground, while larger bags worn on the back are used to consolidate several small bags full. In this way a woman can collect up to thirty-six pounds of roots before she must return to camp. Hemp twine is employed also to make the distinctive Plateau hat, the paλapá, a truncated cone twined very tightly to hold its shape (see fig. 5.23).

Berry collecting requires more rigid collecting containers to prevent the berries from being crushed. "Klikitat" baskets woven of cedar root and imbricated with bleached beargrass leaves (*Xerophyllum tenax;* yaay; see fig. 5.24) and the reddish bark of the bitter cherry (*Prunus emarginata;* tmiš-wáakuł) served well in this capacity. Thus, the bulk of the Plateau diet was harvested with the direct aid of these botanical tools.

Tule mats covered the winter longhouses and were taken down and rolled up for ease of transport to summer camp sites. Here they were used again to cover the summer teepees (see fig. 5.25). Tules are common marsh

var. suksdorfii   var. glaberrimum

Fig. 5.22. Indian hemp (*Apocynum cannabinum;* **taχús**).

plants of low elevations. On favored sites they may grow over ten feet tall, very gradually tapering from the base (see figs. 5.26 and 5.27). A perfectly rectangular mat is formed by alternating the slightly broader basal ends with the tapered ends of the tule segments as the mat materials are laid out. These segments are then sewed, with Indian hemp twine and greasewood (*Sarcobates vermiculatus;* nišxt) twig needles, at two- to five-inch intervals across the entire width of the mat. These cords are tied to a small willow stick at either end of the mat. The edges of the mat are bound by braiding

Fig. 5.23. Chief Mnainak's wife with conical woven hat (Curtis photograph, University of Washington Libraries, neg. 78).

with two hemp strands. A cross-sectional cut through a tule stem reveals its special value as an insulative covering for walls and floors; it resembles styrofoam, a mass of air pockets within the semi-rigid celluloid matrix. Three layers of mats overlapping like shingles and banked at the base with earth kept out cold, wind, snow, and rain.

Tules were not ideal for all purposes. If a rigid open-work mat was needed, for example, as a support for drying the oily salmon, the stiff culms of the common reed (*Phragmites communis*; wápay) were used. If a large, soft container was needed, a cattail (*Typha latifolia*; ščiw) bag was constructed, as for storing large quantities of dried, pounded salmon meal (člay). Lewis and Clark described neat stacks of such salmon meal bags, each lined with salmon skin, at Celilo and near The Dalles in October 1805. Each weighed, in their estimation, one hundred pounds and each stack contained twelve bags. These were arranged neatly with seven forming a circular base supporting the remaining five on top. They counted over a hundred stacks for a total of some sixty tons of dried salmon meal stockpiled at this great salmon entrepôt on the Columbia (Thwaites 1959 [1904], 3:146, 148, 152, 155). These

Fig. 5.24. Beargrass (*Xerophyllum tenax*; **yaay**).

supplies were not yet exhausted when they returned there in April of the following year after wintering on the coast (4:304).

Finally, if an absorbent, neutral-scented material was required, as in separating the sections of a large salmon cut for more efficient drying, giant wild rye (*Elymus cinereus;* šwíčt) culms were selected. This material was also handy for disposable floor coverings and for layering material within the underground ovens when baking camas, black tree lichen, or bear meat. Each of these well-known grass-like plants had its own name. The many other related species of grasses, sedges, and rushes were known simply as waskú, if they were good forage, or číičk, if not.

Medicines

The Sahaptin word for medicine, tawtnúk, includes over seventy-five species of plants (but is not restricted to plants or plant products). The discomfort of disease (páyuwi) for Plateau Indians may be a physical state modifiable by practical medicines and/or a sign of an underlying spiritual disorder. If the latter, the services of a power-gifted Indian doctor or twáti are indicated. There are no specialists in herbal medicine. Individuals acquire from their elders knowledge of medicinal plants, some widely known by name, others in the nature of family secrets or specialties, often unnamed (French 1981). These esoteric remedies do not concern me here, as I am interested primarily in those remedies of wide and established cultural reputation. Such general recognition may be a good clue to their medical efficacy.

One plant stands out in terms of its reported power, the wide range of its applications, and the geographical scope of its use: a species of the now familiar genus *Lomatium,* the fern-leaved lomatium (*L. dissectum;* čalúkš; see fig. 4.11), noted already for its roles as fish poison and spring vegetable. The plant was best known, however, for its medicinal properties, in both human and veterinary treatments. The root was mashed in water to make a hair rinse for itching scalp, while the root pulp could be applied as a poultice to treat infected wounds and boils. In the first instance the toxic properties in the root, which include at least a variety of "coumarin"-like compounds known to paralyze muscle activity (Cox 1983), might kill lice. Its proven antibacterial activity (Matson et al. 1949) would help control infections. A poultice of the root was also used for a horse with saddle sores and to groom a horse's coat. Internal use included drinking a dilute infusion of the root for upper respiratory infections. One young Yakima Indian woman who had

Fig. 5.25. Tule mat covered teepee (Relander Collection, Yakima Valley Regional Library).

Fig. 5.26. Tule or bulrush (*Scirpus acutus;* tḱu).

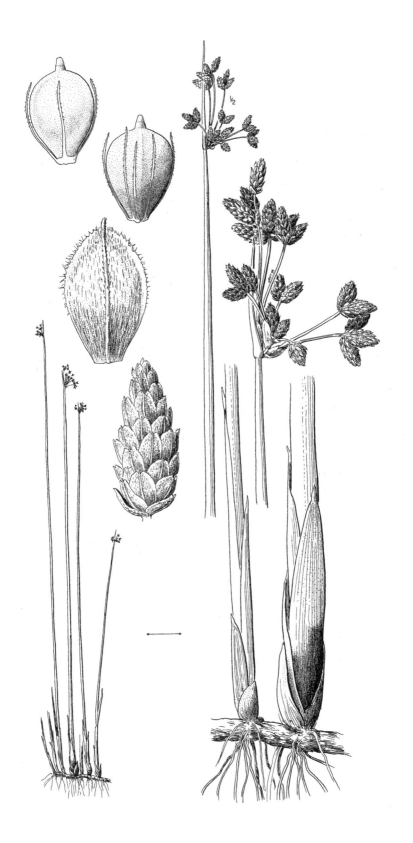

Fig. 5.27. Yakima woman collecting tule (Relander Collection, Yakima Valley Regional Library).

suffered such a treatment at the hands of her grandmother described it as "horribly foul tasting." A piece of root might also be chewed to ease a sore throat, though the root of the related lovage (*Ligusticum canbyi;* áyun; see fig. 4.3) was better known for this purpose. *L. dissectum* was also boiled to produce a curative steam. The Lakes Indians of southcentral British Columbia treated cases of rheumatism, muscle pains, and sprains, as well as pneumonia with this plant prepared in a special steam bath. The roots were washed, then placed on a bed of hot stones on top of which the patient lay (Turner, Bouchard, and Kennedy 1980:68).

Columbia River Sahaptins shared with the Blackfeet of the high Plains (Hellson and Gadd 1974) the technique of forcing a "winded" horse to inhale steam from a boiling pot of *Lomatium dissectum* roots. The horse thereafter would have extraordinary stamina and would be fiercely loyal to the man who performed this therapy.

Many folk remedies are less obviously potent than čalúkš and some may owe their continued acceptance to logical principles at odds with modern medical science. One such principle has been called "sympathetic magic." It is related to the medieval "Doctrine of Signatures." By this logic, some similarity between the illness and its cure is the basis for treatment. Modern mechanistic medical science insists on the demonstration of a cause and effect relation of *contiguity* instead. For example, the field bindweed, *Convolvulus arvensis* (introduced from Europe), is used to prepare a bath for a baby suffering from sleeplessness. The fact that the flowers of this "morning glory" close each night suggests a connection between the behavior of the flower and the desired state of regular sleep to be induced in the patient. We cannot be certain, of course, without laboratory analysis, that the plant might not also have the desired physiological effect, not to mention the psychological power of belief.

Regardless of the effective principle, an analysis of folk medicines reveals those medical problems of most pressing concern to the people. We know that the scourges of smallpox, measles, malaria, influenza, scarlet fever, whooping cough, and tuberculosis were unknown to precontact Plateau Indians. However, they were not entirely disease free, we may be sure, as the variety of their traditional medicines proves. Lewis and Clark noted in particular that many old people suffered blindness (Thwaites 1959 [1904], 3:126). Sure enough, an inventory of mid-Columbia Indian herbal remedies include eight for sore eyes or blindness. Thirteen cures for colds and sore throats may indicate that upper respiratory tract infections were endemic before white contact. Ten treatments for wounds, bruises, or sores suggest the frequency of traumatic injury, while eight "hair medicines" indicate the pervasive presence of that "first domesticated animal," the human louse. Additional remedies are reported for male impotence: the root of the wild sunflower, *Helianthus cusickii* (apparently unnamed), was boiled and drunk to "strengthen the blood" of men so affected. Another remedy served "to prevent the foetus from growing too large," i.e., an infusion of the bittercherry, *Prunus emarginata*. The horsemint (*Agastache occidentalis*) was considered an effective love potion, called pɬax winš-pamá, "potion [to get] your man." The sticky burrs of the cockleburr (*Xanthium strumarium;* čakčákt; see fig. 5.28) might be used to cause one's lover or spouse to "stick" with you.

A final category of medicines are those used for spiritual troubles or malaise. First is the spruce, boiled to make a tea drunk as a spring tonic. This medicine is called wáq̓išwit-anam tawtnuk-i, "medicine for your life." In spiritual crises, such as following the death of a close and much loved relative, one might drink a wild tobacco (*Nicotiana attenuata;* awt-pamá, "for purification"; see fig. 7.2) "tea" to induce vomiting, to free one spiritually of tight emotional bonds. Most widely employed as a defense against the spiritual sickness attributed to "haunting" is the wild rose (*Rosa* spp.; šk̓apášway). Perhaps the rose's formidable thorns provided a sympathetic defensive shield? That the prickly branches of juniper or red cedar may substitute for the rose supports this interpretation. Clearly, however, the Indian concept of "medicine" is more inclusive than our own and recognizes no rigid duality of mind and body. The Indian doctor is general practitioner, pharmacist, psychiatrist, and priest rolled into one, treating the sick person as a whole and social being. Appendix 3 lists the major Columbia River Indian plant remedies.

Just Flowers

I made quite a pest of myself on field trips with my generous Indian hosts, badgering them constantly with the query, "tun i-waník-ša?" "What is its name?"—this for every wild flower and weed that our paths crossed. Once I'd learned the names of the most obvious useful plants, I more and more frequently was told, "It's just a flower" (áwtya ay latít). "Flower" or latít is a residual category in Sahaptin, a response that peremptorily dismisses hundreds of species of small, herbaceous, and culturally insignificant plants. The value of such a category in keeping one's mind clear for thinking about

Fig. 5.28. Cockleburr (*Xanthium strumarium;* **čakčákt**).

the important stuff is obvious. Nevertheless, I was at times dismayed by the fact that some splendid showy wild flowers, such as the grass widow and sagebrush violet, all the orchids, and the gamut of showy buckwheats, were without distinction relegated to this catchall conceptual bin. Could it be, I wondered, that Indian people *see* only that which they define as useful, lacking a purely aesthetic motivation for knowledge?

Clearly, the answer is no. They came up with names for a number of "useless" plants that merited widely recognized names, names often of striking imagination. For example:

globe mallow (*Sphaeralcea munroana*) nusux-mí áčaš
(Literally, "salmon eyes." This flower is a unique dull orange-pink color.)
Indian paintbrush (*Castilleja* spp.) nawinała-nmí latít
(Literally, "Thunder's flower.")
shooting star (*Dodecatheon* spp.) k̓wayk̓way-nmí núšnu
(Literally, "curlew's beak.")
scarlet gilia (*Gilia aggregata*) qmamsalí tkʷátat
(Literally, "hummingbird's food.")
vanilla leaf (*Achlys triphylla*) yaamaš-mí ik̓ʷi-káwas
(Literally, "deer's perfume," as deer are said to lie in it for its pleasant scent. People might also stuff pillows with it.)
lupine (*Lupinus* spp.) wapiyałá
(A favorite for decorating graves.)

It is instructive to compare how strikingly different the Euro-American perceptions are from those of the Indians, while both share a common delight in these striking blooms.

As a final example, consider the diminutive gold star (*Crocidium multicaule;* see fig. 4.12), a tiny "sunflower" scarcely three inches high, growing scattered across the cold muddy slopes beneath the chill winds of March, a sign that we all can recognize as heralding the rebirth of a new year. It is called papčiláw in Sahaptin, which is just its name. The flower plays an important supporting role, not in any economic endeavor, but in the drama of myth. The gold star is "Coyote's eyes" in a charming segment of the Coyote myth cycle.

6

Society

náymu, "kin"

WHEN TEACHING introductory anthropology at the University of Washington, I try to catch the students' attention with the provocative assertion, "Apes have no fathers." This is a telling half-truth. Certainly apes have biological fathers, but, as there is no systematic way for ape "fathers" and their offspring to recognize one another, "fatherhood" can have no social reality in ape society. Ape mothers, on the other hand, by virtue of first bearing and then caring for their offspring, establish a certain and lasting bond between mother and child. The fact that ape "fathers" do not help feed or otherwise care for their offspring is clearly a consequence of this lack of paternity certainty—the concomitant of a society in which mating privileges are not culturally defined and/or socially enforced. Human society is generally distinguished by cultural institutions such as marriage and family in which "fathers," "mothers," "mates," and "children" are socially and ritually recognized. There are culturally defined rights and duties associated with these roles that are enforced by law or the power of public opinion.

In Columbia River Indian society children not only have "mothers" (pča) and "fathers" (pšít), but also four kinds of "grandparents," six basic kinds of siblings, six categories each of "uncles" and "aunts" and of "nephews" and "nieces," and nine types of in-laws; a total of over forty kinds of relatives. Most English speakers, by comparison, recognize about thirty.

A basic finding of anthropology is that the same categories of kin are not everywhere recognized in the same way. One might have assumed that a "brother" is a brother, a "sister" a sister, and a "cousin" a cousin in all societies. On the contrary! Those three English terms are applied to a set of kin relationships that require seven terms in Sahaptin. To understand the differences in perspective between (as well as the common ground beneath) English and Sahaptin kinship systems, we need a more universal language to describe kinship. This language is provided by the anthropologists' kin

type notation, a simple system that allows us to define the range of reference of kinship terms in all known languages.

There are eight basic relations, each symbolized by a capital letter (based
on English, as most anthropologists speak English as their native language):

male	*female*
F (father)	M (mother)
B (brother)	Z (sister)
S (son)	D (daughter)
H (husband)	W (wife)

All kin can now be defined in terms of one or more of these basic relations
linked in series, beginning with *ego* and proceeding link by link to *alter*, the
relative to be named. Thus my Uncle George might be my FB (father's
brother). Using this system we can see that the English term "uncle" (in this
discussion we are concerned only with referential kin terms, not terms of
address) names not one relationship but four, that is, FB (father's brother),
MB (mother's brother), FZH (father's sister's husband), and MZH (mother's
sister's husband). Note also that in English we fail to distinguish paternal
from maternal uncles and "uncles-by-blood" from "uncles-by-marriage."

The Sahaptin terms apply a different logic, as shown in Table 17. The six
Sahaptin terms involve first of all a distinction between father's side and

TABLE 17

English and Sahaptin Uncle and Aunt Terms

♂ = male; ♀ = female

mother's side. As in English, however, uncles and aunts "by blood" are not distinguished from the spouses of "blood" uncles and aunts (with one exception to be discussed below). Curiously, the paternal uncle "by blood" is equated in the Sahaptin terminology with the husband of the maternal aunt, and similarly for the paternal and maternal aunts. This seems illogical at first glance. If it were the case, as it not infrequently is in hunting-gathering societies, that when a man of one family married a woman of another, the groom's sister and brother (if he had any) also married into the family of the bride, then, for their children, a father's brother would also be (or likely become) a mother's sister's husband, and a father's sister might become a mother's brother's wife. So why not use a single term for each pair?

In real life it is not always so easy to guarantee that brothers and sisters— even if they were to exist in precisely the required numbers and be of appropriate ages—would agree to such marriages. Thus, the kinship terms seem to presume an ideal solution to the eternal problem of finding a spouse, an ideal that stresses the value of continued and multiple marriage links between families. This is opposed to our system where primary emphasis is placed on the ideal of individual choice of mates. We will shortly see that the Sahaptin system has another peculiar feature that may have brought this ideal of sibling exchange marriage closer to reality.

Before we get to that, however, we need to note one further peculiarity of Sahaptin aunt and uncle (= "nuncle") terms, a distinct asymmetry. One's FZH is given very special treatment, distinguished not only from the MB but also according to whether *ego* is male or female. As one might expect, this particular relationship is special, as traditionally that particular uncle was expected to provide special instruction to his WBS and WBD (Murdock 1958).[1]

The Columbia River Sahaptin kin term system gives further evidence of a central concern for maintaining the ties between families that are established at marriage—and not only until "death do us part." The sibling-in-law terms are most revealing in this regard. The English system consists of two terms, brother-in-law and sister-in-law. Sahaptin speakers use four terms to span the same genealogical space, as in Table 18. For English

1. The asymmetry built in here is suggestive of what is known as an Omaha kinship system—named for the Omaha Indians of the Mississippi Valley—a system otherwise unknown in our area but found among some California Penutian groups (Aoki 1966:368). It is a subtlety that seems no longer to be relevant in Plateau Indian society.

TABLE 18

English and Sahaptin Sibling-in-Law Terms

	SISTER-IN-LAW		
if connecting relative alive, pnuk	♂ BW	♀ BW	ač
	♂ WZ	♀ HZ	
	BROTHER-IN-LAW		
if connecting relative dead, awít	♀ ZH	♂ ZH	miyú
	♀ HB	♂ WB	

speakers the key issue is the sex of the sibling-in-law. For Sahaptin speakers the sex of the relative is important, but in relation to the sex of ego. If they are of the same sex, one set of terms is used, but if the siblings-in-law are of opposite sex they constitute a special category which we might translate "potential spouse."

Columbia River Indians practiced customs known to anthropologists as the levirate and sororate. The levirate refers to the custom of a man marrying his deceased brother's wife. (From the woman's perspective, a woman marries her deceased husband's brother.) The sororate is the custom in which a man marries his deceased wife's sister (or, a woman marries her deceased sister's husband). When such a custom is honored, one's siblings-in-law of opposite sex—as long as the connecting spouse or sibling is alive—are almost like one's own spouse. In fact, sexual relations with such relatives were not considered offensive. The death of the connecting kin transformed a theoretical possibility into a strong expectation; thus, the need for a change of kinship term.

Such family relations seem very odd to one who has not grown up in such a culture, but they are deeply ingrained in the consciousness of those raised within the system of belief. My first exposure to this fact came as I was trying to arrange an interview with Mary Jim, a knowledgeable, feisty elder (who was about sixty-five years old at the time), a representative of the Snake River Sahaptin people. I asked James Selam if he would contact her about this interview, as I knew they were related. He showed great reluctance and suggested that I should call her myself (which I, as an outsider, was reluctant to do). I some time later learned from Delsie Selam that Mary Jim was James' awít—they had a good laugh about this at James' expense and teased him about his (alleged) dalliances with the woman at every opportunity, though she is quite a few years his senior. In short, a man is expected to have amorous intentions toward his awít, in accord with traditional expectations of marriage.

The levirate and sororate serve to maintain the bonds established between families at the initial marriage, even though one of the original spouses dies. The children, of course, are of continuing concern to both families, but perhaps more important in a hunting-gathering society—societies with low population densities—is the great value of that special trusting relationship that should exist if two families are to give each other their children in marriage.

Polygyny, the practice of a man having more than one wife, was a prerogative of chiefs and other wealthy and influential men on the Columbia Plateau. Sororal polygyny, in which a man marries sisters, sometimes resulted from the practice of the levirate and sororate. For example, if your father's brother were killed by a raiding party of Northern Paiutes, your father might then take his brother's widow as his second wife. Sororal polygyny reflected the primary importance in Plateau marriage of the bonds between the families of the bride and groom, bonds that not even death should sever. While it is easy to appreciate the advantage of plural marriages from the man's point of view—he gains the productive as well as the reproductive power of two women—it is less obvious why women should tolerate it. If cowives are sisters, however, they can count on each other's company and mutual support in the traumatic transition from their own home to that of the groom's family, the normal housing arrangement for Plateau newlyweds. The families of both the bride and groom gain security by strengthening the relation of trust between them.

A man did not always take a second wife from the sisters of his first wife. Plural marriages in which the cowives are unrelated appear in quite a different light to the wives involved, as can be seen from the Sahaptin terms applied to cowives: cowives who are also sisters refer to each other as ƛaks, a general term for a woman's sisters and female friends; unrelated cowives, however, call each other ƛáwi, literally, "enemy"!

Fraternal polyandry, in which a woman marries a set of brothers, has been reported for Northern Paiute and Shoshone people of the Great Basin but is not known to have occurred on the Plateau. In the Great Basin it may be understood as a response to very sparse populations and the concomitant difficulty of finding eligible mates (Steward 1936; Park 1937; Stewart

1937). Polyandry was not disallowed in Plateau society—in fact, the intimacy of the relationship between pnuk, "opposite sex siblings in-law," represented a close approximation to polyandrous marriage. If such marriages did occur, James Selam believes the cohusbands would call one another x̱ay, the general term for a man's brothers and close male friends.

The levirate and sororate had further implications for Sahaptin kinship. It meant that one's "cousins" (to use our all-inclusive term) might likely one day become one's step-siblings. Thus, your father's brother's children become your step-brothers and sisters. In fact, the Sahaptin system is set up so that no change in terminology is required for such a circumstance, as the terms for brothers and sisters apply as well to all but the most distant cousins. As a consequence, a Columbia River Indian has a much larger number of "brothers" and "sisters" (at the expense of cousins) than we do. But he or she also has more kinds of such relatives than we do, as they are distinguished by their relative ages and relative sex (that is, whether their sex is the same as or different from that of ego), as in Table 19.

One last detail should round out the picture. In English we have grandmothers, grandfathers, grandsons, and granddaughters as categories for those lineal relatives two generations apart. Sahaptin also uses four terms for these relatives, but in quite a different pattern from English. There are four kinds of grandparents and four of grandchildren (rather than just two as in English), but the terms are arranged so that each of the four grandparent-grandchild pairs refers to the other by the same term (the terms are self-reciprocal, as is "cousin" in English). Thus four terms serve, and the intimacy of close kin, an intimacy that is distorted neither by parental authority, sibling rivalry, nor sexual politics, is clearly expressed in the reciprocity of these terms (see Table 20). A complete list of Columbia River Sahaptin kin terms is given in Appendix 4, along with a formal analysis of their referential meanings using John Atkins' GRAFIK system of representation (Atkins 1974).

The Division of Labor by Sex

The Plateau Indian economy involved a sexual division of labor that is nearly universal among known hunting-and-gathering peoples. Men fished and hunted large game while women gathered roots and berries and had

TABLE 19
English and Sahaptin Sibling Terms

BROTHER	(FIRST) COUSIN (MALE)		
♂ B+	♂ FBS+	♂ FZS+	
	♂ MBS+	♂ MZS+	pyáp
♀ B+	♀ FBS+	♀ FZS+	
	♀ MBS+	♀ MZS+	
♂ B−	♂ FBS−	♂ FZS−	ɨsxɨp
	♂ MBS−	♂ MZS−	
♀ B−	♀ FBS−	♀ FZS−	pačt
	♀ MBS−	♀ MZS−	

SISTER	(FIRST) COUSIN (FEMALE)		
♂ Z+	♂ FBD+	♂ FZD+	
	♂ MBD+	♂ MZD+	pat
♀ Z+	♀ FBD+	♀ FZD+	
	♀ MBD+	♀ MZD+	
♂ Z−	♂ FBD−	♂ FZD−	ac
	♂ MBD−	♂ MZD−	
♀ Z−	♀ FBD−	♀ FZD−	ɨsíp
	♀ MBD−	♀ MZD−	

Note: The male (δ) and female ($\mathcal{Q}$) symbols preceding each term indicate the sex of speaker. The + and − signs following each term indicate "elder" and "younger" siblings, that is, with respect to the speaker.

primary responsibility for processing all kinds of foods, that is, for cleaning, cooking, and preserving roots, fish, berries, and game. Two questions immediately come to mind: Is such a widespread arrangement "natural"? And if so, does it represent yet another case of the exploitation or control of women by men?

The fact that the cultural assignment of economic tasks to men and women varies but little among near-contemporary hunting-gathering peoples of North America, Africa, and Australia, despite dramatic ecological contrasts and millennia of independent cultural development, strongly sug-

TABLE 20

English and Sahaptin Terms for Grandparents and Grandchildren

	GRANDPARENT		GRANDSON	GRANDDAUGHTER
GRANDFATHER	♂ FF ♀ FF	púša	{ ♂ SS	♂ SD
	♂ MF ♀ MF	tíla	{ ♂ DS	♂ DD
GRANDMOTHER	♂ FM ♀ FM	ála	{ ♀ SS	♀ SD
	♂ MM ♀ MM	káɬa	{ ♀ DS	♀ DD

gests a certain inevitability in these arrangements. Not only are there no cases known in which women hunt and fish by cultural preference while men specialize in gathering and processing foods, but also there are no cases known in which both men and women perform these tasks without distinction.

Before considering why such a division of labor should be the norm for hunting-gathering societies, let us respond to the second question, that of sexual exploitation. This question presumes that the division of labor (however widely practiced) is nevertheless unfair; that the men of the society have somehow imposed a duty upon the women to perform drudgery such as digging roots, cleaning fish, slaving over the hot cooking fire, and taking care of the babies, while reserving for themselves the exciting, dramatic, and most highly valued labor, big-game hunting, fishing, and fighting.

We have already seen that the women's economic contribution is in no objective sense less valuable than that of the men. Furthermore, Sahaptin men also recognize that fact. I asked James Selam on more than one occasion to rank the major Indian foods in terms of their value or importance. He consistently refused to do so, replying that "all the foods are most important." In Plateau Indian thanksgiving feasts, the sacred foods are presented in the following order: čuuš (water), núsux (salmon), pyaxí (bitterroot), lukš or xawš (the lomatium roots), xamsí (bare-stemmed lomatium), and wíwnu (huckleberries). (This is a typical listing, which may vary somewhat, especially in terms of the specific plant foods available.) Though salmon precedes the plant foods and appears to be the single food item that is foremost in their thoughts, the plant foods honored are the more numerous. Plant foods also provide more occasions for first food feasts (káʔwit) than do animal foods.

The division of labor by sex is ritually reinforced in special ceremonies for a boy's first salmon or deer and a girl's first basket of roots or berries. In each case the neophyte must give it all away, including the tools most closely associated with the harvest, the bow-and-arrow—now, the gun—and hunting knife for boys and the digging stick and collecting bags and baskets for girls. These are soon replaced by return gifts from the elders (Schuster 1975:450–52). By this means, boys and girls are recognized in like manner as productive adults who are ready to contribute to the support of their own families at marriage.

The thrill of hunting and fishing is readily appreciated by contemporary Euro-Americans, but the challenges of gathering and of food preparation are lumped with the domestic commonplaces of hauling wood and water. Anthropologists—typically Euro-American males—have also argued that hunting, in particular, holds the key to human evolutionary advance (e.g., Laughlin 1968). They have devised a variety of reasons for believing this, from the alleged cooperative social nature of hunting that "bonds" man to man, to the mental skills of the hunter judged to form the basis for the human being's higher mental faculties. Comparatively little thought has been given to the evolutionary significance of gathering.

Gathering is not a simple matter of pawing in the dirt for roots in the manner of a bear or even of "squirreling" away a winter's store of nuts. Rather, gathering requires a detailed knowledge of the land and of plant habitat associations and life cycles. Roots, berries, and greens can be harvested only at certain times and places. Careful planning is essential so that one may be at the right place at the right time, as is cooperation among women, both for the sake of company and for assistance in acquiring the knowledge on which successful gathering depends. Cooking and drying foods greatly expands their value. Without the elaborate process of baking camas underground, it is virtually worthless as food (Konlande and Robson 1972). The preparation of fish for drying is an art on which the lives of their families depended. The products of the women's gathering efforts—like the products of hunting and fishing—are widely shared, not only around the woman's own hearth, but more widely through regular exchanges among wedding trade partners, at feasts, or through reciprocal hospitality. Gathering thus reinforces human social and intellectual life as much as does hunting or fishing.

The technology of hunting and fishing catches our attention; the skill of the bow hunter; the art of the fisherman knotting his nets. Women have their characteristic technology as well, without which their gathering efforts would fall far short of their family's needs. The digging stick (kápin) is a simple lever, curved so that modest downward, then backward pressure on the handle loosens the rocky matrix that holds the roots. It will not cut through the root or root stalk as a shovel or trowel might. The roots may then be retrieved with a deft movement of the hand without stooping and transferred directly to the twined root-collecting bag tied at her waist (wápas). Though the contemporary kápin is forged of steel rebar with a steel pipe welded on for a handle, its shape is unchanged from the traditional pointed hard wood digging stick with antler handle.

Bags and baskets are technological innovations that are made by and largely for women's use in the Plateau. Women twist the Indian hemp (taxús) fibers into string, which is then used to twine their root-collecting bags and distinctive blunt-topped conical hats. Some few experts among them weave the large, rigid berrying baskets of cedar roots (Kuneki, Thomas, and Slockish 1982). Women also process the skins of deer, elk, and rabbit to make clothing and the leather purses and saddlebags that men carry with them on their travels. It has only recently been recognized that the "invention" of carrying devices such as these represents a critical technological advance on a par with the invention or adoption of bows-and-arrows or of fish nets (Lee 1979).

In short, there is no rational basis for judging the economic contributions of one sex as more important than that of the other. Why then should not men and women do the same work? First, a division of labor produces a more efficient system of production than one in which each person must be a jack-of-all-trades. This principle, of course, is one basis for the great productivity of modern industrial society. Men's and women's work is complementary in a hunting-and-gathering society; a man and a woman together with their children form a nearly self-contained production and consumption unit.

Granting the profit to be derived from some measure of specialization in production, with sharing of the product, why should this be based on sex rather than on personal preference or individual talent? First, the sexual division of productive labor parallels the division of reproductive labor within the human species; the woman's role as bearer and nurturer of children makes mobility far more costly for women than for men. There is a general tendency in all cultures for women to specialize in tasks that may be performed closer to home and to pursue activities less likely to place accompanying infants at risk (Burton, Brudner, and White 1977:229). The Plateau division of labor is thus both natural and equitable, grounded in cooperation, not competition between the sexes.

Village and Regional Political Organization

nišáykt, "village"

Much of the Plateau Indian literature is marred by a persistent misperception. Plateau Indian society is cast in the mold of a medieval European romance. Authors are obsessed with the daring exploits of mounted warriors— red-skinned knights of the round table—and the nobility of tribal chieftains defending their land and honor. Certain "tribes" in particular have been selected for this role in our play, most notably the Nez Perces and the Cayuses. We readers, and the Indian subjects of these accounts, are the victims of ethnocentrism, the fault of seeing another culture through the distorting lenses of our own preconceptions and expectations.

Anthropologists are trained to overcome their ethnocentrism, as far as possible. It is not possible to transcend entirely one's native ways of seeing and to see another culture with perfect objectivity (if such a thing exists). Though anthropologists writing of Plateau Indians have not been free of ethnocentrism, our type case will be drawn from the ranks of the historians, whose writings on Plateau Indians are both more widely known and more extensive than those of anthropologists, and thus more influential for public understanding or misunderstanding.

Robert Ruby and John Brown are historians of the Northwest Indians. Their popular account of the Spokanes (1970), Cayuses (1972), and of Chief Moses of the Columbia Salish (1965) provide a lively introduction to the Indian people of the region. Their historical documentation of the Indians' experiences in the early years of Euro-American contact and settlement is full of vivid detail. Admirably, they attempt to show the Indian side of the story in a balanced historical account. Yet in their enthusiasm for their subjects they fall into a trap. Let us call it the Overlord Syndrome. The Cayuses become, in their account, "Imperial Tribesmen of Old Oregon." It is not sufficient that the Cayuses be intelligent, devout, and courageous, in every way worthy of our respect and admiration, but they must also rule their abject neighbors and dominate the whole region as proof of their superiority. These neighbors that they are said to have dominated, however, include the very Columbia River Indians about whom I write. It is as if we can only appreciate the Cayuses by abusing their neighbors.

Ruby and Brown characterize the Cayuses as a proud people, wealthy in horses: "In their mounts lay not only their nobility but also their mobility, making them *monarchs* [my emphasis] of a vast Pacific Northwest region between the Cascades and the Rocky Mountains" (Ruby and Brown 1972:3). Their self appelation—"Waiilatpu"—is said to mean "Superior People." If so, it would be similar to the self-perception of ethnic groups the world over but certainly not evidence that their neighbors shared this optimistic assessment. However, "Waiilatpu" more likely is derived from a place name, wáylat, plus the Nez Perce locative suffix -pu. This means, according to the interpretive display at the Whitman Mission National Historic Site, "people of the rye grass place," a typical Plateau ethnolinguistic designation.

The Cayuses are furthermore said to be "much hardier than other Indians of the region, . . . [as they] lived in . . . mat houses in summer and mud-covered subterranean houses in winter, subsisting mostly by hunting, fishing, and gathering roots and berries" (Ruby and Brown 1972:4). But we know that such a way of life was common to all Plateau peoples. Again, they contrast the Cayuses with their presumed close relations, the Molalas (about whom even less is known than of the Cayuses), as being "the more aggressive . . . destined for expansion" (p. 4). Yet the Cayuses had virtually lost their language through intermarriage with their Nez Perce and Sahaptin neighbors by the mid-1850s and numbered at best a few hundred during the contact period (see Rigsby 1969). Is that evidence of the expansionist destiny of an aggressive, overweaning people?

Having obtained horses from their "Snake Indian" rivals to the south, they, we are told, "soon developed into formidable horsemen, . . . adding power and opulence to their mobility, the Cayuse broke out of their homeland, driving northward to the Columbia River the peoples standing in their way. For a long time they would *dominate the ragtag bands* [my emphasis] which occupied a twenty-mile belt along the Columbia" (Ruby and Brown 1972:8).

As authority for this reconstruction of events Ruby and Brown cite Thomas Garth (1964). Garth in turn based his interpretation uncritically on a traveler's tale told by a Thomas Farnham, who spent three weeks on the mid-Columbia in the fall of 1839 (1906 [1841]:328–70). Neither Garth nor Ruby and Brown note the inconsistency between their characterization of the Columbia River Indians as "a ragtag band" and Lewis and Clark's experience on that stretch of the river. Lewis and Clark found large, densely populated villages, the people harvesting an abundance of fish and aggressively confident in their dealings with the foreign visitors. Ruby and Brown discount the formidable reputation the Indians of The Dalles and Celilo Falls earned from the early fur-trading parties, who found them anything but easily intimidated. Furthermore, the Columbia River Indians were not confined to a "twenty-mile wide belt" along the river, as Ruby and Brown claim. Rather, they ranged widely, hunting and gathering, into the Blue Mountains and the Cascades each year in the conduct of their seasonal round (see Rigsby 1965:221–28; Suphan 1974a, b).

Ruby and Brown continue to spin their tale of Cayuse political supremacy, alleging even that they extracted tribute from and administered punishment to the people resident at The Dalles (who were Wasco/Wishram and Columbia River Sahaptins with a well-deserved reputation for forcefulness, see also French 1961), who "remained under their control by what they [the Cayuses] claimed to be the right of ownership. Their practice of exacting tribute, in the form of salmon and other goods, from bands in the area served to give them jurisdiction over that stretch of the Columbia. For years to come they would not let its salmon eaters, teeth worn and eyes blinded by river sand, forget their inferiority" (Ruby and Brown 1972:17–18). Strange that Columbia River "salmon eaters" (as if that were a sign of inferiority) of my acquaintance think of the Cayuses as among their relatives and seem unaware of their alleged political subjugation at the hands of the "Imperial Cayuse Tribe." Their experience of imperial power is limited to what they have learned at the hands of the šuyápu (from French *chapeau*, "hat"), as they know the white man.

Ruby and Brown are not alone in this misapprehension. Francis Haines' highly regarded history of the Nez Perces begins by characterizing them as sedentary fishermen (1955: xv, 9, 18, 21, 36) until they acquired horses at about A. D. 1750. He claims that they relied upon fishing for "80–90 percent of their entire food needs for the year, according to some estimates" (p. 12). (I have calculated that fish provided no more than 30 percent of their total food supply [Hunn 1981]; see Table 12). Haines suggests that the horse liberated the Nez Perces from village confinement, allowing them to "dominate" (p. xvii) the western Plateau. "These spirited warriors dominated the entire region from the Cascades to the Rockies [cf. Ruby and Brown's identical claim for the Cayuses; both could not have "dominated" the entire Plateau!] and . . . they dictated the intertribal policies at the great council of tribes held each spring in the Yakima Valley" (p. 48). Haines refers to Nez Perces' feelings of superiority over "the lowly Spokans" (p. 61) and the "unimportant, poverty-stricken [Priest Rapids] branch of Shahaptian stock usually overlooked by the lordly Nez Percés" (p. 192). Yet these same Priest Rapids people included Smohalla, a prophet highly influential among the Nez Perces.

Ecological Constraints on Plateau Politics

In chapter 4 we saw how the Columbia River Indians relied on a carefully scheduled seasonal round requiring considerable mobility from their winter bases along the major rivers. The Nez Perce economy was similar in its broad outlines (Marshall 1977), with the Nez Perces at something of a disadvantage in their restricted access to the rich salmon resources of the Columbia. Thus, to characterize Cayuses and Nez Perces as "wealthier" than their "poverty-stricken" Columbia River relations is ecologically indefensible. Rich in horses they may have been, but so were the Walla Wallas, Umatillas, and Yakimas.

All local groups relied most heavily on such root foods as bitterroot, cous and the other lomatiums, and camas, so access to the salmon fishery very likely was crucial in determining differences in population density and the size of social and political units within the Plateau. In this respect the Cayuses and Nez Perces were at no advantage in comparison with the Columbia River Indians and were likely at some disadvantage. Allegations that the Cayuses and Nez Perces dominated political affairs at The Dalles or in the Yakima Valley summer encampments (presumably at the Weippe Prairie, Kittitas, or Glenwood camas meadows) are supported neither by reliable witnesses nor by theoretical expectations based on sociopolitical or ecological principles.

What are these principles that lead me to doubt claims for Cayuse and Nez Perce hegemony on the Plateau? These principles link resource abundance with population density, and that with technological complexity, the division of labor, surplus production, wealth accumulation, and the concentration of political power. Clearly, these variables are linked, if sometimes in complex ways, in global cultural evolution. Progressively more "effective" hunting-gathering societies, through very gradual population expansion, came to populate virtually the entire global land area by ten thousand years ago, replacing societies incapable of expansion. The Plateau hunting-gathering economies represent an advanced type of this mode of production. Such societies achieved average densities of just one person per fifty square miles in land-locked, strongly seasonal desert and arctic environments, but reached densities of from one to ten per square mile in environments favored by reliable concentrations of food resources (often "locally unearned"), such as the Columbia Plateau, the California Central Valley and southcentral coast, and the Northwest Coast of America. Compare the Cayuses' estimated density of one per ten square miles with that of the Nez Perces: one per three square miles. One per two square miles is estimated for all Sahaptin speakers in the Plateau (see Table 10).

Agricultural production replaced hunting-gathering in much of the tropical and temperate regions. Contrary to popular opinion this was not the result of agriculture being more efficient or more reliable than hunting-gathering as a means of food production. Nonmechanized farming requires more work effort to produce an adequate food supply than does hunting-gathering (Sahlins 1972) and is notoriously subject to the vagaries of weather. Agriculture's evolutionary superiority is due to its ability to produce much more food on a given piece of land than hunting-gathering can, thus supporting—at times rather precariously—human populations of 25 to 500 per square mile, reaching 5,000 per square mile on intensively managed irrigated lands such as in the Java rice paddy zone and on the shores of Lake Xochimilco near the Aztecs' capital in the Valley of Mexico.

As population density increases, the social environment is dramatically altered; the number of fellow humans with whom one can and, indeed, must deal increases in geometric proportion, calling forth new social and political responses. One common response to such population pressures is the *state,* a political system in which members of a dominant community extract by threat of force, taxes or tribute from subordinate communities (Carneiro 1970). We should be very surprised if Plateau hunter-gatherers living at densities substantially less than one person per square mile developed such a form of political domination, one typical of agricultural societies with population densities a thousand times those of the Plateau. In fact, no such system of domination existed among the Indian people on the Columbia Plateau.

The Exercise of Leadership in Plateau Society

As noted, Plateau population densities at the time of first Euro-American contacts were quite typical of inland hunting-gathering peoples worldwide. Their social and political institutions likewise fit that mold.

Families were nearly autonomous both politically and economically. Plateau "chiefs," or more accurately, "village headmen" (miyúux̣/miyáwax̣), at the pinnacle of the indigenous political hierarchy, did not *rule*, rather they exercised authority only so long as they continued to merit the respect of their fellow villagers. Successful headmen attracted larger followings, which in turn increased the economic and political strength of their villages. A successful headman had the means to be generous, a quality expected of leaders by hunter-gatherers the world around.

If particularly notable, a Nez Perce headman (NP: mióx̣at-miox̣at, literally, "little chief") might be named chief (miyóx̣at) of a group of allied villages occupying adjacent sites along a single tributary stream (Marshall 1977:143). The linked villages of such a stream were dominated by a "skyline" (-toyam) after which the allied villages were known. Nez Perce headmen and chiefs were formally elected by consensus at a gathering of the villagers and normally held their positions for life. Yet Plateau people were jealous of their individual autonomy. As the Nez Perces say, "All men are leaders [in their own homes]."

The qualities of an ideal Plateau leader are implied by a Nez Perce synonym for "headman," hamqáqayc (háma, "man"), literally, "man with kind words" (Marshall 1977:141). The eloquence of Indian leaders is legendary, yet words were powerful and should be used sparingly. To deflect the resentment that is engendered by the exercise of authority, village headmen employed "spokesmen" or "heralds" (sínwi-ła, "speaker"; NP: téwyelenewet) to proclaim decisions, announce community projects, and transmit important news, allowing the headman or chief to maintain a dignified reserve.

Just as a chief's rhetorical power was diffused through an intermediary, so also was the exercise of his judicial role. Many villages had a "whipper" (pawawya-łá; NP: wełúwet) who administered discipline. Parents would not punish their own children but might call upon a whipper to administer the needed correctives. A further diffusion of authority involved the division of labor between headmen/chiefs on the one hand and task specific leaders, also called "chiefs" in most of the Plateau literature (for example, "war chief" and "salmon chief" [NP: léwteqnewet]). Each held authority in an area for which he or she was peculiarly talented, by virtue of spiritual gifts. Furthermore, political leaders were rarely also shamans (twáti; N P: tiwét), or "Indian doctors," as they are known in the local English vernacular. Indian doctors possessed extraordinary spiritual powers, giving them the ability (and thus the heavy responsibility) to cure the sick. Thus, power—to the extent that it had to be exercised to maintain peace, health, and social and economic cooperation—was hedged about by "checks and balances" as necessary and effective in their context as the constitutional guarantees of the United States's democracy.

In a system as radically democratic as this there is no place for "Imperial warriors." The stereotypes of Plateau politics I criticized above more closely reflect the social ecology of European monarch and peasant than they do the political realities of Plateau hunter-gatherers.

The Exchange of Kin, Wealth, and Information

Plateau society did not consist of a collection of warring tribes, each jealously defending its territory against aggressive neighbors. It was not a scale model of nineteenth-century Europe. As I have noted, the largest political units were villages and occasional congeries of neighboring villages recognizing a single chief. These units had little formal structure and even less power to control the lives of the coresident families. Yet Plateau society, if acephalous, was not amorphous. It is best understood as a network of ties among individuals and families forged of two strands, a warp of kinship and a weft of exchange.

The ramifying web of kinship ties can be clearly seen in an Indian's family tree (see Table 21). James Selam, for example, was born at Rock Creek, Washington, and raised just across the river in a winter village at táwaš (modern-day Blalock, Oregon). He considers himself to be a tákšpaš-pam, a John Day River Indian, after the regionally dominant village of tákšpaš located just above the John Day River mouth, a dozen miles west of táwaš. His parents hail from the Umatilla and John Day rivers. His grandparents come from as far afield as Priest Rapids and Nez Perce country.

Columbia River Indian kindred exogamy, marrying outside the local bilateral kin group, is derivative of an incest taboo that extended to all recognized kin (with the single exception already noted of one's awít). This guaranteed that most marriages bridged a gap between villages, that many marriages

TABLE 21

Village Affiliations of Three Generations

James Selam slílwal 1919– John Day/Rock Creek	F:	George Selam silám c. 1870–1966 Umatilla	FF:	pačał Umatilla/Wanapam
			FM:	wácwaypam Umatilla/Cayuse
	M:	Sally Sam anwák 1882–1958 John Day	MF:	slílwal John Day/Nez Perce
			MM:	? Nez Perce

Delsie Albert Selam yáystani 1923– Alderdale				FFF: láwax̱alpat
	F:	Isaac Albert waq̓ístax̱at Umatilla/Pendleton	FF:	cáhaya Umatilla/Alderdale
			FM:	tincáat Wanapam/Patterson
	M:	wapstáyu John Day/Rock Creek	MF:	tx̱nášat Patterson
			MM:	yáystani John Day/Blalock
				MMM: tísx̱ckt

crossed the bounds of so-called "tribes" such as Murdock's "Teninos," the Umatillas, or the Yakimas, and that a few marriages each generation linked families with different native languages, such as Sahaptin and Nez Perce, or Sahaptin and Columbia Salish (see Walker 1967c). Between one's own blood kin and one's in-laws an individual could expect a welcome in villages throughout the Plateau, could visit for extended periods, gathering, fishing, and hunting with one's kin. A Cayuse, Nez Perce, or Yakima Indian might "demand" (or so it might appear to a Euro-American observer, one steeped in a tradition emphasizing individual hegemony over property of all kinds) fish at Celilo Falls as his due. Behavior that early observers saw as evidence of Cayuse and Nez Perce political control of Celilo residents might be interpreted more correctly as evidence of the powerful Plateau Indian ethic prescribing generosity among kin.

Exchange among kin is most often what Marshall Sahlins has characterized as generalized reciprocity, that is, one shares what one has without (obvious) expectation of a return (1972:194–95). One does not demand repayment or expect a return on one's gift in the immediate future. It is as if generosity were its own reward. Of course, generous men and women were often rewarded by recognition of their leadership potential. Chiefs must be both willing and able to give beyond normal expectations. A young man, willing and able to give food in abundance to his prospective parents-in-law, gets the bride, as is illustrated in the Wasco story of "Arrow-Point Maker and Tobacco-Hunter" (see Text, p. 220).

As we have noted, this ethical principle is learned early. A boy eats none of the meat from the first deer he kills: he gives the carcass to his elders who ceremoniously distribute it piece-by-piece to a wide set of relatives and fellow villagers. The boy thereby begins the transition to manhood, by first proving his ability to provide meat to his family and his village. Girls likewise turn over their first bags of roots and baskets of berries to their mothers, aunts, or grandmothers for ceremonial distribution.

Despite drastic changes in the traditional Columbia River Indians' lives since the first Euro-American influences were felt on the Plateau, this ethical principle retains much of its original moral force. An elk or deer brought down by rifle fire and transported home on the bed of a pick-up truck is not hoarded in the hunter's freezer but proudly shared among the hunter's kin in his and other households. The subsistence fisherman's salmon harvest likewise ends up spread among households throughout the reservation. Women bring canned huckleberries and bags of root cakes or of baked camas when they drop by to visit relatives and friends, and worshipers in the hundreds are fed from the collective stores of the Indian women each Sunday in the longhouses of the Seven-drums religionists.

Sharing does not stop with traditional food items—now of more symbolic

Arrow-Point Maker and Tobacco-Hunter

(A Wasco story from Ramsey 1977:76–78; courtesy California Folklore Society.)

There was an arrow-point maker on the right side of the Columbia, three miles below [Winquatt]. One day this man cut his finger with flint, so that it bled. He put his finger in his mouth, liked the taste of the blood, ate his finger off, then his hand, pulled the flesh from his arms, legs, and body, and ate it all. At last he had only a little bit of flesh left that was below his shoulders on his back, where he could not reach it. He was a skeleton now; nothing but his bones were left, only his heart hung in his body. He went to the next village and ate all the people. They could not kill him, nothing would penetrate his bones.

Now his wife, carrying a little son, escaped, went south, traveling over the grass, right on the tops of the blades of grass, so that he could not track her for a long time. But at last he found the tracks. The moment he found them, his wife knew it.

She traveled day and night in great fear. The husband gained on her, came nearer and nearer all the time. Far ahead of her was a blue mountain. She hurried on. When she reached the foot of the mountain, she saw a house, and went in. A very old man sat on one side making bows and arrows, and his daughter sat on the other side, making little tobacco-sacks.

The woman called him by a kinship-name, but the old man did not answer. The north wind, which had grown stronger, began to blow terribly, and almost carried the house away, threw down great trees. At last she begged so hard that the old man said, "Hide behind me." That moment the skeleton came in with a frightful wind, walked around the fire, and stamped on the old man's arrows, which broke into bits. The old man grabbed a long arrow-point and thrust it into the skeleton's heart. That instant the skeleton fell to the ground—a pile of bones. The wind stopped blowing when it fell. The old man said to the wife of the skeleton-man, "Come and throw these old bones outdoors."

There was plenty of tobacco growing on the hill above the old man's house. He made arrow-points all the time; and when his quiver was full, he would start out and return with it empty, but with tobacco in his hand. The old man and his daughter lived on smoke, neither ate anything; they lived on smoke from the kind of pipe that is straight. The old man always shot the tobacco; those whom he shot were the Tobacco people. When he brought home the tobacco, his daughter would put it into little sacks, and they would smoke until all was gone. Then he would go off again on another hunt of these people.

The woman and child lived with the old man and his daughter for a long time. When the boy got old enough, he hunted squirrels for his mother. One day when the old man went out, the boy followed him. He saw the old man shoot up at a high rock bluff. The Tobacco people all lived in these high rocks. He crept close, sat behind the old man, took an arrow, and wished it to hit the tobacco. The arrow left his bow at the same instant that the old man's arrow left his bow, and five bunches of tobacco fell down.

The old man was delighted, and danced for joy; he had never shot so many in a whole day. "You are my son-in-law," said the old man, and went home. The daughter was glad that her father had so much tobacco. The old man said, "I don't know but that is an [omen]." The boy laughed to himself. The old man said to his daughter, "This is your husband," and added, "The people of the future will be willing to give their daughters to a good hunter, and the girl must wait until the father and mother find such a man."

The old man now rested, and the young man hunted tobacco for him. He filled the house with tobacco. The old man was satisfied. Then the young boy, his wife and mother, came to the Columbia River. When they came to the village where the young man's father had turned into a man-eater, they found only bones. The young man gathered up the bones, threw paint into the air five times, spoke five times to the sky, and the people all rose up as they were before the man-eater had devoured them.

When the mother was old, she had food given her every day by her daughter-in-law. She grew weak fast, and her son said, "It will be the duty of a daughter-in-law to care for her mother-in-law among the people to come." The mother said, "My daughter and I will go south, and we will be guardian spirits to medicine-women, and will give authority to women to smoke. When a woman smokes, she will be a medicine-woman." The son said, "I will be a guardian spirit to help people. Those whom I help will be good hunters."

than real economic value. The loan of valuable equipment such as cars, trucks, and boats is freely requested of kin and freely granted, no matter how often such equipment has been returned broken or not returned at all in the past. This hunting-gathering norm now not infrequently proves counterproductive for those Indians who strive for success by the standards of the wider American society. It is very difficult to save money or to protect one's capital investments when to do so means refusing to share with needy relatives. Non-Indian standards of competent money management require Indian people to deny the ethical basis of their traditional social life. Indian people today are caught between a cultural rock and an economic hard place.

The Plateau Indian emphasis on generosity as an ideal for social behavior is found among other hunting-gathering peoples such as the San of southern Africa's Kalahari desert and the Australian Aborigines (Lee and DeVore 1968). Such a wide distribution among historically independent societies suggests a strong adaptive payoff for this cultural pattern. I suspect the answer lies in the hypothetical evolutionary mechanism of reciprocal altruism first discussed in detail by Robert Trivers in a 1971 article. The sociobiological challenge to our traditional understanding of Darwinian evolutionary theory is based on the paradox of altruism: that is, true altruism—behaving so as to benefit another individual at genetic cost to oneself—should never evolve. Altruistic behavior should always be overcome by a selfish strategy that takes advantage of the altruist. Most examples of "altruism" have been reinterpreted as genetically selfish, as, for example, when one provides assistance to one's close biological kin. Such kin are, genetically speaking, extensions of the self. Remaining to be explained, however, are cases in which valuable assistance is given to distant kin or to non-kin. The cases of generalized reciprocity we have examined above clearly go beyond what we would expect on the basis of inclusive fitness calculations, that is, calculations of the common genetic interest among close kin. Are we dealing here with a culture defying an iron law of nature? Trivers argues to the contrary.

Generosity toward distant kin or non-kin—potentially altruistic in that one gives away resources essential for survival with no guarantee of return—can prove of adaptive advantage if certain conditions hold. To wit, generosity is to be expected only if the expected benefits to the donor exceed the donor's costs, in other words, only if generosity results in selfish benefit. This will be the case only if generosity is selective, calculated on the likelihood of a balancing return by the beneficiary of one's gifts. This in turn requires careful accounting on an individual basis of a life-time's history of gifts or help given and received and requires as well effective sanctions against those who would abuse the system.

Such safeguards are in fact deeply fixed in primitive societies. Marcel Mauss long ago described the "Power of the Gift" (1967 [1925]) in such societies as based on three moral imperatives: (a) one must give; (b) one must accept a proffered gift; and (c) one must make a return gift. These moral imperatives, if honored by all, should assure that gifts given are profitable to the giver, and the cultural prominence of gift-giving in all human societies suggests how deeply ingrained such imperatives are in human psychology.

Only saints and fools place their entire trust in the effectiveness of moral imperatives. Among the Kalahari San, for example, most conflicts result from perceptions of injustice in the balance of gifts given and received, with dissatisfactions not infrequently smoldering from one generation to the next. Supernatural sanctions are often called upon to discourage those who might disdain the social pressures that encourage morally correct action. For example, the Columbia River Indians stress in mythology the dire consequences of cheating, as in the story of Raccoon and his grandmother (see Text, pp. 186–87). Thus, the dramatic force of myth-telling is used to impress upon the young the necessity of proper action.

Exchanges between unrelated individuals and families often have more the quality of Sahlins' balanced reciprocity, in which the values of gifts and return gifts are carefully and explicitly equated (1972:194–95). For example, marriages were sealed by an elaborate series of exchanges between the families of the bride and groom. Following discreet inquiries as to the acceptability of the proposal, the groom and a delegation of his family paid the bride's family a visit, with each member of the party bringing gifts to bestow upon their kin-counterparts among the bride's people. Gifts were primarily symbolic of a man's role in family provisioning. After a discreet interval the bride's family reciprocated, giving especially gifts associated with the familial roles of women to seal the bargain. Thereupon the groom joined his bride's family for a period of bride service. During this time he was, in effect, on probation to assure that he was willing and able to contribute the man's share to the support of the new family (Schuster 1975:124–28). A marriage established not only a bond between bride and groom but also a whole set of enduring bonds or ritual trading partnerships between particular kin of the bride and of the groom. Even the death of a spouse could not sever these ties. The institution of the levirate and sororate, described above, served to preserve the web of marital partnership.

In death, also, the Columbia River Indians found occasion to reinforce these ties to one another through funeral "give-aways." At modern-day Indian funerals, the kin of the deceased distribute valuables to those who come to honor the dead. The gifts a mourner receives at the occasion of a funeral are returned at the occasion of his or her own funeral.

Material exchanges were not confined to kin. Special relationships of mutual trust, respect, and obligation were recognized among friends and trading partners. Trade was also conducted on a less personal basis, as at major entrepôts such as The Dalles–Celilo area (Spier and Sapir 1930:224–28; French 1961). Surpluses of dried salmon stockpiled by residents of The Dalles were exchanged for commodities of the interior, such as dried roots, berries, and hides (see fig. 6.1). At first Euro-American contact, horses and

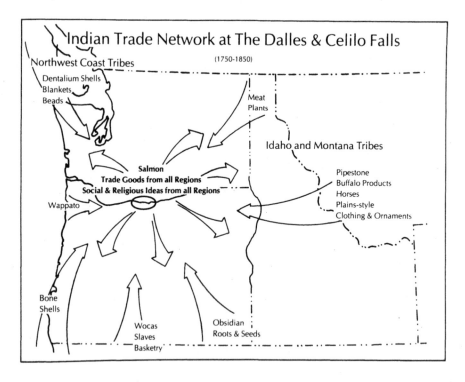

Fig. 6.1. Indian trade network at The Dalles and Celilo Falls (reprinted from *Oregon Indians*, Zucker et al. 1983:43, with permission of the Oregon Historical Society Press).

slaves were much in evidence at these native markets. The first Euro-American traders to visit here encountered sophisticated Chinookan entrepreneurs ready to do business with them.

Slavery

Plateau Indian society was egalitarian and democratic before the coming of the whites; so was that of Athens in its golden age. Yet the gilt of each is somewhat tarnished by the fact of slavery. It is important to bear in mind that the Americans who came as missionaries, soldiers, and settlers to "civilize" the western frontier came from a slave nation: slavery was not abolished in the United States until ratification of the Thirteenth Amendment to the Constitution in 1865—ten years after Isaac Stevens' treaty councils. The great trading center on the Columbia between The Dalles and Celilo Falls was a major slave market during the early decades of the nineteenth century.

Henry Perkins, Methodist missionary at The Dalles, described the trade in graphic terms and railed against it. He tried to stop a party of Wasco Indians that was about to set off for the Klamath country to trade for slaves and was threatened with a whipping for his interference. The previous spring such a slaving party had returned with fourteen captives, "mostly young women & boys—captives of the Chas-ti tribe [the Shasta of northeastern California]. The prime cost of the slaves, was a horse for each or about ten dollars, while slaves stand upon the Columbia at more than double this price" (Perkins n.d. [1838–43], Book 1:11). This comment indicates that the captives were purchased from Klamath intermediaries.

Perkins quotes an Indian slave owner at The Dalles who argued for the necessity of slavery:

> "My children" said he "arise in the morning—they are hungry—they call to a couple of slaves & send them off after food. My children sit down & wait. By & by the slaves return & bring them some breakfast & they eat. Who would get my children food if I had no slaves? Besides" added he "why should we put away our slaves? They are our *brethren* & *sisters*—we *love* them. They are not dogs & horses that we should turn them off to take care of themselves. We do not call them *slaves* [ašwaníya] to their *faces*—if we want them to do any thing we say Brother, do this, or Sister, do that. . . ." (Perkins n.d. [1838–43], Book 1:14)

Perkins is at pains to unmask this benign image of Indian slavery on the Columbia. He compares Indian slavery unfavorably with the conditions of slavery he had witnessed in Brazil and Peru, describes the filth, lassitude, poverty, and degradation suffered by a slave in the service of "the great lordly salmon-eaters along this river" (Book 1:15). He claims that a sick slave is dragged from the house and left to die alone, then thrown to the dogs without ceremony (Book 1:17). He also describes a recent incident in which,

> a young man was accidentally drowned in the great rapids just above here [i.e., at The Dalles proper]. His death was deeply felt by the family, & in their darkness [as the Indians describe the sense of grief] they concluded that they could not do better for him, now that he was gone, than to send his faithful female servant after him. They accordingly led her to the point of rock from which her master had fallen & hurled her into the boiling current." (Perkins n.d. [1838–43], Book 2:21–22)

This practice of sacrificing a slave on the death of the owner was apparently confined to slaves of chiefly families among the Wasco-Wishram people. Spier and Sapir report that "in 1844 a slave boy was bound to the body of the dead chief of the Wasco in the grave house preparatory to burial" (1930:223).

The absolute power to dispose of the life of a slave as if it were any other piece of property may have been more the exception than the rule in the Plateau, according to Verne Ray's review (1939:30–35). Ray notes that slavery was entirely absent among

> "the Sanpoil and Southern Okanogan . . . [who] are outspoken in condemning the practice. Slaves are likewise absent among the Columbia and the Lakes. . . . Only in the extreme northwestern Plateau . . . and among the Wishram [the case described by Perkins] and Klamath are slaves fairly numerous. The western position of these tribes makes it obvious that they are participating in coastal culture in this respect" (Ray 1939:30).

According to Ray virtually all slaves held by Plateau Indians were of non-Plateau nativity, most being war captives taken among peoples of southern Oregon and northeastern California (p. 33). He believes that Plateau slavery is of recent origin, quoting Spier's comment on Klamath slavery, to the effect that, "It is probable that the introduction of the horse stimulated [Klamath] predatory habits and made possible frequent trading visits to the Columbia River people" (Ray 1939:34).

Spier and Sapir let a Plateau Indian slave speak for himself in this autobiographical account. It is the story of a Wishram slave who was taken about 1842 by Klikitats in a raid on a Molala fishing camp in southern Oregon:

"I and my brother were captured in a war between the Klickitat and my tribe. . . . With the Klickitat were Indians from several villages on the Columbia. In those days my people did nothing but prepare for war with Indians from the Columbia [a measure of the political instability subsequent to the introduction of horses, guns, and exotic epidemic diseases] who were in the habit of raiding our people to capture women and children as slaves. . . . I was then a boy of about four years, while my brother was about six.

"We were taken to Sketcútxat, now Vancouver, Washington. I was kept by one family while my brother stayed with another. After a long time I was given to a Wishram family with whom I remained until I was freed [about 1855]. We were so well cared for that my brother and I never had any idea of running away. . . . We both forgot our language. I now talk Wishram and Klickitat. . . . I do not know any of my relatives." (Spier and Sapir 1930:222–23)

Slavery in the Plateau seems to represent the temporary intrusion of an idea foreign to basic Plateau values. The moral ambiguity of slavery is apparent in James Selam's recounting of his tíla's (his MMF) slave-holding career: On one of his daring raids in Northern Paiute country this man kidnapped a boy, intending to raise him as a slave. But he grew attached to the boy and so trained him as a son, teaching him to hunt. When the boy was grown he took him back to his home country and released him. On a subsequent horse-raiding expedition James's tíla again infiltrated a Paiute encampment, but his disguise was exposed by his own one-time foster son who gave him a severe beating. He would not strike back at his "son"; the "son" then tended his wounds and gave him a horse, saying that he had no need to steal it!

7

Religion

tamánwit ku šúkat,
"law and spirit power"

IT IS QUITE POSSIBLE to conclude on the basis of personal familiarity with contemporary Indian people that they are little different from the average American of Irish, Italian, Polish, or Japanese extraction. One may hear a smattering of the old mother tongue in use by grandparents, but parents and children converse in colloquial English about school, sports, jobs, cars, or household tasks while the TV chatters on in the next room (see fig. 7.1). The dusty yards, decorated with nonfunctional motor vehicles and guarded by a loose flock of lean and hungry dogs and cats, are typical of the home environs of the rural poor all over America. (Rusting hulks of dead cars are not without their uses, however, as a ready source of spare parts for the living and a shelter for the menagerie.) A print of James Earle Fraser's famed sculpture, "Trail's End," and the cluster of Indian corn hanging by the kitchen door might be passed off as largely symbolic expressions of a familiar nostalgia for one's "roots" in the past.

Yet I believe this familiarity of the modern Indian home life hides a deep division in world view from the Euro-American norm. This was brought home to me one winter evening as James and Delsie Selam, Sara Quaempts, and I had joined Elsie Pistolhead at her home to record Coyote stories. Elsie Pistolhead is a powerful old woman, with a charismatic aura I could sense at first encounter. She lived alone with a granddaughter, a girl of about fifteen. As the tales progressed—told with great energy and humor by Mrs. Pistolhead, with encouragement and prompting from her audience—the granddaughter grew increasingly restless. Her grandmother several times halted her performance to rebuke the child sharply for her annoyance. Piqued at being ignored by the adults intent on their work, she bolted out the front door. Elsie Pistolhead again broke off the myth-telling, this time shouting at

228

Fig. 7.1. Contemporary Indian life.

the girl in English, "Come back here, child, don't you know, there's dead people outside!" Her granddaughter, cringing, came back in, closed the door, and the tale resumed as if there had never been this interruption.

I felt myself an intruder, transported two centuries back to a mat lodge shrouded by winter's night. I crouched in the back, peering past the family to the fire, beyond which an old woman recounted Coyote's primal adventures, while at my back wind-blown snow and uneasy ghosts whispered in the darkness. But the electric lights and the mechanical humming of my tape recorder soon brought me back to the late twentieth century.

I was reminded of the sprigs of rose (škapášway) or juniper I had often noted inconspicuously tacked to the walls in Indian people's homes, to prevent ghosts (ɬčáča) from disturbing the occupants, I was told. For the same reason an infant's cradle board is constructed with a "fender" of rosewood, and at funerals the empty grave is first spiritually cleansed of ghosts by sweeping with a branch of rose, juniper, or cedar.

Ghosts haunt the living not from spite but because death is lonely, and death is not strong enough to sever completely the emotional attachments of the living to the dead. Ghosts desperately seek the comfort of living human companionship, and the living, especially young children or those who have just lost a close relative, are in real danger that their own "life" will be enticed to join that of the deceased. Harsh measures may be required to wrench the living from this grip of the dead. Elsie Pistolhead recalled as a young woman losing her child and being forced by her mother immediately to go find the rare wild tobacco plant, to brew a bitter tea of it, and to drink it so that she would vomit and thus be freed of the tie forged by having shared food that same day with her dead child. The native tobacco (*Nicotiana attenuata*, see fig. 7.2) is named in Sahaptin for this, its only reported use: awt-pamá, literally, "for purification."

We immigrants, who call ourselves "natives" after one paltry generation on the land, can scarcely fathom what it means to the Indian to walk on a land in which a hundred generations of ancestors have been buried.

Animism

Some scholars claim that religions have evolved universalistic ethical systems from particularistic ones, with monotheistic world churches that stake claims to the souls of all humanity representing the furthest thrust of religious progress. From this perspective the Columbia River Indian traditional religion—tied as it is to particular places and the spirits of particular plants and animals, offering no universal salvation—is primitive, as simple a theology as the society it served. Traditional Sahaptin religion may be called animistic; it is also a species of shamanism. These terms describe aspects of the religious belief and practice of hunter-gatherers all around the world.

Animism was defined by the nineteenth-century anthropological theorist, Sir Edward B. Tylor, in terms of a concept of the spirit that animates living beings (1871). This animate spirit was thought of as being separable from the material body. He concluded that this idea was inferred from the universal experience of dreaming in which one's spirit seems to travel about while the body lies abed. However, in my opinion, Tylor overlooked the theological essence of animism. That essence is a moral principle, not an ontological premise. The heart of animistic religious belief is the following article of faith:

> *People, animals, plants, and other forces of nature—sun, earth, wind, and rock—are animated by spirit. As such they share with humankind intelligence and will, and thus have moral rights and obligations as PERSONS.*

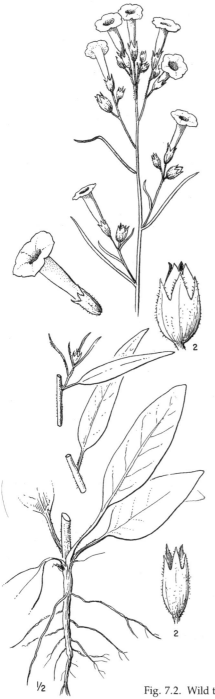

Fig. 7.2. Wild tobacco (*Nicotiana attenuata;* **awt-pamá**).

From this perspective, animism may be judged to represent a more comprehensive morality than that of the established world churches. Animism extends the moral benefits of human society to the entire local ecosystem (Feit 1970).

A Klikitat Indian myth illustrates how this principle is expressed on the Plateau (see Text, opposite). The deer you hunt for your livelihood are *persons* and you must treat them as you would treat an influential human—with respect and consideration for their feelings and needs. Disrespect is offensive to the deer just as it would be to you yourself if so treated by a fellow villager. The consequences of such mistreatment are likewise analogous, the withdrawal of collegial contact, exclusion from the web of mutual support. One's life literally depends upon maintaining whole this socio-ecological web (Nelson 1983).

Animism suggests a rather different view of the world of nature and of the human place in it than does mainstream Euro-American culture. My first interview with James Selam challenged me to see the world thus transformed. James began by speaking of his eldest son who had recently been killed in a car wreck, not in answer to any question from me but out of his own needs. The story was spare in outline, calmly but deliberately told.

He had been sitting up late at home alone the night of the accident when he heard a coyote howl close behind the house (see fig. 7.3) across the pasture toward the hill, though coyotes rarely come by there. He feared then that the coyote bore him a message, news of a death. He went out with his gun in an effort to find it in order to shoot it, thus forestalling fate, but he could see nothing. A few hours later the police called to tell him that Victor, his son, had been killed on the Satus Pass highway.

He spoke then, and still does from time to time, of how bright Victor was, how he was doing so well in college, and of the interest he had shown in his father's store of traditional knowledge. I'm not sure why he volunteered this personal history on our first meeting, though in retrospect perhaps he intended the story to explain why he had agreed to work with an outsider to record his cultural past, lest it be forgotten.

In any case, the coyote spoke to him clearly that night. James's attempt to kill the messenger that brought the bad news is also an understandable, if all-too-human response. This was not the coyote of myth, a roguish archetypal figure of the myth age, but the present-day animal, one's neighbor of the local socio-ecological community, bearing news.

Raven as contemporary bird is also a communicant, but one requires

A Klikitat Indian Coyote Story

Told by Joe Hunt to Melville Jacobs (from Jacobs 1929:200)

There was a woman and a child [Coyote's family]. Coyote would go about hunting; he would shoot and kill all sorts of things. He shot and killed a deer. He butchered it. There were two young ones in its belly. He threw them aside and left them. There the two young deer lay. Rain and snow came upon them. She whom he had killed felt very badly at heart about them [her unborn children]. After that Coyote went all over and shot and killed nothing. He went all about until he was worn out. He was killing nothing at all. He was tired. His family became hungry.

[Coyote] thought, "Why is it indeed that I do not kill anything? I shall defecate my two younger sisters." [The skit which follows is a favorite repeated many times in the local Coyote stories.] That is what he did. He said to them, "Tell me why I have not gone and killed anything here. I am all tired out. I am hungry." The youngest sister said to him, "You always reply [whenever we tell you what you want to know], 'That is the very thing I had forgotten about.' Go and figure it all out yourself." [Coyote countered,] "Aha. Make haste. Tell me. If you do not, it will rain and the rain will break you up." At that they replied, "Oh dear. We will tell you anyhow." [Coyote said,] "Go ahead. Quick. Tell me." The two sisters said to him, "She whom you shot and killed, that deer, and whose fawns you left there at the place where you did the butchering. . . . Well, after then the young fawns cried a great deal. Rain and snow came upon them there. It got cold. She who was the mother of them felt very bad at heart over it, she whom you carried off home. Very, very badly did she feel. She must have gotten very angry at you. That is the cause of your never being able to kill game. But now if you sweat for five days, you will become clean after that. Then you may go hunting. You may kill game again after that." That is what his two sisters told him. In reply Coyote said, "Oh, that is the very thing I had forgotten about. Ready now you! Enter back into me, my younger sisters!"

All right then. Coyote went on and prepared a sweat house. He sweated for five days, five bunches of rocks he used, one bunch for each sweat on each of the five days. Then Coyote went off. "Now I shall hunt deer and I shall shoot and kill it." Thereupon he went off and sure enough he found deer and shot and killed it. He butchered it. He thought to himself, "I shall not again leave young ones who are in its belly, for I shall take it all back home." That is what Coyote did. He took it all back home.

After that he went about all the time, and again he became a successful hunter. He never hungered. For that was what his younger sisters had told him: That is what Coyote did thereafter. "Very well. That is how it will be when the people [the ancestors of today's Indian people] who are coming pretty close now arrive here. That is the way the people will do whenever they shoot and kill game. They will carry all of it back home. They will leave nothing there. They will always sweat [bathe] for hunting. That is the way it shall be. . . . if they should not do so they will not shoot and kill game for many a day. They will go about quite in vain, and they will get all tired out. . . . That is the way the custom will be." That is how Coyote decreed it should be.

special power to decipher a raven's croakings. As a general rule, Plateau ravens bear news of significance over long distances, but without the chill import of the great horned owl's tidings, rendered in Sahaptin as pátkʷatana tanínšin X, "Arrowhead has eaten [i.e., death has taken] X." Meadowlark also speaks to Indians, but he is a tease commenting dryly on the intended ambitions of all humans within earshot. Elsie Pistolhead transcribed a meadowlark that sang over our picnic one spring day when we were root digging near Hardman, Oregon. The bird addressed her by her Indian name, wáwluway, then continued, "You are camped down by the creek," "You've come to dig xawš." The Indians' pleasure in this innocuous conversation indicates the tongue-in-cheek quality of meadowlark talk, a game of wits, a context for self mockery. This is clearly seen in a tale that was told me with barely stifled hilarity by Delsie Selam and Sara Quaempts on the occasion of another meadowlark encounter:

A proud man in riding away from home on a trek one day heard the meadowlark sing out as he crested the hill above his camp, "Your wife is sleeping

Fig. 7.3. James Selam's house.

with another man." As he rode on he heard it repeat, "Your wife is sleeping with another man." And Meadowlark kept repeating this taunt until the man, in a rage, turned his horse around, galloped home, and whipped his wife soundly.

I have asked James if he believes that meadowlarks always tell the truth. This story gives an answer: the truth is in the hearing.

Animism does not make gods of animals. Plateau people do not worship nature in that way. The relationship between people and other animate creatures (including, depending on the context, not only animals but trees, rocks, and winds) is more personal, conceptualized on the model of familiar social relationships among family, villagers, chiefs, shamans, and strangers. It is noteworthy that the Christian God came to be called in Sahaptin, naamí pyap, literally, "our Elder Brother" (Ruby and Brown mistakenly translate it as "Our Father"), a social relationship of great significance, of mutual regard edged by respectful distance, as the elder brother's role implied mild authority.

The earth was "mother," the sun "father," reflecting the nurturant ideal of the parental roles within the Plateau family. The winds come closest to apotheosis. They are depicted in myth as titanic personalities warring among themselves, like Greek gods on Olympus, alternately freezing and thawing the inhabitants of earth. One may entreat them to stop blowing by burning the wood of the pallid evening primrose (kalux̣-mí áčaš, literally, "blueback salmon's eyes," *Oenothera pallida*) as a prayer offering.

The vagaries of weather may also carry a personal message, a sign of the displeasure of a x̣uup-łá or "weather-changer." Dig up x̣uup-łá x̣awš (*Lomatium martindalei*) and the weather will turn bad. This mountain wildflower is of little value as food, quite unlike its namesake x̣awš (*Lomatium cous*, see fig. 5.12). Treat the horned lizard (x̣li-łá-wit, literally, "of the root diggers," fig. 5.9) disrespectfully and expect a return of winter at root digging time. Horned Lizard is a weather changer as well as an Indian doctor, one of those that cures by blowing short puffs of healing breath on the affected body part (pamis-pamisi-łá).

This belief that one's fellow animate beings are sensitive to any hint of disrespect on the part of a human highlights the Plateau social value placed on respect for the autonomy of the individual person. One must cultivate a posture of modesty in one's dealings not only with other people but with all living beings, even the silent oak tree.

James asked me one day if I would help him find a new q̇am-káwas, a "hide scraper," for Elsie Pistolhead as hers was well worn. So we loaded James's chain saw, set out in my old pick-up, and rumbled up into the foothills. We needed to locate a tree of just the right specifications: hard, durable wood; a branch of shoulder height when set on the ground, with a smooth and broadly curved top (see fig. 7.4). Oak is best, but other woods might also serve. I boldly declared that that ought to be an easy task. James smiled and said, "If the trees hear you boast like that you'll never find a q̇am-káwas. All the bent branches will straighten up as you go by." Likewise, if you should boastfully set out to cut teepee poles, all the saplings will be bent! Rather you must say, "Perhaps today I will have the good fortune to find a q̇am-káwas or some nice straight teepee poles." In short, respect the trees and they will not begrudge you their cooperation.

I sense in James—who has a foot in both the animist world and in the mechanistic world of the modern American mainstream—some be-musement, as if he spoke more allegorically than literally in this admonition to respect the trees. Elsie Pistolhead, however, speaks of the same with absolute conviction: one should never even speak of the water ouzel. It is a dangerous bird. I never learned its name from her nor why it was so threatening, though she certainly recognized the gray shadow I pointed

Fig. 7.4. Hide scraper of oak.

out to her one day along the frozen margins of Satus Creek. One simply did
not tempt such powers.

The Vision Quest

Guardian spirit powers (CRS: šúkat; CRS, NWS: taaẋ; NP: wéyekin; Chinook
Jargon: tamánwis) gave the old time Plateau Indians the strength needed for a
successful life. They gave as well the unique talents that distinguished an
individual. Today only a few elders have such allies. Few of those born after
the turn of the century were successful in their spirit quest. Perhaps their
elders then had already lost faith in those powers in the face of the overwhelming power attributed to the white man's God.

In the old days the father or paternal grandfather would send out a child,

if he or she were thought ready for the fateful spiritual encounter. Ida
Nason of Kittitas, born before 1910, tells the story of her mother's quest:

> She was a girl. A young girl. Grandma and two sisters and grandpa and
> mama. . . . All at once then, they decided they gonna move . . . [on] horse-
> back . . . horseback [they went]. They got to the campground where they
> gonna camp and the old man [Ida's mother's father] turns round and tells my
> mother, "Tehanap [her Indian name], you go back again where we come."
> Grandfather, he always had rope made . . . , braided . . . out of horse tail.
> Then he go and tell mama, "I forgot my rope. . . . You have to go back again,
> look for my rope . . ." Mama, she cry, she cry. Dark, dark [it was] dark, and
> grandfather, he was a big [Indian] doctor and he told mama, "You go up
> there . . . where we [have] come." Go . . . dark . . . scared . . . and there was
> [at that time] lots of animals, lots of things in this country. "Go back, it's
> there." (Larsen and Nisbet 1986)

Her solitary quest brought her to the shores of a mountain lake. At sunrise
she heard singing; the voices came from a kind of aquatic insect swarming in
the lake. After five nights alone with the animals and their spirits she came
home, lay down, and slept; she was sick and could not rise. Her father, a
powerful shaman (twáti) set up a pole in the long house; her family painted
her face; then with her father's help she sang her power song (wanp-t) and
they all danced around the pole. She demonstrated her new power by
swinging her long hair through the flames of the lodge fire without it burning. As she danced she gained strength and her people danced with her so
that she might hold on to this power. When later she cured sick people who
came to her—refusing the money they offered—she always used a pan of
water, representing the lake where her spirit animals lived.

The lonely vigil, the vision, the power sickness, and the "coming out"
with the help of a spiritually gifted relative as described by Ida Nason of her
mother's experience, is a, pattern repeated in numerous accounts from
throughout the Plateau (e.g., Ray 1939:68–131, Schuster 1975:114–20). The
present account is temporally compressed, as the sickness and subsequent
acceptance and public exhibition of one's power usually did not occur until
several years after the vision experience (which typically occurred at about
the age of ten years) and were coordinated with the winter season shamanic
power dances (Ray 1939:69–70).

Through most of the Plateau and certainly along the middle Columbia it
was essential that young persons not reveal their visions to anyone on pain
of the power deserting them forever. During the years that intervened be-

tween a vision and the "coming out" of a spirit power, a young person's individual talents and weaknesses became more apparent, providing the child's spiritual guides with a basis for interpreting a child's recollections of the vision experience; one's powers are only publicly revealed in the pattern of one's life.

Contemporary Indian accounts of the operation of spirit powers stress the appropriate relationship between person and power. A man with sharp-tailed grouse power escapes Snake Indian raiders by virtue of his ability to hide in the grass without moving. Jackrabbit power is attributed to one who escapes the enemy by swift running. A shaman known for his ability to handle hot rocks and to drink boiling water might have Sweat Lodge power (Schuster 1975:172). A public demonstration of these powers set the stage for the Indian doctor's curing "work." "Rattlesnake" power produces a "rattlesnake person," who is "onerous and repugnant," widely feared, with powers like sorcery (Schuster 1975:174).

In the old days not everyone was successful in a vision quest. Today the number of those without guardian spirit assistance has grown to include the great majority; moreover, children are now rarely prepared and sent out on quests. Don Umtuch recounted to me a close encounter he had with such a spirit. As a young boy he was exploring the jumbled terrain of the big slide near the northeastern foot of Toppenish Ridge. He heard a voice, but seeing no one, ran home in fear, telling his mother of his experience. At that point, he concluded, the power left him and he never had another chance, to his lasting regret.

Helen Schuster's sources offered a variety of explanations for the decline of spirit power possession, all more or less directly the result of white influences.

> "What spoils young people is being baptised. That chases Indian spirits away. Young folks can't get a spirit now.
> "These kids don't have a feeling for the woods and the mountains. They might inherit a power now, but they can't find one.
> "It's eatin' that white food. It spoils them inside; then they can't get a power.
> "School killed my power. Maybe if I don't talk white way, I'd know things ahead." (Schuster 1975:118)

It is also clear that with the traditional context largely destroyed, young people are no longer able to benefit from the guidance, assistance, and powers of their elders in their own search for meaningful spiritual links to their social and natural environment. Many have found meaning in one or another Christian church (see Walker 1985 [1968]). But for others this loss of contact is a very significant contributing factor to the malaise of reservation life today.

The old religion may be much weakened, but it is not altogether dead yet. Schuster could report as late as 1965 that at least thirty-four elders were known to her Yakima sources to have power songs that required participation at annual winter power dances. In 1985 I heard also that a power dance was planned for the coming early winter. Delsie Selam was somewhat fearful to attend, sharing the distrust of Indian doctors that is pressed forcefully by Shakers and other Christians active on the reservation. Her son, however, wanted her to take him to see it, anxious, with her support, to broaden his appreciation of his spiritual heritage. There is a distinct possibility that the spirit quest may once again give strength to a young Plateau Indian about to embark on his life's career. The recent revival of spirit dancing among Coast Salish Indians in Washington and British Columbia has been credited with real power of psychiatric and social healing (Jilek 1974; Amoss 1978).

We may be inclined, as was Sir Edward Tylor, to discount animism as due to a childlike confusion of objective reality with the subjective reality of dreams, combined with an almost neurotic compulsion to obey a seemingly random set of taboos hedging about one's interactions with nature. I see in animism, rather, a strange but powerfully consistent moral vision that makes us take our place beside those other living creatures whose futures are joined with ours. Such a moral vision seems altogether appropriate for a hunting-gathering people and embodies a wisdom we should seriously consider.

The correlation of religious belief and practice with the realities of social and economic life supports the view that human religious strivings are subject to selection in the service of evolutionary adaptation. Thus we should expect religion to evolve in response to dramatic new environmental challenges or, if unable to adapt, then to be driven to extinction, a spiritual dinosaur. The peoples of the Columbia Plateau endured a change of circumstance as drastic as that which doomed the dinosaurs. Their cultures shuddered, twisted, and crumbled in the face of it, but a series of new religious structures have been built of pieces from the cultural ruins and set in new mortar. The source of these drastic life changes is, of course, the invasion of the isolated New World by an army from the Old. The army was not just a human army composed of intrepid explorers, calculating fur traders, inspired missionaries, greedy miners, and settlers by the millions dreaming of a new life for themselves on the American frontier. The human army was powerfully reinforced by a foreign legion of microbial immigrants. Smallpox viruses, malarial plasmodia, tuberculosis bacilli, as well as the diverse agents of measles, influenza, whooping cough, scarlet fever, and venereal disease. All found the bodies of the Pacific Northwest Indians to be fertile ground. As detailed in chapter 2, a series of epidemics swept off large numbers—conservatively estimated at 30 percent of the total population of the middle Columbia for the first smallpox epidemic about 1780, with gradually lessened impacts until the mid-nineteenth century.

This was more than a biological disaster. Imagine families so ravaged, families that depended on the varied contributions of their adult members, families that lived for their children, that relied on the wisdom of their elders. Imagine also the impact on a village that lost its chief and its doctors, riven by fear of the contagion of social contact. So it was even more a social catastrophe. Most of all it was a spiritual apocalypse. Disease was not understood by the animist as a matter of microbial parasitism leading to physiological dysfunction and death. Disease was a symptom of a moral imbalance or power struggle in the society of animate beings. One might become sick because of the desertion of one's spirit allies (usually in the form of an animal) due to some disrespectful action on the sick individual's part or because of the intrusion of a foreign power (cf. Ray 1939:95–102). Indian doctors cured by enlisting their more powerful and more numerous spirit powers to restore those that had been lost or to overcome destructive powers that had invaded the sick person's body.

Given this frame of reference, imagine the consternation that would be caused by the sudden onset of a disease unlike any previously known, with intense fevers followed by raw pustules covering the body, covering even the eyes, attacking young and old alike, leaving no one unscarred, and killing one in three. Remember that the first smallpox epidemic raged along the Columbia thirty years before the Plateau people had their first face-to-face encounter with whites, Lewis and Clark and their men.

Prophecy

How was this cataclysm to be interpreted? Indian doctors sought to find some cure. Their powers, however, had been tested on endemic illnesses of the body and spirit, conditions very likely responsive to the charismatic ritual dances of healing by which the shamans' power was expressed (cf. Jilek 1974). Against smallpox they were powerless. Only later was a link recognized between these new scourges and the white invaders—invaders, as it were, from another planet. Eventually the connection was impossible to deny. Smohalla, the prophet of Priest Rapids, speaks to this:

> The whites have caused us great suffering. . . . Dr. Whitman many years ago made a long journey to the east [1842] to get a bottle of poison for us. He was gone about a year, and after he came back strong and terrible diseases broke out among us [most notably measles, which is deadly to all ages when introduced into a "virgin population"]. The Indians killed Dr. Whitman [at the so-called Whitman massacre], but it was too late. He had uncorked his bottle and all the air was poisoned. Before that there was little sickness among us, but since then many of us have died. I have had children and grandchildren, but they are all dead. My last grandchild, a young woman of 16, died last month. If only her infant could have lived . . . I labored hard to save them, but my medicine would not work as it used to. (Mooney 1896:724–25)

It is possible that on the aboriginal Plateau, elders might when near death have been revived, that they might have then spoken to the people of a world beyond death. The spectral Plateau myths, "Coyote and the Shadow People" (see Text, opposite) and "Coyote and Eagle Go to the Land of the Dead" (Ramsey 1977:33–35, 81–84) speak of this Orphean journey. When the elders were children, they had sought visions on isolated spots frequented by spirits, and returned with a song, a dance, and a name, tokens of the unseen presence of their spiritual allies. Returnees from the dead likewise brought back new songs, new ritual patterns, transcendentally inspired.

In the face of such new forces of death, the visions of twice-born elders were used to interpret their meaning and to design a response that would reestablish a traditional order. Prophecy was born (or acquired new significance). Its origins cannot be documented historically, as prophecies appear to predate direct white contact or to have roots in aboriginal belief and practice. Prophets predicted the white man's coming, having seen his "iron horses," his sacred books, and all his new things in their dreams. A Spokane prophet spoke: "Soon there will come from the rising sun a different kind of man from any you have yet seen, who will bring with them a book and will teach you everything, and after that the world will fall to pieces" (Wilkes 1845, 4:439).

The first Plateau prophets for whom we have records proclaimed their visions of the future in the last days of the eighteenth century. The Spokane

Coyote and the Shadow People

(A Nez Perce story from Ramsey 1977:33–37; originally in Phinney 1934:283–85; courtesy California Folklore Society.)

Coyote and his wife were dwelling there. His wife became ill. She died. Then Coyote became very, very lonely. He did nothing but weep for his wife.

There the death spirit came to him and said, "Coyote, do you pine for your wife?"—"Yes, friend, I long for her . . ." replied Coyote. "I could take you to the place where your wife has gone but, I tell you, you must do everything just exactly as I say; not once are you to disregard my commands and do something else."—"Yes," replied Coyote, "yes friend, and what could I do? I will do everything you say." There the ghost told him, "Yes. Now let us go." Coyote added, "Yes, let it be so that we are going."

They went. There he said to Coyote again. "You must do whatever I say. Do not disobey."—"yes, yes, friend. I have been pining so deeply, and why should I not heed you?" Coyote could not see the spirit clearly. He appeared to be only a shadow. They started and went along over a plain. "Oh, there are many horses; it looks like a round-up," exclaimed the ghost. "Yes," replied Coyote, though he really saw none, "yes, there are many horses." They had arrived now near the place of the dead. The ghost knew that Coyote could see nothing but he said, "Oh look, such quantities of service berries! Let us pick some to eat. Now when you see me reach up you too will reach up and when I bend the limb down you too will pull your hands down."—"Yes," Coyote said to him, "so be it that thus I will do." The ghost reached up and bent the branch down and Coyote did the same. Although he could see no berries he imitated the ghost in putting his hand to and from his mouth in the manner of eating. Thus they picked and ate berries. Coyote watched him carefully and imitated every action. When the ghost would put his hand into his mouth Coyote did the same. "Such good service berries these are," commented the ghost. "Yes, friend, it is good that we have found them," agreed Coyote. "Now let us go." And they went on.

"We are about to arrive," the ghost told him. "There is a long, very, very long lodge. Your wife is there somewhere. Just wait and let me ask someone." In a little while the ghost returned and said to Coyote, "Yes, they have told me where your wife is. We are coming to a door through which we will enter. You will do in every way exactly what you see me do. I will take hold of the door flap, raise it up, and, bending low, will enter. They you too will take hold of the door flap and do the same." They proceeded in this manner now to enter.

It happened that Coyote's wife was sitting right near the entrance. The ghost said to Coyote, "Sit here beside your wife." They both sat. The ghost added, "Your wife is now going to prepare food for us." Coyote could see nothing, except that he was sitting there on an open prairie where nothing was in sight; yet he could feel the presence of the shadow. "Now she has prepared our food. Let us eat." The ghost reached down and then brought his hand to his mouth. Coyote could see nothing but the prairie dust. They ate. Coyote imitated all the movements of his companion. When they had finished and the woman had apparently put the food away the ghost said to Coyote, "You stay here. I must go around to see some people."

He went out but he returned soon. "Here we have conditions different from those you have in the land of the living. When it gets dark here it has dawned in your land and when it dawns for us it is growing dark for you." And now it began to grow dark and Coyote seemed to hear people whispering, talking in faint tones, all around him. Then darkness set in. Oh, Coyote saw many fires in a long-house. He saw that he was in a very, very large lodge and there were many fires burning. He saw the various people. They seemed to have shadow-like forms but he was able to recognize different persons. He saw his wife sitting by his side.

He was overjoyed, and he joyfully greeted all his old friends who had died long ago. How happy he was! He would march down the aisles between the fires, going here and there, and talk with the people. He did this throughout the night. Now he could see the doorway through which his friend came to him and said, "Coyote, our night is falling and in a little while you will not see us. But you must stay right here. Do not go anywhere at all. Stay right here and then in the evening you will see all these people again."—"Yes, friend. Where could I possibly go? I will spend the day here."

The dawn came and Coyote found himself alone sitting there in the middle of a prairie. He spent the day there, just dying from the heat, parching from the heat, thirsting from the heat. Coyote stayed here several days. He would suffer through the day but always at night he would make merry in the great lodge.

One day his ghost friend came to him and said, "Tomorrow you will go home. You will take your wife with you."—"Yes, friend, but I like it here so much. I am having a good time and I should like to remain here."—"Yes," the ghost replied; "nevertheless you will go tomorrow, and you must guard against your inclination to do foolish things. Do not yield to any queer notions. I will advise you now what you are to do. There are five mountains. You will travel for five days. Your wife will be with you but you must never, never touch her. Do not let any strange impulses possess you. You may talk to her but never touch her. Only after you have crossed and descended from the fifth mountain you may do whatever you like."—"Yes, friend," replied Coyote.

When dawn came again Coyote and his wife started. At first it seemed to him as if he were going alone yet he was dimly aware of his wife's presence as she walked along behind. They crossed one mountain and, now, Coyote could feel more definitely the presence of his wife; like a shadow she seemed. They went on and crossed the second mountain. They camped at night at the foot of each mountain. They had a little conical lodge which they would set up each time. Coyote's wife would sit on one side of the fire and he on the other. Her form appeared clearer and clearer.

The death spirit, who had sent them, now began to count the days and to figure the distance Coyote and his wife had covered. "I hope that he will do everything right and take his wife through to the world beyond," he kept saying to himself.

Here Coyote and his wife were spending their last night, their fourth camping, and on the morrow she would again assume the character of a living person. They were camping for the last time and Coyote could see her very clearly as if she were a real person who sat opposite him. He could see her face and body very clearly, but only looked and dared not touch her.

But suddenly a joyous impulse seized him; the joy of having his wife again overwhelmed him. He jumped to his feet and rushed over to embrace her. His wife cried out, "Stop! Stop! Coyote! Do not touch me. Stop!" Her warning had no effect. Coyote rushed over to his wife and just as he touched her body she vanished. She disappeared—returned to the shadow-land.

When the death spirit learned of Coyote's folly he became deeply angry. "You inveterate doer of this kind of thing! I told you not to do anything foolish. You, Coyote, were about to establish the practice of returning from death. Only a short time away the human race is coming, but you have spoiled everything and established for them death as it is."

Here Coyote wept and wept. He decided, "Tomorrow I shall return to see them again." He started back the following morning and as he went along he began to recognize the places where he and his spirit friend had passed before. He found the place where the ghost had seen the herd of horses, and now he began to do the same things they had done on their way to the shadow-land. "Oh, look at the horses; it looks like a round-up." He went on until he came to the place where the ghost had found the service-berries. "Oh, such choice service-berries! Let us pick and eat some." He went through the motions of picking and eating berries.

He went on and finally came to the place where the long lodge had stood. He said to himself, "Now when I take hold of the door flap and raise it up you must do the same." Coyote remembered all the little things his friend had done. He saw the spot where he had sat before. He went there, sat down, and said, "Now, your wife has brought us food. Let us eat." He went through the motions of eating again. Darkness fell, and now Coyote listened for the voices, and he looked all around, he looked here and there, but nothing appeared. Coyote sat there in the middle of the prairie. He sat there all night but the lodge didn't appear again nor did the ghost ever return to him.

prophecy can be dated rather precisely owing to its well-remembered coincidence with a heavy fall of volcanic ash, which vulcanologists now date to approximately A. D. 1800, plus or minus a year or two (Okazaki, Smith, and Gilkeson 1972).

> Cornelius, a Spokane chief, in 1844 [when visited by the Wilkes expedition] a man of about sixty, gives an account of a singular prophecy that was made by one of their medecine-men, some fifty years ago. . . . Cornelius when about ten years of age, was sleeping in a lodge with a great many people, when suddenly awakened by his mother who called to him that the world was falling to pieces. He then heard a great noise of thunder overhead, and all the people crying out in terror. Something was falling very thick, which they at first took for snow, but on going out they found it to be . . . ashes, which fell to a depth of six inches . . . causing them to suppose that the end of the world was actually at hand. The medecine-man arose, told them to stop their fear and crying, [for] . . . soon there will come from the rising sun a different kind of man from any you have yet seen. . . ." (Wilkes 1845, 4:439)

The Kalispel also remembered this ash fall, reporting that "it rained cinders and fire. The Indians supposed that the sun had burnt up, and that there was an end of all things. The next morning, when the sun arose, they were so delighted as to have a great dance and feast" (Suckley, in Spier 1935:58).

Among the Sanpoil this extraordinary natural phenomenon is associated with certain features of the Prophet Dance worship services described for the Plateau for the mid-1800s.

> The Nespelim chief told me that about 1770 [the date is estimated and no doubt is that of the known 1800 eruption], when his grandmother was a very young girl, a shower of dry dust fell over the country. . . . The people were much alarmed . . . and were afraid it prognosticated evil. They beat drums and sang, and for a time held the "praying" dance [i.e., the Prophet Dance] almost day and night. They prayed to the "dry snow," calling it "Chief" and "Mystery," and asked it [as an animate force] to explain itself and tell why it came. The people danced a great deal all summer and in large measure neglected their usual work. They put up small stores of berries, roots, salmon, and dried meat; and consequently the following winter, which happened to be rather long and severe, they ran out of supplies. (Teit 1930:291–92)

Verne Ray recorded another account of the same event [which he places at about 1800]: "The people called it snow. . . . Everybody was so badly scared that the whole summer was spent in praying. The people even danced—something they never did except in winter [at the guardian spirit performances]. They didn't gather any food but what they had to live on. That winter many people starved to death" (Ray 1933:108, 189).

Another natural cataclysm—the great earthquake of 1872, estimated at 7.5 on the Richter scale and believed to have been centered beneath Lake Chelan—brought a later Sanpoil prophet to prominence, "Skolaskin" (Ray 1936a), another rival (with Smohalla) to the influence of Chief Moses in the Plateau politics of that decade. Leslie Spier, who completed a detailed study of the Plateau Prophet Dance in 1935, argues for the Plateau as a source of inspiration for the Ghost Dance, a well-known messianic religious movement attributed to the teachings of Wovoka, a Northern Paiute prophet of northern Nevada who attracted a wide following among the demoralized remnants of the western tribes about 1890.[1]

The persuasive power of these revelations clearly derives from the fact that they held out one last hope that the apocalypse the white man brought might be reversed and the world restored to its former harmony. So it is curious that these prophetic cults can be traced in the Plateau back to a time before Lewis and Clark's arrival. Could they be aboriginal, representing a recurrent pattern of response to rare natural phenomena such as earthquakes and volcanic eruptions, as Spier argued (1935; Spier, Herskovits, and Suttles 1959)? This seems doubtful. Features of the complex may have a long history before contact, such as the idea of a return from the land of the dead—clearly conceived in myth—and of community dancing. However, the millennarian vision of the imminent end of the world, the destruction of the whites, and the resurrection of the Indian dead seem most likely inspired by a natural cataclysm of far greater import than earthquake and eruption, the invasion of old world disease (Aberle 1959; Walker 1969). Like

---

1. Wovoka's visits to the dead in 1887 and again in 1889 gave force to his revelation that "he was to teach his people to live in love and peace, as a consequence of which there would be a general resurrection of the dead . . . under the guidance of Big Man or Old Man, their chief. . . . He also learned from the dead a dance, which was to be held at regular intervals for five consecutive days, and the performance of which would hasten the approach of the dead, already imminent. The present world would be overwhelmed in flood, when the Indians would find refuge on the mountain tops [while the whites were destroyed], and the earth shaken by quakes." Curious seekers came from as far as the Dakota reserves to hear of this revelation, and they carried back with them instructions as to how to dance this "Ghost Dance." They placed great emphasis on the destruction of the whites and relied upon the "Ghost shirt" to make them invulnerable to the white soldiers' bullets. At Wounded Knee, on the Sioux reservation in South Dakota, their faith was finally broken, as nervous soldiers, fearing renewed war by the Ghost Dance–inspired Indians, massacred the dancers, shredding their "bullet proof" sacred shirts.

earthquakes and volcanic eruptions, the first epidemics of smallpox (preceding Lewis and Clark by nearly thirty years) were inexplicable, unprecedented, and catastrophic signs of a deep rent in the fabric of the living world.

This association of prophetic dreaming and epidemic disease is quite explicit in a number of primary accounts:

> There was an epidemic of smallpox among the Yakima and people were dying and leaving the country. [Leslie Spier estimates that this occurred about 1800; probably the epidemic of 1801 (Boyd 1985:99–100).] One old man, a chief, took sick and was left behind. He died. In his dream he travelled and came to a place where people were gathered eating lots of good things. He was awfully hungry. He came to a kind of gateway and asked for food. The people turned him away and told him it wasn't time for him to come in yet. So they directed him to another place a long way off. He travelled and finally reached there. They told him when he asked for food that they didn't eat there. They looked thin and raw boned and didn't say much. They said, "We are people called angels." They told him to go back where he came from. "We can't take you in," they said. He felt bad and went back. When he came to his place he came to life again. But his people thought he was dead. He followed them. He surprised them. The first place he went to was Hell. The second place was Heaven. (Spier 1935:17)

Oscar Ike of Warm Springs recalled for Cora DuBois that,

> A man died. They kept his body three days and then he came to. He told the people what he saw in heaven and what was right to do. . . . The Creator told him to have this Indian religion every seven days and to sing. They counted seven days and every seventh day danced. This was the first religion. This was a long time back when people were dying like flies. This was how the Washani religion began. (DuBois 1938:9)

The occurrence here of the numbers three and seven in a sacred context contrast with the pervasive significance of the number five in traditional Sahaptin mythology, suggesting Christian influence [in other accounts of prophets' resurrections they are dead for five days].

Another account, this by Martin Spedis, a Wishram, is more specific as to the timing of this foreign influence on the middle Columbia.

> The Indians didn't know about Sunday and keeping track of the week. Some whites came here and made a camp near Big Eddy [a few miles above The Dalles]. . . . They came in canoes. . . . the second white people to come through here. Some bad Indians stole a powder horn from them that was mounted with silver and gold [perhaps this is the item taken in an attack on the Robert Stuart party on July 20, 1812]. It belonged to a white doctor. He got mad

and turned some kind of medicine loose to make disease. [Indian doctors
likewise had power to heal or to sicken others.] The Indians all got sick with a
fever. (DuBois 1938:10)

So the local chiefs went to Fort Vancouver where "some white religious
men . . . gave the Indians a piece of cardboard like the pages on a calendar"
and showed them how to use it to mark the Sabbath. They were also instructed in the necessity for confession [and of the return of the stolen item].
Spedis continues, "This religion spread up the Columbia River way back
east. This religion was a belief in God to help sick people. After that came,
sick people stopped dying. . . . After that religion came everybody was
strict [proper moral behavior and ritual practice was stressed]."

Another earlier inspiration for the Prophet Dance may have been rumors
of white people's great wealth transmitted through the network of inter-
Indian contacts much expanded and intensified by the horse. By 1750 the
fur-trading frontier had broached the Plains, and by 1775 trading vessels of
several European nations had contacted Pacific Northwest coastal groups.
Besides the horse itself and knowledge of its husbandry (including techniques of gelding in the Spanish style [Osborne 1955]), there were iron
tools, glass beads, gold coins, and guns. Guns and horses together set off a
domino-like series of shock waves through the Indian societies in advance of
the whites' arrival, a shock wave of violence of raids and counterraids.

There are suggestions that the first practitioners of prophet dancing saw
the coming whites as miraculous providers. Mary Lane, a Klikitat, told Cora
DuBois of a very early prophetess she had heard about from her grandmother, who founded the Waashani religion in her area:

> In the old days before the whites came, the Indians had many trances. . . .
> That is how the Washani religion got started. . . . A woman on the Columbia
> River had things revealed to her. She died and came back to life and told all she
> had seen. She said a people with white hair and skin and eyes were coming.
> She said they had different materials to work with, different clothing, different
> food that they would give the Indians. They all got excited like Seven Day
> Adventists. They sang and danced all day and all night. They went crazy. They
> burned or threw in the river all their things. They destroyed everything be-
> cause whites were coming to give them everything. They didn't store up any
> food that summer. . . . (DuBois 1938:8)

This aspect of Plateau prophecy bears some striking resemblances to earlier
revitalization movements among Indians in the eastern United States and to
the Cargo cults of Melanesia (Wallace 1956; Aberle 1959; Walker 1969).

The pioneer fur trader David Thompson, the first white man to travel the upper Columbia (in 1811), was greeted everywhere as if he were a god, eagerly awaited. The villagers would dance for him, apparently believing that he represented the realization of their prophetic expectations. Yet even as early as 1811 the Indians' hopes were tempered with fear. Near the Umatilla River the villagers prostrated themselves at his feet, seemingly imploring his mercy. Already the suspicion was spreading among the Indians that the whites were bringing not only new and valuable goods, but also pestilence. This is revealed by a curious encounter Thompson had at the Cascades in the Columbia Gorge on his return trip. From his journal:

> July 28th [1811]. A fine morning. . . . Apparently a young man, well dressed in leather, carrying a Bow and Quiver of Arrows, with his Wife, . . . came to my tent door and requested me to give them my protection. . . . On looking at them, in the Man I recognized the Woman who three years ago was the wife of Boisverd, a Canadian and my servant. . . . She found her way from Tribe to Tribe. . . became a prophetess, declared her sex changed, . . . dressed and armed herself [as a man], and also took a young woman to Wife. . . [See Schaeffer 1965]. When with the Chinooks [she was originally Kootenay], as a prophetess, she predicted diseases . . . which made some of them threaten her life. . . . Four men . . . were waiting for us [at the Casacades]. . . . [They] addressed me, when you passed going down to the sea, we were all strong in life, but what is this we hear, casting their eyes with a stern look on her [the transvestite prophetess], . . . is it true that the white men, . . . have brought with them the Small Pox to destroy us. (Glover 1962:366–67)

This was a strange time, a time of disturbing portents, of rumors of the end of the world as they knew it (which were to prove all too true) that fostered an intense intellectual ferment mixed of large parts of hope and of fear.

šmúx̣ala and His Contemporaries

The truth of the Spokane prophet's warning that the world would fall to pieces was inescapable in the aftermath of the treaty council of 1855 and the skirmishes of the so-called Yakima wars that were ended by Colonel Wright's 1858 campaign through the lands of the Palus, Spokane, and Coeur d'Alene peoples. The uneasy peace of the next twenty years was in part the consequence of the Civil War that briefly distracted settlers and the U.S. military from their pursuit of Manifest Destiny. In the wake of the defeat of the Indian resistance forces in the Plateau, many prophets rose to prominence along the Columbia River (see Table 22). Foremost among

TABLE 22

Time Line for Plateau Prophets and Religious Influences

	Klikitat	Yakima	Skin	Umatilla	Wanapam	Salish	Nez Perce
1780	Smallpox— —
1790	
	St. Helens eruption— — — — — — — — — — — — —(Spokane prophet)
1800	Smallpox (Yakima chief's resurrection)— — — — — — — — — — — —
	Lewis & Clark— — — — — — — — — — — — — —
1810	Thompson (greeted by dancing)— — — — — — — — — — — — -
	Travels of Kutenai prophetess— — — — — — — — — — —-
1820						(Iroquois instruct Flatheads)
1840	
				wiléci	
1850	lišwayláyt				smúxala
1860				lals	
1870	—earthquake of 1872— — — — — — — — — —Skolaskin— — — —
		kútayaqan	
1880			Wishram prophet	
			šxmáya/hununwi	
	(Shaker religion founded /Puget Sound)
1890		Shakers come to Yakima	
			Waashani	
1900	Jake Hunt	
1910	
1920	Feather Dance	
1940	

these—at least in the historical accounts of white observers—was šmúxala (usually spelled "Smohalla"). His home was at p̓na, the main village on the Columbia River at Priest Rapids.

He was neither a chief (miyúux̣) nor a shaman (twáti), but was called iyánča, literally, "one who trains or disciplines" [íyani-, "to train, discipline"]. Born some time after 1810 he was a rather frail, slight, hunchbacked man. The one surviving photograph of Smohalla shows an almost gaunt, "spiritual" face (see fig. 7.5), lacking the imposing fullness that is so impressive in old photographs of his secular rival, Columbia Salish Chief Moses (see fig. 7.6). But like other noted Indian leaders of his day, he had many wives, ten according to Click Relander, his biographer and outspoken admirer.

Smohalla is first mentioned in the historical record in February 1861, in a military report stating that certain fugitive Indians may have taken refuge with "Smoke Hollow." But we mostly know of him and his religion from an ethnographic report by James Mooney published in 1896. This report is based largely on extensive conversations between Smohalla and Major J. W. MacMurray recorded in 1884–85. MacMurray had been sent by the Army command to investigate causes of conflict between whites and Indians in the wake of the completion of the Northern Pacific Railroad across the Plateau, which had opened a flood of immigration into the heart of the Plateau.

Smohalla's extraordinary influence throughout the Plateau was in part because of his ability to enter a trance state from which he revived, having journeyed to the Spirit Land [for this reason believers in the Prophet Dance are often called "dreamers"], bringing back songs and other instructions to his congregation on the necessary forms of worship to hasten the imminent world renewal.

Smohalla is also reputed to have predicted the great 1872 earthquake (as was said as well of Skolaskin, the contemporary Sanpoil prophet) and his reputation was augmented by accurate predictions of eclipses in 1882. Mac-Murray notes, however, that: "He [Smohalla] showed me a [U.S. Naval Observatory] almanac of [1882] and asked me to readjust it for eclipses, as it did not work as it had formerly done" (Mooney 1896:720). Before concluding that Smohalla was cynically manipulating his people we must recall an earlier prophecy to the effect that white men will come with books that tell everything, just before the world's end, and that extraordinary natural phenomena, such as eruptions, earthquakes, and eclipses, were all considered signs of great moment.

Fig. 7.5. Smohalla and his priests (Bureau of American Ethnology, in Relander 1956:96).

Smohalla is remembered still for his eloquent rejection of white civiliza-tion: "My young men shall never work. Men who work cannot dream, and wisdom comes to us in dreams." Challenged that his people were even then hard at work digging camas in the hills, he replied: "This work lasts only a few weeks. Besides it is natural work and does them no harm. But the work of the white man hardens soul and body. Nor is it right to tear up and mutilate the earth as white men do" (Mooney 1896:724). Challenged again to explain how that differed from the Indians digging for roots in the earth with their digging sticks, he responded: "We simply take the gifts that are freely offered. We no more harm the earth than would an infant's fingers harm its mother's breast. But the white man tears up large tracts of land,

Right: Fig. 7.6. Chief Moses of the Columbia Salish (C. A. Bushnell photograph, Relander Collection, Yakima Valley Regional Library).

runs deep ditches, cuts down forests, and changes the whole face of the earth. . . . Every honest man knows in his heart that this is all wrong" (Mooney 1896:724).

Smohalla's "church" at p̓na was a traditional Plateau mat-covered long-house that doubled as family quarters and village meeting hall (see fig. 7.7). He flew his own flag on a tall pole before the lodge, and atop the pole, whenever a service was to be conducted, raised a carved image of his spirit bird, wawšuk-ɫá [the Bullock's oriole, *Icterus galbula bullockii*] (fig. 7.8). This bird had come to him during a vision quest on the summit of grass-topped laliik, the easternmost prominence of Rattlesnake Ridge. This hill, now within the Hanford Nuclear Reservation, commands a view of the conflu-

Fig. 7.7. Pakayatut with Smohalla's flag (Relander Collection, University of Washington Libraries, neg. 9231).

ence of the Yakima and Columbia rivers and the whole surrounding country. The bird is brilliant in black and yellow-orange feathers, a noisy spring
migrant that nests conspicuously in riparian groves along lowland streams.
It is said to call out to the salmon to come upstream and for buds to open. It
turns atop its pole before Smohalla's church—and in front of šxmáya's
longhouse at sḱin at Celilo Falls as well—always to face the sun, a bright
symbol of the Dreamers hopes for a renewal of their lost world.

Mooney witnessed a salmon feast celebrated at the paxutakyúut longhouse
south of Union Gap on the Yakima reservation, a ceremony conducted by
the son of Smohalla's contemporary and colleague, kútayaqan, nephew of the
Yakima leader Kamiakin. This is what Mooney said:

> The regular services take place on Sunday, in the morning, afternoon, and
> evening. Sunday has been held sacred among the Nez Percés and neighboring
> tribes for more than sixty years, as the result of the teachings of the Hudson
> Bay officers. . . . There are also services during the week, besides special peri-
> odic observances, such as the "lament" for the dead, particularly the dead

Fig. 7.8. Smohalla's sacred bird (Relander Collection, University of Washington
Libraries, neg. 9232).

chiefs, in early spring; the salmon dance, when the salmon begin to run in April, and the berry dance, when the wild berries ripen in autumn. The description of the ceremonial of the salmon dance will answer for the others, as it differs chiefly only by the addition of the feast.

The house has the door at the eastern end, as is the common rule in all Indian structures. On the roof, at the east end of the building at Pa'kiut [pax̣utakyúut, below Union Gap], are the flags, the center one blue, representing the sky; another one white, representing the earthly light, and the third yellow, representing the heavenly light of the spirit world. . . . On entering, the worshipers range themselves in two lines along the sides of the building, the men and boys standing along the northern wall, the women and girls along the southern wall, and all facing toward the center. The first man entering takes his place on the north nearest the door; the next one stands just beyond him, and so on; while the women and girls, when their turn comes, make the whole circuit along the northern side, and then, turning at the farther end, take their places in reverse order along the southern wall. In the open space between the rows is a floor-walker, whose business it is to see that everyone is in the right place. All are dressed as nearly as possible in the finest style of the old Indian costume, buckskin and shell ornaments, their faces painted yellow, white, or red with Indian paints [this practice seems to have died out], and carrying eagle feathers in their right hands (see Figure).

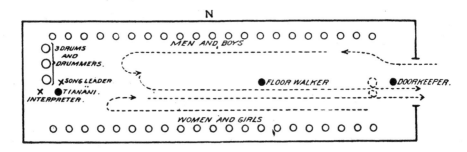

At the farther end, facing the door, sits the high priest, while just behind him stands his "interpreter," and on his left are seated on the ground [nowadays on chairs] the three [now generally seven or more] drummers with their large drums in front of them. The high priest carries a large bell in his left hand and a smaller one in his right.

Dishes of fresh-cooked salmon and jars of water, together with a plentiful supply of other food, are ranged in front of the devotees. After a preliminary ceremony in the nature of a litany, in which the principal articles of their theology are recited in the form of question and answer by the whole body of worshipers, the high priest gives the command, "Take water," when everyone raises a cup of water to his lips. Next comes the command, "Now drink," and each takes a sip. At the words, "Now the salmon," each takes up a portion of fish, which he puts into his mouth at the next command, "Now eat." Last comes the command, "Now help yourselves," which is the signal for a general attack on the provisions.

When everyone has satisfied his hunger, the remains of the feast are cleared away and the "dance" begins. At a signal given by a single stroke of the bell in the left hand of the high priest all stand up in line on either side of the building. At another stroke of the bell all put their right hands on their breasts. Another tap of the bell and the right hand is brought out in front of the body. Another, and they begin to move their right hands backward and forward like fans in front of the breast, and thus continue throughout the dance, keeping time also to the singing by balancing alternately upon their toes and heels, . . . without moving from their places. Ritual songs are sung throughout the remainder of the service, in time with the movements of the dancers and the sounds of the drums, and regulated by the strokes of the bell.

Between songs anyone who wishes to speak steps out into the open space. With a single tap of the bell the high priest then summons his "interpreter," standing behind him, who comes forward and stands beside the speaker, a few feet in front and at the right of the high priest. The speaker then in a low tone tells his story—usually a trance vision of the spirit world—to the interpreter, who repeats it in a loud voice to the company. At the end of the recital the high priest gives the signal with the bell, when all raise their right hands with a loud "Ai!" (Yes!). The high priest himself sometimes discourses also to the people through the interpreter; at other times directly.

The first song is given by all standing motionless, with the right hand on the breast and with eyes cast downward. It may be rendered:

Verily, verily, Our Brother made the body.
He gave it a spirit and the body moved.
Then he counted out the words for us to speak.
Another begins:
Verily, Our Brother put salmon in the water
to be our food.
Another begins:
O, brothers! O, sisters!
When first the light struck this world,
it lighted the world forever.

Our Brother (Nămi Piăp) is the term used in referring to the creating spirit, instead of "our father," as we might expect them to say.

On leaving, at the close of the ceremony, the man nearest the high priest passes around in front of him and down along in front of the line of women, and as he reaches the door he turns around and bows to the high priest. Each man in turn thus files around and passes out, after which the women—first the one nearest the high priest and then the others in regular order—pass out in the same manner. While the worshipers are thus going out, the high priest, standing up, rings continuously the small bell in his right hand, while with the larger bell in his left he gives a single stroke as each one passes through the door. (Mooney 1896:727–31)

I have been a guest at virtually identical services at the Rock Creek longhouse ninety years later. The fidelity of belief and practice that Plateau Waashani demonstrate is striking. Though hope for the imminent return of the all-too-numerous Indian dead coupled with the destruction of the whites and apostasizing Indians has faded, the longhouse religion of sacred dancing, of the seven drums, incorporating ancient rites of thanksgiving for the fruits of the native earth, still draws the faithful by hundreds on feast days and unites a congregation of all ages each Sunday. Smohalla, šxmáya, lals, and their fellow prophets would feel at home were they once again to return to visit their people for Sunday worship.

Plateau Indian Religion Today

The Waashani faithful meet regularly today at thirteen longhouses from Nespelem south to Warm Springs and east to Lapwai. But the core of the faithful live in the ancient Sahaptin country. The people still gather at Priest Rapids, drawn especially to the spring root feaşt for a taste of the Wanapam specialty roots, škúlkul, maxš-lí, and pšáyax (Schuster 1975:77). The old mat longhouse blew down in a storm sometime before 1965 and has been replaced by a quonset hut, oriented to face east, as is traditional for Waashani houses of worship (though traditional winter lodges had doors in the side wall, facing south or toward the river). Sunday meetings are held at Wapato, White Swan, and Satus on the Yakima reservation, and the Toppenish congregation holds services at the Toppenish Community Center. The Rock Creek people recently (1981) built an elegant cinder block building to replace their well worn wood-frame structure, but ordered the center of the floor left bare soil so the dancers could draw strength directly from the Earth.

The Celilo A-frame longhouse, once right on the shore of the Big River at the great fishery, is now cut off from the river by Interstate-80 going north, a river of cars and trucks that passes their door. Yet the worship and fellowship continue. Longhouse congregations elect a leader, sometimes a descendant of a prominent chiefly family long associated with the region represented. These leaders may serve as well as tribal councilmen representing their communities. Leaders, bell-ringers, conduct Sunday worship. A profound knowledge of the rituals and their meanings is expected of them. They must also take care of their people unselfishly, as was expected of chiefs in the past. If anyone of the congregation dies, the leader's first duty is to see personally to the burial rites. No other business should take precedence. As James Selam remarks, "Leaders are slaves to their people."

The Contemporary Religious Scene

The Waashat religion is the Indian religion of the Plateau. James Selam feels that there may have been a slight revival of this traditional religious practice, but that it has yet to regain the position it held a generation ago. At that time longhouses were found in virtually every community along the River. Of course, not only have those longhouses disappeared, but the villages themselves have vanished. A large part of the problem is attributable to the fact that many people were forced or induced to take up residence on the reservations where they were pressured by reservation authorities to abandon traditional religious practices. Indian police were sent to spy out meetings of the traditional religionists; their meetings were disrupted, their drums smashed or burned, and they were admonished to attend Catholic or Protestant services. Agent James Wilbur at Yakima, 1865–80, a devout and intransigent Methodist minister, harried Smohalla and his followers in an attempt to destroy their influence among Wilbur's flock (Schuster 1975:239–41).

Though Wilbur failed to eliminate the Waashani, there are many people on the reservations today whose faith is more Christian than traditional. Among these are the members of the three Shaker congregations (Fitzpatrck 1968) and many who profess a wide variety of Christian allegiances. Mormonism has proven attractive to many Indian people, perhaps in part because the Mormons have a special mission to American Indians, a consequence of their belief that Indians represent one of the lost tribes of Israel.

The Umatilla reservation for some years had no Waashani congregation, though one was reestablished in the 1980s. James Selam attributes this to the effectiveness of Protestant missionary efforts under reservation controls, controls that his River people largely escaped. The Colville reservation is very largely Catholic today (Schultz and Walker 1978), reflecting the greater effectiveness of the "black robes" on the northern edge of the Plateau. Walker's studies of Nez Perce religious factionalism demonstrate the role of competing Christian denominations as foci for competing acculturative strategies, with Protestant allegiance often linked to a more aggressive openness to white ways, while Catholics and "pagans" are seen as more conservative, more traditional.

The Waashat religion has many competitors for the hearts and minds of Indian people today. Unlike many Christian churches, however, the Waashat faith does not demand a dogmatic adherence. One can be a Shaker and go to Waashat services, too. One can be Christian and honor the first fruits of the Earth. Perhaps it is this strength of tolerance, so characteristic of Plateau Indian society, that has made possible the astounding fact of the survival of traditional Indian religious belief and practice well into the 1980s.

Funerals

The wheels of tribal government often appear to move forward haltingly because of the necessity to suspend all business for the conduct of funerals. Death defines more than any single event the life of the Indian community today. In my experience—as an American of Protestant northern European extraction born and raised in the city—funerals are rare, somewhat unpleasant duties. My family is widely scattered across the country and distance mutes the death of cousins, aunts, uncles, and grandparents. My friends are peers of an age when death is exceptional. So death for me is slightly embarrassing, a matter for private contemplation and somber public countenance.

It is different in Indian country. An individual's kindred includes a substantial fraction of the surviving Plateau Indian population. No Plateau Indian dies alone. The result—heightened by the disturbingly high mortality rate among young and middle-aged people due in part to the destructive impact of alcohol—is the impression that funerals are in constant progress.

The ceremony lasts several days and costs the closest survivors dearly, though the tribes help with funeral benefit payments and relatives contribute whatever they have. The "dressing" (wapáwaša, literally, "dress him up," or patkáwaša, "wrapping the body," as with buckskin in the old days) is a private family affair. The body is dressed in its finest buckskin clothing, decorated with Indian jewelry, with eagle feathers attached to the right arm. Then follows a service much like the Sunday worship service during which anyone who wishes may come forward:

If a person wanted to talk, he'd get up here in front of the bellman, to the right, and dance. . . . And when his song was over, he'd interpret what was in his mind. Maybe he was feeling pretty bad and he wanted to relieve himself of these bad feelngs to the Creator. So he'd send a message through this man or woman whose body is lying there and whose life is waiting. They say that as long as the body is lying on top [of the ground] its life does not leave it. But as soon as the body goes into the ground its life leaves it. So a person would get up and speak about how he felt. If he didn't, he might get sick. (James Selam, personal communication, 10 March 1986)

In the Waashani tradition the body is displayed for three days in the longhouse. As during this time the "life" remains in the body, dancing near the coffin is considered disrespectful. During the funeral the closest survivors hold a "give away." All who come to pay respect, but especially those who have been most respectful to the deceased throughout his life, receive gifts: blankets, shawls, kitchen utensils, personal items that belonged to the dead person. These personal effects are all given away. As James Selam explained, you give away the couch the person used to sit on, the bed he slept in, the dishes he ate from, everything that reminds you of him. This breaks the power of the dead person's "ghost," which bothers the living, distracting them from the necessity to continue with their lives. The funeral "give away" also ensures that a person's death enriches those who knew him just as in his life he generously shared whatever he had with others.

The body is buried in an Indian cemetery in an informally defined family plot. The grave is dug by the men of the family, then the empty grave is swept clear of "ghosts" with a wand of rosewood by the officiating religious leader. Traditional families take great care that the last rites are conducted in a manner as faithful to their traditions as they know how. If the dead man were a war veteran, it is essential that an appropriate military rite also be performed. As James Selam is a well-known V.F.W. leader as well as being staunchly traditional, he is frequently called upon to perform this military service.

Indian graveyards have a particular quality. There are no irrigated and manicured lawns. Just bare earth and sere bunch grasses, bent before the winds (see fig. 7.9). Such graveyards are often set on a prominence from which the ancestral lands may be broadly surveyed. Graves are mounded with earth; many are unmarked beyond that small hill of earth. Others have bare bleached wooden headboards devoid of public markings. Twentieth-century graves are more often marked with elaborate headstones, highly personalized with color photographs of the deceased and symbols of the

Fig. 7.9. Satus cemetery.

person's allegiances in life. James's brother Bennie's headstone features a baseball bat and mitt (he loved baseball and was in demand as a catcher), a dip net (he was a fisherman), and a bell with eagle feathers (representing his Waashani allegiance). Fresh graves are strewn with mementoes of the deceased—favorite toys, hard won trophies—and graced with the ubiquitous plastic flowers that are expressly forbidden in so many white cemeteries. Memorial day has come to be recognized throughout Indian country as the time to clean and redecorate the graves of one's ancestors, a responsibility that is taken very seriously.

The Sweat Lodge

James Selam's youngest son, Ernie, had often invited me—perhaps "challenged" would be a better term—to come sweat with him and his dad at

dawn. I worried that James might see this as an unwelcome intrusion into the heart of his Indianness. But when he affirmed Ernie's bantering challenge, I decided to give it a try. I had been out to inspect his sweat lodge (xʷyáyč), a hundred yards down a weed-grown path from his house, set amongst reeds and wormwood on the banks of the main irrigation canal. A wall of plywood sheets gave privacy from the passing traffic on Highway 22, enclosing the lodge, fire pit, and rain barrel for bathing. There were low benches to sit on and wooden plank walkways to keep the mud off the bathers' feet. My first sweat was on a summer morning with sunrise coming early, the air refreshingly cool as the hills turned from gray to mauve.

James had been out at 4 A.M. to set the fire to heat the river cobbles, and the stones were now lying deep in superheated coals. Ernie and two young cousins stood naked by the fire, bathing in the herb-steeped water from the tank. We joined them, the morning air biting our skin. Ernie then placed a half-dozen stones inside the lodge in a stone-lined hearth just to the left of the entrance. As he lifted them from the fire on the tines of a pitchfork they glowed dully and sparked. A darker stone, of vesicular basalt, was set on top of the pile. Then we crawled in. James first, settling himself next to the hearth, a bowl of water handy. Ernie followed me in and pulled down the heavy rug that served as a door.

I sat on a bed of fir boughs and drew in their heavy balsam scent, a powerful physical and spiritual cleansing agent in the Indians' view. A strong dry heat radiated into the confined darkness. A dim light suffused from random gaps in the willow frame structure's covering. We sat for a time in silence, meditating, inhaling, sensing the heat. Then James intoned a prayer of greeting to the Lodge, to púša, paternal grandfather, as the person of the Lodge is familiarly known. The Lodge is a powerful spirit *person*. He then hit the rocks with a few

Fig. 7.10. Sweat lodge construction.

Fig. 7.11. James Selam at his sweat lodge.

drops of water dipped from the bowl and snapped with his fingers. The steam rushed up, almost choking me. I broke out in a profuse sweat, as the steam seemed to draw out the accumulated impurities from my body.

Many traditional Plateau families have a sweat lodge enclosure in their yards (see figs. 7.10 and 7.11; cf. Walker 1966). James Selam's is perhaps more rustic than most, as he lives at the edge of a marsh among fields. Sweating should be performed daily, though the press of contemporary business often interferes. Many sweat now more conveniently in the evenings rather than at dawn, but James prefers the old way. Dawn bathing was part of the traditional discipline fathers and father's fathers instilled in their children. The practice was revealed to Coyote in Myth times, as an essential preparation for hunting: sweat five mornings before embarking on a hunt and respect the spirits of your prey and you will be successful. No doubt the cleansing effects of sweating made the human hunter less readily detected by the sharp noses of his prey.

Sweating was also an adjunct of Indian healing. The Indian doctor would sweat with the patient, employing particular herbs in the bathing waters in conjunction with special prayers to Sweat Lodge to effect a cure. Tragically, this traditional healing practice only quickened death for the victims of smallpox and malaria (Boyd 1985:138–39, 141), whose bodies were racked with dangerously high fevers.

James hit the hot stones five times. The vesicular basalt stone whistled as the water that collected in its pores boiled: the singing of "the Old Man," the Lodge himself, emanated in this way from the rock. Then James called out, aaaww, "now." Ernie pushed the rug up over the doorway and we crawled out into the rich light of early morning, our bodies steaming. James advised us to sit for a while before jumping into the canal, to ease the shock. He commented on the contrasting sweating styles of his acquaintances. Some try to "burn you out," using excessive heat in a display of superior personal endurance. This, he felt, was disrespectful to Sweat Lodge and harmful to the body. He recommended a moderate and gradual treatment.

The canal was cold and flowing hard toward the culvert under the highway. To get it over with I leaped in with a hearty splash. For that James awarded me the name wišpúš, "beaver," as they make a similar splash with their tails to warn of danger. People were known by such names in the past, commemorating some amusing but memorable moment in their lives.

I believe the Indian sweat lodge represents most clearly the special quality of Indian religious practice: a personal encounter marked by the natural rhythm of daybreak; a conjunction of natural forces of water and fire. A spiritual force personified in everyday objects and events; spiritual and physical cleansing indivisible. Daily life is a form of worship, as if our morning shower were a prayer to life.

Sweat lodges have recently been built on prison grounds and in city parks in an effort to reclaim Indian souls lost and cut off from the land (Seven 1988). And the lodge can fight the ravages of alcohol. After you have sweated, the day stretches clear out ahead of you; your body feels suspended and your mind is clear, a perfect antithesis of a hangover. When James has been drinking he seems almost to *fear* the sweat lodge; when he starts sweating again we know he's free of it.

8

From the Treaties to Today

paʔaníx̣ʷat, **"treaty"**

THE TREATIES guaranteed the "exclusive use" of reservation lands to the signatory Indians and today provide a legal basis for the continued existence of a Plateau Indian way of life. However, those reservation lands represent less than 10 percent of the land area originally occupied by ancestral Plateau peoples (see fig. 2.6). Inevitably a large fraction of the Plateau peoples were forced to abandon their homes and to move onto lands where they had neither traditional rights nor ancestral ties, often against the fervent wishes of the people who were indigenous to those reservation areas.

Such conflicts have been particularly acute on the Colville Reservation where indigenous Sanpoil-Nespelem, Okanagan, and Colville Indians were moved aside to accommodate the followers of Chief Moses' Columbia Salish people and Joseph's Nez Perce and Palus followers. Joseph's people were prevented from settling on the Nez Perce Reservation—what little was left of it after the land grabs of 1863 and 1872—by the resistance of the Protestant followers of Lawyer. Their relocation in the heart of Sanpoil-Nespelem territory generated persistent factional divisions at Colville that have sometimes interfered with effective political action, as during the bitter disputes over termination in the 1950s (Ross 1968). At the Yakima and Warm Springs reservations the problems have been less acute, perhaps because the original residents were more extensively intermarried with the newcomers.

Life Between the Reservations

Many Columbia River Indians refused to leave their productive fishing sites to be confined on reservations far removed from their ancestors' graves and their familiar sources of food and materials. Some are still living off-reservation on homesteads acquired after the homestead laws were amended in 1884 to allow Indian participation. A few Indians live at *in lieu* fishing sites in the Columbia Gorge such as Cook's Landing near the Little White Salmon River mouth and at Underwood where the White Salmon River joins the Columbia. These sites were purchased by the federal government to replace fishing sites inundated by Bonneville Dam.

The Wanapam or Priest Rapids people signed no treaty and some four households still live there near the traditional village site of p̓na, where Smohalla held forth. Many Palus and Snake River people likewise spurned the treaties, though Governor Stevens had authorized a Palus Indian, Koo-lat-toose, as "Chief of the 'Palouses'" to represent and sign for them at the Walla Walla Council (Doty 1978 [1855]:36). Click Relander gives us a sympathetic account of the last independent Palus:

> Many believed that Sam [Fisher] was the last full-blooded Palouse. His Indian name was Yosyostulekasen (Something Covered with Blue).
>
> Sam refused to cut his long braids and he danced the *Washat* at the infrequent later-day feasts on the Columbia, or over around Cayuse in Oregon. He danced well, too, although he was eighty-four. Sam kept to the tumbled-down cabins in the old village, deserted now excepting for occasional small gatherings of part-bloods who sought sanctuary from a world that was constantly growing more bewildering to them. He served his time there and that was all. . . .
>
> Sam sold some beaver pelts and the game warden came to take him to court. In broken English he told his story. He expected no justice and wasn't pleading for mercy.
>
> Sam told of the old-time wealth of his people—the wealth of the land, food and water that belonged to everyone born of dust.
>
> "My father and his father's father lived here. They and my people lived here. They were here a long time ago and for a long time. When they grew old, they died and returned to their Mother.
>
> "A long time ago the Palouses killed deer and beaver. We fished in the river. That was how we got food and clothing. There was no one to tell the Indian what he could do and what he could not do.
>
> "The salmon came every year and so did deer and beaver, the way the Watcher intended it should be. And we used them as they were intended to be used.
>
> "But when the big herds of cattle wandered over the Palouse Hills and when the sheep came later, they ate all the grass—even to the very doors of our lodges—so the deer no longer came.

"The white man built dams that choked the rivers; only a few salmon could come.

"Now I am accused of killing beaver. I did.

"You say it is not the law to kill beaver. I ate the flesh because I needed food. So did my family. I sold the skins because I needed money to buy clothes for my wife and children. When I did this, I stole nothing that belonged to the white man."

The man many said was the last Palouse died believing as Smowhala believed—not life and death, but death, then life. (Relander 1956:119–20)

Today there are Palus descendants (of those who were with Joseph when he was finally captured) on the Colville Reservation; others settled with Nez Perce relatives on the Nez Perce Reservation. A few ended up at Yakima: Mary Jim is one of these. She was born and raised along the Snake River on her family's homestead allotment, which is now buried under the Ice Harbor dam pool. Her emotional ties to this homeland—bleak as it may seem to us—are still the overriding concern of her life. She is trying hard to retain— at a distance—a public and ritual tie to her family's land and burial ground. To this end she hosts an occasional feast on the old place to which she invites all those who will lend a sympathetic ear.

Other Yakima enrollees trace their roots to the village of k̓ʷsís, literally, "the point" at the junction of the Snake and Columbia rivers. When Lewis and Clark visited here in 1805 they found a bustling community. The site is now Sacajawea State Park, named for Lewis and Clark's Shoshone guide. Traditional claims to the site are being pursued with renewed vigor.

Delsie Selam and Sara Quaempts call Alderdale at the mouth of Alder Creek on the Columbia their first home, a site they know as náwawi. When the John Day Dam inundated the local fisheries they moved to the Yakima Reservation, but they continue to clean and decorate their families' graves at the river each Memorial Day and own trust allotments there, which they have leased to white ranchers.

The Rock Creek community—represented among the treaty signers by "Shee-ah-cotte"—is a coherent group with members now divided between Warm Springs and Yakima reservation enrollment. Some reside on trust lands near Goldendale. Rock Creek people gather each Sunday at their new stone longhouse at q̓mił (the "Kamilt-pah" of the treaty) just up the canyon from the Columbia. Though no longer permanently resident on Rock Creek, the community meets regularly and addresses issues of collective concern.

These are focused on continued access to their burial ground (now on land owned by a non-Indian family), memorials to their ancestors whose graves are now drowned by The Dalles and John Day dams, and the maintenance of their longhouse and its congregation. Rock Creek people elect a chief who serves with the Celilo and Klikitat chiefs on a Columbia River Council of Chiefs.

Helen Schuster in 1965 was told by a young Rock Creek wáašani drummer that, "We mostly come up to White Swan or Satus (on the Yakima Reservation) now, there's so few of us left to carry on in Rock Creek" (Schuster 1975:390). She also estimated a total of 200 active wáašani adherents at Yakima. By contrast I have counted over 250 in attendance at Rock Creek for spring Waashat thanksgiving services (in 1977 and 1980). Though this number exceeds those regularly attending Sunday services there, it suggests the continuing strength of traditionalist off-reservation communities along the mid-Columbia. The Rock Creek community today encompasses a somewhat broader spectrum of people than it did at contact, as river people from Patterson (nišxt) to Celilo Falls (škin) are included.

The Celilo community in Oregon is a focal point for the descendants of the lower Deschutes River and Celilo Falls people. Their new longhouse serves for wáašani worship and as a meeting place for Columbia River Indian fishermen. Before The Dalles Dam covered the falls in 1957, it was a scene of intense activity during the salmon runs, with men cavorting on cables and platforms with just a safety rope as a hedge against a fall into the maelstrom of the rushing waters, manipulating their long-handled dip nets from the edges of makeshift wooden platforms cantilevered over the flood. The hereditary salmon chief, lawát (that is, "Belly") known to the whites as Chief Tommy Thompson, supervised and regulated Indian fishing here until the last, ordering fishing opened or closed each day and season. In later days, however, as fishermen displaced from up and down the river and its tributaries came to Celilo eager for a share of its bounty, the traditional order of fishing and associated rights gave way somewhat. New platforms were constructed where there had been no recognized fishing sites before and the traditional proprietary rights of river people were contested by "treaty Indians" whose traditional access to Celilo's fish had been by courtesy of the recognized local owners. Indian dip net fishing continues today from platforms built on the rocks just below The Dalles Dam, at the "Lone Pine" fishery, one of the five Bonneville in lieu sites. Here the river still flows free for a short distance before merging with the Bonneville dam pool. The spot

is known to the Indians as wacúqʷs (wacáqʷs in Wasco-Wishram), and was
originally under Chinookan control. Here a weathered clapboard ruin, a
turn-of-the-century Indian Shaker church, sits incongruously beside a modern motel at the foot of The Dalles highway bridge, overlooking the Indian
fishermen still tending their nets.

There are scattered Klikitat homesteads at or near traditional village or
fishing sites up the Klickitat and White Salmon rivers from the Columbia as
at Husum (the aboriginal village of "Nakrepunk") on the White Salmon.
Klikitat descendants still use twenty-one fishing platforms at the falls on the
Klickitat River two miles above its mouth, a traditional fishery called łátaxat,
and they maintain their burial ground nearby. In 1987 the Klikitats gathered
to install Wilbur Slokish, Sr., as traditional chief, the first elected since the
position had fallen vacant in 1945 (see fig. 8.1). Slokish is a direct descendant
of the Sla-kish who represented the Klikitats at the treaty council in 1855.
Chief Slokish is an enrolled Yakima Indian, but asserts that though "I live in
the Yakima Valley, . . . I am still a Klickitat Indian" (*The Oregonian*, 6 April
1987, p. B7).

Johnny "Jumbo" Jackson was elected Klikitat subchief. He makes his
home at an in lieu fishing site at the mouth of the White Salmon River. He
guards that boat launch area there—posted "Indian Use Only"—as best he
can from the numerous white boaters and fishermen who continue to use
the site to launch their boats. He complains that his protests about white
encroachment on this vestige of aboriginal territory have fallen on deaf ears
at the BIA regional office. The government has responded with an eviction
notice. Jackson and his fellow Yakima's can fish there but cannot *live* there,
the government has ruled.

Farther downstream at Cook's Landing near the mouth of the Little White
Salmon, Columbia River Indians have formed a corporation, Treaty Indians
of the Columbia, Inc., to push for the recognition of their fishing rights,
documented in a film—"Little White Salmon River Indians" (Community
Eye Productions 1972)—that tells their side of the story. In 1985, five Indian
fishermen from Cook's Landing led by David Sohappy, Sr.—a codefendant
in the landmark 1969 *U.S.* vs. *Oregon* case—were convicted in federal court
of illegal sales of salmon to an undercover agent of the National Marine
Fisheries Service (the notorious "Salmonscam" case), discussed below.
Sohappy and his extended family are subject to the same eviction order
served on Johnny Jackson. They have filed a countersuit (1987). The Indian
wars continue in the courts!

Fig. 8.1. Contemporary Columbia River chiefs (photograph by Jeanie Senior, published in *The Oregonian*, April 6, 1987).

The Columbia River Indians demonstrate a little known side of Indian survival today. These people are neither reservation nor urban Indians. They may share reservation benefits as enrolled members and have strong family ties to the reservations (often to more than one reservation), but their strongest ties remain with their ancestral homes on the Big River.

Life on the Reservations

The reservations are the core of Plateau Indian cultural continuity, providing a physical, social, and economic refuge in the face of tremendous pressures for assimilation. On some reservations Indian societies number in the thousands (see Table 23) in contrast to the scattered families still living off-reservation in the Plateau. Reservation-based Indians have resources for needed legal, political, and social actions that non-reservation Indians lack. On the other hand, reservation Indians were exposed to more concerted efforts at religious conversion during the period of missionary control of the Indian agencies, pressures that Indians who remained at traditional village sites off the reservation escaped. Reservation Indians were often cut off from traditional economic pursuits and persecuted for continuing allegiance to traditionally oriented values and practices. Thus the off-reservation Indians—though few in number and often virtually invisible to non-Indian society—maintain a particularly strong commitment to and close association with traditional culture.

The treaties that established the Yakima, Umatilla, and Warm Springs reservations were ratified in 1859. According to the treaty language, the affected Indians had one year to abandon their homes off-reservation and to move within its confines. Reservation life at Yakima for the next twenty-five years would be dominated by the six-foot-four-inch, 200-pound presence of "Father" James Wilbur, a Methodist minister and teacher. Wilbur's career at Yakima began in 1860 as a teacher in the reservation school, but he soon came into conflict with the Indian agent who fired him. Wilbur went to Washington, D.C., gained a personal interview with President Lincoln, and succeeded in being named agent in his rival's place.

Wilbur was dedicated to his civilizing mission with the fervor of the true believer. He waged a verbal war against the heathen forces epitomized by Smohalla, the pagan prophet at Priest Rapids, as well as against Father St. Onge, the "papist agent" whose Ahtanum mission (first established in 1849, where St. Onge served from 1867–71) presented stiff competition to the Methodist latecomers. Eventually President Grant himself intervened on behalf of the Methodists, as it was federal policy during Grant's administration to assign each Indian agency to one or another Protestant denomination. As was true throughout the missionary period on the western frontier, the line between "civilizing" and "converting" was none too clear.

Despite Wilbur's efforts, Smohalla remained at large and exerted a strong influence on the Yakima Reservation. There was a strong reservation wáašani following under the guidance of Smohalla's contemporary and colleague, Chief Kamiakin's nephew Kotiakan (kútayaqan), who rang the bell for Waashat services at his longhouse at Parker just south of Union Gap. By 1881

TABLE 23
Southern Plateau Indian Reservations

Washington

Yakima	Pop.: 7,500 (1980)	Treaty: 1855
c/o Yakima Agency	Area: 1,134,830 acres	
P.O. Box 632	Groups: Sahaptin, Wishram	
Toppenish, WA 98948	Govt.: tribal council	

Colville	Pop.: 4,500 (2,750 resident)	Exec. Order: 1872
c/o Colville Agency	Area: 1,087,271 acres	
P.O. Box 111	Groups: Okanagan-Colville,	
Nespelem, WA 99155	Columbia, Nez Perce, Palus	
	Govt.: tribal council	

Spokane	Pop.: 1,500 (500 resident)	Exec. Order: 1887
c/o Spokane Agency	Area: 138,750 acres	
P.O. Box 86	Groups: Spokane	
Wellpinit, WA 99040	Govt.: tribal council	

Kalispel	Pop.: 150	Exec. Order: 1887
c/o N. Idaho Agency	Area: 4500 acres	
P.O. Drawer 277	Groups: Kalispel	
Lapwai, ID 83540		

Oregon

Warm Springs	Pop.: 1,750	Treaty: 1855, 1865
Warm Springs Agency	Area: 639,898 acres (1979)	
P.O. Box 1239	Groups: Sahaptin, Wasco,	
Warm Springs, OR 97761	N. Paiute	
	Govt.: tribal council	

Umatilla	Pop.: 500	Treaty: 1855
Umatilla Agency	Area: 85,322 acres (1979)	
P.O. Box 520	Groups: Umatilla, Walla Walla,	
Pendleton, OR 97801	Cayuse	
	Govt.: tribal council	

TABLE 23 (*continued*)

Burns Paiute Colony c/o Warm Springs Agency	Pop.: 150 Area: 11,944 acres Groups: Burns N. Paiute	Exec. Order: ?
Klamath	Pop.: 450 Original Area: 860,930 acres	Treaty: 1865 Terminated: 1961
Idaho Nez Perce c/o N. Idaho Agency	Pop.: 750 Area: 92,685 acres Groups: Nez Perce Govt.: tribal council	Treaty: 1855, 1863, 1868 Exec. Order: 1875
Coeur d'Alene c/o N. Idaho Agency	Pop.: 600 Area: 69,435 acres Groups: Coeur d'Alene Govt.: tribal council	Exec. Order: 1889
Kootenai c/o N. Idaho Agency	Pop.: ? Area: 2,680 acres Groups: Kootenai Govt.: by Flathead Tribe	Treaty: 1855
Fort Hall Fort Hall Agency Fort Hall, ID 83203	Pop.: 3,000 Area: 523,917 acres Groups: Shoshone, Bannock, Blackfoot Govt.: tribal council	Treaty: 1868
Montana Flathead Flathead Agency Box A Pablo, MT 59855	Pop.: 3,000 Area: 140,000 acres Groups: Flathead, Kootenai Govt.: tribal council	Treaty: 1855

Sources: Klein (1978); Zucker, Hummel, and Høgfoss (1983).

Wilbur had to admit that, of a reservation population of 2,628, only 697 were full-time farmers and another 1,057 combined farming with fishing for subsistence. The remaining 874 still pursued a traditional and transient existence, settling on the reservation only for the winters (Schuster 1975:237–38). However, by 1895 only 10 percent of the reservation population (by then reduced further to 2,000) were considered still "wild" Indians. A fundamental economic transformation was wrought among the reservation Indians in these few decades. It was an accommodation forced also by the tightening noose of settlement around the reservation that made a dependence upon the traditional round of hunting, fishing, and gathering increasingly difficult.

Wilbur's retirement in 1883 marked the beginning of an acceleration of threats to the treaty guarantee of "exclusive use" of reservation lands, which Wilbur, to his credit, had vigorously defended. The situation at Yakima at this time is repeated on reservations throughout the Plateau. In 1883 the Northern Pacific Railroad completed its track right across the eastern border of the Yakima Reservation, completing a transcontinental route to Puget Sound. A flood of immigration into the reservation border area followed. By 1889 white farmers on Ahtanum Creek just north of the reservation (and just above Kamiakin's original village) had diverted so much of the creek's water to irrigate their properties that Indians downstream had none left with which to water their herds (Schuster 1975:256). Rights to the water flowing past the reservation are now the object of intense litigation as irrigation districts, hydropower generation companies, and fisheries interests contest control of the finite water resources of Plateau rivers.

The settlers' demands for more and more land led to the passage of the Dawes' Severalty Act (a.k.a., General Allotment Act) by Congress in 1887. The pious justification for this abrogation of treaty guarantees was that it would encourage the Indians' transition to a civilized way of life by virtue of the alleged moral force of private property ownership, a powerful element of the "liberal" political ideology of that day. The hidden agenda was clearly otherwise. All reservation lands remaining after each enrolled tribal member received his or her 80 acres of farmland or 160 acres of grazing or timber land was to be declared *surplus*. The government was then authorized to buy this from the tribes for distribution by sale or homestead title to the citizenry at large. Furthermore, the Indians' allotted acres—after a period of up to twenty-five years in trust status—could be converted to *fee patent* ownership, that is, their lands could be freely bought and sold. The first such fee patent allotments became available for sale on the Yakima Reservation in 1906, with the passage of the Burke Act allowing accelerated fee patent conversion of Indian allotments, and by 1907 three non-Indian towns—Toppenish, Wapato, and Parker—had been established within the reservation boundaries on plots purchased from Indian allottees (Schuster 1975:257). By 1911, 290 allotments had been sold to non-Indians, virtually every allotment that had been converted to fee patent ownership by that time. This included 10,000 acres of irrigated farmland within the Wapato Irrigation Project, a scheme constructed without tribal approval, taking reservation land and water illegally (consult McWhorter's passionate indictment of this in his book, *The Crime Against the Yakima*, published in 1913, and Schuster 1975:249–62).

In 1914 the allotment rolls were closed, but the damage had been done. The best agricultural lands of the reservation had become a checkerboard of Indian and white ownership with whites resident within the reservation boundaries outnumbering resident Indians ten to one. Whites now own the most productive 10 percent of all Yakima Reservation lands (Schuster 1975:265). The Umatilla Reservation has experienced even more severe erosion of its land base (see fig. 8.2). The Warm Springs Reservation, due to the shortage of decent farmland within its boundaries, retained nearly all its territory as trust land (see fig. 8.3).

The next two decades saw a minor reversal of reservation Indian fortunes with the passage of a bill granting all Indians full citizenship rights, including the right to vote (1924). This law was justified as an expression of gratitude for Indian people's loyal service in World War I. In 1934, under President Franklin Roosevelt's depression administration, a "New Deal" for Indians was initiated with the passage of the Johnson-O'Malley and Wheeler-Howard acts. The first act mandated federal support for Indian education, health, and welfare and continues to provide essential resources to impoverished reservation communities. The second, better known as the Indian Reorganization Act or IRA, explicitly rejected the assimilationist philosophy that had motivated the Dawes Act and past BIA administrative policies (such as the forced separation of Indian children from their parents in order that they might be "educated" at distant BIA Indian boarding schools).

The right of Indians to be Indians was asserted in the IRA (under BIA supervision, however) and tribes were invited to submit plans for tribal self-government. Roosevelt's appointment of the activist John Collier as Commissioner of Indian Affairs (a post he held until 1945) assured strong administrative backing to these legislative innovations.

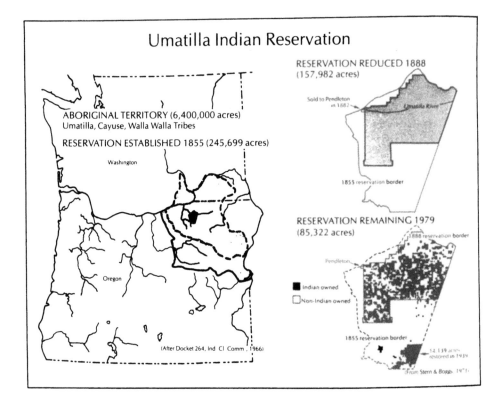

Fig. 8.2. Umatilla Reservation (reprinted from *Oregon Indians,* Zucker et al. 1983:100, with permission of the Oregon Historical Society Press).

Many tribes, however, were suspicious of this new direction. The Umatillas refused until 1949 to submit a self-government plan, some denouncing the act as "communist inspired," a rhetorical response of many Republicans to New Deal proposals. The Warm Springs Indians joined the program in 1938 and the Yakimas submitted their plan in 1944.

At Yakima, all adult enrollees were constituted as a General Council of the Nation; this council delegated administrative and executive authority to an elected Tribal Council of fourteen members chosen by majority vote for four-year terms. The Yakima tribal government has proved an excellent example of participatory democracy in action. The General Council acts as a jealous watchdog ready to react to any hint of Tribal Council mismanagement or

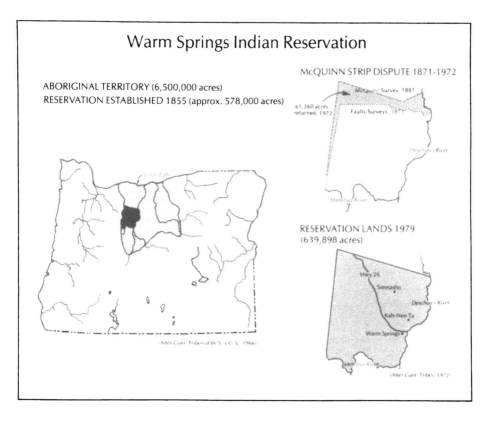

Fig. 8.3. Warm Springs Reservation (reprinted from *Oregon Indians*, Zucker et al. 1983:99, with permission of the Oregon Historical Society Press).

misuse of power. In this, they carry forward the traditional suspicion that Plateau hunter-gatherers held toward those who exercised power.

Warm Springs opted for a somewhat similar executive structure, which included electing three chiefs for life and other councilmen who serve specified terms; executives are appointed by this council. There is also a General Council of the Confederated Tribes. Though traditional Plateau politics were radically "democratic," political action was not mandated by majority vote as in the United States, but by an often long and informal pursuit of consensus. Consensual democracy does not grant the majority the right to force collective actions on the minority; traditional "acephalous" Plateau society could not long survive in the face of a disgruntled minority. Contemporary reservation politics reflect this conflict between two distinct visions of democratic government.

The national political pendulum swings to and fro, and after World War II national sentiment shifted again toward the assimilationist position that Indians should, like it or not, join the American "mainstream." The termination of reservations policies of the Eisenhower years were codified in the Termination Act of 1953. That same year saw the passage of another federal bill (Public Law 280) transferring legal responsibility for Indian education, welfare, and justice to six state governments, including Oregon (but not Washington, Idaho, or Montana). A special exception was made for the Warm Springs tribe. This federal initiative to terminate reservations found little support among Plateau Indians except at Colville where an off-reservation, "progressive" faction nearly succeeded in winning a vote for the termination of the Colville Reservation and the distribution of its assets (including reservation lands of 1,000,000+ acres, among the largest in the Northwest) as cash shares on a per capita basis to the tribal membership.

Termination lost support in the 1960s with yet another swing of the ideological pendulum. The regnant concept today is "Indian self-determination." The Indian Self-Determination and Education Assistance Act of 1975 defined the current policy, directing all federal agencies "to allow Indian tribes and organizations to contract for, and administer themselves, those federal services and funds that were available to them" (Zucker, Hummel, and Høgfoss 1983:136).

Diabetes: A Modern Epidemic

The biological assaults on Plateau Indian populations did not cease with the waning of the brutal epidemics of smallpox, measles, and assorted scourges of the first century of contact. Today a new and more insidious biological hazard has begun to take a heavy toll. This is the modern epidemic of diabetes.

Diabetes first caused concern among Papagos in the 1940s, a medical problem rarely noted before that time among Native Americans. Today Papagos have achieved the unwelcome distinction of having the highest diabetes rate of any human population. It has reached epidemic proportions subsequently among a number of Native American groups, the Yakima among them, and is now a major cause of adult mortality on many Indian reservations (Sievers and Fisher 1981). It may not kill outright, but is closely correlated with an increased incidence of heart disease, high blood pressure associated with obesity, and gall bladder disease. Add to that the similarly insidious impact of high alcoholism rates and high suicide and accident rates attributable to deculturation (i.e., the destruction of older cultural meanings without replacement by any meaningful new alternative taken from the dominant cultural tradition) and one can begin to understand why Native American life expectancy at birth in the United States lags six years behind that of the white majority (Sievers and Fisher 1981:196).

How are we to understand this sudden appearance of a complex of diseases that were previously unknown or rare among Native Americans? The essential clue in this instance may lie in dietary changes. Indian people today have ready access to an abundance of processed foods that are high in short-chain carbohydrates and animal fats but low in long-chain carbohydrates and fiber. Such processed foods are conspicuously marketed in our supermarkets and have now largely replaced traditional greens, roots, fish, and berries in the Indians' diet. Traditional foods had a higher fiber content and were rich in essential vitamins and minerals well preserved by indigenous drying techniques. Healthy fish oils were the primary source of fats. Such foods provided all essential nutrients, including ample calories (see Table 15, p. 177). However, it is hard work to find these foods and to harvest and process them. There were times of abundance and times when food was scarce, notably in the late winter.

My impression is that Indian people today still eat as if they were hunting, fishing, and gathering for their sustenance. Food is sacred; it is not to be wasted, even if the quantities available are in excess of immediate needs; food is to be shared generously. These social and cultural factors encourage overconsumption under modern conditions of reliable and ready supply. However, it is apparently not simply a matter of overeating. A study of Papago diet indicated that even when they consume no more calories than their non-Indian neighbors, Indian people put on more weight more quickly. One theory that has gained credibility in recent years is that of diabetes as a "thrifty genotype," first proposed by James Neel, a well-known geneticist.

Neel proposed that human hunting and gathering populations may have developed a genetic susceptibility to diabetes because a "diabetes gene" complex increased their biological fitness under environmental conditions of alternating feast and famine (1962). The diabetes genes under such dietary conditions allow the body to build up fat reserves readily when food is abundant, reserves that may then be metabolized to keep the body going when food calories are in short supply. Individuals lacking this diabetes gene complex are less able to store body fat during periods of abundance and thus more quickly exhaust their fat reserves during famine.

Laboratory studies of mice provide some support for this argument. Mice with the diabetes gene complex survive at much higher rates when fed a diet that contains just half the calories of the normal laboratory diet, while mice without the diabetes genes readily succumb under those conditions. Increase the caloric intakes, however, and the non-diabetic mice thrive while the diabetic mice begin to exhibit the harmful diabetic symptoms we know so well (Tucker 1983).

Thus, American Indians may have evolved both social and genetic mechanisms designed to enhance an individual's survival in lean times. The social mechanisms stressed the fundamental moral values of generosity and sharing, of feasting with friends and relatives as long as supplies hold out, while the physiological mechanisms acted as a caloric savings account. Today, however, these tendencies contribute to the poor health of Native Americans. What can be done to correct this problem? How can American Indians escape this latest crippling biological legacy of white contact, which ironically gains force in the midst of an American society of abundance and superior medical technology? There is certainly no simple answer. Perhaps if Plateau Indians recognize the causes of this problem they can take steps to improve their diets, in particular, by reviving an interest in native foods, especially the roots and greens that are nearly as abundant and readily available today as they were before white settlement.

Fishing Rights

The latest chapter in the saga of the Columbia River Indians is the struggle for fishing rights. Residents of the Pacific Northwest have heard a great deal of debate about the Boldt decision, a judicial ruling handed down by Judge George Boldt of the Federal District Court in Tacoma, Washington, in 1974. His decision was subsequently clarified and strongly affirmed by the U.S. Supreme Court in 1979. Few appreciate the key roles played by Columbia River Indians in the legal battles leading up to and following the Boldt decision. As early as 1887 the Yakima Tribe sued to gain access to a "usual and accustomed" fishing site on the Columbia River at Celilo Falls (*Yakima Tribe* vs. *Taylor*). A settler named Taylor, in fencing his property, had blocked that traditional right of access. The Supreme Court of Washington Territory ordered the fence removed (Cohen 1986:54–55).

The first litigation dealing with Indian fishing rights in the Pacific Northwest to reach the U.S. Supreme Court was the case of *U.S.* vs. *Winans*, heard in 1905. As in the Taylor case, Mr. Winans had blocked Indian access to a fishing site covered by treaty. Winans objected to the Indians taking fish near his state-licensed fish wheel and argued that the superior technology he employed entitled him to an exclusive right to fish at that site.[1] Justice Joseph McKenna spoke for the court in rejecting that argument, ruling in favor of the treaty Indian fishermen. His decision established several key legal precedents that remain basic to treaty interpretation to this day:

1. He affirmed that the treaties remained in force despite the conferral of statehood on Washington Territory.

2. He articulated the principle that Indian treaties must be "interpreted in the way that the Indians would have understood" them (Cohen 1986:55); "all ambiguities must be resolved in the Indians' favor . . . consistent with the general legal doctrine that . . . contracts . . . between parties with unequal bargaining, . . . will [be interpreted] . . . in favor of the weaker one" (Cohen 1986:141).

3. His decision defined the "reserved rights doctrine," that in signing treaties Indian tribes granted rights *to* the United States, not vice versa; thus all rights not specifically ceded in the treaties were reserved to the tribes (Cohen 1986:56).

4. His ruling left open the possibility that states might nevertheless have the right to regulate Indian fishing in certain circumstances; this last issue is still very much a focus of contention today.

Columbia River Indians have not won every fishing rights case they were party to, however. In 1916 the Washington State Supreme Court upheld the conviction of a Yakima Indian fisherman, Towessnute by name, for fishing without a license and for gaffing salmon, both in violation of state fishing regulations. Justice Bausman's opinion opened with

---

1. Fish wheels were water wheels equipped with wire-mesh baskets turned by the current. Salmon swimming against the current were caught in the baskets, lifted by the wheel, then shunted to the shore down a trough. The record catch for a fish wheel near The Dalles was 35 tons in a day and 209 tons in a season (Donaldson and Cramer 1971:91), roughly equivalent to the harvest of 200 Indian fishermen.

this salvo: "The premise of Indian sovereignty we reject . . ." (quoted in Cohen 1986:57). (This intransigence by state government—especially the Washington State government—continued into the late 1970s, when the Washington State Supreme Court issued an order prohibiting state fisheries officials from enforcing Judge Boldt's federal court ruling.) But in 1921 the U.S. Supreme Court again upheld Indian treaty rights in the case of *Seufert Brothers* vs. *U.S.*, another case arising out of conficts between Indian fishermen and fish wheel operators.[2]

A third Columbia River Indian fisheries case reached the Supreme Court in 1942, the case of Sampson Tulee versus the State of Washington. Tulee, a Yakima Indian, invited arrest by catching salmon with a dip net and selling it without a state license. The U.S. Supreme Court overturned the state high court ruling and decreed that state license fees were not essential for the exercise of the state's right to regulate fishing in the interest of conservation and constituted an illegal charge for the exercise of a legal right. *Tulee* vs. *Washington* marks the beginning of a tradition of non-violent resistance by Indian fishermen in order to force the courts to define and uphold their rights in the face of defiant state government officials, both executive and judiciary.

A 1958 case, *Maison* vs. *The Confederated Tribes of the Umatilla Reservation*, also addressed the issue of states' rights to regulate Indian fishing. Three Umatilla Indian fishermen were arrested for fishing during a state-ordered closed season. (H. G. Maison was named as superintendent of the Oregon State Police.) The Tribe won its case and was sustained by the Ninth Circuit Court on appeal. Judge Montgomery Koelsch wrote the Circuit Court opinion which established the rule that states could regulate Indian fishing only if such regulation was indispensable for conservation of the resource (Cohen 1986:68–69). In short, Indian fishing could be restricted only after all possible restrictions had been enforced on non-Indian fisheries.

The landmark case of *Sohappy* vs. *Smith*—later consolidated as the *U.S.* vs. *Oregon*, heard by Judge Robert Belloni—began with a calculated act of civil

2. The Seufert Brothers, Frank and Theodore, were pioneer fish and fruit packers at The Dalles. Their company, established in 1881, erected its first fish wheel in 1885 and at one time operated nineteen stationary wheels, seventeen scow-mounted wheels, and four seining operations in the Columbia River between The Dalles and Celilo Falls. Their cannery at Fifteen Mile Creek, across from where the Dalles Dam powerhouse now stands, had a capacity of thirty-two tons of salmon per day. Wheels were outlawed on the Columbia in the late 1920s and early 1930s (Donaldson and Cramer 1971:82–96; Smith 1979:95–96).

disobedience. Richard Sohappy, a Yakima tribal member and a richly decorated war veteran, with his uncle, David Sohappy, Sr., both residents of the embattled Cook's Landing community in the Columbia Gorge, invited arrest by gill netting in the Columbia River in defiance of state fishing regulations. The federal government entered the case on behalf of the Columbia River treaty tribes in support of the Sohappys. Judge Belloni's ruling broke new ground in requiring states to regulate fishing in such a way as to guarantee the Indians a "fair and equitable share of all fish which it permits to be taken from a given run" (quoted in Cohen 1986:78–79).

The ambiguity inherent in the phrase "fair and equitable share" was subsequently resolved by the 1974 Boldt ruling. In Boldt's decision that share was defined as an *equal* share of the harvestable fish destined to reach treaty fishing sites.[3]

Boldt's opponents argue that this provision is grossly unfair, as it allocates 50 percent of the fish to only 0.03 percent of the population. It must be noted, however, that most of the remaining 50 percent share is allocated to a small special-interest group also comprising less than 0.03 percent of the region's population, non-Indian commercial fishermen (Zucker et al. 1982:170). It also must be noted that the 50 percent applies to harvestable fish returning to usual and accustomed fishing sites. Not included is the huge offshore catch (which intercepted 71 percent of the total Columbia River runs during 1970–74) that until recently was largely unregulated. If we subtract the catch of non-Indian commercial and sports fishermen operating below Bonneville Dam (another 14.2 percent) and subtract 9.6 percent for escapement, the Indians' share is whittled down to a scant 5.3 percent of the river's fish (see Table 24).

Judge Belloni applied Boldt's judgment to the Columbia River and then in 1977 ordered the concerned state and tribal governments to develop a trial five-year Joint Management Plan in an attempt to enhance the Columbia River fishery for the benefit of all parties. As part of the plan, the Technical Advisory Committee was established to make recommendations to the Columbia River Compact, a committee composed of representatives of the fish and game commissions of Washington and Oregon that has regulated fish-

3. Specifically excluded by Boldt from this 50–50 calculation were fish caught by Indians on their reservations, fish caught to meet Indians' ceremonial and subsistence needs, and fish reserved for "escapement," i.e., that fraction judged essential for maintaining spawning populations (Cohen 1986:12). The U.S. Supreme Court reversed Boldt's ruling on the first two points in upholding his decision in 1979 (Cohen 1986:114).

TABLE 24

Catch Distribution of Fall Chinook Destined for the Upper Columbia River
(1970–1974 average) (Zucker et al. 1983:167)

56.2% Ocean Commercial			14.8% Ocean Sport		19.5% Columbia River			9.6% Escapement
41.4% Canadian Troll & Nets	10.8% Washington Troll & Nets	4.0% Other	10.4% Washington & Puget Sound	4.4% Other	3.8% Sport	10.4% Non-Indian Commercial Catch	5.3% Treaty Indian Catch	

ing on the Columbia River since 1918 (Cohen 1986:124; Stanford 1987). The tribes responded by forming their own Columbia River Inter-Tribal Fish Commission (CRITFC) "to coordinate their fisheries management policies and to provide tribal decision-makers with technical information" (Cohen 1986:125).

It soon became clear, however, that Columbia River salmon could not be managed in isolation from a larger context, one encompassing the offshore waters of western North America. Columbia River fishermen, Indian and non-Indian alike, were fighting over the scraps left by a "voracious ocean troll fishery" that harvested prior to 1980 an estimated 64 percent of the salmon produced in the Columbia River above Bonneville Dam (Cohen 1986:127). In 1979 the Columbia River treaty tribes (Yakima, Warm Springs, Umatilla, Nez Perce, and Shoshone-Bannock) sued the Secretary of Commerce to require the Pacific Fisheries Management Council (responsible for regulating the off-shore fisheries of California, Oregon, and Washington) to impose tighter restrictions on ocean trollers. Though the Department of the Interior sided with the tribes, the Justice Department chose to defend Commerce in the case. Nevertheless, the courts sided with the Indian plaintiffs, ruling that the Boldt decision gave priority to treaty fishing rights over the political and economic concerns guiding Commerce Department decisions.

Though Judge Belloni's five-year plan was a failure, it has encouraged a greater degree of cooperation between Indian and non-Indian parties in fisheries management. There has been a dramatic expansion of the role of tribal representatives in fisheries management in the past decade, first on the Columbia River on a par with state officials, then in the federal management of off-shore fishing, and most recently in the negotiation of international agreements between the United States and Canada (Cohen 1986:169–70). Columbia River tribes are now represented on the International Pacific Salmon Fisheries Commission.

Salmonscam

The right of treaty tribes to regulate off-reservation fishing by their own members was firmly established by the Boldt ruling. Some tribes, such as Yakima and Warm Springs, had established and enforced fishing regulations for their members as soon as their tribal governments were constituted under the provisions of the IRA. These tribal regulations governed who could fish, where and when they could fish, and specified allowable gear.

Tribal regulation, however, has not always been willingly accepted by individual tribal members. Plateau Indians come from a tradition leery of the exercise of authority, a tradition that places a high value on individual autonomy. Furthermore, contemporary tribal governments—legally the repositories of treaty rights—do not represent traditional institutions of social control. Fishing sites on the Columbia were originally held by locally resident families, while fishing practices were regulated in accord with a sacred law enunciated by Coyote in myth and enforced by informal social and supernatural sanctions. Some Columbia River Indian traditionalists to this day deny the legitimacy of tribal authority on *their* river.

Now that Columbia River fishing regulations are formulated with significant tribal inputs, defying those regulations may pit Indian against Indian and could threaten gains achieved through previous legal challenges. The recent cause célèbre, the salmonscam trials of David Sohappy, Sr., and his codefendants, exposes these raw nerves.

In 1981 the National Marine Fisheries Service, an arm of the beleaguered Commerce Department, initiated an undercover "sting" operation designed to expose David Sohappy, Sr., and his Cook's Landing community as a band of Indian outlaw poachers. Federal agents posing as blackmarket fish-buyers purchased fifty-three tons of illegal fish (about six thousand fish in all, mostly spring Chinook salmon, valued at some $150,000) from Indians at Cook's Landing. More than a dozen were convicted in federal court of violating provisions of the Lacey Act, passed in 1981, which made interstate trafficking in illegal fish a felony. But all were found not guilty of related charges of conspiracy. David Sohappy, Sr., and his son were given maximum sentences of five years in prison (Cohen 1986:133–35).

The Fisheries Service justified the sting by the fact that 40,000 bright fall Chinook salmon, about half the total upriver run, "disappeared" each year between Bonneville Dam and their spawning grounds above McNary Dam. The sting, however, did not solve the mystery it was intended to solve. The illegal fish caught—6,000, not 40,000—were spring, not fall, Chinook salmon. And the number of missing fish was no less after the arrests at Cook's Landing. It is now suspected that many of the 40,000 "lost fish" were not really lost at all; some were discovered to be spawning in the Deschutes River and another fraction may have been lost by statistical error. The following year anti-poaching patrols on the river were increased 50 percent: 93 percent of those caught fishing illegally proved to be non-Indians (Cohen 1986:134–35).

Despite these facts, Senators Gorton and Jackson of Washington and Hatfield and Packwood of Oregon called on the Secretary of the Interior to evict the Indians from the in lieu site at Cook's Landing, branding it "the last remaining focal point for illegal fishing activity on the Columbia River" (quoted in Stanford 1987, Part 1, p. A29).

The fact remains that the Cook's Landing Indians sold fish in violation not only of state regulations but of tribal regulations as well. They sought and were granted a largely symbolic retrial before the Yakima Nation tribal court. This retrial of six of the original defendants during the spring of 1987 was first of all an assertion of the Tribe's superior right to enforce its own fishing regulations. It also pitted modern secular tribal authority and compromise against claims of an absolute, traditional, and personal spiritual authority. It set tribal rights based on treaty language in opposition to individual and familial rights grounded in unwritten cultural traditions.

Sohappy's claim that his actions were governed by his traditional religious beliefs seems an incongruous justification for the sale of $150,000 worth of sacred salmon to a federal undercover agent. Nevertheless, a jury of Sohappy's peers empaneled by the Yakima tribal court exonerated the salmonscam defendants. The jury concluded that they had been entrapped by the federal agent and that Indian religious values took precedence over the white man's law. The defendants were then remanded to federal prison for the duration of their heavy sentences.

Boldt Phase II

The latest spice to be added to this political stew is known as "Boldt Phase II." Judge Boldt set aside two questions for a subsequent phase of judicial review: (1) whether the treaty-based fishery allocation should include hatchery-bred fish, and (2) whether the treaties required the protection of the salmon's habitat in order to guarantee adequate fish for future generations of Indian people (Cohen 1986:5–6). The second issue is of the most sweeping significance. If answered in the affirmative it could grant Indian tribes an interest in virtually all land and resource use decisions affecting salmon habitat, including but not limited to timber harvesting, water and power allocation, pesticide and herbicide application, and nuclear waste disposal. Such an outcome would no doubt be met with an outburst of fear and anger by non-Indians that would dwarf the storm that greeted Boldt's decision in Phase I.

On the other hand, sharing responsibility for the management of our Pacific Northwest habitat with the descendants of its original human inhabitants presents an opportunity to appreciate this land and its resources from a more complex perspective. Some environmental groups are already on record in support of Phase II. Hazel Wolf of the Federation of Western Outdoor Clubs declared that, "The successful outcomes of this lawsuit [Phase II] would provide a new source of environmental control of value to the entire community" (quoted in Cohen 1986:141). George Boldt died in 1984 but the case that bears his name lives on, now the responsibility of Judge William Orrick. In 1980 Judge Orrick issued preliminary rulings on these issues, affirming that hatchery fish replaced wild fish populations covered by treaty guarantees and thus should be included in the pool from which the Indian share is drawn. He also ruled that "the state could not deny the Indians' right to fish by destroying the environment, anymore than it could deny that right by other means" (Cohen 1986:142).

The treaties reserved for the Columbia River Indians the continuing right to fish at usual and accustomed sites. However, that guarantee means nothing if there are no fish to be caught. The Dalles Dam, completed in 1957, buried Celilo Falls under sixty feet of still water and struck a knock-out blow to the Columbia River Indians' traditional subsistence economy. Though the Yakima Tribe received $15 million in compensation (approximately $3,270 per member), no amount of money could compensate for the loss of this great fishery (Schuster 1975:294). Relander reports that unemployment on the Yakima Reservation increased 45 percent as a direct consequence of the Dam (1962:12). Priest Rapids Dam, completed in 1962, buried another key Indian fishery as well as the most sacred points of contact linking the Wanapam people to their past.

The taming of the mighty Columbia began with the construction of Rock Island, Bonneville, and Grand Coulee dams, massive New Deal public works projects designed to lift the nation out of the despair of the Great Depression, gigantic sculptures glorifying progress. Today eleven dams stretch across the mid-Columbia and another four sap the strength of the lower Snake River. Only the Hanford Reach on the Columbia flows free. These dams have transformed rural life in the Columbia basin. The Grand Coulee alone irrigates over half-a-million acres of arid steppe, while all the dams together generate electricity to meet the demands of 10,000,000 people and have made floods but a distant memory (Lange 1987).

The continuing industrialization of the River year-by-year reduces the long-term viability of the Columbia River fishery. Fish ladders allow salmon to struggle upriver as far as Chief Joseph Dam just below the Grand Coulee, but more than a thousand miles of spawning gravels upriver are cut off forever (see fig. 8.4). A famed run of giant spring Chinook salmon that spawned high on the Columbia was exterminated when the Grand Coulee opened for business in 1941. And fish ladders are no help to the salmon fry on their journey to the sea. As many as 30 percent are chewed up by turbines or asphyxiated in the hyperaerated waters below each dam. Biologists estimate that 15 million salmon spawned in the Columbia 100 years ago and that just 2.5 million spawn in the River today. Many might be saved if enough water could be flushed over the dams during the critical down-

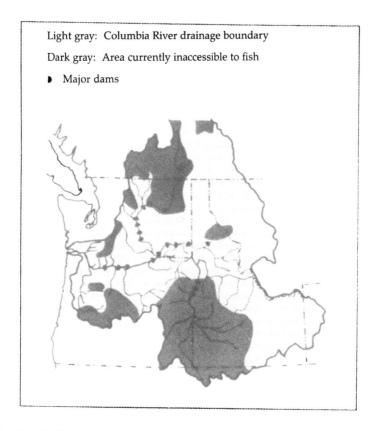

Light gray: Columbia River drainage boundary

Dark gray: Area currently inaccessible to fish

▶ Major dams

Fig. 8.4. Declining fish runs in the Columbia Basin (reprinted from *Oregon Indians,* Zucker et al. 1983:168, with permission of the Oregon Historical Society Press).

stream migration period. However, economists estimate the cost of such measures at over $20 million in lost hydroelectric power revenue, a "tax" of one dollar for every salmon in the river. For one tenth that sum the Army Corps of Engineers has been able to barge 15 million fry past the lower dams (Fobes 1987:8). In the battle of the big money the salmon fishery is a loser. Protection of the river's salmon resource then must be justified by legal and moral arguments rather than strictly economic ones.

A 1982 case quickly put this principle to the test. The Yakima Nation requested the Kittitas Reclamation District watermaster to assure a sufficient flow of water from the Cle Elum Irrigation Dam on the upper Yakima River to save sixty Chinook salmon redds in the stream below the dam. Farmers downstream protested, arguing that all the reservoir's water should be diverted to guarantee that their irrigation needs would be met. Appeals to the Ninth Circuit Court have so far resulted in a split decision (Cohen 1986:146–49). It will likely be many years before the dust settles. The legacy of Judge Boldt's Phase II is in opening the door to the possibility that Indian people may once again serve as stewards of Mother Earth, guarding her great jugular vein, the Columbia River.

Bibliography

Aberle, David F. 1959. "The Prophet Dance and Reactions to White Contact." *Southwestern Journal of Anthropology* 15:74–83.

Ackerman, Lillian Alice. 1982. "Sexual Equality in the Plateau Culture Area." Ph.D. dissertation, Washington State University, Pullman.

American Anthropological Association. 1976 [1971]. "Statement on Ethics." Washington, D.C.

American Friends Service Committee. 1970. *Uncommon Controversy: Fishing Rights of the Muckleshoot, Puyallup, and Nisqually Indians.* University of Washington Press, Seattle.

Ames, Kenneth M., and Alan G. Marshall. 1980–81. "Villages, Demography and Subsistence Intensification on the Southern Columbia Plateau." *North American Archaeologist* 2:25–52.

Amoss, Pamela. 1978. *Coast Salish Spirit Dancing: The Survival of an Ancestral Religion.* University of Washington Press, Seattle.

Anastasio, Angelo. 1972 [1955]. "The Southern Plateau: An Ecological Analysis of Intergroup Relations." *Northwest Anthropological Research Notes* 6:109–229. (Originally 1955, Ph. D. dissertation, University of Chicago.)

Aoki, Haruo. 1966. "Nez Perce and Proto-Sahaptian Kinship Terms." *International Journal of American Linguistics* 32:357–68.

Aoki, Haruo. 1979. "Nez Perce Texts." *University of California Publications in Linguistics* 90.

Arno, Stephen F., and Ramona P. Hammerly. 1977. *Northwest Trees.* The Mountaineers, Seattle.

Atkins, John R. 1974. "GRAFIK: A Multipurpose Kinship Metalanguage." In *Genealogical Mathematics,* edited by P. A. Ballonoff, pp. 27–51. Mouton, The Hague.

Baenen, James A. 1968. "The Conflict over Nez Perce Hunting and Fishing Rights." *Northwest Anthropological Research Notes* 2:44–82.

Bailey, Reeve M., and Carl E. Bond. 1963. "Four New Species of Fresh Water Sculpins, Genus *Cottus,* from Western North America." *Occasional Papers* No. 634. Museum of Zoology, University of Michigan, Ann Arbor.

Beavert, Virginia. 1974. *The Way It Was: Anaku Iwacha, Yakima Indian Legends.*

Consortium of Johnson O'Malley Committees of Region IV, State of Washington. Franklin Press, Yakima, Washington.

Beavert, Virginia, and Bruce Rigsby. 1976. *Yakima Language Practical Dictionary*. Johnson-O'Malley (JOM), Consortium of Committees, Region IV, Toppenish, Washington. Prototype.

Benson, E. M., J. M. Peters, M. A. Edwards, and L. A. Hagen. 1973. "Wild Edible Plants of the Pacific Northwest." *Journal of the American Dietetic Association* 62:143–47.

Berlin, Brent, and Paul Kay. 1969. *Basic Color Terms: Their Universality and Evolution*. University of California Press, Berkeley.

Boas, Franz. 1934. *Geographical Names of the Kwakiutl Indians*. Columbia University Press, New York.

Boas, Franz. 1940. *Race, Language, and Culture*. Macmillan, New York.

Borden, Charles E. 1979. "Peopling and Early Cultures of the Pacific Northwest." *Science* 203:963–70.

Boyd, Robert T. 1985. "The Introduction of Infectious Diseases among the Indians of the Pacific Northwest, 1774–1874." Ph.D. dissertation, University of Washington, Seattle.

Boyd, Robert T., and Yvonne P. Hajda. 1987. "Seasonal Population Movements along the Lower Columbia River: The Social and Ecological Context." *American Ethnologist* 14:309–26.

Bright, William. 1960. "Animals of Acculturation in the California Indian Languages." *University of California Publications in Linguistics* 4:215–46.

Brown, Cecil B. 1985. "Mode of Subsistence and Folk Biological Taxonomy." *Current Anthropology* 26:43–62.

Burton, Michael L., Lilyan A. Brudner, and Douglas R. White. 1977. "A Model of the Sexual Division of Labor." *American Ethnologist* 4:277–51.

Call, Tracey G., and John Green. 1956. "Spasmolytics from Plants. I: Suksdorfin A and Columbianin." *Montana Academy of Sciences* 16:49–51.

Carneiro, Robert L. 1970. "A Theory of the Origin of the State." *Science* 169:733–38.

Chance, David H. 1973. "Influences of the Hudson's Bay Company on the Native Cultures of the Colville District." *Northwest Anthropological Research Notes* 7 (1), part 2 (Memoir No. 2).

Cohen, Fay G. 1986. *Treaties on Trial: The Continuing Controversy over Northwest Indian Fishing Rights*. University of Washington Press, Seattle.

Colson, Elizabeth. 1953. *The Makah Indians*. University of Minnesota Press, Minneapolis.

Cook, Sherburne F. 1955. "The Epidemic of 1830–1833 in California and Oregon," *University of California Publications in American Archaeology and Ethnology* 43:303–26.

Couture, Marilyn Dunlap. 1978. "Recent and Contemporary Foraging Practices of the Harney Valley Paiute." M.A. Thesis, Portland State University, Portland, Oregon.

Coville, Frederick V. 1904. "Notes on the Plants Used by the Klamath Indians of Oregon." *United States National Museum Report.* Washington, D. C.

Cox, Rachel. 1983. "Chemical Investigations into the Ichthyotoxic Effect of *Lomatium dissectum.*" B. A. thesis, Reed College, Portland, Oregon.

Cox, Ross. 1831. *Adventures on the Columbia River.* Two vols. H. Colburn and R. Bentley, London. Reprinted Binfords and Mort, Portland, Oregon, 1975.

Cressman, Luther S. 1977. *Prehistory of the Far West: Homes of Vanished Peoples.* University of Utah, Salt Lake City.

Cressman, Luther S., et al. 1960. "Cultural Sequences at The Dalles, Oregon: A Contribution to Pacific Northwest History," *American Philosophical Society Transactions* 50:10.

Curtin, Jeremiah. 1909. *Wishram Texts.* Brill, Leiden.

Curtis, Edward Sheriff. 1911a. *The Yakima. The Klickitat. Salishan Tribes of the Interior. The Kutenai.* Vol. 7 of *The North American Indian,* edited by Frederick W. Hodge. 20 vols. Plimpton Press, Norwood, Massachusetts. Reprinted, Johnson, New York, 1970.

Curtis, Edward Sheriff. 1911b. *The Nez Perces. The Wallawalla, Umatilla, Cayuse. The Chinookan Tribes.* Vol. 8 of *The North American Indian,* edited by Frederick W. Hodge. 20 vols. Plimpton Press, Norwood, Massachusetts. Reprinted, Johnson, New York, 1970.

Daugherty, Richard D. 1973. *The Yakima People.* Indian Tribal Series, Phoenix, Arizona.

Davies, John. 1980. *Douglas of the Forests: The North American Journals of David Douglas.* University of Washington Press, Seattle.

Deloria, Vine, Jr. 1969. *Custer Died for Your Sins: An Indian Manifesto.* Macmillan, New York.

Desmond, Gerald R. 1952. *Gambling among the Yakima.* Catholic University Anthropological Series No. 14. Catholic Univ. of America, Washington, D. C.

Dixon, C. W. 1962. *Smallpox.* J. & H. Churchill, London.

Donaldson, Ivan J., and Frederick K. Cramer. 1971. *Fishwheels of the Columbia.* Binfords and Mort, Portland, Oregon.

Doty, James. 1978 [1855]. *Journal of Operations of Governor Isaac Ingalls Stevens of Washington Territory in 1855.* Ye Galleon Press, Fairfield, Washington.

Drury, Clifford Merrill, ed. 1958. *The Diaries and Letters of Henry H. Spalding and Asa Bowen Smith Relating to the Nez Perce Mission, 1838–1842.* Arthur H. Clark, Glendale, California.

Drury, Clifford Merrill. 1979. *Chief Lawyer of the Nez Perces, 1796–1876.* Arthur H. Clark, Glendale, California.

Dubois, Cora. 1938. "The Feather Cult of the Middle Columbia." *General Series in Anthropology* No. 7. George Banta, Menasha, Wisconsin.

Elmendorf, William. 1965. "Linguistic and Geographic Relations in the Northern Plateau Area." *Southwestern Journal of Anthropology* 21:63–77.

Everette, Will E. n.d. [1883]. "Indian Languages of North America: Yakima." Manuscript, Smithsonian Institution, Washington, D. C.

Fahey, John. 1974. *The Flathead Indians.* University of Oklahoma Press, Norman.

Farnham, Thomas J. 1906 [1841]. "Travels in the Great Western Prairies, the Anahuac and Rocky Mountains, and in the Oregon Country." In *Early Western Travels, 1748–1846,* vols. 28, 29, edited by R. G. Thwaites. Arthur H. Clark, Cleveland, Ohio.

Feit, Harvey. 1970. "The Ethno-ecology of the Waswanipi Cree: or How Hunters Can Manage Their Resources." In *Cultural Ecology: Readings on the Canadian Indians and Eskimos.* McClelland and Stewart, Toronto.

Filloon, Ray M. 1952. "Huckleberry Pilgrimage." *Pacific Discovery* 5(3):4–13.

Fitzpatrick, Darleen Ann. 1968. "The 'Shake': The Indian Shaker Curing Ritual among the Yakima." M.A. thesis, Department of Anthropology, University of Washington, Seattle.

Fobes, Natalie. 1987. "The Saga of Salmon: An Epic Struggle to Survive Man." *The Seattle Times,* November 22, 1987, special report, pp. 1–12.

Fowler, Catherine S. 1986 [1982]. "Food-Named Groups among Northern Paiute in North America's Great Basin: An Ecological Interpretation." In *Resource Managers: North American and Australian Hunter-Gatherers,* edited by N. M. Williams and E. S. Hunn, pp. 113–29. Australian Institute of Aboriginal Studies, Canberra.

Franklin, Jerry F., and C. T. Dyrness. 1973. *Natural Vegetation of Oregon and Washington.* Forest Service General Technical Report PNW-8. U.S. Department of Agriculture, Washington, D. C.

French, David H. 1961. "Wasco-Wishram." In *Perspectives in American Indian Culture Change,* edited by E. H. Spicer, pp. 337–430. University of Chicago Press, Chicago.

French, David H. 1981. "Neglected Aspects of North American Ethnobotany." *Canadian Journal of Botany* 59:2326–30.

French, David H., and Kathrine S. French. n.d. [1979]. "Warm Springs Sahaptin Medicinal Plants: A Summary." Manuscript, Department of Anthropology, Reed College, Portland, Oregon.

Frisch, Jack A. 1978. "Iroquois in the West." In *Handbook of North American Indians,* vol. 10, *Northeast,* edited by B. G. Trigger, pp. 544–46. Smithsonian Institution, Washington, D.C.

Garth, Thomas R. 1964. "Early Nineteenth Century Tribal Relations in the Columbia Plateau." *Southwestern Journal of Anthropology* 20:43–57.

Geyer, C. A. 1845–46. "Notes on the Vegetation and General Characteristics of the Missouri and Oregon Territories, During the Years 1843 and 1844." *London Journal of Botany* 4:479–92, 653–62; 5:22–41, 198–208, 285–310, 509–24.

Giannettino, Susan. 1977. "The Middleman Role in the Fur Trade: Its Influence on Interethnic Relations in the Saskatchewan-Missouri Plains." *Canadian Journal of Anthropology* 7:22–33.

Gibbs, George. 1978 [1854]. *Indian Tribes of Washington Territory.* Ye Galleon Press, Fairfield, Wash. Originally in G. McClellan, "Report of Exploration of a Route for the Pacific Railroad from St. Paul to Puget Sound," House Executive Document No. 129, Serial No. 736, 33rd Congress, 1st Session, Washington, D. C. Pp. 419–65.

Glover, Richard, ed. 1962. *David Thompson's Narrative, 1784–1812.* Champlain Society, Toronto.

Grayson, Donald K. 1977. "Pleistocene Avifaunas and the Overkill Hypothesis." *Science* 195:691–93.

Greenberg, Joseph H. 1987. *Language in the Americas.* Stanford University Press, Stanford.

Gunther, Erna. 1926. "An Analysis of the First Salmon Ceremony." *American Anthropologist* 28:605–17.

Gunther, Erna. 1928. "A Further Analysis of the First Salmon Ceremony." *University of Washington Publications in Anthropology* 2:129–73.

Haines, Francis. 1937. "The Nez Percé Delegation to St. Louis in 1831." *Pacific Historical Review* 6:71–78.

Haines, Francis. 1938. "The Northward Spread of Horses among the Plains Indians." *American Anthropologist* 40:429–37.

Haines, Francis. 1955. *The Nez Percés: Tribesmen of the Columbia Plateau.* University of Oklahoma Press, Norman.

Hart, J. 1976. *Montana—Native Plants and Early Peoples.* Montana Historical Society, Helena.

Heizer, Robert. 1942. "Walla Walla Expeditions to the Sacramento Valley." *California Historical Quarterly* 21:1–7.

Hellson, C., and Morgan Gadd. 1974. *Ethnobotany of the Blackfoot Indians.* Canadian Ethnology Service Paper No. 19. National Museums of Canada, Ottawa.

Hewes, Gordon. 1973 [1947]. "Indian Fisheries Productivity in Pre-Contact Times in the Pacific Salmon Area." *Northwest Anthropological Research Notes* 7:133–55.

Hitchcock, C. Leo, Arthur Cronquist, Marion Ownbey, and J. W. Thompson. 1955. *Vascular Plants of the Pacific Northwest, Part 5: Compositae.* University of Washington Press, Seattle.

Hitchcock, C. Leo, Arthur Cronquist, Marion Ownbey, and J. W. Thompson. 1959. *Vascular Plants of the Pacific Northwest, Part 4: Ericaceae through Campanulaceae.* University of Washington Press, Seattle.

Hitchcock, C. Leo, Arthur Cronquist, Marion Ownbey, and J. W. Thompson. 1961. *Vascular Plants of the Pacific Northwest, Part 3: Saxifragaceae to Ericaceae.* University of Washington Press, Seattle.

Hitchcock, C. Leo, Arthur Cronquist, Marion Ownbey, and J. W. Thompson. 1964. *Vascular Plants of the Pacific Northwest. Part 2: Salicaceae to Saxifragaceae.* University of Washington Press, Seattle.

Hitchcock, C. Leo, Arthur Cronquist, Marion Ownbey, and J. W. Thompson. 1969. *Vascular Plants of the Pacific Northwest, Part 1: Vascular Cryptogams, Gymnosperms, and Monocotyledons.* University of Washington Press, Seattle.

Hitchcock, C. Leo, and Arthur Cronquist. 1973. *Flora of the Pacific Northwest: An Illustrated Manual.* University of Washington Press, Seattle.

Hunn, Eugene S. 1979. "Sahaptin Folk Zoological Classification: A Persistent Paradigm." *Folk Classification Bulletin* 3(1):3–4.

Hunn, Eugene S. 1980. "Sahaptin Fish Classification." *Northwest Anthropological Research Notes* 14:1–19.

Hunn, Eugene S. 1981. "On the Relative Contribution of Men and Women to Subsistence Among Hunter-Gatherers of the Columbia Plateau: A Comparison with *Ethnographic Atlas* Summaries." *Journal of Ethnobiology* 1:124–34.

Hunn, Eugene S., and David H. French. 1981. "*Lomatium:* A Key Resource for Columbia Plateau Subsistence." *Northwest Science* 55:87–94.

Hunn, Eugene S., and David H. French. 1984. "Alternatives to Taxonomic Hierarchy: The Sahaptin Case." *Journal of Ethnobiology* 4:73–92.

Hunn, Eugene S., and David H. French. n.d. [1977]. "Sahaptin Color Terms." Manuscript, Department of Anthropology, University of Washington, Seattle.

Hymes, Virginia. 1976. "Word and Phrase List of Warm Springs Sahaptin." Manuscript, Warm Springs Confederated Tribes, Warm Springs, Oregon. 2d edition.

Jacobs, Melville. 1929. "Northwest Sahaptin Texts." *University of Washington Publications in Anthropology* 2:175–244.

Jacobs, Melville. 1931. "A Sketch of Sahaptin Grammar." *University of Washington Publications in Anthropology* 4:85–292.

Jacobs, Melville. 1934. "Northwest Sahaptin Texts, Part 1." *Columbia University Contributions to Anthropology* No. 19 (English).

Jacobs, Melville. 1937a. "Northwest Sahaptin Texts, Part 2." *Columbia University Contributions to Anthropology* No. 19 (Sahaptin).

Jacobs, Melville. 1937b. "Historic Perspectives in Indian Languages of Oregon and Washington." *Pacific Northwest Quarterly* 28:55–74.

Jermann, Jerry V., and Roger D. Mason. 1976. "A Cultural Resources Overview of the Gifford Pinchot National Forest of South-Central Washington." Office of Public Archaeology, Institute for Environmental Studies, University of Washington, Seattle.

Jesset, Thomas E. 1960. *Chief Spokan Garry, 1811–1892, Christian, Statesman, and Friend of the White Man.* T. S. Denison, Minneapolis, Minnesota.

Jilek, Wolfgang G. 1974. *Salish Indian Mental Health and Culture Change: Psychohygienic and Therapeutic Aspects of the Guardian Spirit Ceremonial.* Holt, Rinehart and Winston of Canada, Toronto.

Joseph, Chief. 1983 [1879]. "Chief Joseph's Own Story." Foreword by D. MacRae. Shorey Publications, Seattle Washington. Originally published with an Introduction by the Rt. Rev. W. H. Hare, D. D., Bishop of South Dakota, in *The North American Review,* April 1879.

Josephy, Alvin M., Jr. 1965. *The Nez Percé Indians and the Opening of the Northwest.* Yale University Press, New Haven.

Keeley, Patrick B. 1980. "Nutrient Composition of Selected Important Plant Foods of the Pre-Contact Diet of the Northwest Native American Peoples." M.S. thesis, University of Washington, Seattle.

Kent, Susan. 1980. "Pacifism—A Myth of the Plateau." *Northwest Anthropological Research Notes* 14:125–34.

Kew, M. n.d. [1976]. "Salmon Abundance, Technology and Human Populations on the Fraser River Watershed." Manuscript, Department of Anthropology and Sociology, University of British Columbia, Vancouver.

Kinkade, M. Dale. 1967. "On the Identification of the Methows (Salish)." *International Journal of American Linguistics* 33:193–97.

Kinkade, M. Dale. 1981. *Dictionary of the Moses-Columbia Language.* Colville Confederated Tribes, Nespelem, Washington.

Kip, Lawrence, 1971 [1855]. *Indian Council at Walla Walla.* Facsimile reproduction by The Shorey Book Store, Seattle, Washington. Originally published by Whitton and Towne, San Francisco, California.

Kirk, Ruth, and Richard D. Daugherty. 1978. *Exploring Washington Archaeology.* University of Washington Press, Seattle.

Klein, Barry T., ed. 1978. *Reference Encyclopedia of the American Indian.* 3d edition, vol. 1. Todd and Rye, New York.

Konlande, J. E., and J. R. K. Robson. 1972. "The Nutritive Value of Cooked Camas as Consumed by Flathead Indians." *Ecology of Food and Nutrition* 2:193–95.

Kroeber, Alfred L. 1939. "Cultural and Natural Areas of Native North America." *University of California Publications in American Archaeology and Ethnology* 38:1–242.

Kuhnlein, Harriet V., and Nancy J. Turner. 1986. "Cow-Parsnip (*Heracleum lanatum* Michx.): An Indigenous Vegetable of Native People of Northwestern North America." *Journal of Ethnobiology* 6:309–24.

Kuneki, Nettie, Elsie Thomas, and Marie Slockish. 1982. *The Heritage of Klickitat Basketry: A History and Art Preserved.* Oregon Historical Society Press, Portland.

Lamb, Sydney. 1958. "Linguistic Prehistory in the Great Basin." *International Journal of American Linguistics* 24:95–100.

Lange, Larry. 1987. "The B.P.A.: 50 Years of Water over the Dam." *The Seattle Post-Intelligencer,* August 6, 1987, pp. A4–A5.

Larsen, Pat, and Sandie Nisbet, eds. 1986. *Everything Change, Everything Change: Recollections of Ida Nason, an Elderly Plateau Indian Woman.* Ellensburg Public Library, Ellensburg, Washington. [Ida Nason videotape transcript; portion quoted courtesy of Ellensburg Public Library]

Laughlin, William S. 1968. "Hunting: An Integrating Biobehavioral System and Its Evolutionary Importance." In *Man the Hunter,* edited by R. B. Lee and I. DeVore, pp. 304–20, Aldine, Chicago.

Lee, Daniel, and Joseph Frost. 1968 [1844]. *Ten Years in Oregon.* Ye Galleon Press, Fairfield, Washington.

Lee, Richard B. 1979. *The !Kung San: Men, Women, and Work in a Foraging Society.* Cambridge University Press, London.

Lee, Richard B., and Irven DeVore, eds. 1968. *Man, the Hunter.* Aldine, Chicago.

Leechman, J. D., and M. R. Harrington. 1921. "String Records of the Northwest." *Indian Notes and Monographs* No. 16.

Lesley, Craig. 1984. *Winterkill.* Dell, New York.

Lewis, Henry. 1973. "Patterns of Indian Burning in California: Ecology and Ethnohistory." *Anthropological Papers* No. 1. Ballena Press, Ramona, California.

Lewis, Henry. 1977. "Maskuta: The Ecology of Indian Fires in Northern Alberta." *Western Canadian Journal of Anthropology* 7:15–52.

Lomawaima, K. Tsianina. 1987. "Oral Histories from Chilocco Indian Agricultural School, 1920–1940." *American Indian Quarterly* 11:241–54.

Lyman, R. Lee. 1984. "A Model of Large Freshwater Clam Exploitation in the Prehistoric Southern Columbia Plateau Culture Area." *Northwest Anthropological Research Notes* 18:97–107.

Marshall, Alan G. 1977. "Nez Perce Social Groups: An Ecological Interpretation." Ph.D. dissertation, Washington State University, Pullman.

Martin, Calvin. 1978. *Keepers of the Game: Indian-Animal Relationships and the Fur Trade.* University of California Press, Berkeley.

Martin, Paul S. 1973. "Pleistocene Overkill." *Science* 179:969.

Matson, G. A., A. Ravve, J. M. Sugihara, and W. J. Burke. 1949. "Antibiotic Studies on an Extract from *Leptotaenia multifida* [= *Lomatium dissectum*]." *Journal of Clinical Investigation* 28:903–8.

Mauss, Marcel. 1967 [1925]. *The Gift: Forms and Functions of Exchange in Archaic Societies.* Translated by I. Cunnison. W. W. Norton, New York.

McBeth, Sally. 1983. *Ethnic Identity and the Boarding School Experience of West-Central Oklahoma American Indians.* University Press of America, Washington, D. C.

McClellan, George B. 1854. "Report of Exploration of a Route for the Pacific Railroad from St. Paul to Puget Sound." House Executive Document No. 129, Serial No. 736, 33rd Congress, 1st Session, Washington, D. C.

McWhorter, Lucullus V. 1913. *The Crime against the Yakimas.* Republic Printers, Yakima, Washington.

Meilleur, Brien A., Eugene S. Hunn, and Rachel L. Cox. n.d. [1989]. "*Lomatium dissectum:* Multipurpose Plant of the Pacific Northwest." *Journal of Ethnobiology,* in press.

Meinig, D. W. 1968. *The Great Columbia Plain: A Historical Geography, 1805–1910.* University of Washington Press, Seattle.

Merk, Frederick, ed. 1968. *Fur Trade and Empire: George Simpson's Journal, Entitled "Remarks connected with the Fur Trade in the Course of a Voyage from York Factory to Fort George and Back to York Factory, 1824–1825, with Related Documents."* Rev. ed. The Belknap Press, Cambridge, Massachusetts.

Merriam, Alan P. 1967. "Ethnomusicology of the Flathead Indians." *Viking Fund Publications in Anthropology* No. 44.

Miller, Christopher L. 1985. *Prophetic Worlds: Indians and Whites on the Columbia Plateau.* Rutgers University Press, New Brunswick, New Jersey.

Minore, Donald. 1972. "The Wild Huckleberries of Oregon and Washington—A Dwindling Resource." *Forest Service Research Paper* No. 143. U.S.D.A., Forest Service, Portland, Oregon.

Mooney, James. 1896. "The Ghost-Dance Religion and the Sioux Outbreak of 1890." *Fourteenth Annual Report of the Bureau of Ethnology*, Part 2, pp. 641–1136.

Murdock, George P. 1938. "Notes on the Tenino, Molala, and Paiute of Oregon." *American Anthropologist* 40:395–402.

Murdock, George P. 1958. "Social Organization of the Tenino." *Miscellanea Paul Rivet: Octogenario Dicata*, pp. 299–315. Mexico.

Murdock, George P. 1965. "Tenino Shamanism." *Ethnology* 4:165–71.

Murdock, George P. 1980. "The Tenino Indians." *Ethnology* 19:129–49.

Neel, James V. 1962. "Diabetes mellitus: A 'Thrifty' Genotype Rendered Detrimental by 'Progress'?" *American Journal of Human Genetics* 14:353–62.

Nelson, C. M. 1973. "Prehistoric Culture Change in the Intermontane Plateau of Western North America." In *The Exploration of Cultural Change: Models in Prehistory*, edited by C. Renfrew, pp. 371–90. Duckworth, London.

Nelson, Richard K. 1983. *Make Prayers to the Raven: A Koyukon View of the Northern Forest.* University of Chicago Press, Chicago.

Norton, H. H., E. S. Hunn, C. S. Martinsen, and P. B. Keely. 1984. "Vegetable Food Products of the Foraging Economies of the Pacific Northwest." *Ecology of Food and Nutrition* 14:219–28.

Okazaki, Rose, Henry Smith, and Raymond Gilkeson. 1972. "Correlation of West Blacktail Ash with Pyroclastic Layer T from the 1800 AD Eruption of Mt. St. Helens." *Northwest Science* 46:77–89.

Osborne, D. 1955. "Nez Perce Horse Castration." *Davidson Journal of Anthropology* 1:113–22.

Pace, Robert E., compiler. 1977. *The Land of the Yakimas.* Yakima Indian Nation Tribal Council, Toppenish, Washington.

Palmer, Gary. 1975. "Shuswap Indian Ethnobotany." *Syesis* 8:29–81.

Palmer, Gary. 1978. "Cultural Ecology in the Canadian Plateau: Estimates of Shuswap Indian Salmon Resources in Pre-Contact Times." *Northwest Anthropological Research Notes* 12:5–8.

Palmer, Gary. 1985. "Coeur d'Alene Exceptions to Proposed Universals of Anatomical Nomenclature." *American Ethnologist* 12:341–59.

Palmer, Joel. 1906 [1847]. "Palmer's Journal of Travels over the Rocky Mountains, 1845–1846." In *Early Western Travels, 1748–1846*, edited by R. G. Thwaites, vol. 30. Arthur H. Clark, Cleveland, Ohio.

Pandosy, Marie Charles. 1862. *Grammar and Dictionary of the Yakima Language.* Cramoisy Press, New York (ed. and trans. G. Gibbs and J. G. Shea).

Park, Willard Z. 1937. "Paviotso Polyandry." *American Anthropologist* 39:366–68.

Parker, Samuel. 1846 [1838]. *Journal of an Exploring Tour beyond the Rocky Mountains.* J. C. Derby, Auburn, New York.

Peattie, Donald Culross. 1950. *A Natural History of Western Trees.* Bonanza Books, New York.

Perkins, Henry K. W. n.d. [1838–43]. "Diary and Letters." Edited by Robert T. Boyd. Manuscript, Pacific Lutheran University, Tacoma, Washington.

Perkins, Henry K. W. 1843. "History of the Oregon Mission." *The Christian Advocate and Journal,* September 13, 1843.

Perkins, Henry K. W. 1850. "Wonderful Work of God among the Indians of the Oregon Territory: An Account of the Conversion of Five Hundred of These Natives." In *History of the Missions of the Methodist Episcopal Church,* ed. W. P. Strickland, pp. 120–59. L. Swormstedt and J. H. Power, Cincinnati, Ohio.

Phinney, Archie. 1934. *Nez Percé Texts.* Columbia University Contributions to Anthropology Vol. 25.

Pierce, Joe. 1965. "The Field Situation in Oregon." *Canadian Journal of Linguistics* 10:120–28.

Ramsey, Jarold. 1977. *Coyote Was Going There: Indian Literature of the Oregon Country.* University of Washington Press, Seattle.

Raven, Peter H., Brent Berlin, and Dennis E. Breedlove. 1971. "The Origins of Taxonomy." *Science* 174:1210–13.

Ray, Verne F. 1933. "The Sanpoil and Nespelem: Salishan Peoples of Northeastern Washington." *University of Washington Publications in Anthropology* No. 5.

Ray, Verne F. 1936a. "Kolaskin Cult: A Prophet Movement of 1870 in Northeastern Washington." *American Anthropologist* 38:67–75.

Ray, Verne F. 1936b. "Native Villages and Groupings of the Columbia Basin." *Pacific Northwest Quarterly* 27:99–152.

Ray, Verne F. 1937. "The Bluejay Character in the Plateau Spirit Dance." *American Anthropologist* 39:593–601.

Ray, Verne F. 1938. "Tribal Distribution in Eastern Oregon and Adjacent Regions." *American Anthropologist* 40:384–95.

Ray, Verne F. 1939. "Cultural Relations in the Plateau of Northwestern America." *Publications of the Frederick Webb Hodge Anniversary Publication Fund* Vol. 3. Southwestern Museum, Los Angeles, California.

Ray, Verne F. 1942. "Culture Element Distributions: XXII, Plateau." *University of California Anthropological Records* 8:99–258.

Ray, Verne F. 1960. "The Columbia Indian Confederacy: A League of Central Plateau Tribes." In *Culture in History: Essays in Honor of Paul Radin,* edited by S. Diamond, pp. 771–89. Columbia University Press, New York.

Relander, Click. 1956. *Drummers and Dreamers.* Caxton Printers, Caldwell, Idaho.

Relander, Click. 1962. *Strangers on the Land.* Franklin Press, Yakima, Washington.

Rigsby, Bruce J. 1965. "Linguistic Relations in the Southern Plateau." Ph.D. dissertation, University of Oregon, Eugene.

Rigsby, Bruce. 1969. "The Waiilatpuan Problem: More on Cayuse-Molala Relatability." *Northwest Anthropological Research Notes* 3:68–146.

Rigsby, Bruce. n.d. "Sahaptin Grammar." *Handbook of North American Indians,* vol. 17, *Languages,* edited by I. Goddard. Smithsonian Institution, Washington, D. C. In press.

Roe, Frank Gilbert. 1955. *The Indian and the Horse.* University of Oklahoma Press, Norman.

Ross, Alexander. 1956 [1924]. *The Fur Hunters of the Far West.* Edited by K. A. Spaulding. University of Oklahoma Press, Norman.

Ross, John Alan. 1968. "Political Conflict on the Colville Reservation." *Northwest Anthropological Research Notes* 2:29–91.

Rostlund, Erhard. 1952. "Freshwater Fish and Fishing in Native North America." *University of California Publications in Geography,* vol. 9. University of California Press, Berkeley.

Ruby, Robert H., and John A. Brown. 1965. *Half-Sun on the Columbia.* University of Oklahoma Press, Norman.

Ruby, Robert H., and John A. Brown. 1970. *The Spokane Indians, Children of the Sun.* University of Oklahoma Press, Norman.

Ruby, Robert H., and John A. Brown. 1972. *The Cayuse Indians: Imperial Tribesmen of Old Oregon.* University of Oklahoma Press, Norman.

Rude, Noel. n.d. [1986]. "Some Klamath-Sahaptin Grammatical Correspondences." Manuscript, Department of Linguistics, University of Oregon, Eugene.

Ruhlen, Merritt. 1987. "Voices from the Past." *Natural History* 96(3):6–10.

Sahlins, Marshall. 1972. *Stone Age Economics.* Aldine, Chicago.

Sapir, Edward. 1921. *Language: An Introduction to the Study of Speech.* Harcourt, Brace and World, New York.

Sapir, Edward. 1929. "Central and North American Languages." In *Encyclopedia Brittanica,* 14th edition, vol. 5, pp. 138–41.

Schalk, Randall F. n.d. "Salmon and Steelhead Usage in the Columbia Basin before 1850." *Northwest Environmental Journal.* In press.

Schlessman, Mark A. 1978. "Systematics and Reproductive Biology of *Lomatium farinosum* (Geyer ex Hooker) Coulter & Rose (Umbelliferae)." *Madroño* 25:1–9.

Schlessman, Mark A. 1980. "Systematics of the Tuberous Species of *Loma-tium*." Ph.D. dissertation, University of Washington, Seattle.

Schlessman, Mark A., and Lincoln Constance. 1979. "Two New Species of Tuberous Lomatiums (Umbelliferae)." *Madroño* 26:37–43.

Schoning, R. W., T. R. Merrell, Jr., and D. R. Johnson. 1951. "The Indian Dip Net Fishery at Celilo Falls on the Columbia River." Contribution No. 17. Oregon Fish Commission, Portland.

Schroedl, Gerald F. 1973. "The Archaeological Occurrence of Bison in the Southern Plateau." *Reports of Investigations*, No. 51. Laboratory of Anthropology, Washington State University, Pullman.

Schultz, John L., and Deward E. Walker, Jr. 1967. "Indian Shakers on the Colville Reservation." *Research Studies* 35(2):167–72. Washington State University, Pullman.

Schuster, Helen H. 1975. "Yakima Indian Traditionalism: A Study in Continuity and Change." Ph.D. dissertation, University of Washington, Seattle.

Schuster, Helen H. 1982. *The Yakima: A Critical Bibliography*. Indiana University Press, Bloomington.

Scott, Leslie, M. 1928. "Indian Diseases as Aids to Pacific Northwest Settlement." *Oregon Historical Quarterly* 29:144–61.

Senior, Jeanie. 1987. "New Klickitat Tribal Chief Pledges Role in Columbia River Issues." *The Oregonian*, April 6, 1987, p. B7.

Seven, Richard. 1988. "Ritual of Rebirth." *The Seattle Times/Seattle Post-Intelligencer*, January 24, 1988, pp. K1–K6.

Sievers, Maurice L., and Jeffrey R. Fisher. 1981. "Diseases of North American Indians." In *Biocultural Aspects of Disease*, ed. H. Rothschild, pp. 191–252. Academic Press, New York.

Simoons, Frederick J. 1961. *Eat Not This Flesh, Food Avoidances in the Old World*. University of Wisconsin Press, Madison.

Smith, Courtland L. 1979. *Salmon Fishers of the Columbia*. Oregon State University, Corvallis.

Smith, Eric Alden. 1983. "Anthropological Applications of Optimal Foraging Theory: A Critical Review." *Current Anthropology* 24:625–51.

Spier, Leslie. 1935. "The Prophet Dance of the Northwest and Its Derivatives: The Source of the Ghost Dance." *General Series in Anthropology* No. 1. George Banta, Menasha, Wisconsin.

Spier, Leslie, ed. 1938. "The Sinkaietk or Southern Okanagon of Washington." *General Series in Anthropology* No. 6. George Banta, Menasha, Wisconsin.

Spier, Leslie, Melville J. Herskovits, and Wayne Suttles. 1959. "Comment on Aberle's Thesis of Deprivation." *Southwestern Journal of Anthropology* 15:84–88.

Spier, Leslie, and Edward Sapir. 1930. "Wishram Ethnography." *University of Washington Publications in Anthropology* 3:151–300.

Spinden, Herbert Joseph. 1908. "The Nez Percé Indians." *Memoirs of the American Anthropological Association* 2:165–274.

Stanford, Phil. 1987. "The Trials of David Sohappy." *The Oregonian,* April 12, 1987.

Steward, Julian H. 1936. "Shoshone Polyandry." *American Anthropologist* 38:561–64.

Steward, Julian H. 1938. *Basin-Plateau Aboriginal Socio-political Groups.* Bureau of American Ethnology Bulletin No. 120, Smithsonian Institution, Washington, D. C.

Steward, Julian, and Erminie Wheeler-Voegelin. 1974. *The Northern Paiute Indians.* Garland Publishers, Inc., New York.

Stewart, Omer C. 1937. "Northern Paiute Polyandry." *American Anthropologist* 39:368–69.

Storer, Tracy I., and Robert L. Usinger. 1963. *Sierra Nevada Natural History: An Illustrated Handbook.* University of California Press, Berkeley.

Suphan, Robert J. 1974a. "Ethnological Report on the Wasco and Tenino Indians Relative to Socio-Political Organization and Land Use." In *Oregon Indians II,* edited by D. A. Horr, pp. 9–84, Garland Publishing, New York. Originally docket number 198, defense exhibit number 17, before the Indian Claims Commission.

Suphan, Robert J. 1974b. "Ethnological Report on the Umatilla, Walla Walla, and Cayuse Indians Relative to Socio-Political Organization and Land Use." In *Oregon Indians II,* edited by D. A. Horr, pp. 85–180, Garland Publishing, New York. Originally docket number 264, defense exhibit number 18, before the Indian Claims Commission.

Suttles, Wayne. 1951. "The Early Diffusion of the Potato among the Coast Salish." *Southwestern Journal of Anthropology* 7:272–88.

Swadesh, Morris. 1959. "Linguistics as an Instrument of Prehistory." *Southwestern Journal of Anthropology* 15:20–35.

Teit, James A. 1900. "The Thompson Indians of British Columbia." *Memoirs of the American Museum of Natural History* 2:163–392.

Teit, James A. 1906. "The Lillooet Indians." *Memoirs of the American Museum of Natural History* 4:193–300.

Teit, James A. 1909. "The Shuswap." *Memoirs of the American Museum of Natural History* 4:443–789.

Teit, James A. 1928. "The Middle Columbia Salish." *University of Washington Publications in Anthropology* 2:83–128.

Teit, James A. 1930. "The Salishan Tribes of the Western Plateaus." *Forty-fifth Annual Report of the Bureau of American Ethnology,* edited by Franz Boas, pp. 23–396.

Thompson, Laurence. 1973. "The Northwest." In *Native Languages of the Americas,* edited by T. A. Seboek, vol. 1, pp. 359–425. Plenum Press, New York (*Current Trends in Linguistics* No. 10, Mouton, The Hague).

Thwaites, Reuben Gold, ed. 1959 [1904]. *Original Journals of the Lewis and Clark Expedition, 1804–1806.* Antiquarian Press, New York.

Timbrook, Jan. 1982. "Use of Wild Cherry Pits as Food by the California Indians." *Journal of Ethnobiology* 2:162–76.

Trivers, Robert L. 1971. "The Evolution of Reciprocal Altruism." *Quarterly Review of Biology* 46:35–57.

Tucker, William. 1983. "Crosscurrents." *Science 83*:92–94.

Turner, Nancy J. 1977. "Economic Importance of Black Tree Lichen (*Bryoria fremontii*) to the Indians of Western North America." *Economic Botany* 31:461–70.

Turner, Nancy J. 1987. "General Plant Categories in Thompson and Lillooet, Two Interior Salish Languages of British Columbia." *Journal of Ethnobiology* 7:55–82.

Turner, Nancy Chapman, and Marcus A. M. Bell. 1973. "The Ethnobotany of the Southern Kwakiutl Indians of British Columbia." *Economic Botany* 27:257–310.

Turner, Nancy J., Randy Bouchard, and Dorothy I. D. Kennedy. 1980. *Ethnobotany of the Okanagan-Colville Indians of British Columbia.* British Columbia Provincial Museum, Victoria, B. C. Occasional Paper No. 21.

Turner, Nancy J., Laurence C. Thompson, M. Terry Thompson, and Annie York. n.d. "Knowledge and Usage of Plants by the Thompson Indian People of British Columbia." British Columbia Provincial Museum, Victoria, in press.

Turney-High, Harry Holbert. 1937. "The Flathead Indians of Montana." *American Anthropological Association Memoir* No. 48.

Turney-High, Harry Holbert. 1941. "Ethnography of the Kutenai." *American Anthropological Association Memoir* No. 56.

Uebelacker, Morris L. 1984. *Time Ball: A Story of the Yakima People and Their Land.* The Yakima Nation, Yakima, Washington.

United States Army Corps of Engineers. 1952. *Columbia River and Tributaries, Northwestern United States.* 8 vols. House Document No. 531, 81st Congress, 2nd Session. Washington, D. C.

Walker, Deward E., Jr. 1966. "The Nez Perce Sweat Bath Complex: An Acculturational Analysis." *Southwestern Journal of Anthropology* 22:133–71.

Walker, Deward E., Jr. 1967a. "Mutual Cross-Utilization of Economic Resources in the Plateau: An Example from Aboriginal Nez Perce Fishing Practices." *Washington State University, Laboratory of Anthropology, Report of Investigations* No. 41.

Walker, Deward E., Jr. 1967b. "Nez Perce Sorcery." *Ethnology* 6:66–96.

Walker, Deward E., Jr. 1967c. "Measures of Nez Perce Outbreeding and the Analysis of Cultural Change." *Southwestern Journal of Anthropology* 23:141–58.

Walker, Deward E., Jr. 1969. "New Light on the Prophet Dance Controversy." *Ethnohistory* 16:245–56.

Walker, Deward E., Jr. 1970. "Sorcery among the Nez Perces." In *Systems of North American Witchcraft and Sorcery*, edited by D. E. Walker, Jr., pp. 267–95. Univ. of Idaho, Moscow (Anthropological Monographs No. 1).

Walker, Deward E., Jr. 1985 [1968]. *Conflict and Schism in Nez Perce Accultura-tion: A Study of Religion and Politics.* Washington State University Press, Pullman. Rev. ed.

Walker, William. 1833. "Letter to G. P. Disoway." *The Christian Advocate and Journal and Zion's Herald* 7:105.

Wallace, Anthony F. C. 1956. "Revitalization Movements." *American Anthro-pologist* 58:264–81.

Washington, Nat W. n.d. [1976]. "Tsukulotsa (*Lomatium canbyi*): Key to Un-derstanding Central Washington Nonriverine Archaeology." Paper pre-sented at the 29th Annual Northwest Anthropological Conference, April 10, 1976, Ellensburg, Washington.

Watt, B. K., and A. L. Merrill. 1963. *Composition of Foods.* Handbook No. 8, United States Department of Agriculture, Washington, D. C.

Whorf, Benjamin Lee. 1950. "An American Indian Model of the Universe." *International Journal of American Linguistics* 16:67–72.

Wilkes, Charles. 1845. *Narrative of the United States Exploring Expeditions Dur-ing the Years 1838–1842.* Lea and Blanchard, Philadelphia, Pennsylvania.

Wolf, Eric. 1959. *Sons of the Shaking Earth.* University of Chicago Press, Chicago.

Work, John. 1923. *The Snake Country Expedition of 1830–1831.* Edited by F. D. Haines, Jr. University of Oklahoma Press, Norman.

Wydoski, Richard S., and Richard R. Whitney. 1979. *Inland Fishes of Washing-ton.* University of Washington Press, Seattle.

Zucker, Jeff, Kay Hummel, and Bob Høgfoss. 1983. *Oregon Indians: Culture, History, and Current Affairs: an Atlas and Introduction.* Western Imprints, Oregon Historical Society, Portland.

Appendix 1.

Sahaptin Animal Terms

THIS IS a systematic listing by both Latin and English vernacular names. The Sahaptin forms cited are not exhaustive of all variants but represent the most common ones. Terms recorded from Sahaptin speakers of other than mid-Columbia River dialects are included in brackets. If no dialect is specifically indicated, the term is in use by mid-Columbia speakers. Synonyms may be indicated following a slash. Sahaptin terms in double quotes are descriptive phrases not true names. The letters "sp" following a genus name indicate an unspecified or unknown species of that genus; the letters "spp" following the genus name indicate that more than one species of the genus is included in the denotation of the term; if a genus or higher order taxon name occurs alone, all the species of that taxon that occur locally are so included without distinction. Sometimes the term refers prototypically to one (or more) species, but may be used to indicate additional species as well. In such cases, the peripheral species are listed after the plus (+) sign or, if not in order, are cited following a > sign. A question mark (?) following a term indicates uncertainty as to the term's referential meaning.

ASCHELMINTHES (cavity worms)
  NEMATOMORPHA (horsehair worms)
    Gordioidea (freshwater horsehair worms)
              nawinała-nmí šuu, "thunder's whiskers"
MOLLUSCA (mollusks)
  SCAPHOPODA (tusk or tooth shells)
    Dentaliidae (tusk shells)
      Dentalium pretiosum (Indian money tusk)
              áxšaxš
  GASTROPODA (univalves)
  PELECYPODA (bivalves)

311

Eulamellibranchia
  Heterodonta (clams)
    šáx̣u
  Schizodonta (freshwater clams)
    x̣istú
ANNELIDA
  OLIGOCHAETA (earthworms)
    sáysay (in part)
  HIRUDINEA (leeches)
    [NWS: ḱúpša]
ARTHROPODA
  ARACHNIDA (arachnids)
  Scorpionida (scorpions)
    watwalacíka/pakasapɬi-ɬá/q̓špa-lí
  Acarina (mites and ticks)
    Parasitiformes (ticks)
      áč̓pɬ
  Phalangida (harvestmen/daddy-long-legs)
    káatlam-wúx̣a (+ wax̣alx̣alí), "long-leg" (+ "spider")
  Araneae (spiders)
    wax̣alx̣alí
    Araneomorphae (true spiders)
      Theridiidae (comb-footed spiders)
        Latrodectus spp. (black widow spiders)
          females: tišpún
          males ?: tispúl-tispul, "little tišpún"
CRUSTACEA (crustaceans)
  Malacostraca
  Isopoda (sowbugs and pillbugs)
    pina-wa-x̓iyawi-ɬá, "plays dead"
  Decapoda
    Reptantia (crayfishes, lobsters, and crabs)
      ḱastilá
MYRIAPODA
  Diplopoda (millipedes) & Chilopoda (centipedes)
    wux̣a-putaaptit-ní, "hundred-legged"
INSECTA (insects)

Odonata (dragonflies and damselflies)
    papacáki/watiqaylak-ɫá
Orthoptera (crickets and grasshoppers)
  Acrididae (short-horned grasshoppers)
    íɫš [w s s: íṭš]
    Oedipodinae (band-winged grasshoppers)
      tátx̣ [w s s: tx̣tx̣]
  Gryllidae (crickets)
    Oecanthinae (green tree crickets)
      sík-sík [= the following?]
   Gryllinae + (field crickets)
      síɫk-síɫk
  Gryllacrididae (cave and camel crickets)
    Rhaphidophorinae (camel crickets)
      taš
  Mantidae (mantises)
    Litaneutria minor (Scudder) ?
      [N w s: tyawntyam]
Dermaptera (earwigs)
  Forficulidae
      [umS: mišyú papaʔaš-ɫá, "enters ear"]
Anopleura (sucking lice)
  Pediculidae (human lice)
    Pediculus humanus humanus (human body louse)
      apúlk
    Pediculus humanus capitis (human head louse)
      apín [w s s: apń]
Hemiptera (true bugs)
  Gerridae (water striders)
      čuušnaknuwi-ɫá, "water guardian"
  Pentatomidae (stink bugs)
      tuʔuk-lí
Homoptera (cicadas, leaf hoppers, and scale insects)
  Cicadidae (cicadas)
      čal-ɫá/šapa-čuuɫa-ɫá, "make thirsty"
Neuroptera (nerve-winged insects)
  Corydalidae (dobsonflies and fishflies)

"troutflies"

    papsťá

Dysmicohermes sp. ? larvae (hellgrammites)

    [NWS: úšʔuš]

Coleoptera (beetles)

  Gyrinidae (whiligig beetles)

    [NWS: kławáw-kławaw]

  Silphidae (carrion beetles)

    q̇ayq̇áy

  Buprestidae (metallic wood-boring beetles)

    x̣ax̣áykʷ, "silver, money"

    Buprestis aurulenta (golden buprestis)

      "male"

    Chalcophora spp. ?

      "female"

  Tenebrionidae (darkling beetles)

    Eleodes spp. ("stink bugs")

    tiiš

  Scarabaeidae (scarab beetles)

    Polyphylla crinita (Coastline June beetle)

    łxáwkaał

Trichoptera (caddisflies)

    larvae: x̣amłúy

Lepidoptera (butterflies and moths)

  Papilionoidea (butterflies)

    walak-wálak

  "moths"

    ilkʷš-pała-łá, "fire-lover"

Diptera (flies)

  Culicidae (mosquitoes)

    adults: wawá

    larvae/pupae: k̇aspak̇aspa-łá, "twitcher"

  Anisopodidae, Mycetophilidae, Sciaridae ("gnats")

    [klS: wuskaláy/umS: típtip]

  Dixidae, Chaoboridae, Chironomidae ("midges")

    [prS: "hish-hish"?]

  Tabanidae (horse and deer flies)

Tabanus spp. (horse flies)
łštxni

Chrysops spp. (deer flies)
ɨstxlí-ɨstxli

Muscidae (house flies)

Musca domestica (common house fly)
muxláy

smaller flies
muxláy-muxlay

Siphonaptera (fleas)
ášnam

Hymenoptera (ants, bees, and wasps)

Formicidae (ants)

in general: kliwisá

Camponotus spp. (carpenter ants)

in particular: kliwisá

small, black ant species
tamšúy

Vespidae (wasps, in part)

Vespinae (yellowjackets and hornets)

Vespula sp. (yellowjacket, bald-faced hornet)
atníwa

Apidae (bees, in part)

Apinae (honey bees)

Apis mellifera (the honey bee) [introduced]
atníwa (= above)

Bombus spp. (bumblebees)
lawašmúk

CHORDATA (vertebrates)

AGNATHA (boneless fishes)

Petromyzontiformes (lampreys)

Petromyzontidae

Lampetra (*Entosphenus*) *tridentata*
[+ *L. ayresi, L. richardsoni* ?]
k̓súyas/asúm [WSS: asṁ]

CHONDRICHTHYES (cartilaginous fishes)

"sharks" [WSS: sux̌x-ła (see also "whale")]

OSTEICHTHYES (bony fishes)

Acipenseriformes (sturgeons)

Acipenseridae

Acipenser transmontanus (white sturgeon)

[+ *A. medirostris* ?]

wílaps

Salmonidae (salmon, trout, whitefish, and Dolly Varden)

Prosopium williamsoni (mountain whitefish)

sɨmay [wss: sṁay]

Salmo in general [not anadromous], including:

S. *trutta* (brown trout [introduced])

S. *clarki* (cutthroat trout)

S. *gairdneri* (rainbow trout)

ayáy/[= aytmɨn ?] [wss: x̣úlx̣ul, but see sucker]

Salmo gairdneri (rainbow trout) [not anadromous] in particular

[wss: ɨaɬáa-ɨaɬaa/peS: wawaɬám)

"mountain trout" in particular

[NWS: aytmɨn]

Salvelinus malma (Dolly Varden)

áščinš

"salmon" in general (*Oncorhynchus* and anadromous *Salmo* spp.]

núsux̣

Salmo gairdneri (steelhead) [anadromous]

šušáynš

Oncorhynchus gorbuscha (pink or humpback salmon)

[ucS: wác̓ya]

Oncorhynchus kisutch (coho or silver salmon)

sɨnx̣ʷ/sínux̣

Oncorhynchus tschawytscha (chinook or king salmon)

tkʷínat

jacks: tkʷilát-tkʷilat

Oncorhynchus nerka (sockeye or blueback salmon)

kálux̣

Oncorhynchus keta (chum or dog or white salmon)

mɨɬúla

Osmeridae (smelts)

Thaleichthys pacificus (eulachon)

[NWS: wiɬx̣ɨna]

Cyprinidae (minnows and carp)

    Cyprinus carpio (carp) [introduced]

        nči-psaní, "big scale"

    Carassius auratus (goldfish) [introduced]

        [umS: xayxayx-mí, "of silver, money"]

        luča-nmí x̣úlx̣ul, "red trout"

    Acrocheilus alutaceus (chiselmouth)

        lálapti

    Richardsonius balteatus (red-sided shiner)

        ṗała-lí, "flat"

    Rhinichthys osculus, R. cataractae, and *R. falcatus*

        muk̓ʷiyá ?

    Ptychocheilus oregonensis (northern squawfish)

        luk̓ʷáa

    Mylocheilus caurinus (peamouth)

        čukš, "obsidian"

Catostomidae (suckers)

    Catostomus macrocheilus (large-scale sucker)

        x̣uun

    Catostomus columbianus (bridge-lip sucker)

        yayk

    "Klamath sucker"

        [wss: c̓wam]

Cottidae (sculpins), in general, including:

    Cottus confusus, C. beldingi, C. rhotheus, C. cognatus,

      C. asper, C. marginatus, C. bairdi

        k̓ʷašlá

AMPHIBIA (amphibians)

  Caudata (salamanders and newts)

    Salamandridae (newts)

      Taricha granulosa (rough-skinned newt)

        škʷiyá

    [+ Ambystomatidae (mole salamanders), including:

      Ambystoma macrodactylum (long-toed salamander) ?

      A. tigrinus (tiger salamander) ?]

  Anura (frogs and toads)

    larvae in general (tadpoles)

        yawatakíls

Bufonidae (true toads)
   Bufo boreas (western toad)
      ámtanat, "bride"/pamtá, "woman's nephew"
Ranidae (true frogs)
   Rana catesbeana (bullfrog) [introduced]
      yuu-ɬá, "shouter"
   Rana cascadae (Cascade frog)
   R. pipiens (leopard frog)
   R. pretiosa (spotted frog)
Hylidae (tree frogs)
   Hyla regilla (Pacific tree frog)
      aluq̓ʷát
[+ Pelobatidae (archaic toads), including *Spea intermontana*
   (Great Basin spadefoot) ?]
[+ Leiopelmatidae (bell toads), including *Ascaphus truei*
   (tailed frog) ?]
REPTILIA (reptiles)
  Testudines (turtles), in general, including
  Emydidae (box turtles)
   Clemmys marmorata (western pond turtle)
   Chrysemys picta (painted turtle)
      alašík
  Squamata (lizards and snakes)
  Lacertilia (lizards)
  Iguanidae
   Phrynosoma douglassi (short-horned lizard)
      xliɬáwit, "of root-diggers"
   Sceloporus (spiny lizards), including:
    S. graciosus (sagebrush lizard)
    S. occidentalis (western fence lizard)
   Uta stansburiana (side-blotched lizard)
      watik̓ásasa
  Scincidae (skinks)
   Eumeces skiltonianus (western skink)
      lamt wáɬwas watik̓ásasa, "blue-tail lizard"
  Anguidae
   Elgaria [*Gerrhonotus*] (alligator lizards), including:

    E. coerulea (northern alligator lizard)

    E. multicarinata (southern alligator lizard)

        ɫuulnawa-ɫá, "jumps at you"?/> watiḱásasa

Ophidia (snakes)

        in general: pyuš [excluding the rattlesnake]

Boidae (boas)

    Charina bottae (rubber boa)

        [klS: papučalí]

Colubridae

    Coluber constrictor (racer)

        [wss: pawilawayx-ɫá "racer"; kls: ḱʷayḱʷi]

    Diadophis punctatus (ringneck snake)

        [klS: palšq̓ʷay ?]

    Lampropeltis zonatus (California mountain kingsnake)

        [klS: kímkaš]

    Pituophis melanoleucus (gopher snake)

        [nws: ppaw/crs: nč̓i-pyúš/wss: pyúuyax]

    Thamnophis (garter snakes), including:

        T. elegans vagrans (wandering garter snake)

        T. sirtalis fitchi (valley garter snake)

        pyuš

Viperidae (pit vipers)

    Crotalus viridis oreganus (northern Pacific rattlesnake)

        waxpúš

AVES (birds)

        in general: kákya

Gaviiformes (loons)

  Gaviidae (loons)

    Gavia immer (common loon)

        waan

Podicipediformes (grebes)

  Podicipedidae (grebes)

        > xátxat, "duck" ?

Pelicaniformes (pelicans and cormorants)

  Pelicanidae (pelicans)

    Pelecanus erythrorhynchos (American white pelican)

        >wišana-ɫá, "traveler" (see snow goose)

Ciconiiformes (ibises, storks, herons, etc.)
Ardeidae (herons)
Ardea herodias (great blue heron)
múq̓a
Anseriformes (ducks, geese, and swans)
Anatidae (ducks, geese, and swans)
Cygnini (swans)
Cygnus columbianus (whistling/tundra swan)
C. buccinator (trumpeter swan)
wawqilúk
Anserini (geese)
Chen caerulescens (snow goose)
wišana-ɬá, "traveler"
Branta canadensis (Canada goose)
ákak
Anatini (ducks)
in general: x̣átx̣at
Anas platyrhynchos (mallard)
x̣átx̣at
Mergus merganser (common merganser)
táštaš
Falconiformes (hawks, eagles, falcons, etc.)
Cathartidae (New World vultures)
Cathartes aura (turkey vulture)
q̓špa-lí
Gymnogyps californianus (California condor)
čanahúu/pačanahú
Accipitridae (hawks and eagles)
Pandioninae (osprey)
Pandion haliaetus (osprey)
q̓iq̓ínu ?
Accipitrinae
Haliaeetus leucocephalus (bald eagle)
k̓ámamul
Circus cyaneus (northern harrier or marsh hawk)
> wapnyawa-ɬá, "comes out at you" (see prairie falcon)
Accipiter striatus (sharp-shinned hawk)

A. cooperii (Cooper's hawk)

A. gentilis (northern goshawk)

> wapnyawa-ɬá, "comes out at you" (see prairie falcon)

Buteo jamaicensis (red-tailed hawk)

[+ *B. swainsoni* (Swainson's hawk)]

[+ *B. lagopus* (rough-legged hawk)]

qíluš

Buteo regalis (ferruginous hawk)

ítatat ?/> qíluš (see red-tailed hawk)

Aquila chrysaetos (golden eagle)

x̣ʷaamá, "high above"

Falconidae (falcons)

Falco sparverius (American kestrel or sparrow hawk)

yítyit

Falco mexicanus (prairie falcon)

wapnyawa-ɬá, "comes out at you"

Galliformes (grouse, quail, partridges, and pheasants)

Phasianidae

Phasianinae (partridges and pheasants)

Perdix perdix (gray or Hungarian partridge) [introduced]

Alectoris chukar (chukar) [introduced]

q̓axnu-wáakuɬ, "like the sharp-tailed grouse"

Gallus gallus (red junglefowl or chicken) [introduced]

likúuk/wašwášnu

Phasianus colchicus (ring-necked pheasant) [introduced]

[no Sahaptin name]

Tetraoninae (grouse)

Dendragapus canadensis (spruce grouse)

[N W S: miyáwax̣, "chief"]

Dendragapus obscurus (blue grouse)

pti

Bonasa umbellus (ruffed grouse)

sapaníca/> wašwášnu

Centrocercus urophasianus (sage grouse)

payúmš, "dances together"

Tympanuchus phasianellus (sharp-tailed grouse)

q̓áx̣nu

Meleagridinae (turkeys)
>   *Meleagris gallopavo* (wild turkey) [introduced]
>   qʷalqʷal-ɬá, "gobbler"/ɬíiɬki, "snotty-nose"
Odontophorinae (quail)
>   *Callipepla californica* (California quail) [introduced]
>   *Oreortyx pictus* (mountain quail)
>   pátaši, "crested"
Gruiformes (cranes, rails, and coots)
>   Rallidae (rails and coots)
>   *Fulica americana* (American coot)
>   skʷalkʷalí
Gruidae (cranes)
>   *Grus canadensis* (sandhill crane)
>   [N W S: paʔax-lí, "the gray one"]
Charadriiformes (shorebirds)
>   Charadriidae (plovers)
>   *Charadrius vociferus* (killdeer)
>   tiit, "fart"
Scolopacidae (sandpipers, curlews, etc.)
>   *Actitis macularia* (spotted sandpiper)
>   wítwit
>   *Numenius americanus* (long-billed curlew),
>   q̇ʷáyq̇ʷay
Laridae (gulls and terns)
>   *Larus delawarensis* (ring-billed gull)
>   *L. californicus* (California gull)
>   k̇aylás-k̇aylas/caspúla
Columbiformes (pigeons and doves)
>   Columbidae
>   *Columba livia* (rock dove/domestic pigeon) [introduced]
>   miimim-wáakuɬ, "like the mourning dove"
>   *Columba fasciata* (band-tailed pigeon)
>   [klS: wíɬqin]
>   *Zenaida macroura* (mourning dove)
>   miimím
Strigiformes (owls)
>   Tytonidae (barn owls)

Tyto alba (barn owl)
    q̓apq̓ap-ɬá, "clacker"?
Strigidae (true owls)
  Otus flammeolus (flammulated owl)
  O. kennicottii (western screech owl)
    alapáp/uus ?
  Bubo virginianus (great horned owl)
    miimánu
  Nyctea scandiaca (snowy owl)
    quyx̣ miimánu, "white large owl"
  Glaucidium gnoma (northern pygmy owl)
    > alapáp/uus ?
  Athene cunicularia (burrowing owl)
    papú/ppu
  Strix occidentalis (spotted owl)
  Asio otus (long-eared owl)
  A. flammeus (short-eared owl)
    > miimánu ?
  Aegolius acadicus (northern saw-whet owl)
    > alapáp/uus ?
Caprimulgiformes (whip-poor-wills and nighthawks)
  Caprimulgidae
    Chordeilinae (nighthawks)
      Chordeiles minor (common nighthawk)
        p̓iim
    Caprimulginae (whip-poor-wills)
      Phalaenoptilus nuttalli (common poorwill)
        wawiyúk̓k
Apodiformes
  Apodidae (swifts)
    > ɬíx̣ɬix̣, "swallow"
  Trochilidae (hummingbirds)
    qmamsa-lí
Coraciiformes
  Alcedinidae (kingfishers)
    Ceryle alcyon (belted kingfisher)
      šáxšax̣
Piciformes (woodpeckers)

Picidae

 Melanerpes lewis (Lewis's woodpecker)

   síwsiw

 Picoides pubescens (downy woodpecker)

 P. villosus (hairy woodpecker)

 [+ *P. albolarvatus* (white-headed woodpecker) ?]

 [+ *P. tridactylus* (three-toed woodpecker) ?]

 [+ *P. arcticus* (black-backed woodpecker) ?]

   pips

 Colaptes auratus (common flicker)

   taxt

 Dryocopus pileatus (pileated woodpecker)

   wanánpas ?

Passeriformes (perching birds)

   in general: cikʷá-cikʷa [for small, unnamed species]

Tyrannidae (tyrant flycatchers)

 Tyrannus verticalis (western kingbird)

 T. tyrannus (eastern kingbird)

   twícawałcawał

Hirundinidae (swallows)

   łíx̣łix̣

Corvidae (jays, crows, and ravens)

 Perisoreus canadensis (gray jay)

   yapaš-pała-łá, "fat lover"

 Cyanocitta stelleri (Steller's jay)

   x̣ʷáṣ̌x̣ʷay

 Nucifraga columbiana (Clark's nutcracker)

   lal

 Pica pica (black-billed magpie)

   áč̓ay

 Corvus brachyrhynchos (American crow)

   áʔa

 Corvus corax (common raven)

   x̣úx̣ux̣

Paridae (chickadees)

 Parus atricapillus (black-capped chickadee)

 P. gambeli (mountain chickadee)

   č̓ítatat/latítalwit, "the people are coming!"

Sittidae (nuthatches)
  Sitta canadensis (red-breasted nuthatch)
  [+ *S. carolinensis* (white-breasted nuthatch) ?]
      nátnat/látlat
Certhiidae (creepers)
  Certhia americana (brown creeper)
      > nátnat/látlat
Troglodytidae (wrens)
  Catherpes mexicanus (canyon wren)
  [+ *Salpinctes obsoletus* (rock wren) ?]
      x̣ali-x̣áli/taymúusya, "news-bearer"
Cinclidae (dippers)
  Cinclus americanus
      [not named; tabooed]
Muscicapidae (Old World flycatchers)
  Turdinae (thrushes)
    Sialia mexicana (western bluebird)
    S. currucoides (mountain bluebird)
        yulyúl
    Catharus fuscescens (veery)
    C. ustulatus (Swainson's thrush)
    C. guttatus (hermit thrush)
        x̣ʷii̱ ?
    Turdus migratorius (American robin)
        wísqaqa
Emberizidae (sparrow family)
  Emberizinae (sparrows)
    Junco hyemalis (dark-eyed junco)
        puuyáy, "of snow"
  Icterinae (blackbirds, orioles, and meadowlarks)
    Agelaius phoeniceus (red-winged blackbird)
        x̣ix̣ámx̣ʷ
    Sturnella neglecta (western meadowlark)
        x̣ʷii̱x̣ʷii̱
    Xanthocephalus xanthocephalus (yellow-headed blackbird)
    Euphagus cyanocephalus (Brewer's blackbird)
        > x̣ix̣ámx̣ʷ
    Icterus galbula (northern oriole)

wawšuk-łá, "shakes it down"
Fringillidae (finch family)
   Carduelinae
     Carduelis tristis (American goldfinch)
     [yks: maxɨ́š, "yellowish"]
MAMMALIA (mammals)
  Insectivora (shrews and moles)
   Soricidae (shrews)
     > lákas, "mouse"
   Talpidae (moles)
     Scapanus orarius (coast mole)
     xunaxuna-łá/iiʔani-łá
  Chiroptera (bats)
     in general: čátakš/> kákya, "bird"
  Lagomorpha (pikas, rabbits, hares, and cottontails)
   Ochotonidae (pikas)
     Ochotona princeps (pika)
     > xuup-łá, "weather changer"
   Leporidae (rabbits, hares, and cottontails)
     Lepus americanus (snowshoe hare)
     > xuup-łá, "weather changer"
     Lepus californicus (black-tailed hare)
     čmuk-wáłwas wilalík, "black-tail jackrabbit"
     Lepus townsendii (white-tailed hare)
     plaš-wáłwas wilalík, "white-tail jackrabbit"
     Sylvilagus nuttallii (Nuttall cottontail)
     S. floridanus (eastern cottontail) [introduced]
     [+ *S. idahoensis* (pigmy rabbit)?]
     aykʷs
  Rodentia (rodents)
   Sciuromorpha (mountain beavers, marmots, squirrels, and chipmunks)
   Aplodontiidae
     Aplodontia rufa (mountain beaver)
     [NWS: šq̓ʷla]
   Sciuridae (marmots, squirrels, and chipmunks)
    Sciurinae

Marmota flaviventris (yellow-bellied marmot)
čɨkčɨknu

Marmota caligata (hoary marmot)
[NWS: wáwšiłun]

Citellus townsendii (Townsend ground squirrel)

C. washingtoni (Washington ground squirrel)
čii-łá, "whistler"

Citellus beldingi (Belding ground squirrel)
čiiłá-wáakuł, "like čii-łá"

Otospermophilus beecheyi (California ground squirrel)
wáški

Callospermophilus lateralis (golden-mantled ground squirrel)

C. saturatus (golden-mantled ground squirrel)
amɨt

Eutamias minimus (least chipmunk)

E. amoenus (yellow pine chipmunk)

E. townsendii (Townsend chipmunk)
ɨmɨs

Sciurus carolinensis (eastern gray squirrel) [introduced]
> wáški ?

Sciurus griseus (western gray squirrel)
qánqan

Tamiasciurus douglasii (chickaree)

T. hudsonicus (red squirrel)
sinmí

Pteromyinae (flying squirrels)
Glaucomys sabrinus (northern flying squirrel)
łánłan

Geomyidae (pocket gophers)
Thomomys talpoides (northern pocket gopher)
tapunayt-łá, "coming out [of the ground]"

Heteromyidae (pocket mice and kangaroo rats)
Perognathus parvus (Great Basin pocket mouse)
> lákas, "mouse"

Dipodomys ordii (Ord kangaroo rat)
[wwS: "sim-tup-tup" ?]

Castoridae (beavers)

Castor canadensis (beaver)
> wišpúš

Myomorpha
Cricetidae
Cricetinae
Reithrodontomys megalotis (western harvest mouse)
Peromyscus oreas (forest deer mouse)
P. maniculatus (deer mouse)
Onychomys leucogaster (northern grasshopper mouse) ?
> lákas

Neotoma cinerea (bushy-tailed wood rat)
> wuší/ináw, "boy"

Microtinae
Lagurus curtatus (sagebrush vole)
Phenacomys intermedius (heather vole)
P. longicaudus (red tree mouse)
Clethrionomys gapperi (Gapper red-backed mouse)
C. occidentalis (western red-backed mouse)
Microtus longicaudus (long-tailed meadow mouse)
M. oregoni (Oregon meadow mouse)
M. richardsoni (water rat)
M. montanus (montane meadow mouse)
> lákas

Ondatra zibethicus (muskrat)
> ptis

Muridae (old world rats and mice) [introduced]
> lákas

Zapodidae (jumping mice)
Zapus trinotatus (Pacific jumping mouse)
Z. princeps (western jumping mouse)
> [N W S: yámas, "little deer"]

Hystrichomorpha
Erethizontidae (porcupines)
Erethizon dorsatum (porcupine)
> šíšaaš

Cetacea (whales, dolphins, and porpoises)
> sucx-łá, "splitter" [known by hearsay only]

Carnivora (carnivores)

Fissipedia (land carnivores)

Canidae (dogs, foxes, wolves, and the coyote)

Vulpes fulva (red fox)

Urocyon cinereoargenteus (gray fox)

    x̣ɨpa

    red phase of red fox

      luc̓á, "red"

    silver, gray, or black phase of red fox ?

      tuuptúup

Canis lupus (wolf)

    x̣áliš

    timber wolf variety ?

      [w s s: č̓iwa-č̓iwa]

Canis latrans (coyote)

    spílya

    small variety

      spilyá-spilya, "little coyote"

Canis familiaris (domestic dog)

    k̓usí-k̓usi, "little horse"

Ursidae (bears)

Euarctos [Ursus] americanus (black bear)

    yáka

Ursus horribilis [chelan] (grizzly bear)

    wapaan-łá, "paws the ground"

Procyonidae (raccoons)

Procyon lotor (raccoon)

    k̓aalás

Mustelidae

Martes americana (marten)

    wałtx̣-łá, "climber"

Martes pennanti (fisher)

    šimłíš

Mustela vison (mink)

    ptyaw

Mustela frenata (long-tailed weasel)

M. erminea (ermine)

    in summer pelage

      watáy

in winer pelage

čítała

Gulo luscus (wolverine)

wašapa-ní, "packer"

Taxidea taxus (badger)

šíki

Mephitis mephitis (striped skunk)

Spilogale putorius (spotted skunk)

tiskáy

Lutra canadensis (river otter)

nukšáy

Felidae (cats, cougar, lynx, bobcat)

Felis cattus (house cat) [introduced]

p̓uus/kitís

Felis concolor (cougar/puma/mountain lion)

k̓ʷaawí

Lynx canadensis (Canadian lynx)

x̣úpx̣up

Lynx rufus (bobcat)

pí̓čɨm

Pinnipedia (seals and sealions)

Phocidae (seals)

Phoca vitulina (harbor seal)

wálčayu

Perissodactyla

Equidae (horses, donkeys, and mules)

Equus asinus (donkey) [introduced]

cákas, "jackass"/> limíil, "mule"

Equus asinus X *Equus caballus* (mule) [introduced]

múla/limíil, "mule"

Equus caballus (horse)

k̓úsi [includes many named varieties]

stallion [bull of cattle also]: talá-yi, "has balls"

calf [of elk and cattle also]: q̓áyq̓ay

máamɨn, > "mormon" ? (appaloosa)

pátumx̣i/patk̓ʷáylaki (baldface/blazed face)

lučá, > lučá, "red" (bay)

liláw-lilaw (bay with white belly)

čmuk, "black" (black)

šuuka-wáakuɫ, "like sugar" (bluish-white with white mane and eye)

šk̓ʷí-šk̓ʷi (brown)

paʔáx̣ (buckskin)

páatk̓ʷiki (buckskin with dark back stripes; or uniformly orangish ?)

šiwíw-šiwiw (chestnut sorrel)

čmáakʷ, > čmuk, "black" (dark)

čmuk-ɫámtax̣, "black head" (dark headed)

k̓iix̣-k̓íix̣ (dun colored)

puʔúx̣, "gray" (dusty colored, faded blue-gray)

taqa-wáakuš, "like ?" (faded whitish)

lamt, "blue/green" (gray)

wíwlu/wiwlu-wáakuɫ, "huckleberry-like" (huckleberry roan with light on haunches)

kayús, "cayuse" (Indian pony)

kawx-káwx (palomino)

támšiɫpi/támx̣̌aki (pinto, spotted)

qaaš-qáaš (roan/strawberry roan)

maq̓áš "yellow" (sorrel)

luča-ɫámtx̣/luča-ɫámtx̣ qaaš-qáaš, "bay-headed roan" (strawberry roan with red head)

qaʔáw-qaʔaw/quyx̣, "white" (white)

Artiodactyla

　Suidae (pigs)

　　Sus scrofa (domestic pig)

　　　huq̓húq̓/kušúu

　　newborn: kusú-kusu

　Cervidae (deer, elk, and moose)

　　in general, especially as food: iwínat

　　Cervus canadensis (elk/wapiti)

　　　wawúkya

　　bull: wawúkya

　　cow: tašímka

　　calf [of horse and cattle also]: q̓áyq̓ay

　　Alces alces (moose)

　　　[w s s: šašík]

Odocoileus (deer)
   buck: yukaasíns, "has horns"
   spike buck: ɨstí, "pointed"
   two-point buck: qx̣a, "forked"
   doe: yáamaš
   fawn: mups
Odocoileus hemionus hemionus (mule deer)
      yáamaš
Odocoileus hemionus columbianus (black-tailed deer)
      x̣alk
Odocoileus virginiana (white-tailed deer)
      čatwilí
Antilocapridae (pronghorns)
   Antilocapra americana (American pronghorn/antelope)
      wáwataw
Bovidae (cattle, sheep, goats)
   Ovis aries (domestic sheep) [introduced]
      limitú
   Ovis canadensis (bighorn sheep)
      tnuun
   Capra hircus (domestic goat) [introduced]
      šiip-wáakuɬ, "sheep-like"/šúuwi, "bearded"
   Oreamnos americanus (mountain goat)
      waw
   Bison bison (buffalo/bison)
      cúuɬm
   bull [of cattle and horse also]: talá-yi, "has balls"
   Bos taurus (cattle) [introduced]
      músmuscɨn
   bull [of horse and bison also]: talá-yi, "has balls"
   cow: músmuscɨn
   calf [of horse and elk also]: q̓áyq̓ay

Appendix 2.

Sahaptin Plant Terms

THIS IS an alphabetical listing by both English vernacular and Latin names. Each English name is keyed to the appropriate Latin term. The Sahaptin forms cited are not exhaustive of all variants but represent the most common ones. Only terms recorded by the author from Sahaptin speakers of the mid-Columbia River area (Celilo Falls to Alderdale) are included here.

The letters "sp" following a genus name indicate an unspecified or unknown species of that genus; the letters "spp" following the genus name indicate that more than one species of the genus is included in the denotation of the term; if a genus or higher order taxon name occurs alone, all the species of that taxon that occur locally are so included without distinction. Sometimes the term refers prototypically to one (or more) species, but may be used to indicate additional species as well. In such cases, the prototype is indicated with an asterisk (*) and peripheral species are listed after the plus (+) sign. The exclamation point (!) indicates that the species is recognized but not named. A question mark (?) following a term indicates uncertainty as to the term's referential meaning.

Each species listed is also categorized as to its cultural relevance, as follows: "f" for food plants; "m" for medicinal plants; "p" for poisonous plants, and "t" for plants used in technological applications. Plants with none of these letters indicated are important only in other ways, such as ecological indicators or mythological references. I also indicate whether a species in cultivated (c), introduced (i), and/or weedy (w).

Abies lasiocarpa*   patátwi; papš if large [m, t]; also
  A. amabilis   includes *Pseudotsuga menziesii*
  A. procera   (and *Picea engelmannii* ?);
  A. grandis   branches: patátwi [m]
Acer circinatum   twanúwaš, "dip-net plant" [t]
  A. glabrum var. *douglasii*
Acer macrophyllum   šq̓ɨmš [t]
Achillea millefolium   wapɨn-wápɨn [m]
Achlys triphylla   "yamaš-mí ik̓ʷikáwas," "deer's
                                  perfume"
Agaricus sp.   apán [f]
Agastache occidentalis   płax wɨnš-pamá, "magic [to get a]
                                  man" [m]
Agropyron spicatum*   > waskú [fodder] (includes many
                                  grasses)

Alder (= *Alnus*)
alder, mountain (= *Alnus incana*)
alder, red (= *Alnus rubra*)
alder, Sitka (= *Alnus sinuata*)
alder, white (= *Alnus rhombifolia*
alfalfa (= *Medicago sativa*)
Allium in general   šaak, šɨšáak, šišáak [f]
Allium spp., wild species   tanán šaak, "Indian onion" [f]
  + *A. acuminatum*
Allium douglasii   q̓ʷláwi [f]
Allium macrum   šámamwi [f]
  A. pleianthum
  A. scylloides
Allium sativum (c)   šaak, šɨšáak, šišáak [f]
Alnus   psúni, psuuní [t, m]
Amelanchier alnifolia*   kkáasu [t];
  + *Amelanchier* spp.   fruit: ččaa [f]
Angelica spp.   > alamíla (*Cicuta douglasii)
antelope-brush (= *Purshia tridentata*)
Antennaria spp.   "ik̓ʷikáwas," "perfume"
Apocynum cannabinum   taxús [t]
apple (= *Pyrus malus*)

Aquilegia formosa   łiłík-łiłik, "small pine nuts" [smoke]
arborvitae (= *Thuja plicata*)
*Arceuthobium campylopodum**   "maxáł", "yellowish"
  + *Arceuthobium* spp.
Arctium minus (iw)   > čakčákt (**Xanthium*)
Arctostaphylos nevadensis   łiłk [smoke]
  A. *uva-ursi*
arrowhead (= *Sagittaria latifolia*)
Artemisia douglasiana   puʔúx-puʔux, "gray" [m];
  A. *ludoviciana*   or q̓tuní [t]
Artemisia tridentata   tawšá [m, t]
Artemisia arbuscula   tawšá-tawša, "little sagebrush"
  A. *cana*
  A. *rigida*
  A. *tripartita*
ash (= *Fraxinus latifolia*)
ash, mountain (= *Sorbus* spp.)
Asparagus officinalis (c, iw)   qiláa-qilaa, "bent"
aspen (= *Populus tremuloides*)
avens, three-flowered (= *Geum triflorum*)
Balsamorhiza careyana   pášx̣aš [f]
  B. *sagittata*
*Balsamorhiza hookeri**   p̓líwa [f]
  + B. *incana* &
  + B. *serrata*
balsamroot (= *Balsamorhiza* spp.)
basket-grass, Indian (= *Xerophyllum tenax*)
bearberry (= *Arctostaphylos* spp.)
beargrass (= *Xerophyllum tenax*)
bedstraw (= *Galium* spp.)
bee-plant, yellow (= *Cleome lutea*)
Berberis aquifolium   łk̓áwk̓aw [f, m]
B. *nervosa*   šk̓áwk̓aw [f, m]
Betula occidentalis   psuni-wáakuł, "alder-like"
                                               > psuní (**Alnus*)

bigroot (= *Marah oreganus*)
bilberry (= *Vaccinium* spp.)
bilberry, dwarf (= *V. scoparium*)

bilberry, low (= *V. caespitosum*)
bilberry, red (= *V. parvifolium*)
bilberry, tall (= *V. membranaceum*)
bindweed (= *Convolvulus arvensis*)
birch (= *Betula occidentalis*)
bisquit-root (= *Lomatium cous*)
bistort (= *Polygonum bistortoides*)
bitter-brush (= *Purshia tridentata*)
bitterroot (= *Lewisia rediviva*)
blackberry (= *Rubus ursinus*)
blackcap (= *Rubus leucodermis*)
black sage (= *Purshia tridentata*)
blueberry (= *Vaccinium* spp.)
blueberry, Alaska (= *V. alaskaense*)
blueberry, Cascade (= *V. deliciosum*)
blueberry, early (= *V. ovalifolium*)
blueberry, thin-leaved (= *V. membranaceum*)
bracken (= *Pteridium aquilinum*)
brake-fern (= *Pteridium aquilinum*)

Brodiaea douglasii	aɬpípi, anaɬpípi [f]
B. howellii	
Brodiaea hyacinthina	síɬx̌ʷs [f]
Bryoria fremontii	k̓unč, k̓ʷɨnč [f]
Bryoria spp.	k̓unč-wáakuɬ, "like k̓unč" [m ?]

bulrush (= *Scirpus* spp.)
bulrush, hardstem (= *Scirpus acutus*)
bulrush, softstem (= *Scirpus validus*)
bunchgrass (cf. *Agropyron spicatum*)
burdock (*Arctium minus*)
cabbage, skunk (= *Lysichitum americanum*)
cactus (= *Opuntia* spp.)

Calamagrostis spp. ?	aytalú (cf. *Triticum*)
Calochortus macrocarpus	nunás, nuunás [f]

camas (= *Camassia quamash*)
camas, death (= *Zigadenus*)

Camassia quamash	wák̓amu, x̣maš, x̣maaš [f]

carrot (= *Daucus carota*)
carrot, Indian (= *Perideridia*)

*Castilleja miniata** nawina-ła-nmí latít, "thunder's
  + *Castilleja* spp. ? flower"
cat-tail (= *Typha latifolia*)
Ceanothus velutinus wíčakλ [t, m]
cedar, Alaska (= *Chamaecyparis nootkatensis*)
cedar, western red (= *Thuja plicata*)
cedar, yellow (= *Chamaecyparis nootkatensis*)
Celtis reticulata talaǩú
Cercocarpus ledifolius čiši-wáakuł, "like bitterbrush" [t]
Chaenactis douglasii waxalxali-pamá, "for spider";
    waxalxali-mí, "of spider" [m]
checker-mallow (= *Sphaeralcea munroana*)
Chenopodium spp. > čiič̓k [*GRAMINAE]
cherry, bitter (= *Prunus emarginata*)
cherry, choke- (= *Prunus virginiana*)
cherry, domestic (= *Prunus avium*)
Chimaphila menziesii tanuxit-pamá, "for TB" [m]
  C. umbellata
chocolate tips (= *Lomatium dissectum*)
chokecherry (= *Prunus virginiana*)
Chrysothamnus pišxú, pisxú, psxú [t]
  C. nauseosus puʔúx-puʔux pišxú, "gray
    rabbitbrush"
  C. viscidiflorus lamt pišxú, "green rabbitbrush"
Cicuta douglasii alamíla [p]
cinquefoil, slender (= *Potentilla gracilis*)
Cirsium undulatum qut-qút
  C. canadense (iw)
  C. vulgare (iw)
  + *Cirsium* spp.
Citrullus vulgaris (c) málals
Claytonia lanceolata anipáš [f]
Clematis liqusticifolia tamqikskúla, tamq̓ikskúla,
    tamqlikskúla [m, t]
Cleome lutea tiskay-nmí tiit, "skunk's musk" [m]
clover, big-head (= *Trifolium macrocephalum*)
clubmoss (= *Lycopodium*)

cocklebur (= *Xanthium strumarium*)
columbine (= *Aquilegia formosa*)
Convolvulus arvensis (iw)   nčuu-ɫá, "sleep-maker" [m]
corn (= *Zea mays*)
Cornus stolonifera   luča-ní, "the red one" [m];
                                           fruit: wiwál [f, m]
Corylus cornuta   kkúuš-aaš [t];
                                           seed: kkuuš [f]

cottonwood (= *Populus trichocarpa*)
cous (= *Lomatium cous*)
cow-parsnip (= *Heracleum lanatum*)
Crataegus columbiana ?   kula-kúla [f]
Crataegus douglasii   išnɨm-áašu, šnɨ́m-aašu;
                                           fruit: išnɨ́m [f]
Crocidium multicaule   papčiláw [myth]
Cucumis melo var. *cantalupensis* (c)   latiwalá, "good smell"
Cucurbita spp. (c)   skʷáašiš

currant, golden (= *Ribes aureum*)
currant, squaw (= *Ribes cereum*)
currant, wax (= *Ribes cereum*)
Cymopterus terebinthinus   šyapɨ́špš [m]
dandelion, false (= *Microseris troximoides*)
Daucus carota (c, iw)   sawitk-wáakuɫ, "like Indian carrot"
death-camas (= *Zigadenus*)
deer-foot (= *Achlys triphylla*)
desert parsley (= *Lomatium* spp.)
desert parsley, fern-leaved
    (= *Lomatium dissectum*)
desert parsley, large-fruited
    (= *Lomatium macrocarpum*)
devil's club (= *Oplopanax horridum*)
dock, veiny (= *Rumex venosus*)
dock, winged (= *Rumex venosus*)
Dodecatheon   kʷaykʷay-nmí núšnu, "curlew's
                                                             beak"

dog-tooth violet (= *Erythronium grandiflorum*)
dogwood, creek (= *Cornus stolonifera*)

dwarf mistletoe (= *Arceuthobium* spp.)

Echinodontium tinctorium   nuknúkt, nukʷnúkʷt [t, m]

elderberry, black (= *Sambucus racemosa*)

elderberry, blue (= *Sambucus cerulea*)

elderberry, red (= *Sambucus racemosa*)

Elymus cinereus   šwičt [t]

Equisetum hyemale*   wapáy-wapay, "little reed" [myth]

E. arvense   siikʷ-síikʷ [t, m]

  E. telmateia

  + *Equisetum* spp.

evening-primrose (= *Oenothera pallida*)

Evernia vulpina (= *Letharia vulpina*)

false-agoseris (= *Microseris troximoides*)

"false-dandelion" (= *Microseris troximoides*)

false hellebore (= *Veratrum*)

false-yarrow (= *Chaenactis douglasii*)

fawn-lily (= *Erythronium grandiflorum*)

fern (= POLYPODIACEAE)

fern, bracken (= *Pteridium aquilinum*)

filbert (= *Corylus cornuta*)

fir, true (= *Abies*)

fir, Douglas (= *Pseudotsuga*)

fir, grand (= *Abies grandis*)

fir, noble (= *Abies procera*)

fir, silver (= *Abies amabilis*)

fir, subalpine (= *Abies lasiocarpa*)

Fomes spp.   maqš-máqš [t]

Fragaria vesca   suspán-aaš; fruit: suspán [f]

  F. virginiana

Fritillaria pudica   síkni [f]

fritillary (= *Fritillaria pudica*)

fungus (cf. *Agaricus*,
    Echinodontium, Fomes,
    Polyporus, mushroom)

Galium   tišxpanú, lusta-lústa, "sticky"

Geranium viscosissimum   tamcí, "sweetener" [f]

Geum triflorum   suspan-wáakuɬ, "strawberry-like"
                                                [m]

giant-hyssop (= *Agastache occidentalis*)

Gilia aggregata   qmamsalí tkʷátat, "hummingbird's food"

goldstar (= *Crocidium multicaule*)
gooseberry (= *Ribes lacustre*)
gooseberry (= *Ribes* spp.)

GRAMINAE   čiíčk [if not useful]; may also include other grasslike plants without "flowers"; forage grasses are waskú

grass (= GRAMINAE)
grass, giant wild rye (= *Elymus cinereus*)
grass, bear- (= *Xerophyllum tenax*)
grass, reed- (= *Calamagrostis* spp.)
greasewood (= *Sarcobates vermiculatus*)
"greasewood" (cf. *Purshia tridentata*)
ground-cherry (= *Physalis longifolia*)
grouseberry (= *Vaccinium scoparium*)
hackberry (= *Celtis reticulata*)
hawthorn (= *Crataegus*)
hawthorn, black (= *Crataegus douglasii*)
hawthorn, Columbia (= *Crataegus columbiana*)
hawthorn, red (= *Crataegus columbiana*)
hazelnut (= *Corylus cornuta*)

Helianthus annuus (c, iw)   "pašxaš-wáakuł," "like balsamroot"

Helianthus cusickii   "činukit-yaw tawtnúk," "VD medicine" [m]

hellebore, false- (= *Veratrum*)
hemlock (tree) (= *Tsuga*)
hemlock, poison (= *Cicuta douglasii*)
hemp, Indian (= *Apocynum cannabinum*)

Heracleum lanatum   tx̣u [f, m]

Holodiscus discolor   pɨx̣wayč-pamá, "for bracing"; "tax̣čxt-pamá tawtnúk," "diarrhea medicine" [t, m]

honeysuckle, bearberry (= *Lonicera involucrata*)
horse-mint (= *Agastache occidentalis*)
horsetail (fern) (= *Equisetum* spp.)

huckleberry (= *Vaccinium* spp.)
huckleberry, big (= *Vaccinium membranaceum*)
huckleberry, blue-leaf (= *Vaccinium deliciosum*)
huckleberry, Cascade (= *Vaccinium deliciosum*)
huckleberry, dwarf (= *Vaccinium caespitosum*)
huckleberry, oval-leaf (= *Vaccinium ovalifolium*)
Indian balsam (= *Lomatium dissectum*)
Indian basketgrass (= *Xerophyllum tenax*)
Indian celery (cf. *Lomatium grayi, L. dissectum, L. nudicaule*)
Indian-paintbrush (= *Castilleja* spp.)
Indian pond lily (= *Nuphar polysepalum*)
Indian rhubarb (= *Heracleum lanatum*)
joint grass (= *Equisetum hyemale*)
juniper (= *Juniperus*)
juniper, Rocky Mountain (= *Juniperus scopulorum*)
juniper, western (= *Juniperus occidentalis*)

Juniperus occidentalis	puuš, púuš-aaš [t, m];
J. scopulorum	fruit; puuš [m]

kinnikinnik (= *Arctostaphylos* spp.)
knotweed, alpine (= *Polygonum phytolaccaefolium*)
larch (= *Larix occidentalis*)

Larix occidentalis	kimíla [t, m]
Lathyrus spp.	lapwa-wáakuɬ, "like peas"
Letharia vulpina	maqɨɬ, "yellowish" [t, m]
Lewisia rediviva	pyax̣í [f, m]

lichen, black tree (= *Bryoria fremontii*)
lichen, green tree (= *Bryoria* spp.)
lichen, staghorn (= *Letharia vulpina*)
lichen, wolf (= *Letharia vulpina*)
licorice-root (= *Ligusticum*)

*Ligusticum canbyi** + *L. grayi* ?	áyun [m]
Lilium columbianum	pananát [f, m]

lily, Columbia (= *Lilium columbianum*)
lily, fawn- (= *Erythronium grandiflorum*)
lily, mariposa (= *Calochortus macrocarpus*)
lily, Oregon (= *Lilium columbianum*)
lomatium, bare-stem (= *L. nudicaule*)

lomatium, Canby's (= *L. canbyi*)
lomatium, Donnell's (= *L. donnellii*)
lomatium, fern-leaved (= *L. dissectum*)
lomatium, few-fruited (= *L. martindalei*)
lomatium, Gray's (= *L. grayi*)
lomatium, Hamblen's (=
    L. farinosum var. *hambleniae*)
lomatium, John Day Valley (= *L. minus*)
lomatium, large-fruit (= *L. macrocarpum*)
lomatium, Martindale's (= *L. martindalei*)
lomatium, Piper's (= *L. piperi*)

Lomatium canbyi	lukš [f]; Priest Rapids variety: škúlkul [f]
L. cous	x̲awš [f]
L. dissectum	čalúkš [m, f, t]
L. donellii ?	háti [p]
L. farinosum var. *hambleniae*	max̲šlí, max̲šní [f]
L. gormanii	sasamíła, łałamíła [f ?]
L. grayi	latít-latit, "many flowers" [f]; root: atuná [f, m]; stem: wáʔwɨnu [f]
L. macrocarpum	púła [f, m, p]; if flowering: wɨnš púła, "male púła"; if not: tílaaki púła, "female púła" ("male" not eaten)
L. martindalei	! [weather changer]
L. minus	nak̓únk [f]
L. nudicaule	x̲amsí [f, m]; leaf shoots: płíš-płiš [f, m]; mature stem: ašwaníya, "slave"
L. piperi	mámɨn [f]
Lonicera involucrata	wapaanła-nmí tkʷátat, "grizzly's food"; yaka-nmí tkʷátat, "black bear's food"

lovage (= *Liqusticum*)
lupine (= *Lupinus*)

Lupinus spp.	wapiyałá [grave decorations]

Lysichitum americanum watiptíp [t, m]

manroot (= *Marah oreganus*)

manzanita (= *Arctostaphylos*)

maple (= *Acer*)

maple, big-leaf (= *Acer macrophyllum*)

maple, Douglas' (= *Acer glabrum* var. *douglasii*)

maple, vine (= *Acer circinatum*)

Marah oreganus x̱ax̱alq̓k [m]

mariposa lily (= *Calochortus macrocarpus*)

Medicago sativa (iw) alpaʔálpa

Mentha arvensis šux̱a-šúx̱a [f, m]

Microseris troximoides mɨ́c̓úna [f]

Mimulus guttatus pamaywax̱-pamá, winanuut-pamá,

  + *Mimulus* spp. "for swimming" [m]

M. guttatus var. *depauperata* > "maqɨ́š latít", "yellow flower" [t]

mint (= *Mentha arvensis*)

mistletoe, dwarf (= *Arceuthobium*)

mock orange (= *Philadelphus lewisii*)

monkey-flower (= *Mimulus*)

morning-glory (= *Convolvulus* spp.)

moss, tree (= *Bryoria* spp.)

moss, water wax̱úš, wax̱úuš

mountain-ash (= *Sorbus*)

mountain balm (= *Ceanothus velutinus*)

mountain-mahogany (= *Cercocarpus ledifolius*)

mule's-ears (= *Wyethia amplexicaulis*)

mullein (= *Verbascum thapsus*)

mushroom (cf. *Agaricus, Polyporus, Fomes*)

mushroom, cottonwood (= *Polyporus*)

mushroom, oyster (= *Polyporus*)

mushroom, poisonous tiyax̱ʷalílat [p]

Myriophyllum spicatum yawastakíns [m]

nettle (= *Urtica dioica*)

Nicotiana attenuata awt-pamá, "for purification" [m]

*Nicotiana tabacum** táwax̱ [m]

  + *N. quadrivalvis*

Nuphar polysepalum kalamát

oak (= *Quercus garryana*)

ocean-spray (= *Holodiscus discolor*)

Oenothera pallida   kalux̣-mí áčaš, "blueback salmon's
                                                       eyes"

onion (= *Allium* spp.)

onion, domestic (= *Allium sativa*)

onion, Hooker (= *Allium acuminatum*)

onion, tapertip (= *Allium acuminatum*)

onion, rock (= *Allium macrum*)

onion, Douglas' (= *Allium douglasii*)

onion, many-flowered (= *Allium pleianthum*)

onion, scilla-like (= *Allium scilloides*)

Oplopanax horridum   šqapqápnu-waaš, "rash bush" [m,
                                                       p]

Opuntia polyacantha   ištɨš [f, t]
   O. fragilis

Oregon grape (= *Berberis*)

Osmorhiza occidentalis   siwíw, síwsiw, stiwíw [f, m]

Paeonia brownii   k̓tk̓ɨt [m]

paintbrush, Indian (= *Castilleja* spp.)

paintbrush, scarlet (= *Castilleja miniata*)

parsnip, pestle (= *Lomatium nudicaule*)

pea, domestic (= *Pisum sativum*)

pea, wild (= *Lathyrus* spp.)

peach (= *Prunus persica*)

peony (= *Paeonia brownii*)

Perideridia gairdneri   sawítk, "tawtnúk wax̣ʷayč-pa,"
                                                       "medicine for ?" [f, m]

Philadelphus lewisii   sáx̣i [t, m]

Phleum pratense (c, iw)   timatí

Phlox hoodi   "tamašam-pamá," "lithosol plant"
   + *Phlox* spp. ?

Phragmites communis   wápay [t, m]

Physalis longifolia ?   sápčɨmliki

pine (= *Pinus*)

pine, lodgepole (= *Pinus contorta* var. *latifolia*)

pine, ponderosa (= *Pinus ponderosa*)

pine, western white (= *Pinus monticola*)

pine, whitebark (= *Pinus albicaulis*)

pineapple weed (= *Matricaria matricarioides*)
pinedrops (= *Pterospora andromeda*)
Pinus spp.   tápaš, tápaaš;
                                        cone: pananík, palalík;
                                        seedling: tapáy-tapay
Pinus albicaulis   nɨník-aaš;
                                        nut: nɨník [f]
Pinus contorta var. *latifolia*   kalám-kalam, qalám-qalam; > "tapaš-
                                        wáakuł," "ponderosa-like";
                                        "tapáš-tapaš," "little
                                        ponderosa" (?) [t, m]
Pinus monticola   > tápaš
*Pinus ponderosa**   tápaš [t, m, f]; inner bark:
                                        sukʷaymit [f]

pipsissewa (= *Chimaphila*)
Pisum sativum   lapwá
poison-hemlock (= *Cicuta douglasii*)
poison ivy (= *Rhus radicans*)
poison oak (= *Rhus diversiloba*)
Polygonum bistortoides?   k̓usí-k̓usi 'dog' [m]
P. phytolaccaefolium   tamaxplá, tamaxp-łá "reduces
                                        swelling " [m]

POLYPODIACEAE   "paq̓ʷɨnk-pamá," "for covering" (cf.
                                        **Pteridium*)

Polyporus sp. ?   łintɨt [f]
poplar (= *Populus trichocarpa*)
Populus tremuloides   niní [t]
P. trichocarpa   xapxáp, xpxáp, xápxap [t, m]
potato (= *Solanum tuberosum*)
potato, Indian (= *Claytonia lanceolata*)
prince's-pine (= *Chimaphila*)
Prunus avium (c)   tmɨš-wáakuł, "like chokecherry"
Prunus emarginata   ɨšnípš [t, m]; > tmɨš-wáakuł
Prunus virginiana   tmɨš-aaš, tmáašu;
                                        fruit: tmɨš [f, m]

Pseudotsuga menziesii   papš [> *Abies*, maybe *Picea*] [t];
                                        patátwi [if small, cf. *Abies*]

Pteridium aquilinum	> "paq̓ʷɨnk-pamá," "for covering" [t]
Pterospora andromeda	"tutanik-pamá," "for hair" [m]
Pteryxia terebinthina (= *Cymopterus terebinthinus*)	
puffball (= *Fomes* spp.)	
Purshia tridentata	čɨší [t, m]
pussy-toes (= *Antennaria*)	
Pyrus malus (c)	ápɨls
quaking-aspen (= *Populus tremuloides*)	
Queen Anne's lace (= *Daucus carota*)	
Quercus garryana	čuníps, kápɨn-aaš, "digging-stick tree" [t]; acorn: wawačí [f, m]
rabbit-brush (= *Chrysothamnus*)	
rabbit-brush, gray (= *C. nauseosus*)	
rabbit-brush, green (= *C. viscidiflorus*)	
raspberry (= *Rubus idaeus*)	
raspberry, blackcap (= *Rubus leucodermis*)	
reed (= *Phragmites communis*)	
reedgrass (= *Calamagrostis*)	
*Rhus diversiloba**	łɨmtq̓áx̣, łamtḱáx, łamtqáx̣-yaš [p]
+ *R. radicans*	
Rhus glabra	tantɨ́t [m]
Ribes aureum	x̣án-aaš; fruit: x̣an [f]
R. cereum	sx̣íyap [f]
*R. lacustre**	pínuš-aaš; fruit: pínuš [f]
+ *Ribes* spp.	
Rosa gymnocarpa	šḱapášway; fruit: sčápa, sčápa [f]
R. nutkana	
R. woodsii	
Rosa gymnocarpa ?	pɨx̣anu-pamá šḱapášway, "mountain forest rose"
rose (= *Rosa*)	
Rubus idaeus	šáx̣at-aaš; fruit: lučá šáx̣at, "red raspberry" [f]
R. leucodermis	šáx̣at-aaš; fruit: čmuk šáx̣at, "black raspberry"; šáx̣at, sáx̣at [f]

R. *parviflorus* — tuna-túna [f]

R. *ursinus* — wisík-aaš;

Rumex — fruit: wisík [f]

R. *venosus* — waq̇ilmáx̣ [t]

Russian thistle (= *Salsola*)

rye, giant wild (= *Elymus cinereus*)

ryegrass (= *Elymus cinereus*)

sage, gray ball (= *Salvia dorrii*)

sagebrush, big (= *Artemisia tridentata*)

sagebrush, cut-leaf (= *Artemisia tripartita*)

sagebrush, dwarf, (= *Artemisia arbuscula*)

sagebrush, hoary (= *Artemisia cana*)

sagebrush, silver (= *Artemisia cana*)

sagebrush, stiff (= *Artemisia rigida*)

sagebrush, threetip (= *Artemisia tripartita*)

sagewort (= *Artemisia douglasii, A. ludoviciana*)

Sagittaria latifolia — "wapato" [no Sahaptin term known]

Salix spp. — ttax̣š [t, m] [includes all species of willows except *S. amygdaloides*]

Salix babylonica (c) — kɨkí ttax̣š, "drooping willow"

Salix exiqua — puʔúx̣-puʔux̣ ttax̣š, "gray willow" [t, m]

Salix monticola ? — pɨx̣anu-pamá ttax̣š, "mountain willow"

Salix amygdaloides — haháw [t]

salmonberry (= *Rubus spectabilis*)

Salsola kali — šapyá-šapya

Salvia dorrii — q̇ašq̇aš-lí [m]

Sambucus cerulea — mɨłɨp-aaš [t]; fruit: mɨłɨp [f]

Sambucus racemosa — čmɨt [f]

Sarcobates vermiculatus — nɨšx̣t [t]

Scirpus acutus — tk̇u [t]

    S. validus

scouring-rush (= *Equisetum hyemale*)

Sedum lanceolatum   "kɨtu wayx̣ti-ɬá miyánaš," "quick
   S. oregonum   runner child" [m]
   + *Sedum* spp.
serviceberry (= *Amelanchier alnifolia*)
Shepherdia canadensis   kula-kúla [f]
shooting star (= *Dodecatheon*)
skunk-cabbage (= *Lysichitum americanum*)
snowberry (= *Symphoricarpos*)
soapberry (= *Shepherdia canadensis*)
Solanum tuberosum (c)   lapatáat
soopolallie (= *Shepherdia canadensis*)
Sorbus scopulina   kʷalkʷála-yaaš;
   S. sitchensis   fruit: kʷalkʷála
spatterdock (= *Nuphar polysepalum*)
Sphaeralcea munroana   šušaynš-mí áčaš, "steelhead's
                                   eyes"; nusux̣-mí áčaš,
                                   "salmon's eyes"

springbeauty (= *Claytonia lanceolata*)
spring-gold (= *Crocidium multicaule*)
spruce (= *Picea engelmannii*)
sticky-laurel (= *Ceanothus velutinus*)
stonecrop (= *Ledum lanceolatum*)
stovepipe weed (= *Equisetum hyemale*)
strawberry (= *Fragaria*)
sumac (= *Rhus glabra*)
sunflower, common (= *Helianthus annuus*)
sunflower, Cusick's (= *Helianthus cusickii*)
"sunflower" (cf. *Balsamorhiza*)
sweet-cicely (= *Osmorhiza occidentalis*)
*Symphoricarpos albus**   saxi-wáakuɬ, saxisax̣i-wáakuɬ, "like
   + *Symphoricarpos* spp.   syringa" [m]
syringa (= *Philadelphus lewisii*)
tamarack (= *Larix occidentalis*)
Tauschia hooveri   pank̓ú [f]
Taxus brevifolia   wawanínš [t]
thimbleberry (= *Rubus parviflorus*)
thistle (= *Cirsium*)
thornapple (= *Crataegus*)

Thuja plicata   nank [t, m]
tiger lily (= *Lilium columbianum*)
timothy (= *Phleum pratense*)
tobacco, cultivated (= *Nicotiana tabacum*)
tobacco, wild (= *Nicotiana attenuata*)
tobacco, Indian (= *Arctostaphylos* spp.)
tobacco-root (= *Valeriana edulis*)
Trifolium macrocephalum   alpaʔalpa-wáakuɬ, "like alfalfa"
*Trillium ovatum**   sapaniċá [m]
    + *T. petiolatum*
Triticum aestivum (c)   > aytalú
Tsuga heterophylla   waqutqút, "hooker" [t, m, f, myth]
    T. mertensiana
tule (= *Scirpus* spp.)
tumbleweed (= *Salsola kali*)
turkey-beard, western (= *Xerophyllum tenax*)
twin-berry (= *Lonicera involucrata*)
Typha latifolia   šċ̌iw, čč̌iw [t, p]
Urtica dioica   alaʔála [m]
Vaccinium caespitosum   ililmúk-aaš; fruit: ililmúk, ɬɨɬmúk [f]
    V. deliciosum
*Vaccinium membranaceum**   wíwnu;
    + *Vaccinium alaskaense*   fruit: wíwnu [f, m]
Vaccinium ovalifolium   q̇ašiš-lí, q̇šɨš-lí, q̇šɨš-lí, huʔuš-lí
Vaccinium parvifolium   lúċa-luċa wíwnu, "red huckleberry";
                                                      luċa-luċa-lí, "the red one" [f]
Vaccinium scoparium   wiwlú-wiwlu, "little huckleberry" [f]
valerian, edible (= *Valeriana edulis*)
Valeriana edulis   k̇ʷíya [f]
vanillaleaf (= *Achlys triphylla*)
Veratrum californicum   mimún [m]
    V. viride
Verbascum thapsus (iw)   wasikayk-ɬá [m]
virgin's-bower (= *Clematis liqusticifolia*)
wake-robin (= *Trillium ovatum*)
wapato (= *Sagittaria latifolia*)
water-hemlock (= *Cicuta douglasii*)
water-lily, yellow (= *Nuphar polysepalum*)

water-milfoil, spiked (= *Myriophyllum spicatum*)
wheatgrass (= *Agropyron spicatum*)
whortleberry (= *Vaccinium scoparium*)
wild begonia (= *Rumex venosus*)
wild cucumber (= *Marah oreganus*)
willow (= *Salix*)
willow, coyote (= *Salix exiqua*)
willow, mountain (= *Salix monticola*)
willow, peach-leaf (= *Salix amygdaloides*)
willow, slender (= *Salix exiqua*)
willow, weeping (= *Salix babylonica*)
wokas (= *Nuphar polysepalum*)
wormwood (= *Artemisia* spp.)

Wyethia amplexicaulis   pii, pípi [f, m]
Xanthium strumarium   čakčákt, "clinging"
yampah (= *Perideridia*)
yarrow (= *Achillea millefolium*)
yellow bell (= *Fritillaria pudica*)
yew (= *Taxus brevifolia*)
Zea mays   sɨ̓łxʷs-wáakuł, "like hyacinth brodiaea"

Zigadenus elegans   alapíšaš [p]
     Z. paniculatus
     Z. venenosus

Appendix 3.

Some Plateau Medicinal Plants

Species	Disease	Part/Preparation
Abies grandis grand fir	colds, fever	inner bark
A. lasiocarpa subalpine fir	make hair grow; purification	boil; wash or drink use in sweat lodge
Abies spp. or *Pseudotsuga* or *Picea* fir or spruce	chest colds	
Acer glabrum Douglas maple	diarrhea	drink infusion
Achillea millefolium yarrow	diarrhea eye wash swelling barrenness	boil; drink infusion root, leaves; infusion leaves; poultice boil, drink
*Achlys triphylla** vanilla leaf	cataracts	leaves
Alnus incana thin-leaf alder	purify blood	bark; drink infusion
Alnus rhombifolia white alder	"female problems"	
Aquilegia formosa columbine	perfume	smoking mixture
Arceuthobium campylopodum dwarf mistletoe	dandruff	infusion; wash
Arctostaphylos patula manzanita	cathartic; appetite	drink tea

Species	Disease	Part/Preparation
Artemisia douglasiana sagewort	itches, sores	

Artemisia tridentata
    sagebrush
	colds, fever,
	        headache
		leaves; boil, drink

	prevent gray hair	wash w/infusion
Astragalus spp. locoweed, milk-vetch	hemorrhage	root
Balsamorhiza sagittata arrowleaf balsamroot	fever, chills	root; boil, drink
Balsamorhiza serrata toothed balsamroot	T B	root; chew
Berberis aquifolium tall Oregon grape	upset stomach	
Berberis nervosa low Oregon grape	paralysis rheumatism	root; bathe w/infusion root; drink infusion
Betula occidentalis water birch	pimples, sores	
Blepharipappus scaber blepharipappus	bloody diarrhea	w/acorns, willow
Bryoria fremontii black tree lichen	arthritis	boil; poultice

Ceanothus velutinus
    mountain balm
	cold, flu, fever	boil; drink to induce
		        sweating

	dandruff	leaves; rinse hair
Chaenactis douglasii false-yarrow	burns, wounds, sores rash, pimples; spider bite	as dressing
Chimaphila umbellata prince's pine	T B	boil, drink
Clematis liqusticifolia western clematis	make hair grow; dandruff, hair loss	leaves, stem; infusion

Cleome lutea
    yellow bee plant
	colds	flower, branch; drink
		    infusion

C. *platycarpa* golden spiderflower	children's colds fever	drink infusion mash, rub on body
Convolvulus polymorphus morning-glory	hair tonic	

Species	Disease	Part/Preparation
Cornus nuttallii Pacific dogwood	laxative, emetic	bark
Cornus stolonifera creek dogwood	eye problems colds bleeding	use in sweat bath berries; eaten
Cymopteris terebinthinus [Umbelliferae]	sores, colds	root; chew
Echinodontium tinctorium a woody fungus	keep skin from chapping	apply to skin
Elymus cinereus giant wild rye	hair tonic	boil, wash
Epilobium paniculatum willow-herb	dandruff, falling hair	spring shoots; wash
Equisetum hyemale scouring rush	v d, diuretic	stalks; boil, drink
Erigeron linearis fleabane	sores	greens; pound, poultice
Erythronium grandiflorum yellow fawn-lily	uncertain	no details
Fragaria vesca/ *F. virginiana* wild strawberry	hurt eyes, blind fever	leaf; boil, wash root; drink infusion
Gaillardia aristata blanket-flower	wounds; fever	
Geum triflorum three-flower avens	t b	no details
Gilia aggregata skyrocket gilia	kidneys hair and scalp	boil, drink
Goodyera oblongifolia rattlesnake plantain	boils	poultice
Haplopappus resinosus goldenweed	hemorrhage; tonic	
Heracleum lanatum cow's parsnip	sores, swelling	root; pound, poultice
Helianthus cusickii Cusick's sunflower	male impotence wasting, t b	root; no details root; chew

Species	Disease	Part/Preparation

Holodiscus discolor/
H.dumosus
    ocean-spray
	diarrhea	flowers, inner bark;
		    boil, drink tea

Hydrophyllum capitatum ball-head waterleaf	tonic, appetitie	root; chew
Iris missouriensis wild iris	eyewash toothache	 root

Juniperus communis
    common juniper
J. occidentalis/
J. scopulorum
    juniper
	counter magic
	fever
	colds, sore throat,
	    flu, VD, kidneys
	cough, fever
	
	laxative; colds
		wash baby w/infusion
		drink infusion
		boil; drink to sweat
		    before sleeping
		leaves, inner bark;
		    boil, drink infusion
		berries; boil, drink

Larix occidentalis
    larch
	TB, laryngitis	young shoots; drink
		    infusion

Letharia vulpina wolf lichen	sores, boils swelling, bruises hemorrhage	boil; poultice as hot poultice boil, drink
Ligusticum canbyi/ *L. grayi* lovage	sorethroat, TB, colds pneumonia toothache	root; chew, use in sweat lodge drink infusion root; in cavity
Lilium columbianum tiger lily	for good luck	root; hold in mouth
Linum perenne wild flax	hair tonic	for children
Listera convallarioides twayblade	boils	poultice

Lomatium dissectum
    fern-leaved
        lomatium
	dandruff, lice
	sores, boils
	colds, etc.
	sore throat
	fever, emetic
	winded horse
	saddle sores
		root; infusion, rinse
		root; mash, poultice
		root; drink infusion
		root; chew
		root; chew
		root; boil, inhale steam
		root; infusion rinse

Species	Disease	Part/Preparation
Lomatium grayi Gray's lomatium	colds	root; chew, swallow
Lomatium macrocarpum large-fruited lomatium	TB	tops; eat
Lomatium nudicaule bare-stem lomatium	headache, colds	seeds; boil, inhale
Lomatium triternatum nine-leaved lomatium	emetic; VD ?	root
Lonicera involucrata twinberry	emetic	
Lotus purshiana Spanish-clover	eyes	
Lupinus leucophyllus lupine	skin rash	infusion
Lycopodium annotinum/ L. clavatum clubmoss	make hair grow	wash w/infusion
Lysichitum americanum skunk cabbage	swelling, pain of joints	leaf; mash, poultice
Marah oreganus wild cucumber	sores; eyes	root; no details
Mentha arvensis wild mint	cough, colds, eyes	infusion; drink, wash
Mentzelia laevicaulis blazing-star	burns	for children
Mimulus guttatus monkey-flower	wounds; eyes	mature plants; infusion
Monardella odoratissima monardella	cough, colds, fever	infusion
Myriophyllum spicatum water-milfoil	dandruff	
Nicotiana attenuata wild tobacco	purgative at death of close relation	tops; boil, drink
	raw sores	w/hot water as poultice
Oplopanax horridum devil's-club	TB	wood; boil, drink

Species	Disease	Part/Preparation
Osmorhiza occidentalis	headache	infusion; rinse hair
sweet-cicely	coughs, colds	root; chew
Paeonia brownii	eye problems	top of root; wash w/
Brown's peony		infusion
	worms, fever, TB	root; chew, boil & drink
Penstemon deustus	dandruff	mash, boil, wash,
hot-rock penstemon		
Philadelphus lewisii	eyes	bark
syringa	irritated skin	leaves; wash
Phlox hoodii	itching	infusion; wash
phlox		used in sweat bath
Picea engelmannii	high fever	
spruce		
Pinus contorta	spring tonic	drink infusion
lodgepole pine	boils, swelling	pitch; apply topically
Pinus ponderosa	boils, flu	pitch, young shoots
ponderosa pine		
Polygonum aviculare	hair tonic	infusion
knotweed	backache; VD	drink infusion
Polygonum bistortoides	eye problems	root; boil, wash
American bistort		
P. phytolaccaefolium	swelling	poultice
alpine knotweed		
Populus trichocarpa	sores; hand, face	buds; no details
black cottonwood	fever	inner bark
Prunus emarginata	prevent too large fetus	w/*Berberis*, boil, drink
bitter cherry	rheumatism	
P. virginiana	diarrhea	
chokecherry		
Pseudotsuga mensiezii	rheumatism; warts	bark; burn on skin
Douglas fir	chest colds	(see *Abies*)
Pterospora andromeda	dandruff, falling hair	hair tonic
pinedrops		
Purshia tridentata	emetic; flu, fever	seeds, roots; tea
bitter-brush	laxative	
	itch	bathe skin w/infusion

Species	Disease	Part/Preparation
Pyrola picta wintergreen	boils	mash, poultice
Quercus garryana Garry oak	diarrhea	acorns; cook, eat w/willow
Rhamnus purshiana cascara	laxative, emetic	bark
Rhus glabra smooth sumac	eye problems VD, TB, kidneys	root
Rosa nutkana/ R. *gymnocarpa/* R. *woodsi* wild rose	cough, flu ward off ghosts burns, sore navel	hips; infusion, drink branch; keep in house galls; burn, powdered
Rumex spp. wild dock	toothache	root; roast, apply
Salix exiqua Coyote willow	dandruff sores	leaf, shoot; mash
Salix spp. willow	bleeding pain of insect bites coughs, colds hair tonic diarrhea	leaves and new growth inner bark root w/acorns
Salvia dorrii gray ball sage	colds; esp. babies	chest pack
Sambucus cerulea blue elderberry	loss of appetite	
Sorbus spp. mountain-ash	fever	berries; cook, eat
Symphoricarpos albus snowberry	eyes bed wetting TB	berry, branch; wash w/ infusion berry, branch; drink infusion drink as tea
Thuja plicata western red cedar	hemorrhage, eyes, belly ache hair tonic cough syrup	drink infusion roots, bark

Species	Disease	Part/Preparation
Tolmiea menziesii youth-on-age	boils	
Trillium ovatum wake-robin	eye problems, remove object from eye	root
Urtica dioica nettle	arthritis, rheumatism, backache, paralysis	counterirritant
Vaccinium membranaceum black mountain huckleberry	trenchmouth	juice; gargle
Veratrum viride	POISONOUS	
V. californicum false hellebore	prevent gray hair; scalp sores, lice rheumatism, sores	rinse hair w/infusion root; poultice
Wyethia amplexicaulis mule's-ears	emetic	
Zigadenus venenosus death camas	POISONOUS; emetic; skin rash or sore	root; small amount apply w/tobacco

In part from French and French n.d. [1979]. (For additional Plateau plant medicines see Turner, Bouchard, and Kennedy 1980 and Turner et al., n.d.)

Appendix 4.

Columbia River Sahaptin Kinterms

FOLLOWING IS a comprehensive (but not exhaustive) listing of Columbia River Sahaptin kinship terms. If the term of address differs significantly from the term of reference, the address term will be given in parentheses below the referential term. Each term is "defined" by a listing of included kin types and by a GRAFIK formula (Atkins 1974). The formula states a logical rule for classifying each type of kin named. The horizontal arrow ($\rightarrow$) indicates a parent-child link; the arrow points to the child. Double-headed arrows ($\leftrightarrow$) stand for sibling links, i.e., a (non-identical) child of a parent of a person ($\leftarrow \rightarrow$). Superscripted "i" and "k" indicate that the relationship so marked may be repeated one or more times (the superscript "k-1" implies that the relationship is repeated one or more times or is not present at all, i.e., when k = 1, k − 1 = 0). Repeated sibling links ($\leftrightarrow^k$) should be read as ($\leftarrow^k \rightarrow^k$), e.g., a (non-identical) child of a (non-identical) child of a parent of a parent of a person ($\leftrightarrow^{k=2}$). Standard symbols for male (δ) and female (φ) are used to indicate the sex of referent, speaker, or intervening relative where needed. The plus and minus signs indicate that the formulae within the vertical bars (or parentheses) are to be read forwards (right-to-left) or backwards (left-to-right), respectively. A formula marked +/− may be read in either direction. A + attached to a sibling link points to the elder sibling. A marriage link is indicated by a double horizontal line ($=$), which, if marked with an "x" ($\overset{x}{=}$) is optional.

Parents:

pča	M	$	\varphi$	$\rightarrow$	$	+$
(íła)				
pšít	F	$	\delta$	$\rightarrow$	$	+$
(túta)				

Children:

pap   ♂'s D |♂   →   ♀|−
(ɨsa)

išt   S, D | → |−
(tta)

Siblings/Cousins:

pat   Z+; MZD+, MBD+, FZD+, |♀+$\overset{k}{\longleftrightarrow}$ |+
(nána)   FBD+, etc.

pyap   B+; MZS+, MBS+, FZS+, |♂+$\overset{k}{\longleftrightarrow}$ |+
(yáya)   FBS+, etc.

isíp   ♀'s Z−; ♀'s MZD−, ♀'s |♀+$\overset{k}{\longleftrightarrow}$ ♀|−
(níya)   MBD−, ♀'s FZD−, ♀'s
           FBD−, etc.

ac   ♂'s Z−; ♂'s MZD−, ♂'s |♂+$\overset{k}{\longleftrightarrow}$ ♀|−
(nɨ́ča)   MBD−, ♂'s FZD−, ♂'s
           FBD−, etc.

pačt   ♀'s B−; ♀'s MZS−, ♀'s |♀+$\overset{k}{\longleftrightarrow}$ ♂|−
(nɨ́pa)   MBS−, ♀'s FZS−, ♀'s
           FBS−, etc.

ɨsxɨ́p   ♂'s B−; ♂'s MZS−, ♂'s |♂+$\overset{k}{\longleftrightarrow}$ ♂|−
(nɨ́ka)   MBS−, ♂'s FZS−, ♂'s
           FBS−, etc.

Grandparents/Grandchildren:

káła   MM: MMM, MFM; MMZ, |♀$\overset{k-1}{\longleftrightarrow}$ $\overset{i}{\longrightarrow}$♀→ |±
            MFZ; ♀'s DD, ♀'s DS; ♀'s
            DDD, ♀'s SDD, ♀'s DDS,
            ♀'s SDS; ♀'s ZDD, ♀'s
            ZDS, ♀'s BDD, ♀'s BDS;
            etc.

ála   FM: FMM, FFM; FMZ, FFZ; |♀$\overset{k-1}{\longleftrightarrow}$ $\overset{i}{\longrightarrow}$♂→ |±
            ♀'s SD, ♀'s SS; ♀'s DSD,
            ♀'s SSD, ♀'s DSS, ♀'s SSS;
            ♀'s ZSD, ♀'s ZSS, ♀'s
            BSD, ♀'s BSS; etc.

tíla   MF: MMF, MFF; MFB, MMB; |♂$\overset{k-1}{\longleftrightarrow}$ $\overset{i}{\longrightarrow}$♀→ |±
            ♂'s DD, ♂'s DS; ♂'s DDD,

	♂'s SDD, ♂'s DDS, ♂'s SDS; ♂'s ZDD, ♂'s ZDS, ♂'s BDD, ♂'s BDS; etc.	
púša	FF: FMF, FFF, FMB, FFB; ♂'s SD, ♂'s SS; ♂'s DSD, ♂'s SSD, ♂'s DSS, ♂'s SSS; ♂'s ZSS, ♂'s ZSD, ♂'s BSD, ♂'s BSS; etc.	$\mid ♂ \leftrightharpoons^{k-1} \quad \rightharpoondown_i ♂ \rightarrow \quad \mid \pm$

Aunts/Uncles/Nieces/Nephews:

paxáx (xáxa)	MZ; FBW; ~M; etc.	$\mid ♀ \underset{=}{\overset{x}{=}} \overset{k-1}{\leftrightharpoons} \underset{=}{\overset{x}{=}}$	♀→		$\mid +$
pši (písi)	♀'s ZD; HBD; ♀'s ~D; etc.	$\mid ♀ \underset{=}{\overset{x}{=}} \overset{k-1}{\leftrightharpoons} \underset{=}{\overset{x}{=}}$	♀→	♀	$\mid -$
itt (íti)	♀'s ZS; HBS; ♀'s ~S; etc.	$\mid ♀ \underset{=}{\overset{x}{=}} \overset{k-1}{\leftrightharpoons} \underset{=}{\overset{x}{=}}$	♀→	♂	$\mid -$
pišíš (šíša)	FZ; MBW; etc.	$\mid ♀ \underset{=}{\overset{x}{=}} \overset{k}{\leftrightharpoons} \underset{=}{\overset{x}{=}}$	♂→		$\mid +$
pawát (páway)	♀'s BD; HZD; etc.	$\mid ♀ \underset{=}{\overset{x}{=}} \overset{k}{\leftrightharpoons} \underset{=}{\overset{x}{=}}$	♂→	♀	$\mid -$
pámta (pámta)	♀'s BS; HZS; etc.	$\mid ♀ \underset{=}{\overset{x}{=}} \overset{k}{\leftrightharpoons} \underset{=}{\overset{x}{=}}$	♂→	♂	$\mid -$
pitx (káka) (píti)	MB; ♂'s ZD, ♂'s ZS; etc. (addressing senior relation) (addressing junior relation)	$\mid ♂ \quad \overset{k}{\leftrightharpoons}$	♀→		$\mid \pm$
swax	♀'s FZH; WBD	$\mid ♂ \underset{=}{=} \overset{k}{\leftrightharpoons} \underset{=}{=}$	♀→	♀	$\mid \pm$
psɨs or pitx	♂'s FZH; WBS	$\mid ♂ \underset{=}{=} \overset{k}{\leftrightharpoons} \underset{=}{=}$	♀→	♂	$\mid \pm$
pimx (mɨ́xa)	FB; MZH; ~F; etc.	$\mid ♂ \underset{=}{\overset{x}{=}} \overset{k}{\leftrightharpoons} \underset{=}{\overset{x}{=}}$	♂→		$\mid +$
paxyáx (páya)	♂'s BD, ♂'s BS; WZD, WZS; ♂'s ~D, ♂'s ~S; etc.	$\mid ♂ \underset{=}{\overset{x}{=}} \overset{k}{\leftrightharpoons} \underset{=}{\overset{x}{=}}$	♂→		$\mid -$

Spouses:

| ášam | W | $\mid ♀$ | = | $\mid +$ |
| am | H | $\mid ♂$ | = | $\mid +$ |

Siblings-in-Law:

| ayč | HZ, ♀'s BW | $\mid ♀ (\underset{=}{=} \overset{k}{\leftrightharpoons})^{\pm}$ | ♀$\mid \pm$ |
| miyú | WB, ♂'s ZH | $\mid ♂ (\underset{=}{=} \overset{k}{\leftrightharpoons})^{\pm}$ | ♂$\mid \pm$ |

pnuk	WZ, HB, ♀'s ZH, ♂'s BW, while connecting kin lives	$\|♀(\!=\!\overset{k}{\leftrightarrow}\,)^{\pm}$	$♂\|^{\pm}$
awít	WZ, HB, ♀'s ZH, ♂'s BW, when connecting kin dead	$\|♀(\!=\!\overset{k}{\leftrightarrow}\,)^{\pm}$	$♂\|^{\pm}$

Spouses of Siblings-in-Law:

x̣aks	HBW; a woman's female friend; HW, literally 'sister'	$\|♀\overset{x\ k-\dagger}{=\!=\!=}$	$\overset{x}{=\!=}$	$♀\|^{\pm}$
x̣ay	WZH; a man's male friend	$\|♂\overset{x\ k-\dagger}{=\!=\!=}$	$\overset{x}{=\!=}$	$♂\|^{\pm}$
tax̣úntway	HZH, WBW; friend of the opposite sex	$\|♀\overset{x\ k}{=\!=\!\leftrightarrow}$	$\overset{x}{=\!=}$	$♂\|^{\pm}$

Parents-in-Law/Children-in-Law

pnayč	HF, HM; SW	$\|$	$\rightarrow\!=\!=$	$♀\|^{\pm}$
pišaš	WF; ♂'s DH	$\|♂$	$\rightarrow\!=\!=$	$♂\|^{\pm}$
šwax̣	WM; ♀'s DH	$\|♀$	$\rightarrow\!=\!=$	$♂\|^{\pm}$
píwnaš	DHM, DHF, SWM, SWF	$\|$	$\rightarrow\!=\!=\!\leftarrow$	$\|^{\pm}$

Appendix 5.
The Yakima Treaty, June 9, 1855

*Treaty between the United States and the Yakama Nation of Indians.
Concluded at Camp Stevens, Walla-Walla Valley, June 9, 1855. Rati-
fied by the Senate, March 8, 1859. Proclaimed by the President of the
United States, April 18, 1859.*

JAMES BUCHANAN,

PRESIDENT OF THE UNITED STATES OF AMERICA,

TO ALL AND SINGULAR TO WHOM THESE PRESENTS SHALL COME, GREETING: June 9, 1855.

WHEREAS a treaty was made and concluded at the Treaty Ground, Preamble.
Camp Stevens, Walla-Walla Valley, on the ninth day of June, in the
year one thousand eight hundred and fifty-five, between Isaac I. Stevens,
governor, and superintendent of Indian affairs, for the Territory of Washington, on the part of the United States, and the hereinafter named head
chief, chiefs, headmen and delegates of the Yakama, Palouse, Pisquouse,
Wenatshapam, Klikatat, Klinquit, Kow-was-say-ee, Li-ay-was, Skin-pah,
Wish-ham, Shyiks, Oche-chotes, Kah-milt-pah, and Se-ap-cat, confederate
tribes and bands of Indians, occupying lands lying in Washington Territory, who, for the purposes of this treaty, are to be considered as one
nation, under the name of "Yakama," with Kamaiakun as its Head
Chief, on behalf of and acting for said bands and tribes, and duly
authorized thereto by them; which treaty is in the words and figures
following, to wit:

Articles of agreement and convention made and concluded at the treaty Contracting
ground, Camp Stevens, Walla-Walla Valley, this ninth day of June, in the parties.
year one thousand eight hundred and fifty-five, by and between Isaac I.
Stevens, governor and superintendent of Indian affairs for the Territory
of Washington, on the part of the United States, and the undersigned
head chief, chiefs, headmen and delegates of the Yakama, Palouse,
Pisquouse, Wenatshapam, Klikatat, Klinquit, Kow-was-say-ee, Li-ay-was,
Skin-pah, Wish-ham, Shyiks, Oche-chotes, Kah-milt-pah, and Se-ap-cat,
confederated tribes and bands of Indians, occupying lands hereinafter
bounded and described and lying in Washington Territory, who for the
purposes of this treaty are to be considered as one nation, under the
name of "Yakama," with Kamaiakun as its head chief, on behalf of and
acting for said tribes and bands, and being duly authorized thereto by
them.

ARTICLE I. The aforesaid confederated tribes and bands of Indians Cession of
hereby cede, relinquish, and convey to the United States all their right, lands to the
title, and interest in and to the lands and country occupied and claimed United States.
by them, and bounded and described as follows, to wit:

Commencing at Mount Ranier, thence northerly along the main ridge Boundaries.
of the Cascade Mountains to the point where the northern tributaries of
Lake Che-lan and the southern tributaries of the Methow River have their
rise; thence southeasterly on the divide between the waters of Lake
Che-lan and the Methow River to the Columbia River; thence, crossing
the Columbia on a true east course, to a point whose longitude is one
hundred and nineteen degrees and ten minutes (119° 10′,) which two
latter lines separate the above confederated tribes and bands from the
Oakinakane tribe of Indians: thence in a true south course to the

forty-seventh (47°) parallel of latitude; thence east on said parallel to the main Palouse River, which two latter lines of boundary separate the above confederated tribes and bands from the Spokanes; thence down the Palouse River to its junction with the Moh-hah-ne-she, or southern tributary of the same; thence, in a southesterly direction, to the Snake River, at the mouth of the Tucannon River, separating the above confederated tribes from the Nez Percé tribe of Indians; thence down the Snake River to its junction with the Columbia River; thence up the Columbia River to the "White banks," below the Priest's rapids; thence westerly to a lake called "La Lac;" thence southerly to a point on the Yakama River called Toh-mah-luke; thence, in a southwesterly direction, to the Columbia River, at the western extremity of the " Big Island," between the mouths of the Umatilla River and Butler Creek; all which latter boundaries separate the above confederated tribes and bands from the Walla-Walla, Cayuse, and Umatilla tribes and bands of Indians; thence down the Columbia River to midway between the mouths of White Salmon and Wind Rivers; thence along the divide between said rivers to the main ridge of the Cascade Mountains; and thence along said ridge to the place of beginning.

Reservation. ARTICLE II. There is, however, reserved, from the lands above ceded for the use and occupation of the aforesaid confederated tribes and bands of Indians, the tract of land included within the following boundaries, to wit:

Boundaries. Commencing on the Yakama River, at the mouth of the Attah-nam River; thence westerly along said Attah-nam River to the forks; thence along the southern tributary to the Cascade Mountains; thence southerly along the main ridge of said mountains, passing south and east of Mount Adams, to the spur whence flows the waters of the Klickatat and Pisco rivers; thence down said spur to the divide between the waters of said rivers; thence along said divide to the divide separating the waters of the Satass River from those flowing into the Columbia River; thence along said divide to the main Yakama, eight miles below the mouth of the Satass River; and thence up the Yakama River to the place of beginning.

Reservation to be set apart, &c. and Indians to settle thereon;
whites not to reside thereon. All which tract shall be set apart, and, so far as necessary, surveyed and marked out, for the exclusive use and benefit of said confederated tribes and bands of Indians, as an Indian reservation; nor shall any white man, excepting those in the employment of the Indian Department, be permitted to reside upon the said reservation without permission of the tribe and the superintendent and agent. And the said confederated tribes and bands agree to remove to, and settle upon, the same, within one year after the ratification of this treaty. In the mean time it shall be lawful for them to reside upon any ground not in the actual claim and occupation of citizens of the United States; and upon any ground claimed or occupied, if with the permission of the owner or claimant.

Guaranteeing, however, the right to all citizens of the United States, to enter upon and occupy as settlers any lands not actually occupied and cultivated by said Indians at this time, and not included in the reservation above named.

Improvements to be paid for by the United States. And provided, That any substantial improvements heretofore made by any Indian, such as fields enclosed and cultivated, and houses erected upon the lands hereby ceded, and which he may be compelled to abandon in consequence of this treaty, shall be valued, under the direction of the President of the United States, and payment made therefor in money; or improvements of an equal value made for said Indian upon the reservation. And no Indian will be required to abandon the improvements aforesaid, now occupied by him, until their value in money, or improvements of an equal value shall be furnished him as aforesaid.

ARTICLE III. And provided, That, if necessary for the public convenience, roads may be run through the said reservation; and on the Roads may be made. other hand, the right of way, with free access from the same to the nearest public highway, is secured to them; as also the right, in common with citizens of the United States, to travel upon all public highways.

The exclusive right of taking fish in all the streams, where running Privileges secured to Indians. through or bordering said reservation, is further secured to said confederated tribes and bands of Indians, as also the right of taking fish at all usual and accustomed places, in common with citizens of the Territory, and of erecting temporary buildings for curing them; together with the privilege of hunting, gathering roots and berries, and pasturing their horses and cattle upon open and unclaimed land.

ARTICLE IV. In consideration of the above cession, the United States Payments by the United States; agree to pay to the said confederated tribes and bands of Indians, in addition to the goods and provisions distributed to them at the time of signing this treaty, the sum of two hundred thousand dollars, in the following manner, that is to say: sixty thousand dollars, to be expended under the direction of the President of the United States, the first year after the ratification of this treaty, in providing for their removal to the reservation, breaking up and fencing farms, building houses for them, supplying them with provisions and a suitable outfit, and for such other objects as he may deem necessary, and the remainder in annuities, as follows: for the first five years after the ratification of the treaty, ten thousand dollars each year, commencing September first, 1856; for the next five years, eight thousand dollars each year; for the next five years, six thousand dollars per year; and for the next five years, four thousand per year.

All which sums of money shall be applied to the use and benefit of said how to be applied. Indians, under the direction of the President of the United States, who may from time to time determine, at his discretion, upon what beneficial objects to expend the same for them. And the superintendent of Indian affairs, or other proper officer, shall each year inform the President of the wishes of the Indians in relation thereto.

ARTICLE V. The United States further agree to establish at suitable United States to establish schools, points within said reservation, within one year after the ratification hereof, two schools, erecting the necessary buildings, keeping them in repair, and providing them with furniture, books, and stationery, one of which shall be an agricultural and industrial school, to be located at the agency, and to be free to the children of the said confederated tribes and bands of Indians, and to employ one superintendent of teaching and two teachers; to build two blacksmiths' shops, to one of which shall be attached a tin mechanics' shops, shop, and to the other a gunsmith's shop; one carpenter's shop, one wagon and ploughmaker's shop, and to keep the same in repair and furnished with the necessary tools; to employ one superintendent of farming and two farmers, two blacksmiths, one tinner, one gunsmith, one carpenter, one wagon and ploughmaker, for the instruction of the Indians in trades and to assist them in the same; to erect one saw-mill and one flouring- saw-mill and flouring-mill, mill, keeping the same in repair and furnished with the necessary tools and fixtures; to erect a hospital, keeping the same in repair and provided hospital. with the necessary medicines and furniture, and to employ a physician; and to erect, keep in repair, and provided with the necessary furniture, the buildings required for the accommodation of the said employees. The said buildings and establishments to be maintained and kept in repair as aforesaid, and the employees to be kept in service for the period of twenty years.

And in view of the fact that the head chief of the said confederated Salary to head chief; house, &c tribes and bands of Indians is expected, and will be called upon, to perform many services of a public character, occupying much of his time, the United States further agree to pay to the said confederated tribes and bands of Indians five hundred dollars per year, for the term of twenty years after the ratification hereof, as a salary for such person as the said confederated tribes and bands of Indians may select to be their head chief; to build for him at a suitable point on the reservation a comfortable house and properly furnish the same, and to plough and fence ten acres of land. The said salary to be paid to, and the said house to be occupied by, such head chief so long as he may continue to hold that office.

Kamaiakun is the head chief. And it is distinctly understood and agreed that at the time of the conclusion of this treaty Kamaiakun is the duly elected and authorized head chief of the confederated tribes and bands aforesaid, styled the Yakama nation, and is recognized as such by them and by the commissioners on the part of the United States holding this treaty; and all the expenditures and expenses contemplated in this article of this treaty shall be defrayed by the United States, and shall not be deducted from the annuities agreed to be paid to said confederated tribes and bands of Indians. Nor shall the cost of transporting the goods for the annuity payments be a charge upon the annuities, but shall be defrayed by the United States.

Reservation may be surveyed into lots, and assigned to individuals or families. ARTICLE VI. The President may, from time to time, at his discretion, cause the whole or such portions of such reservation as he may think proper, to be surveyed into lots, and assign the same to such individuals or families of the said confederated tribes and bands of Indians as are willing to avail themselves of the privilege, and will locate on the same as a permanent home, on the same terms and subject to the same regulations Vol. x. p. 1044. as are provided in the sixth article of the treaty with the Omahas, so far as the same may be applicable.

Annuities not to pay debts of individuals. ARTICLE VII. The annuities of the aforesaid confederated tribes and bands of Indians shall not be taken to pay the debts of individuals.

Tribes to preserve friendly relations; ARTICLE VIII. The aforesaid confederated tribes and bands of Indians acknowledge their dependence upon the government of the United States, and promise to be friendly with all citizens thereof, and pledge themselves to commit no depredations upon the property of such citizens.

to pay for depredations; And should any one or more of them violate this pledge, and the fact be satisfactorily proved before the agent, the property taken shall be returned, or in default thereof, or if injured or destroyed, compensation may be made by the government out of the annuities.

not to make war but in self-defence; Nor will they make war upon any other tribe, except in self-defence, but will submit all matters of difference between them and other Indians to the government of the United States or its agent for decision, and abide thereby. And if any of the said Indians commit depredations on any other Indians within the Territory of Washington or Oregon, the same rule shall prevail as that provided in this article in case of depredations against citizens. And the said confederated tribes and bands of Indians to surrender offenders. agree not to shelter or conceal offenders against the laws of the United States, but to deliver them up to the authorities for trial.

Annuities may be withheld from those who drink ardent spirits. ARTICLE IX. The said confederated tribes and bands of Indians desire to exclude from their reservation the use of ardent spirits, and to prevent their people from drinking the same, and, therefore, it is provided that any Indian belonging to said confederated tribes and bands of Indians, who is guilty of bringing liquor into said reservation, or who drinks liquor, may have his or her annuities withheld from him or her for such time as the President may determine.

Wenatshapam fishery reserved. ARTICLE X. *And provided*, That there is also reserved and set apart from the lands ceded by this treaty, for the use and benefit of the aforesaid confederated tribes and bands, a tract of land not exceeding in quantity one township of six miles square, situated at the forks of the Pisquouse or Wenatshapam River, and known as the "Wenatshapam fishery," which said reservation shall be surveyed and marked out whenever the President may direct, and be subject to the same provisions and restrictions as other Indian reservations.

When treaty to take effect. ARTICLE XI. This treaty shall be obligatory upon the contracting parties as soon as the same shall be ratified by the President and Senate of the United States.

Index

CPSIA information can be obtained
at www.ICGtesting.com
Printed in the USA
BVHW08s2227300818
525485BV00001BA/3/P